WILLIE P

WILLIE PEP

*A Biography
of the 20th Century's
Greatest Featherweight*

Mark Allen Baker

McFarland & Company, Inc., Publishers
Jefferson, North Carolina

Unless otherwise noted, photos are from the author's collection.

ISBN (print) 978-1-4766-8552-6
ISBN (ebook) 978-1-4766-4710-4

Library of Congress and British Library
cataloguing data are available

Library of Congress Control Number 2022037249

On the cover: an early publicity photograph of Hartford's most promising featherweight. Willie Pep often claimed an amateur record of 59–3–3, in 65 bouts (author's collection)

Printed in the United States of America

*McFarland & Company, Inc., Publishers
Box 611, Jefferson, North Carolina 28640
www.mcfarlandpub.com*

To ROBERT ROY BAKER (1901–1966),
my grandfather,
whose favorite boxer was Willie Pep

Table of Contents

Acknowledgments

"The living owe it to those who no longer can speak to tell their story for them," the Polish-American poet Czeslaw Milosz once quipped. This work fulfills a piece of my role as a boxing historian; moreover, I promised Willie Pep I would do this back in 1995. My appreciation to everyone associated with this title at McFarland.

Covering the life and boxing career of Pep in the detail they merit, but also at a publishable length, was a real challenge. It was a little like jamming a sailfish into a sardine can. Leading a fast-paced life, Willie Pep never sat still. He had 242 professional bouts and more than 60 amateur/semi-pro contests. Two unbeaten streaks of 60-plus fights are alone enough to make any historian cringe at the thought of documenting each contest. Yet Willie Pep was no ordinary fighter, and such an incredible accomplishment merits the labor.

Boxers can be judged in large part by their record, but when comparing greats (all of whom have impressive records), there is subjectivity involved, as in scoring a bout. Judges sometimes see things differently. There's little argument, though, that Willie Pep was the greatest featherweight boxer ever.

Those who know me understand my proud association with the International Boxing Hall of Fame in Canastota, New York. My service has been rewarding because of these incredible individuals: Edward Brophy, Jeffrey S. Brophy, Chris Bowers, Rachel Shaw, and Mike Delaney. I would like to single out in particular the efforts of Jeffrey S. Brophy, for his outstanding research and ongoing friendship, and Edward Brophy, for his years of friendship and dedication to the sweet science.

This book would not have been possible without the assistance of the Library of Congress. Chronicling America, a Website providing access to select digitized newspaper pages and produced by the National Digital Newspaper Program, was another outstanding source. Adding to my periodical research was newspapers.com by ancestry, which filled the gaps left behind by other sources.

The International Boxing Research Organization (IBRO) was organized in May 1982 for the express purpose of establishing an accurate history of boxing; compiling complete and accurate boxing records; facilitating the dissemination of boxing research information; and cooperating in safeguarding the individual research efforts of its members by application of the rules of scholarly research. They have been successful because when they are needed, they are there. Thank you to my fellow IBRO members.

Living in the historic state of Connecticut, birthplace of Willie Pep, I am fortunate to have a great support system. My gratitude to all the independent bookstores in Connecticut for supporting local authors, especially Bank Square Books in Mystic.

Larry Dasilva (Nutmeg TV), Larry Rifkin (WATR), Teresa Dufour (CTSTYLE, on ABC 8), Wayne Norman (WILI–AM), Roger Zotti (*The Resident*, IBRO), The Authors Guild, IBRO, Heritage Auctions, and *USA Boxing News*, thank you for your inspiration and advocacy of my work.

There are many talented individuals, in and around the sport of boxing, who don't get the credit they deserve. Recognizing this, the state of Connecticut created their own Boxing Hall of Fame located inside Mohegan Sun Resort & Casino in Uncasville. I wish to express my appreciation to everyone associated with the organization for their support.

Having spent considerable time with my subject, I am honored to present an account of his boxing life. We spent the day together on July 7, 1995, in Canastota, New York, and talked for hours like two old friends who hadn't seen one another in decades.

Strength and inspiration were drawn from my friends and family. My thanks to friends Dana Beck and Brian Brinkman, Rick Kaletsky, Ann and Mark Lepkowski, Jim Risley and Steve Ike.

To my family, Marilyn Allen Baker, Aaron, Sharon and Elliott Baker, Elizabeth, Mark, Paisley and Monroe Taylor, and Rebecca Baker: thank you for your love and support. To Richard Long, my wonderful father-in-law, who has always been a second in my corner: I am grateful for your support.

In loving memory of: Ford William Baker, James Buford Bird, Flavil Q. Van Dyke III, Deborah Jean Long, David Arthur Mumper, Nancy L. Allen, Thomas P. Allen, and Richard Alan Long.

To my wife Alison, I will modify a line from Edna St. Vincent Millay: "They say when you are missing someone that they are probably feeling the same, but I don't think it is possible for you to miss me as much as I always seem to miss you."

Preface

The year 2022 marks the centennial of the birth of one of the greatest pugilists who ever lived, Willie Pep, a boxer described by one word: spectacular. With complete disregard for the laws of gravity, he created a style all his own. Majestic, he didn't enter a confrontation, he choreographed it. Nobody had ever seen a prizefighter move with such elegance. Seamlessly gliding across the canvas, the fighter was to the sweet science what Fred Astaire was to motion pictures. As an impossible target to capture, yet alone engage—he was "Pep-petual motion"—he not only frustrated his opponents, he made them look foolish.

On July 7, 1995, I spent nearly an entire day in Canastota, New York, with Guglielmo (William) Papaleo, aka Willie Pep. Ed Brophy (or Eddie, as Willie always called him), the director of the International Boxing Hall of Fame, had contacted me the evening before and asked me to host the 72-year-old Pep at the museum. Little did I know that it would be one of the greatest days of my life.

Making the over 230-mile pilgrimage from his house in central Connecticut to upstate New York, Pep appeared as sharp as ever when I greeted him at the door. Having prepared hours of questions for the man, I was nervous. Yet it wasn't long before I felt I had known Pep my entire life. We talked about everything—and I mean everything—under the sun for hours. Having written and published a few books, I optimistically told him that I would one day write a book about him.

Holding the distinction of being the only person to serve the International Boxing Hall of Fame as an author, historian, chairperson, sponsor, volunteer, and biographer, I felt inspired, as I did with my biographies of Oscar "Battling" Nelson, Abe Attell, and Lou Ambers, to write an account of the boxing life of Willie Pep.

My inspiration was enhanced by living in the state of Connecticut, not far from where Willie was born. (If I refer to him as Willie in this book instead of Pep, it is not that we were intimate pals; it is because that was the way fight fans—who felt intimate with him—referred to the elite pugilist.) Constantly reminded of the fighter as I pass the street corners he worked (as a young bootblack), venues he fought in (as an amateur, semi-pro, and professional), and even his former houses, I wanted everyone to understand how beloved he remains in Connecticut, and for that matter, all over the world. With his charm and self-deprecating humor, Willie Pep managed to touch the souls of nearly everyone he came in contact with, and he earned the immortality he desperately sought.

There is a movement to erect a statue in his honor, as well there should be. It should be a bronze, life-size statue, similar to the statue of Nathan Hale that stands outside the Wadsworth Atheneum Museum of Art in Hartford, and it should be

placed on a pedestal of equal height outside the former Auditorium at 331 Wethersfield Avenue. Willie Pep, one of Connecticut's favorite sons, was a talent worthy of a
monument.

This book will appeal to boxing fans of all ages all over the world (especially to
residents of New England, New York, and Florida), and to those studying ethnicity in
sports. It does so by presenting the sport tastefully and in great detail. With complete
respect for the subject and his family, this work does not dwell on any aspect of his
personal life that did not enter the public domain.

Over a year in the making, this chronological tale is based on contemporane-
ous newspaper accounts of events in the life of Willie Pep. Please take advantage of
the comprehensive references that are in the Appendix. They include: A. A Canastota
Scrapbook; B. Guglielmo Papaleo—Boxing Record; C. Skills Overview; and D. Official Records of Associated Members of the International Boxing Hall of Fame, along
with Chapter Notes, Bibliography and Index.

With my 25th book, fourth biography and ninth boxing title, I am thankful for
the opportunity to explore the life of this amazing man. As an acolyte of Willie Pep, I
will forever be in his corner. He was one of the finest pugilists ever, and without question the greatest featherweight to enter a boxing ring.

Introduction

If success was a puzzle, Guglielmo Papaleo had all the pieces. He began with superb genetics, a father who had a passion for the sweet science. He was born in the right place, central Connecticut, at the right time, the 1920s—Hartford lay claim to a world light heavyweight champion and two featherweight world champions during the same decade. The footsteps, or these pieces if you will, along with everyone and everything needed to construct a champion, existed, if they could be assembled.

Papaleo, who felt he was born with leather mitts, believed boxing was his calling. Realizing that Dominic J. "Pete" Perone held the key to a successful amateur career, the youngster pressured the association, leading to the Connecticut State Amateur Flyweight Championship (1938). It was in that same year that Bert Keane, *Hartford Courant* sports editor and columnist, predicted stardom for Willie Pep—he was the first to publicly make that prognostication.

As the line of demarcation between amateur, semi-pro, and professional boxing blurred, Pep decided, at age 17, to turn professional. Quickly realizing that his early fight managers could only take him so far, he began searching for a solution. Thankfully, that was when Lou Viscusi decided to dedicate himself to the task (1942). As much of a politician as a fight manager, Viscusi guided the talented youngster all the way to the world featherweight championship. And he accomplished the task before Pep, under the rules in place, was even old enough to hold the title.[1]

When Viscusi and Pep invited trainer Bill Gore to the picnic, the triumvirate was complete. Gore molded Pep the way Michelangelo crafted David. As the perfect pugilist, Pep was soon a contender. When the trio set their sight on Chalky Wright and the featherweight championship of the world, it was essentially over. The title belonged to them—the pugilistic trinity was that talented.

Behind the featherweight champion were his friends and family, an extraordinary group that evolved with the champion's career. In addition to his close friends, there were associates like Bill Lee, sports editor for the *Hartford Courant*. Lee proved almost as key to the success of Willie Pep as Gore and Viscusi. Throughout Pep's incredible career, Lee never turned his back on "The Champ."

Families which include multiple marriages can create complexities.[2] Positive or negative, they can impact a person's behavior or even their job performance. Yet they were a part of life for some people, including this extraordinary featherweight boxer.

Pep's personal charm resonated with everyone he met. It was a recipe that began with the genetics of his parents, before stirring in a bit of Henny Youngman, Jake LaMotta, and Rocky Graziano, then adding a pinch of George Raft and Edward G. Robinson. Naturally, elements of his personality were enhanced by his friends, family, and surroundings. As he matured, his self-deprecating humor (supplemented by one-liners) was delivered in swift staccato bursts. That was because Willie Pep understood an audience like he interpreted an opponent: An entertainer's style should be inviting, never challenging to an attention span, and always capable of putting a smile on the face of a spectator.

Pep abhorred restraint in nearly every form; consequently, he was not afraid of challenging authority or the power attached to it. As a nonpareil pugilist, he fed off the euphoria attached to beating the odds, pushing himself to the furthest extent of his physical or mental endurance, and challenging boundaries. As an elite professional athlete, he understood the selfishness attached to his behavior, even if the consequences weren't always considered.[3]

Like all the champions who had gone before him, Pep had his vices. And they cost him. They transformed his reputation, personal life, and bank account. Yet through it all, he persevered. Willie knew they were there, he just, or so he believed, had to keep them in check. Thankfully, a common trait shared by elite boxers such as Pep was the ability to compartmentalize—to be successful, they had no other choice.

Winning for Willie Pep was a given: moreover, he made it look routine. Ask yourself: How many fighters can say the same? His mark of not one, but TWO, winning streaks, each over 60 victories will never be matched or surpassed. As the victories piled up, they enhanced his marketability—better said, Lou Viscusi's job got much easier—that is, if holding your ground during negotiations against Mike Jacobs was ever simple for a fight manager.[4] Never burning any bridges, Viscusi had a pocket filled with favors from promoters all around the country and even into Canada. It was these favors that prolonged the career of his premier meal ticket.

As a ring impresario, Pep was unrivaled. He systematically destroyed his opposition like a parasite that not only feeds on one of its host's body parts but destroys them from the inside out. Round by round, his adversaries withered away in a hopeless death march. Trying to hit Pep was like trying to strike a hummingbird with a slingshot. After all, an opposer can't hit what he can't catch. Moreover, he was boxing's version of three-card monte: now you see him, now you don't. Cold and calculating, Willie Pep controlled his opponents before letting them self-destruct. When he was asked if he was as Machiavellian outside a ring as in, an enigmatic smile painted his face.

During his first featherweight title reign, Pep successfully defended against Sal Bartolo (twice), Chalky Wright, Phil Terranova, Jock Leslie, and Humberto Sierra. All five challengers were far more than just speed bumps. During his second rule, he triumphantly defended against Eddie Compo, Charley Riley, and Ray Famechon. Once again, every challenger was a worthy opponent. His nemesis, besides Father Time, was Joseph "Sandy" Saddler, an elite pugilist. If you had to pick an archrival, Saddler was a supreme selection.

Willie Pep's accepted International Boxing Hall of Fame record stands at: 230–11–1, with 65 knockouts. It earned him induction into the institution as part of its inaugural class (1990). Battling over a generation (1940–1966), his 26 years in professional boxing allowed him to appear on boxing fight cards with everyone from Fritzie Zivic, who fought Lou Ambers, to Joe Frazier, who fought Muhammad Ali. In his book *Boxing's Greatest Fighters*, historian Bert Randolph Sugar ranked Willie Pep third all-time. Only Henry Armstrong and Sugar Ray Robinson were ranked higher.

If Willie Pep's career had ended in 1951, he was guaranteed immortality (record 152–3–1); moreover, his masterpieces had been painted. Fortunately for a new generation of fight fans, it did not. Following his final loss to Sandy Saddler, his career was all about numbers (each success moving him higher up the victory ladder), not to mention survival. He was fighting for the dough, and he admitted it. Pep dreaded retirement. Knowing he could not replace the adulation, remuneration, and excitement he received in the ring left him unsatisfied and unsettled. To be forgotten, in his mind, would be the ultimate insult.

Staying close to the ring, and the memories, was his security blanket. Award dinners, banquets, and fund-raisers, not to mention a few jobs, made ring retirement tolerable—as did induction into every conceivable elite boxing institution. Masked by an arsenal of one-liners was a complex man, hell-bent on satisfying *his* desires. Yet through it all, his allure was undeniable.

The advent of the International Boxing Hall of Fame in Canastota and Pep's induction as part of the inaugural class revitalized the man. The outpouring of adulation for the elite fighter was beyond compare. While generations had passed since he wore the featherweight crown, he was "The Champ." And he always will be.

ONE

A Machinist's Son

"Dare to live the life you have dreamed for yourself. Go forward and make your dreams come true."—Ralph Waldo Emerson

Salvatore Papaleo was a dreamer. There were times when he would leave his Middletown residence to walk down by the water. Searching for a comfortable place along the riverbank, he would sit and stare across the Connecticut River at a vista that reminded him of northern Italy. His thoughts would drift as he watched the operation of the unique swing truss bridge. Built in 1872, it was the first bridge spanning the river at Middletown. Used by the New York, New Haven and Hartford Railroad, it never failed to mesmerize an audience along the shore with its versatility.

Standing five feet five inches, with brown eyes and black hair, Salvatore Papaleo was a handsome man whose broad shoulders made him appear taller.[1] He never questioned whether it was a good decision to leave Italy; he knew—even as a teenager—that it was. Like many, he, along with his family, hoped to sow the seeds of the American dream.

Italian Immigration—Overcoming Racism

The road to that dream would not be easy for Salvatore Papaleo, primarily because of stereotypic views. At the beginning of the 20th century, sociologists were trying hard to better understand America's immigration. However, it wasn't easy because of the lack of concise information. Prompted by a recent increase in Italian immigration, scholars sought answers. Some believed people of Italian parentage accounted for about a million immigrants in 1901, as compared to about 6.9 million of German and nearly five million of Irish.

Enter Frederick J. Turner, Ph.D., director of the School of History at the University of Wisconsin, who in 1901 believed the causes for this influx of Italians were chiefly: the economic distress of Southern Italy; the remarkable cheapening of transatlantic transportation; the organization of emigration agencies; and the industrial revolution in the United States (during the past two decades). Great corporations were responsible for the importation of cheap labor for mines, railroad building, street making, and manufacture.[2]

It was employment that drove the exodus to both the United States and other parts of Europe. Taking a closer look, *Los Angeles Times* noted:

In 1891, the Italian immigration to the United Sates amounted to over 76,000, and the returning Italians were estimated at about 10,000. Of the 94,700 Italians who landed here from July 1, 1893, to the end of 1895, about 21,700 had been in the country before.[3]

For many, their initial journey was to reinforce claims about the country and its opportunities. Family patriarchs often made the lengthy passage first to obtain gainful employment. Saving enough money for a trip back to Italy, they would then confidently return to America with their family.

Dr. Turner was also quick to note that Italy suffered from over-population, excessive taxation, and agricultural oppression (land tenure).[4] The bulk of the Italian immigrants came from southern Italy, nearly five times as many for the year ending June 30, 1900. Provinces fueling the exodus included: Abruzzi (particularly the region of Compobasso), Campania (particularly Salerno), Basilicata, Calabria, and Sicily. Did it matter where they came from? Dr. Turner wasn't certain, so he referenced the views of others.

Unfortunately, upon arrival in America, many immigrants faced prejudice. Turner, in his piece for the *Los Angeles Times,* even quoted an Italian writer's partisan opinion regarding the bulk of the immigration:

> It is chiefly the oppressed and miserable laborer of the least advanced part of Italy. The race is mixed with Greek and Arab blood: in physique and health they are inferior to the north Italians; education and morals are below those of the north; the standard of comfort is of the lowest; foul hovels, a diet of chestnuts and polenta and wages of 15 or 20 cents a day are characteristic of these people. Between one-half and one-third of these south Italian adults cannot read or write. They bring, on an average, less than $10 per capita, and hardly more than the pack on their back. Indeed, often they are in debt for their passage money. The proportion of paupers and criminals whose migration is assisted or winked at by the authorities is considerable.[5]

Wisely, Turner countered with some of his own positive views of Italian immigration, which included a desire for improved distribution to better suit their skills, and their contribution to industrial development. However, his own preconceptions also surfaced in the *Los Angeles Times*:

> The contributions of the south Italian to American racial characteristics are of doubtful value, judged from the ethical point of view of the stocks that have heretofore made the nation. They are quick witted, but supple in morals. Centuries of misrule have taught them self-preservation by deception. The impetuosity and revengeful spirit of the region will not easily be put aside.[6]

Trying hard to redeem his credibility—he was losing the fight and he knew it—he added:

> And yet it is easy to draw too dark a picture of these people. At their best they are [a] lighthearted, sunny race, capable of the hardest work and endurance, eager to better their condition. It must always be borne in mind that their worse traits are in part due to centuries of oppression, and that with freer and more favorable conditions in this country the nationality may reveal its strength.[7]

Printed in a major newspaper at the turn of the 20th century, this was an appalling and fallacious perspective that many Italian immigrants, including Salvatore Papaleo, had to endure. It wasn't fair; nonetheless, prejudice during this era was common and difficult to defuse. To negate its impact, Papaleo sought a suitable location to call home. A place void of intolerance yet abounding in opportunity. And he found it in New England.

Middletown, Connecticut

Located in Middlesex County in the central part of the state, Middletown, a mere 16 miles south of Hartford, was originally called by its Native American name, Mattabeseck. Its present name was given in 1653, a simpler time, over a hundred years before its central settlement was incorporated as a city. From a bustling sailing port to even an industrial center, the city, with its over 40 square miles, managed to transform commerce to meet the needs of its growing population.

Named for being halfway between Hartford and Saybrook (colony) on the west bank of the Connecticut River, Middletown had a growing population of 9,589 in 1900. In the midst of a demographic transformation, the city had experienced a wave of Irish, followed by a large number of Italian immigrants—many from the town of Melilli, Sicily (a sister city), drawn to the area by its employment opportunities. The benefactors clearly were Middletown's factories and farms, in desperate need of workers. By 1911, the Italian population of

The strength and perseverance of the immigrants who settled in Middletown, Connecticut, was truly amazing. As a reminder, this plaque was dedicated in 1990.

Middletown was estimated at about 4,000. There was strength in numbers, and the community knew it.

In the latter half of the 19th century, manufacturing, especially finely crafted metal hardware, was the mainstay of the city's economy. This ranged from marine hardware and typewriters to early automobile manufacturing.

Birth of a Champion

Guglielmo Papaleo was born on September 19, 1922, on lower Court Street in Middletown, Connecticut, to parents Salvatore Papaleo (Sal, 1896–1966) and Maria Marchese Papaleo (Mary, Mary Ann, 1901–1983).[8] The name Guglielmo was the Italian form of the masculine name William. He was the couple's first child. Both parents were born in Italy. Salvatore arrived in the United Sates prior (estimated at one year) to his wife—she arrived in 1915 or 1916.[9] Political tensions were rising in Europe, and like many Italians, they were concerned; World War I began in 1914 and ended in 1918. Following a stop in Worcester, Massachusetts, Salvatore found his way to Middletown, where he had relatives and associates.[10]

Married on May 26, 1917, in Middletown, the couple made their home there.[11] Living along Water Street (Dekoven Drive), the Papaleos were a stone's throw from the Connecticut River and within walking distance to satisfy their needs. They were one of many Italian families living on city streets such as Portland, St. John, Green, Ferry and Washington. It felt like home and the perfect environment to raise a family. Salvatore was even recruited for Middletown's Home Guard.

Hoping his love of sports would translate to his son, Salvatore assisted the process by teaching the youngster how to box. Not surprisingly, young Guglielmo adorned a pair of boxing gloves by the age of five, and before the age of ten he had his own complete set of sporting togs. And they fit. That's where Mrs. Papaleo, needle and thread in hand, entered the picture. While she was happy that her husband taught their son how to defend himself, she nevertheless feared the possibility of an injury.

Believing that employment opportunities were better in Hartford, Salvatore moved the family to the city's east side before the close of the decade. It appeared like a wise decision from numerous perspectives. Middletown, especially areas near the river, had experienced considerable flooding in 1927. While parts of Hartford, East Hartford, and Wethersfield were hit hard by the rising waters, hundreds had to evacuate the East side of Middletown. The water, which was rising an average of three inches an hour, cut off much of the city's electrical supply. Naturally, everyone in the city was concerned about the possible repercussions, from disease to the availability of clean drinking water.

With a growing family, Salvatore sought higher ground, not to mention larger quarters. Welcoming the birth of a daughter, Francis Papaleo, in 1928, followed later by their last child, Nicholas, in 1936, the family found solace in Hartford. The couple were entrenched in their roles: As a hard-working laborer, Salvatore was good with his hands and honed his skills as a machine operator, while charming Maria Marchese Papaleo, with her dark hair, brown eyes, and broad shoulders, tended to the home front.

Maternalistic and hard-working, Maria always wanted the best for her family. If that meant a bit of personal sacrifice, as her Catholic upbringing had taught her, then that would indeed be the case.

Hartford and the Great Depression

The stock market crash of 1929 contributed to the Great Depression of the 1930s. Folks did what they could to make ends meet during those ten years. Much of the labor unrest created by the situation was pacified by the election of Franklin D. Roosevelt in 1932. His efforts to combat the financial crisis and put folks back to work fostered a series of efforts, including the National Recovery Act (NRA), the Civilian Conservation Corps (CCC), and the Works Progress Administration (WPA).

In Connecticut, these programs were under the control of Governor Wilbur L.

A detailed view of 108–150 Main Street in Middletown, Connecticut. Although the storefronts changed over the years, the architecture was familiar to generations who lived in the city (Library of Congress, Photos from Survey HABS CT-326).

Cross, former provost of Yale University. More of a scholar than a politician, Cross was a skilled negotiator and empathetic to the needs of state residents. Often recalled in conjunction with the construction of the Merritt Parkway (the northward continuation of the project bears his name), Cross was also effective at disaster relief.[12]

As the family patriarch, Salvatore Papaleo felt that the capital city of Hartford better suited the needs of the family. By 1930, the family was renting a house on Fairmount Street. Five years later, needing more space, they rented a house at 35 Portland Street. The evolution in lifestyle mimicked family income. In 1937, Salvatore was making $15 a week working for the Works Progress Administration (WPA). (By the early 1940s, he was employed by the Carling Tool Company on Capital Avenue in Hartford. Not long after, he suffered stomach ulcers that impacted his ability to work.)

As a youngster, Guglielmo was enterprising, energetic, and tenacious. To grab some coin, he and his buddies, one of whom was Giulio "Johnny Duke" Gallucci, would sell newspapers or shine shoes on the thoroughfares of Hartford. Staking claim to their street corners (often Ann and Asylum, or along Front Street) was of prime importance to the youngsters, and if that meant holding their ground against a challenge, then so be it. Quick afoot, the boys learned all the tricks of how to distract, or dodge the competition (or on occasion the authorities) in order to maximize their profit.

One day Guglielmo had his bootblack money taken from him by a larger and more convincing juvenile. The humiliating incident enticed the youngster to refine his defensive skills. While the story changed over time—one version had a judge suggesting to the minors that physical education might be better use of their time than creating a ruckus at a downtown corner—the conclusion remained the same: It wasn't long before Papaleo and Gallucci were pounding a heavy bag inside a gym.

Passions can be vices or virtues depending upon your perspective. In addition to pugilism, Papaleo found comfort in gambling. Taking a fancy to shooting craps (a dice game played for money), the teenager "liked the action," or exhilaration. It was a euphoria that shadowed him for life. And, shadows, like destiny, were impossible to outrun.

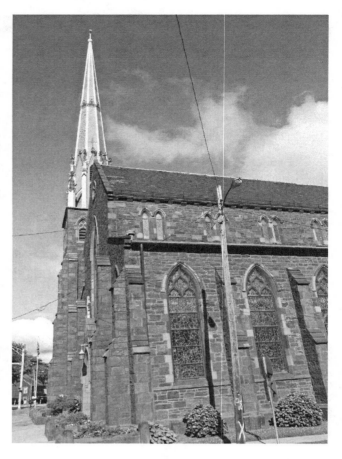

This view of Saint John Church (1852), the Mother Church of the Roman Catholic Diocese of Norwich, located in Middletown, was familiar to the Papaleo family.

As an ordinary student, Guglielmo was not thrilled by school. Despite weighing 105 pounds, he preferred athletics over academics any day of the week. The trick was finding a sport for his size. In some instances, the desire didn't match the need: He could field and run fast enough to make the baseball team, but he didn't have the power to hit. Nevertheless, he understood that he was blessed with good genetics, so individual sports such as boxing became an option.

Connecticut Boxing

For an adolescent looking for a ring education during the early decades of the 20th century, Connecticut was the perfect place. From Bridgeport to Willimantic, boxing was taught, conducted, and enjoyed. It seemed to hit a pinnacle of popularity during the 1920s. This came courtesy of three extraordinary pugilists, not to mention those who supported them.

Ukrainian-born Louis "Kid" Kaplan, who resided in Meriden, possessed natural skills. When he found a mentor, not mention sparring partner, in featherweight Charlie Pilkington, a former New York State Champion, Kaplan used his expertise to capture the featherweight championship of the world (1925–1926).

Over in the light heavyweight division, their champion, Jack Delaney from Bridgeport, reigned supreme. Back in 1924, under the direction of Pete Reilly, Delaney decisioned future light heavyweight champion Tommy Loughran. That victory had set him on a course to the championship (1927).[13]

Meanwhile, the 1927 National AAU featherweight championship was won by another Connecticut youth, Christopher "Bat" Battalino of Hartford. He would also become featherweight champion of the world in 1929. In a glimpse of destiny, Salvatore Papaleo took his son to watch the popular Italian phenom train in Hartford—ethnic pride forever played a central role in the popularity of the sport.

While every culture had their fair share of extraordinary athletes, some were quick to brag louder than others. It was justified, since the Italian youth who loved boxing had plenty of outstanding pugilists to emulate. Those born prior to 1920 included: Luigi D'Ambrosio, aka Lou Ambers (1913–1995); Salvatore Engotti, aka Sammy Angott (1915–1980); Mike Ballerino (1901–1965); Christopher "Bat" Batalino (1908–1977); Melio Bettina (1916–1996); Luigi Nicola Buccassi, aka Lou Bogash (1901–1978); Anthony "Tony" Canzoneri (1908–1959); Primo Carnera (1906–1967), Francesco Conte, aka Frankie Conley (1890–1952); Raffaele Giordano, aka Young Corbett III (1905–1993); Frankie Covelli (1913–2003); Samuel Lazzaro, aka Joe Dundee (1903–1982); Giuseppe Corrara, aka Johnny Dundee (1893–1965); Vincenzo Lazzara, aka Vince Dundee (1907–1949); Domenico Galento, aka Tony Galento (1910–1979); Frankie DiGennaro, aka Frankie Genaro (1901–1966); Angelo Geraci, aka Bushy Graham (1905–1982); Thomas Rocco Barbella, aka Rocky Graziano (1919–1990); and, many, many more.[14] The dignity, affection and self-respect that was expressed through one's ethnic or culture heritage thrived during the era.[15]

Was Guglielmo Papaleo at the right place at the right time? It certainly appeared that way, but only time would tell.

Amateur Ambition[16]

If amateur boxing belonged to one man in Connecticut during the 1930s, it would have to be Dominic J. "Pete" Perone. In the 1920s, he opened his first boxing gym on Windsor Street in Hartford. It was located on the second floor of a building occupied by a sewing emporium. The pugs loved it, whereas the Lipmans, who owned the sewing shop on the first floor, weren't always happy with the noise or the clientele it drew. It was there that Perone got a grasp on Connecticut's amateur fight picture. Later, accompanied by Lenny Marello, he would open the Charter Oak Athletic Club, at the corner of Trumbull and Main Street in Hartford.

Working during the day for G. Fox & Company, the renowned department store, then turning his energy to boxing in the evening, Perone was tireless. As he became involved in all facets of the fight game—from trainer to manager—it was only a matter of time until he took on the role of matchmaker. His venue of choice was Capitol Park, a multi-faceted outdoor facility at the end of Wethersfield Avenue in Hartford.

Conveniently located at the conclusion of the trolley line, it was an all-star attraction that also included a restaurant and a swimming pool. With tickets scaled from 25 to 75 cents, boxing at Capitol Park proved the perfect entertainment for the time.

Later, Perone turned to other venues for his amateur boxing shows, such as South Park (Hartford), Foot Guard Hall (Hartford), and Stanley Arena (New Britain). He imported boxing teams from all around the area, including New Haven, Norwalk, Plainfield, and Torrington, to name a few. Among the better Connecticut pugs were: "Codfish" Balesano (Hartford), "Goldfish" Balesano (Hartford), Gene Bonin (Willimantic), Tommy Brouillard (Danielson), "Big Boy" Carilli (Hartford), Benn Carr (Meriden), Jackie Clark (Hartford), Herman Dixon (Hartford), Harry Gentile (Hartford), Jimmy Gorman (Hartford), Joey Iannotti (New Haven), Bobby "Poison" Ivy (Hartford), Claude King (Hartford), Julie Kogon (New Haven), Joey Marcus (Windsor Locks), "Unknown" Morgan (Hartford), Spiro Morris (Bridgeport), Mike Murphy (East Hampton), and Joe Polowitzer (Windsor Locks).

In 1937, wanting to put his pugilistic skills to the test, Guglielmo Papaleo engaged in a variety of bootleg boxing battles, the first of which took place in Danbury. Trying hard to mask his avocation from his parents, or at least his mother, he typically hid the cash he earned in his socks or shoes. One day, his mother spotted the money. Concerned, she told her husband. Questioning the youth about the origin of the cash, Salvatore, a former amateur boxer, believed his son's explanation. He actually encouraged him to continue participating in the sport.

Speaking of battles, on May 3, 1938, Salvatore Papaleo, of 35 Portland Street, and Bernard Weinstein, of 146 Portland Street, were charged with breach of peace. Never afraid to take a stand, Salvatore wasn't going to quit now. The family tree appeared to be an apple.

As a young bootblack, Guglielmo had been led by fate to a downtown gym, where he had an opportunity to watch a popular amateur named Bobby "Poison" Ivy. Taking a fancy to the fighter, Papaleo aspired to be like him.

Bobby "Poison" Ivy

As the featherweight state champion, Bobby "Poison" Ivy was simply dominant. Born Sebastian DeMauro in Hartford on December 7, 1915, he was drawn to the sport early in life. Managed by Pete Reilly, who also handled Bat Battalino, Jack Delaney, Freddie Miller, André Routis, and Pete Scalzo, the youngster turned pro in January 1938. Standing five feet six and a half inches, his defensive skills compensated for his lack of power. After losing his pro debut, Ivy posted an impressive record of 11–2–1 in 1938. Becoming a workhorse for Reilly, Ivy went 16–4–1 in 1939. His loses, which were often more impressive than his victories, came at the hands of Sal Bartolo, Tony Dupre, an undefeated Marty Servo, and Joey Fontana—all quality fighters.[17]

On June 21, 1938, William S. Papaleo, as his name would read on the roll call, graduated from Henry Barnard Junior High during an early afternoon ceremony.[18] As is it for any teenager, it was a milestone in his life, even if it wasn't a priority (he spent two years at Hartford High). With nearly two dozen amateur/bootleg boxing battles under his belt, the only thing he wanted handed to him was a winner's share.

At the age of 15½, Willie Papaleo, seeking better instruction, walked into Pete

Looking at these two newsboys, working in downtown Hartford in 1924, it isn't hard to imagine Guglielmo Papaleo and Giulio Gallucci working the same streets (Library of Congress, LC-DIG-nclc-04059, color digital file from b&w original print).

Perone's gym one day and told the proprietor his story. He had spent a year at another gym, and a catchweight loss to Angelo Rodano—it occurred in Papaleo's 22nd amateur battle and was his first defeat—prompted the visit. Taking one look at the diminutive Papaleo, the amateur boxing advocate told the youngster to scram. After hearing similar stories from hundreds of pugs, Perone had no time for sympathy. Nevertheless, the next day Papaleo returned. He believed, he had to. Impressed by the teenager's tenacity, Perone told the kid to get in the ring.[19] Liking a bit of what he saw, Perrone agreed to provide some instruction. Honestly speaking, Perrone had more talent available to him than he knew what to do with. Ring time, especially for aspiring youngsters like Papaleo, was at a premium.

Since an amateur pugilist was defined as a person who engaged in boxing on an unpaid or non-payment basis, the word "unpaid" was subject to interpretation. It became common during this era for promoters and matchmakers to dance around the definition. For example, Dominic J. "Pete" Perone chose to gift the participants of his boxing shows. This method of appreciation helped the promoter sustain competitive fight cards while also incentivizing participants. A common offering was a watch or some similar form of appreciation. Following the promotion, if Perone knew certain boxers needed cash, he would offer to buy back the gift.[20] It was a fine line, but boxing has always walked that line.

On June 30, 1938, matchmaker Pete Perone, under the auspices of the Garden Athletic Club, placed Willie Papaleo on a promotion held at Capitol Park.[21] This was not Willie's first amateur bout—that, as previously mentioned, took place in

Danbury, Connecticut—but it was his first significant fight card. It was also the largest promotion of the summer at the outdoor venue, drawing 2,700 fight fans. Most were there to watch the volatile "Red" Doty—who was dropped three times before recovering—knock out the Cisco Kid. As always, Doty fought as if he was starring in an action film.

Nervous, Willie Pep, tipping the scales at 113, grabbed a decision victory over Henry Reese of South Windsor. Not overly impressed by Papaleo's performance, Perone nevertheless matched him on his next amateur card, held over at South Park on July 7. There he fought Holyoke, Massachusetts fighter Dennis Lyon to a draw. Both fighters scaled at 114. Again, the exposure was good as more than 3,000 fight fans packed the event that featured Al Stevens knocking out Bill Martin, Dennis Junior pounding out a victory over Johnny Ginaforte, and dubious "Red" Doty, who hit the canvas three times during the opening round, once again battling his way to victory. Pep, not satisfied by his performance, was less impressed when they spelled his name wrong in the local newspaper (Willie Pepe).

Rain washed away Pep's July 14 battle at Capitol Park in Hartford—he was to meet George "Georgie" Stone, who happened to be the state flyweight champion.[22] Pep's battle against Stone was rescheduled for Capitol Park on July 28. Surprisingly Stone, who possessed a crafty left upper cut and was quick on his feet, couldn't match his opponent punch for punch. Pep, tipping two pounds heavier at 116, seized the three-round decision. New Haven's Joe Iannotti topped the card that drew nearly 2,000 attendees.

Leaving Hartford, Pep captured a decision victory over Willimantic fighter Young Levine (Lavigne) on August 2. This time the event was held at Sandy Beach Arena out in Rockville. Back at Capitol Park two days later, Pep took a second-round TKO victory over Wilbraham, Massachusetts boxer Spike Murphy. An early body assault did the damage as the Hartford scrapper, tipping at 114, delivered a seemingly endless barrage of solid rights. Gradually moving up on Perone's fight cards, Pep's performances were now being highlighted by the press and noted by fight fans.[23]

Perone signed three state amateur champions for his Thursday evening weekly program at Capitol Park on August 11. Pep outpointed the familiar face of state amateur flyweight champion Georgie Stone, from Willimantic. In other bouts, "Big Boy" Carilli, state amateur heavyweight champion, nearly killed Massachusetts boxer Frankie Miller, and "Red" Doty demolished New Britain boxer Bobby Ellis. Henry Davis, state bantamweight champion, was scheduled to meet Joe Iannotti, but it fell through. Despite the card alterations, the exciting evening drew an estimated 2,500 fight fans.

Sitting in the Capitol Park audience was Bert Keane, the *Hartford Courant* columnist. No stranger to ringside, Keane could spot a talented fighter from across the Connecticut River. When he viewed the crafty Pep, who claimed to have reached the age of 16, he saw "a natural."[24] Keane predicted stardom for the youngster in less than three years.

Word of Keane's discovery traveled quickly through the sports department at the newspaper, and Pep garnered a headline on August 16. The article previewed Capitol Park's regular 12-bout amateur card and presumptuously compared Pep to elite Connecticut fighter Bat Battalino—by no means easy shoes to fill. Hartford's fighting "baby," as Pep was labeled, would meet Chuck Wolack from East Hampton on

August 18. Scaling at 115, three pounds heavier than his antagonist, Pep's speed alone allowed him to grab the decision. Though he was scheduled to meet Young Levine) at Capitol Park on August 25, the bout was scrubbed.

September, always a busy month for boxing, would prove challenging for Pep. Greeting the recognized face of South Windsor fighter Henry Reese, Pep (labeled Joe Pep in a newspaper preview), opened the month with a decision victory though the triumph was lackluster. Nevertheless, it was a win. Preparing for the Connecticut Amateur Boxing Championships (CABC) that were scheduled for the middle of the month, Pep squeezed in a bout, and a victory, over Georgie Stone, who was training for the same, over in Norwich at the Duwell Athletic club. Slated next to meet Collinsville boxer Joe Barisano the following week in Capitol Park, Pep felt he was on his game.

Still comfortable anchoring his promotions with knockout artists "Big Boy" Carilli and "Red" Doty, Perone wanted Pep on the card as an entertaining lead into his September 8 feature—Capitol Park was one of the CABC tournament venues. Pep didn't disappoint, as he took the decision victory over Joe Barisano.

Annual Connecticut Amateur Boxing Championships (CABC)

The annual Connecticut Amateur Boxing Championships marked the end of the summer. The preliminary rounds were scheduled for Capitol Park on September 16. Joining Willie Pep as an early entrant in the flyweight (112 pounds) class were Shadow Franciamore of Thompsonville, Earl Roys of Bristol, Georgie Stone of Willimantic (1938 champ), and Vito Tallarita of Thompsonville. Later, Joe Barisano of Collinsville and Henry Reese of South Windsor were added. Willie Pep, as fate had it, drew a bye during the first round.

On September 21, 1938, one of the deadliest and most destructive tropical cyclones (Category 3) ever to strike Long Island, New York, and New England made landfall. Whereas Long Island acted as a buffer against large ocean surges, the small shoreline towns to the east of New Haven experienced tremendous destruction. In New London, the winds and storm surge struck first, followed by the waterfront catching fire and burning out of control for 10 hours. Upstate didn't fare any better. For example, some of Willie Pep's friends unexpectedly rowed a boat across Hartford's flooded Bushnell Park. The destruction appeared to impact the lives of every Connecticut resident.

To little surprise, weather contributed to the postponement of the second round of the tournament, which was finally held on October 13 at the New Haven Arena. Gene Tunney, retired undefeated heavyweight champion, assisted in the refereeing duties during the preliminary rounds. The Connecticut resident was given a huge ovation from an audience estimated at about 4,000. (To stay fresh, as they say, Pep seized a decision victory over Zeno Hardy at the Arena in New Haven on September 30). In the semi-final, Willie Pep simply destroyed Vito Tallarita, dropping him for a five count in the second round and a nine count in the third. This left only Earl Roys of Bristol between Pep and the 112-pound championship. True to form, Pep did not disappoint and took the three-round decision—he lit up like a light bulb following the victory. With his first major ring success, Willie Pep basked in the attention.

In November, the Connecticut State Amateur Flyweight Champion took three battles. In New Britain, Pep participated in the opener of the indoor season of the Patrolmen and Firemen's Association at the Stanley Arena. The card was primarily an amateur feature but included one professional bout. Scaling at 120, Pep grabbed an impressive TKO victory over Buddy Lesso at the 1:50 mark of the second round. On November 11, he headed over to Norwich to battle the familiar face of Georgie Stone. Tipping at 120, two pounds heavier than his opponent, Pep carried off a decision victory. Finishing the month on November 17, Pep defeated Joel (Joey) Meyers, of New York, back in New Haven on a pro-amateur fight card.

A typical Friday night out for the 16 year old was going to the diner with a few male friends. Conversation centered around music, sports, and naturally girls. Dating wasn't a priority because most young men lacked jobs and therefore the finances required. Listening to the radio, be it baseball or boxing, also filled the time. Speaking of time, Pep was as cautious about getting a good night's sleep as watching his weight.

Ray Roberts, aka Sugar Ray Robinson

The feature bout at the Duwell (also spelled Du-Well) Athletic Club on December 2, 1938, saw Dan Wilson of New York outpoint Young Sharkey of Willimantic. Buried in the newspaper results was that one Ray Roberts, of New York, tipping at a believed 123 pounds, took a decision victory over Willie Pep, of Hartford, who scaled a reported pound lighter.[25] According to Pep, it was his 42nd amateur fight. As Connecticut amateurs were essentially allowed to fight for money, the City pugilists simply loved traveling north.

The club was located on the second floor of an old car barn located on North Main Street in Norwich, Connecticut.[26] The poorly ventilated and unheated hall was large enough to accommodate a ring, surrounded by four sets of bleachers, but not much else. Below it, on the south end of the building, was the Checkerboard Feed Company. Suffice it to say that the combination of feed and sweat discharged a distinctive fragrance.

At 105 pounds, Willie Pep wasn't overly anxious to fight any member of the Salem-Crescent Athletic Club, yet alone a lanky fighter called Ray Roberts. With Pep outweighed by at least 20 pounds, when his manager confirmed the match, Pep's jaw nearly hit the floor. At the opening bell, the welterweight was all over Pep like bees to honey. It took every ounce of energy for the Hartford fighter to make the distance. Pep rode the bike, witnessed a Bolo punch that thankfully missed, and ducked punches as if he had water in both ears. Afterwards, the Hartford pug took the loss hard. Putting a buck inside his front pocket, he gave the remaining eight dollars, or what was left of the loser's share, to his manager. But he never forgot the name Ray Roberts. Later, he learned the true identity of Mr. Roberts: his real name was Walker Smith, Jr., and he was fighting under the moniker Sugar Ray Robinson.

It was a year that many Connecticut residents, especially those impacted by the hurricane, hoped to forget. As the powerful storm rolled up the East Coast, it killed nearly 700 people, while damaging or destroying more than 50,000 houses. Property losses were estimated at over $300 million.

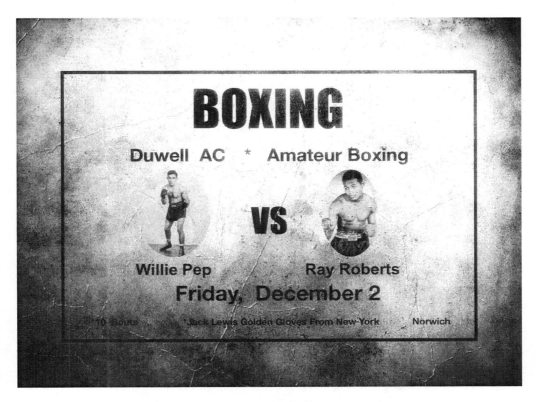

BOXING

Duwell AC * Amateur Boxing

VS

Willie Pep   Ray Roberts

Friday, December 2

10 Bouts   Jack Lewis Golden Gloves From New York   Norwich

If we had only known! It was amateur boxing at its finest on Friday, December 2, 1938, at the Duwell Athletic Club in Norwich, Connecticut. Lanky Ray Roberts, aka Sugar Ray Robinson, stepped inside a ring and disposed of Willie Pep.

The Pep household was a bit hectic during the holidays. Willie's sister, Frances Josephine Papaleo, age 10, and brother Nicholas, age two, occupied most of the attention of the adults. That was fine with Willie, age 16, who preferred to be out and about with friends rather than babysitting. Growing up quickly and providing some financial support for the family, Willie wasn't your average teenager.

1939

As the 1930s drew to a close, amateur boxing had faced its share of issues during the decade. Led by the state of New York, many officials were trying hard to gain authority over bootleg boxing, which was out of control earlier in the decade. For example, beginning on September 1, 1931, NYSAC (New York State Athletic Commission) handed down reform that stated: all amateur bouts would be limited to three rounds only (referees could not extend bouts); club fees, for a city such as Buffalo, were set at $250 a year; referees, judges, and physicians must be licensed at $25 a year; referees would be paid $15 a night, while judges would receive $10; and two experienced and licensed seconds would be mandated. For years, the regulations were simply ignored until NYSAC finally met a price point acceptable to bootleg promoters. No doubt prompting that acquiescence were the aggressive actions taken by authorities to shut down bootleg shows. Safety was a major issue, as was a fighter's status. The definitions of amateur, semi-professional, and professional boxing needed to be clarified.

By the end of the decade, there was also a concern that the State Athletic Commission was quantity-driven instead of quality. The sheer frequency of boxing shows was straining available talent. Commission rules prohibited a fighter from entering a ring more than a few times a week. Yet it was clear that this regulation was not being upheld.[27]

In addition to Perone, major participants in Connecticut amateur boxing during this period included: Ed Hurley (Hartford), Frank Alicky (Torrington), Al Caroly (New Haven), Mickey Dance (Waterbury) Joe DeMaria (Thompsonville), Dick Gray (New Haven), Charlie Pilkington (Meriden), Maurice Podoloff (New Haven), Henry Rothplatt (Rockville), and Johnny Voccola (Bridgeport). Connecticut State officials included Frank Coskey (Commissioner), Basil Fitzpatrick (deputy), and "Dinny" McMahon (Chief Inspector). Whereas a peaceful coexistence between state promoters and officials was sought, it didn't always take place; incidentally, more than once, Charlie Pilkington had to be separated from Dinny McMahon.

Weekly amateur shows were held in Bridgeport, Crystal Lake (Rockville), Danbury, Hartford, Meriden, New Britain, Norwich (winter schedule), Thompsonville, Torrington, Waterbury, and West Haven. When veteran matchmaker Lou Viscusi announced that he would be promoting regular professional boxing shows at Foot Guard Hall on Tuesday evenings beginning on January 17, 1939, it surprised few.[28] Having arrived in Hartford the previous year, he handled notable professional fighters Jimmy Leto and Steve Carr.[29] Optimistic that he could draw the promising amateur talent in the city to his stable, including Lou Dell, Bobby Ivy, and Jackie LaSalle, Viscusi's intentions were obvious.

As the year began, Pep was back at the Duwell AC on January 20. Tipping at 118, two pounds heavier than his opponent, he knocked out Georgie Stone in the opening round. Although he was gratified by the victory, boxing wasn't the only thing on the mind of the adolescent. Steady work, plus a regular paycheck from an employer, would provide greater support for his family. So Willie Pep pulled back from the fight picture.[30] It wasn't easy to do.

When the Connecticut State Amateur Championship began in May, Pep was not entered. In those weight classes of interest to the youngster: Earl Roys won the Featherweight (open) championship, Nick Schaffer picked up its Featherweight novice class crown, Russ Barnes was the Bantamweight (open) champion, and Joe Wasnick took the bantam novice title.

As the months passed. Pep yearned to return to the fight game. Taking a few bootleg battles, he found himself in Manchester at the Red Man's Arena on July 1. A loss to Earl Roys, who tipped two pounds lighter at 112, convinced the teenager to reestablish his priorities. Had he been in shape, he never would have lost to Roys, and he knew it.

Working himself back into condition, Pep sought to meet, then defeat, both amateur bantamweight champions, Russ Barnes (open category) and Joey Wasnick (novice).[31] He had something to prove and was hell-bent on doing it. Wasnick was scheduled to meet Pep on July 20; however, he was replaced by New Haven's Bill Dayton. Pep took out Dayton by way of an impressive third-round TKO. Next, he knocked out Roughhouse Vivienzo in the third round at Red Men's Hall in Manchester on July 28. It was the beginning of what he hoped would be a challenging and prolific fight schedule.

On August 3, Willie Pep, scaling at 121, snatched a points victory over bantam champ Russ Barnes of Windsor Locks, who scaled at 129. The bout was one of 12 contests featured on the weekly semi-pro boxing card at Capitol Park. Many of the skirmishes featured members of the Worcester, Massachusetts, boxing team that traveled south for the event. Delighted, no, ecstatic to defeat Barnes, Pep claimed his title whether anyone liked it or not.[32]

After knocking out Roughhouse Vivienzo in the third round at Capitol Park on August 10, Pep was inked to meet Joey Schultz of Meriden the following week at the same venue. Both fighters entered the ring at 120 pounds. The pair battled hammer and tongs over the first two rounds. When Pep spotted an opening in the third round, he fired a ravaging left to the gut of Schultz that dropped the fighter for an anguishing full count.

A man on a mission, Willie Pep, scaling at 123, opened September with a dominant points victory over New Rochelle's Joey Clapps, who was four pounds heavier. The contest took place at White City Stadium in West Haven on September 1. Next, in a fantastic display of determination, Pep, floored for a humiliating eight count in the opening round by Shelton fighter Dom Centerino, fought his way back to earn a draw. Despite the verdict by Referee George Proto, many spectators at White City Stadium in New Haven disagreed: They believed Pep earned the victory. Willie merely shook his head at Proto and left the ring.[33] Moving to the New Haven Arena on September 15, Pep, scaling at 123, dominated and defeated Joe DeJohn of Ansonia, who tipped three pounds heavier. It was an impressive three-round verdict. In his final bout of the month, on September 21 in New Haven, Willie Pep got what he wanted: a decisive three-round victory over Dom Centerino. If any opponent intended to demean him between the ropes, they had better rethink their strategy. As a belated birthday gift, the victory was perfect.

With fall approaching, Willie was more select with his bouts. He finished October in New Haven, on the 26th, by taking a third-round TKO over Mickey Pronto. However, he didn't fight again until December 1. Scaling at a post-holiday 130, Pep drew New Britain boxer Henry Davis, who was two pounds lighter. Conducted under the auspices of the Red Man Athletic Club (AC) in Manchester, it was an exceptionally competitive semi-pro boxing card.[34]

The Christmas holiday was a time of reflection for the teenager. Regardless of the opinions of others, Willie Pep knew he was ready to take his game to the next level.

1940

The "classy Hartford featherweight," as Pep was labeled by the *Journal*, would have his hands full with Buddy Donovan, the clever Yonkers Irishman.[35] The pair planned to do battle on January 4, in the main event at the Arena in New Haven. The reasoning was that Donovan clobbered Angelo Rodano, while Pep only drew against the Stamford pug (unverified bout). However, logic never found a home in a boxing ring. Pep punished Donovan over four rounds and took an unpopular decision.

As the line of demarcation between amateur, semi-pro, and professional boxing blurred, Willie Pep began toying with his options. Why not? Being on fight cards that included professional fighters, as he was for his first-round TKO over Vito Tallarita on March 1 in New Haven, he viewed the differences first-hand. The disparity, as he saw it, was in the paycheck and not in the ring.

Making the decision somewhat easier was the State Athletic Commission decision that initiated new fee requirements on July 1: All managers had to pay an annual fee of $25, regardless of a fighter's earnings. Prior to this, a manager only paid $25 for a license if his fighter had earnings in excess of $300. The fighters paid a $10 license fee. According to some, including the newly organized Connecticut Boxing Alliance, the Commission's fees and farcical control were out of line.

Following a Friday night, opening round TKO victory over Springfield, Massachusetts boxer Jimmy Stenta, at the Sandy Beach Arena in Crystal Lake, Pep drew to a close his illustrious amateur career. It was over.

Combining a supportive family, good genetics, outstanding instruction and opportunity, Willie Pep pieced together a brilliant amateur career: In 65 bouts, he posted a *claimed* record of 59–3–3. He was the 1938 Connecticut State Amateur Flyweight Championship and claimant to the 1939 Connecticut State Amateur Bantamweight Championship, so nobody disputed his ring prowess. In a class by himself, he had no doubt of his success as a professional boxer. With nothing left to prove, it was time to lift the bar of proficiency.

Two

Establishing Proficiency,
1940–1941

"A name pronounced is the recognition of the individual to whom it belongs. He who can pronounce my name aright, he can call me, and is entitled to my love and service."—Henry David Thoreau

No stranger to the Hartford fight scene, Willie Pep, following months of contemplation, decided to turn professional in July 1940. The semi-pro class he had participated in had nothing left to offer. Many participants, including those in his classification, were unhappy with the way the State Athletic Commission was conducting *their* business.[1]

When matchmaker Lou Viscusi, who had an impressive five-bout card scheduled for Thursday, July 25, at Bulkeley Stadium, offered Pep an opportunity to open the program, the youngster lit up like a Christmas tree. And of all places, Bulkeley Stadium. The 17-year-old pugilist just shook his head in disbelief.[2]

Thrilled but anxious, Pep, scaling at 123½, took a unanimous four-round decision over Joey Marcus, who tipped two pounds heavier. Setting a brisk pace early in the bout, Pep took control. Marcus, who could be a scrapper at times, wasn't landing at the same level of accuracy. Regardless, the crowd of nearly 1,300 appeared to thoroughly enjoy the professional debut of both fighters.

On the card as well, Larry Lovett took a six-round points victory over Danny Roberts, Mickey Williams grabbed a six-round points victory over Leo Dulmaine, an undefeated Marty Servo took a sixth-round technical knockout victory over Eddie Zivic, and Ernest "Cat" Robinson seized a thrilling ten-round points verdict over Carl Dell. Servo, with his movie star looks, drew an

An early publicity photograph of Hartford's most promising featherweight. Willie Pep often claimed an amateur record of 59–3–3, in 65 bouts.

23

Featherweights don't get much better than this trio of elite Connecticut pugilists. From left to right, publicity photographs of: Louis "Kid" Kaplan, Christopher "Bat" Battalino, and Willie Pep.

impressive female contingent to the event—to little surprise, few of the participants failed to notice. When it became clear that Zivic could no longer defend himself, referee Louis "Kid" Kaplan stopped the contest. The end came between the fifth and sixth rounds.

As one might imagine, the event was exhilarating for Willie Pep. Just fighting inside Bulkeley Field, over on the south end of the city near Little Italy, was impactful enough. But making his debut on a fight card topped by an undefeated fighter such as Marty Servo (Mario Severino), a cousin of former lightweight champion Lou Ambers, added to the excitement. Servo, like Ambers, was managed by the incomparable Al Weill. Last year, the connected fight manager was responsible for taking boxer Joey Archibald to the top of the featherweight division. Although Pep was exhausted from the evening when he arrived at home, images of the event danced nonstop through his head and delayed his sleep.[3]

Promoter Lou Viscusi, satisfied with Pep's performance, inked him to meet New Haven's Joey Wasnick at Bulkeley Stadium on August 8. Scaling a pound heavier than his opponent, Pep, who tipped at 124, delivered a precision right hand to the chin

A plaque commemorating Morgan G. Bulkeley Stadium, which was demolished in 1960. Located in Hartford, the venue not only hosted Pep's first three professional bouts, but was also the site of Babe Ruth's final baseball game.

of Wasnick that sent the fighter to dreamland in the third round.[4] A crowd of more than 1,200 turned out for the card that was topped by Ernest "Cat" Robinson and Carl Dell. Although the feature bout failed to recreate the excitement of their previous encounter, the card remained a success.

The big boys always drew a crowd, and that was indeed the case on August 29 at Bulkeley Stadium, as Hamden's Nathan Mann knocked out Hartford's Larry Lovett. A crowd of 4,200 watched the popular heavyweight—known best as a Joe Louis knockout victim in 1938—defend his New England crown by flooring Lovett five times. There must have been something in the Connecticut air, as Willie Pep, in the four-round opener, dropped Springfield, Massachusetts pug Tommy Burns three times in the first round.[5] Error-free left hooks created the damage and forced Referee Louis "Kid" Kaplan to stop the battle in the initial term. Using his two-pound advantage (124½ pounds), Pep delivered rapid precision punches that overpowered his opposer.

On September 5, it was out to Waterbury, 33 miles southwest of Hartford, to meet the familiar face of Joey Marcus at Randolph-Clowes Stadium. Honestly, neither the match nor the entire card made much sense. Pep's manager, Lenny Marello, no stranger to the Connecticut fight game as he partnered with Hy Malley to handle Christopher "Bat" Battalino, appeared to be fulfilling a favor. While the Windsor Locks fighter, who was 2½ pounds heavier at 126½, did fight his heart out, the four-round unanimous decision went to Pep.[6] The crowd of more than 2,200 fans enjoyed the preliminaries but weren't happy with the main event, an eight-round yawner that saw Larry Lovett take an unimpressive points victory over Charley Eagle.

It was back to Bulkeley Stadium on September 19 for a Viscusi promotion topped by Nathan Mann versus Larry Lovett. Tending to his stable of fighters (especially Jimmy Leto), Viscusi inked Pep, a fighter he was growing fond of, for a six-round slot on the card against Springfield's Jackie Moore. Not Viscusi's first choice, as Moore was making his professional debut, but the matchmaker was running out of time and needed a body. Pep, in his first six-round effort, used it as target practice on the way to a unanimous decision. The promotion drew an enthusiastic crowd of 4,300 fight fans, despite the crisp September air.[7]

Scheduled to meet Windsor Locks boxer Billy Marcus, Pep instead met Jimmy Ritchie on October 3 at Municipal Stadium in Waterbury. The Hartford boxer disposed of his Windsor Locks foe via TKO at the 2:02 mark of the third term—the bout was scheduled for six rounds. Pep would rather have met Marcus, but he understood that it was Ritchie's final recorded professional fight. The promotion, sponsored by the Mutual Aid Association of the Waterbury Police Department, drew more than 5,500 fight fans. The main event ended in controversy as Waterbury's Eddie Dolan, ahead in points, drew Hartford boxer Jimmy Leto. Hey, it's boxing.

On October 24, Willie Pep dominated New York fighter James McGovern to capture a four-round victory at the Arena in New Haven.[8] Flooring his opponent twice on the way to victory, the Hartford boxer's left hook was on target all evening. Despite two nine counts, McGovern, who substituted for Henry Davis, managed to go the distance. On the card, much to the delight of Pep, was Bobby "Poison" Ivy, who knocked out Johnny Buff in the second round of their co-feature.[9] As an early ring mentor, Ivy, who was also being handled by Marello, had many of the refined skills Pep desired.

Promoter Lou Viscusi booked Pep for two battles at the Stanley Arena in New Britain in November. On the 22nd, Pep, scaling at 129, punched out a sixth-round TKO over Springfield's Carlo Daponde (DePonte), who tipped at 132. It was Pep's damaging left hook that closed one eye of Daponde and crushed his muzzle. Referee Louis "Kid" Kaplan, noting the destruction, had little choice but to wave it off. Pep's retaliatory assault was prompted by being dropped in the opening minute of the battle to a nine count. More embarrassed than injured, the Hartford fighter responded by making mincemeat out of the countenance of his opponent.[10] A week later, Pep met Bristol, Rhode Island, pugilist Frank (Al) Topazio. At the 2:45 mark of the fifth round, it was a victory for Pep.[11] Delighted by the win, Pep still appeared anxious to get home and dig into the Thanksgiving leftovers his mother had set aside.

Taking one fight in December, Willie Pep knocked out New York tomato can (fighter with poor or diminished skills) Jimmy Mutone at the 1:45 mark of the second session. A blast to the breadbasket, followed by a solid left to the face of Mutone was responsible for the siesta. The contest took place on December 6 at the Stanley Arena in New Britain. In one of those hard-to-believe moments, Tony Canzoneri, former featherweight and lightweight champion, refereed the semi-final of the evening between Mike Angieri and Al Evans. Pep, who was only three years old when Canzoneri began his professional career, was raised on stories about the ring idol and was delighted to have a chance to meet him. The elite fighter was in the "Hardware City" for a banquet, conducted by the New Britain Italians, at the Stanley Hotel. Canzoneri, a three-division world champion, was revered by his culture for his skills, versatility, and longevity.[12]

1941

With the world on the verge of war, nobody was overly concerned about boxing in 1941. You could try to look the other way, and some did. But it wasn't easy, as the headlines were a constant reminder every morning in the dailies. Those who saw the writing on the wall volunteered early to begin their military service, while others— including more than 100,000 noncitizens—who were eligible chose to wait until they were called.

Undefeated at 10–0, Willie Pep began his year at the Valley Arena in Holyoke, Massachusetts. It was a hotbed for boxing, and any pug who wanted to be somebody eventually fought at the venue. Matched against Joe Echevarria, aka José Echevarría, a tomato can out of New York City, the Hartford boxer used him for target practice on January 13. When the lackluster six-round decision went in his favor, it wasn't a surprise. Echevarria had won only four fights since 1939. Both fighters weighed in at near 129, with a half-pound edge to the Hartford boxer. In his first professional battle outside the state of Connecticut, Pep enjoyed the experience and the increased exposure. Leaving the comfort of Connecticut, as even Pep knew from his amateur days, was always a risk. Thankfully, his manager knew the caliber of his opposition before taking the fight.

In contrast to Echevarria, Pep was scheduled to meet the undefeated Jackie Harris, from Boston, on January 28 back in the (New Haven) Arena. Quickly establishing himself as a knockout artist, Harris had recently sent Joey Marcus horizontal in less than a round. If Pep was looking for a challenge, this was it. (One might question what his handlers were thinking by booking Pep for six rounds against the Irishman.) However, a case of the flu stopped Harris before he ever entered the ring. Taking his place was fledgling Rhode Island boxer Augie Almeida. Pep played the left jab early, staking his claim while waiting to unload with that deadly left hook of his. Dropping Almeida for a five count in the second term, the Hartford boxer appeared satisfied with a strategy of cumulative destruction over an all-out attack. Referee Billy Conway, noting that Almeida was failing to defend himself, waved it off at the 2:20 mark of the sixth round. The event, which drew fewer than 2,000 fans, was capped by Johnny Compo's thrilling, systematic victory—the Elm City fighter tied up his opposer like a detained murder suspect—over Bobby Ivy.[13]

What's in a Name?

There was once a belief that "all press is good press," though that could certainly be debated. Some of the media boys, including the *Hartford Courant*'s W. J. "Bill" Lee, one of the better Connecticut sports minds, believed that Guglielmo Papaleo, aka Willie Pep, might be better off to adopt another moniker. To Lee's credit, he loved the youngster and believed in his potential, but he preferred a more intimidating nickname, such as Will "The Hitman" Leo or "Billy the Butcher" Papaleo. That, however, was about the only flaw Lee found in Pep's armor.

Lee, like other members of the press, fancied Bobby "Poison" Ivy as the next featherweight star (plus who doesn't love the moniker?); consequently, Pep, at least for now, was in the on-deck circle. The problem with Ivy was not his moniker, but his inability to stay in control in the ring. At least that was how some critics saw it. When he lost his head, he lost the fight.

Off went Willie Pep to Holyoke for the month of February. He was getting used to the 35-mile northern trek. On February 10, the Hartford boxer, who tipped at 128 for a one-pound advantage, knocked out Holyoke's Don Lyons in the second round. Lyons wasn't a tomato can, but he also wasn't much of a challenge; he lasted less than four and a half minutes. Pep simply spotted an angle and took it. Picking up some sparring cash, both Pep and Bobby Ivy were working with ring veteran Norment Quarles over at the Charter Oak Gym in Hartford. The Richmond, Virginia, fighter was in town to do battle against former lightweight champion Lou Ambers at the Armory on February 14.

Speaking of the "Herkimer Hurricane," Ambers, with his endless bobbing and weaving defense, had an enormous influence on Pep.[14] The ring veteran was one of the first fighters to recognize the value of ducking a punch instead of taking it. Al Weill, who handled Ambers, was a former ballroom dancer and lectured his fighters on improving their footwork; ergo, few fighters ever obtained the defensive skills of Lou Ambers. Marty Servo, also on the Armory fight card, was serving in the Army while trying to sustain a boxing career.

Puerto Rican prospect Ruby Garcia was Pep's next opponent at the Arena on February 17. With six consecutive knockout victories—five in the opening round—Garcia appeared to be a legitimate ring contender and hoped to prove it. Yet Pep, scaling at 129½, managed a six-round unanimous decision over his antagonist, who tipped at 131 and was the odds-on favorite. Dropped for a startling nine count—yep, you read that correctly—in the fifth round, Pep managed to take a united verdict thanks to a prolific and undeniable performance. After the fall, the Hartford boxer attacked Garcia as if his life depended on it—the decision certainly did. On their feet for most of the battle, the crowd, many having made the jaunt from Hartford, were thrilled with the contest.

If the recipe worked once, then it could work again, or so Willie Pep believed. In a rematch, he defeated Ruby Garcia via a six-round unanimous decision at the Valley Arena in Holyoke. It took place on March 3, and both fighters scaled at 129 pounds. Yet it came at a price. Garcia, with his lightning-quick right hand and accurate left jab, sliced Pep's right eye in the fourth round and his nose in the fifth. It was the first time Pep, as a professional, fought the same fighter in back-to-back battles.[15] Desperate for healing time, Pep didn't fight again until the end of the month.

Boxing impresario Lou Viscusi assembled an entertaining fight card for Tuesday evening, March 25, at Foot Guard Hall in Hartford. Topping the list was a rematch between East Sider Bobby Ivy and New Haven boxer Johnny Compo. To prepare, Willie Pep had been sparring with stablemate Bobby Ivy (both fighters were handled by Pete Perone and Lenny Marello). An overflow crowd turned out for the event that saw Ivy, who had lost in the pair's first battle, destroy Compo. Meanwhile, Pep, tipping at 130, a 4½-pound disadvantage, grabbed a six-round victory over Marty Shapiro in the semi-final. A novice from Bridgeport, Shapiro fought a slipshod battle against his Hartford opponent. Hoping to use his weight advantage to yield a Hail Mary final blow, Shapiro failed and looked foolish. Pep finished March, on the 31st, back at the Arena in Holyoke, by knocking out Brooklyn boxer Joey Gatto. A trusty left hook to the chin was responsible for the verdict at the 2:20 mark of the second round. Having hit the canvas briefly in the first round (no count), Pep, scaling at 127½, dropped his adversary, who tipped two

Governor's Foot Guard Hall, which still stands at 159 High Street in Hartford, was the site of a few of Willie Pep's professional ring battles.

pounds lighter, multiple times in the second round. As the main event of the evening, on a weak undercard, it drew about 1,700 fans.

Scheduled to meet Danny Carabella, the former National Golden Gloves featherweight champion, on April 14 at the Arena in Holyoke, Willie Pep was utterly thrilled. It was the six-round feature on a seven-bout card. However, Carabella took ill and was replaced by Harlem fighter Henry Vasquez. Still a teenager, Vasquez nevertheless was a dangerous substitution, and the Hartford battler knew it. At a 1½-pound disadvantage, Pep took the first two rounds, stayed out of range for the next two, then turned on the engines during the final rounds to take the six-round unanimous decision. Back at Foot Guard Hall on April 22, Willie Pep was part of an interesting card that featured three undefeated fighters: Marty Servo, Pep, and Freddie Cabral. As fate had it, all three fighters remained that way. Scaling at 128, a three-pound disadvantage, Pep controlled his opponent, punching bag Joey Silva, over six rounds to take the victory. Silva, who bobbed and weaved but not much else, did manage to draw blood from the nose of his adversary.

You had to hand it to Lou Viscusi for not giving up on Jimmy Leto. The talented welterweight, who began his career in Tampa, Florida, back in 1924, had compiled

over 100 victories against about 25 defeats, and the sanguine manager was still trying to get him a title shot against Fritzie Zivic. Leto topped a May 6 card at Foot
Guard Hall that included Norwalk sensation Angelo Rodano—yep, the same youngster who handed Guglielmo Papaleo an early amateur defeat and had recently compiled a dozen straight professional victories—and Willie Pep. Unfortunately, the pair
weren't fighting each other. At the 1:30 mark of the second round of a scheduled
six-round contest, Pep knocked out Lou Puglese, who substituted for Joey Stack. Both
fighters scaled at 127 pounds. A Pep right hand did the damage and dropped the Philadelphia pug like an oversized anchor. In a twist, not to mention growing interest in
having Pep alter his moniker, the fighter was announced as Willie Papaleo.[16]

Participating in the annual Springfield Boys Health Camp boxing show in the
Valley Arena at Holyoke on May 12, Willie Papaleo, scaling at 127½, took a six-round,
uninspiring decision over New York punching bag Johnny Cockfield, who tipped at
129. For Papaleo, who couldn't care less about the perceived identity crisis, which by
the way was in sharp contrast to the racial indignity of Cockfield, who was referred
to by his skin color, the fight game at this stage of his career was all about an impressive payday.

Pep was scheduled to meet Worcester boxer Harry Hintlian at Red Men's Arena
in Manchester, Connecticut, on June 12, but the six-round bout was rained out.[17] It
was rescheduled for June 19. Tipping at 129½, Pep grabbed the six-round verdict over
Hintlian, who scaled at 132. Having given up on his surname alteration, Willie Pep
was placed on an attractive card held at Bulkeley Stadium on June 24. Tipping at
127½, the Hartford pugilist delivered a targeted right hand to the chin of neophyte
Boston boxer Eddie DeAngelis that sent him to dreamland in the third round. Pep
struck his adversary so hard that Referee Frank Petrolle ignored a count. Prior to the
kayo, DeAngelis had hit the canvas twice in the second round for short counts, and
twice in the third for nine counts. Speaking of seeing stars: They were out in Hartford
as Louis "Kid" Kaplan refereed the main event that saw Bobby Ivy defeat Harry Jeffra. In Jeffra's corner was former heavyweight legend Jack Dempsey. If you had to pick
an adjective that described Pep's performance at this point in his career, it would be
"spectacular."[18]

On July 15, veteran Jimmy Gilligan, from Buffalo, met Willie Pep at Bulkeley Stadium in an eight-round semi-final event. Scaling at 128½, a one-pound advantage,
Pep won every round on his way to a unanimous decision. Frankly, Gilligan, who was
sent to a nine count in the second term, was lucky to make the distance.[19] Pep, who
was being signed to fights with an extraordinary frequency, seemed to thrive on the
pace.

Part of an exciting evening of boxing at Bulkeley Stadium on August 5, Willie Pep, scaling at 129, or nearly five pounds heavier than his opponent, stopped Paul
Frechette at the 1:40 mark of the third round.[20] Pep had floored the Bangor, Maine
boxer for two nine counts earlier in the round, and Referee Billy Conway had little
choice but to wave it off.[21] Six days later, at the Carpet City Arena in Thompsonville
(20 miles north of Hartford), Willie Pep knocked out Puerto Rican boxer Eddie Flores
in the first round of their scheduled eight-round clash. At the 2:30 mark, the Hartford fighter landed an outstanding right cross to the face of his adversary, followed by
a targeted left hook. Four days later, on August 15, Pep agreed to replace New Haven
fighter Mickey Williams in his bout against Terry Amico at the Meadowbrook Arena

in North Adams, Massachusetts. However, the card promoted by Jimmy Quinton was rained out.

Taking a break from the boxing circuit, Willie Pep wanted to enjoy some of the money he had been earning. At 19, his final year as a teenager, he knew there was life beyond the ring, he just needed time to find it. Meanwhile, Lenny Marello contracted his fighter to one of the featured eight-round battles at the New Haven Arena on September 25. It was a great opportunity, as the first event of the new season always drew plenty of attention. Willie Pep, who tipped at 125½ and outweighed his adversary by two pounds, stopped Irish Jackie Harris at the 2:37 mark of the opening round. Knowing that the Boston fighter had never failed to go the distance, the 1,500 spectators on hand were stunned by the action. Working behind a commanding left jab, Pep patiently waited, then unloaded a powerful right uppercut that sent Harris down for a nine count. Arising, the groggy hub fighter was nothing more than a target. Pep unloaded the chamber and sent him back to the canvas. Although Harris arose again, Referee Lou Bogash, sensing the damage, waved it off.[22]

Lou Viscusi's endless effort to land a featherweight title fight for Bobby Ivy was indicative of his style. He was simply relentless in his pursuit; it was becoming his trademark. By the third week in September, it looked as if that match might happen at either Bulkeley Stadium or the State Armory in Hartford. The politics of negotiation went like this: Al Weill managed Joey Archibald, the featherweight champion of the world. Since Weill and Viscusi were like peas and carrots, Weill agreed to allow Archibald to fight contender Chalky Wright—but only if Wright agreed to meet Bobby Ivy for the title should he defeat Archibald. Well, when Wright knocked out Archibald, his manager Eddie Walker was held to the carpet, as they say. Naturally, Viscusi felt Walker owed Ivy an opportunity. Plus, Ivy had earned it by defeating Archibald (in a non-title bout), Harry Jeffra, and Angelo Radano in succession. Walker knew this and didn't want his fighter in the ring with Ivy, but he also knew he owed Weill, an exceptionally connected player in the fight game, a favor. Viscusi, in an excellent position, would just have to wait and see.

Matchmaker George Sheppard inked Willie Pep to an eight-round clash, at the New Haven Arena on October 9, against Mexican Carlos "Bandit" Manzano. It wasn't expected to be much of a contest, and it wasn't. The Hartford boxer dominated every round and even sent his opponent to the canvas for a five count in the seventh session. Back in Hartford on October 21, Pep agreed to an eight-round bout at Foot Guard Hall against Providence pug Al Dionne. Matchmaker Pete Perrone was handling the card and hoped that Pep would pack them into the venue, but it didn't work out that way. Brooklyn fighter Conny Savoy (Connie Savoie), little more than a sacrificial offering, substituted for Dionne. Combinations by Pep in the second round dropped his opponent for a nine count, then to a five count, and finally the fight was stopped with Savoy sitting on the canvas, trying to recall the make and license plate of the truck that hit him.

In a bizarre and unexpected twist, Willie Pep and "a couple wise guys" as he called them, got a car and headed to California. The journey, which took four days and four nights, was filled with twists and turns. Needing money, Pep hooked up with Manuel Ortiz for sparring in trade for pocket cash. Pep claimed he was paid a dollar a round. Booked on a November 7 fight card at Hollywood Legion Arena, Pep, who was supposed to meet Kent Martinez, ended up picking up a four-round decision over Buddy Spencer, not to mention 50 bucks. Placed on the fight card courtesy of Bill Gore, a gentleman from Rhode Island who happened to catch the youngster sparring, Pep got a lucky break in more ways than one. The highlight of the trip, at least for Pep, was meeting film actor George Raft. Known for his portrayals of gangsters in crime melodramas of the 1930s and 1940s, Raft enjoyed the attention even though he had no idea who anyone in the group was or why they were in California. Raft's big break came when cast as the second lead in the 1932 classic, *Scarface*. His character, Guino Rinaldo, became known for flipping a coin during various scenes, and Pep, as well as his Connecticut friends, always enjoyed mimicking the behavior.

Returning home at the end of November, Viscusi had originally booked Pep for a November 25 bout at Foot Guard Hall, but it fell through. The Hartford fighter ended up appearing in an eight-round semi-windup at Holyoke's Valley Arena against Brooklyn boxer Davey Crawford on November 24. Noticeably a bit out of shape—the California air can do that to a fella—Pep, who tipped at 127, was able to dance his way to a decision. It was not without consequences, however, as the Hartford feather suffered a nasty slice over his left eye that required stitches.[23]

A bit before 8:00 on Sunday morning, December 7, 1941, a surprise military strike by the Imperial Japanese Navy Air Service against the United States naval base at Pearl Harbor in Honolulu, Territory of Hawaii, ushered in America's formal entry into World War II the following day. Life as everyone knew it changed. The headline on the front page of the *Hartford Courant* on December 8, 1941 read "Japs Declare War, Bomb U.S. Bases, President Meets Congress Today."

Change was clearly in the air on every front. Word was that Pep's management was shifting responsibilities. First, Lou Viscusi relinquished the affairs of Bobby "Poison" Ivy. Next, it was announced that Pete Reilly would handle "Poison." Reilly wanted to handle Pep as well, but Viscusi wouldn't stand for it. Viscusi, who had other things in mind, wanted greater control of the fighter. And Viscusi would commemorate the change: On December 8 came news that Guglielmo Papaleo would be making his first appearance inside Madison Square Garden. His opponent would be Ruby Garcia. It would be a preliminary bout on the Fritzie Zivic versus Young Kid McCoy fight card. Viscusi claimed that this was his doing, thanks to his friendship with Benny Jacobs, Uncle Mike's (Jacobs') nephew.[24]

On December 12, in his Garden debut, Willie Pep , scaling at 126½, took a challenging four-round decision over Puerto Rican Ruby Garcia, who tipped at 127¾. A badly sliced right cheek that occurred in the second round ignited the Hartford feather. Pep's precision left hook carried him to victory, as did his legs. Garcia's constant in-fighting was countered by Pep's wise and swift exits, wisely as the Hartford boxer endured some damaging blasts. It was one of those contests where four rounds felt like forever.

So the world was at war, and Willie Pep, who was destined to have his part in it, was fighting his way into title contention, and Lou Viscusi, who was running out of time and knew it, still had a favor in his back pocket.

THREE

The War Years,
Part 1, 1942–1943

"When I was a young fellow I was knocked down plenty. I wanted to stay down, but I couldn't. I had to collect the two dollars for winning or go hungry. I had to get up. I was one of those hungry fighters. You could have hit me on the chin with a sledgehammer for five dollars. When you haven't eaten for two days you'll understand."—Jack Dempsey

War was an all-encompassing crusade that transformed our nation. People were mobilized and directed toward serving a single goal: reaching complete industrial capacity to service the needs of the conflict. This meant that all critical activities, such as farming, labor, and manufacturing, needed to be brought under government control. The use of personal pronouns such as *I* and *me* were quickly replaced by *us* and *we*.

It was difficult to believe, at least for some, that by the conclusion of 1943, America would have 65 million people servicing the war effort. Discretionary income, not to mention leisure time, was at a premium. Thankfully, in addition to servicing that effort, folks attempted to balance their lives with what few pre-war interests remained. Professional sports, which the President of the United States—also the Commander in Chief—believed served a useful purpose, needed to find a way to continue. At the same time, preservation without many key participants such as champions and contenders would be no simple task.

Would Chalky Wright of New York, the featherweight champion, fight in Hartford in January 1942? And if so, whom would he fight? These were just a couple of questions on the minds of Connecticut fight fans. Naturally, the first name that came to mind was Bobby Ivy. Pete Reilly, Ivy's manager, believed that Hartford, as a location, was out of the question. Meanwhile, the guilefully soft-spoken Lou Viscusi, who had been keeping in touch with Eddie Walker, Wright's manager, was strategically crafting a scenario. If the champion fought in Hartford, regardless of the opponent, Viscusi wanted the promotion. More important, he wanted Wright's decision-makers comfortable with the Connecticut fight game and everyone around it. Were his intentions sincere? Yes. Was there more to it than just the promotion? You betcha!

Opening the fight year in Fall River, Massachusetts, Willie Pep was slated to meet tomato can Mexican Joey Rivers over eight rounds at the Casino.[1] It would be a warm-up battle for his second appearance at Madison Square Garden on January 16. It was time, he believed, to remove the holiday ring rust. Scaling at 129, a one-pound disadvantage, Pep happened to open a cut over his opponent's left eye in the opening round. Unfortunately for Rivers, his corner never got the laceration under control, and the fight was waved off in the fourth term. On to Madison Square Garden.

Sensational! Inside New York's prestigious boxing venue, Willie Pep did not disappoint. Dropping Sammy Parrotta, a stablemate of headliner Fritzie Zivic, three times, once in the opening round and twice in the second, Pep skillfully fought behind his left hand and picked up the four-round decision. Bolting out of his corner like Bat Battalino at the opening gong, Pep unloaded on his adversary, who outweighed him by nearly nine pounds. Surprised, Parrotta arose quickly from his initial visit to the canvas. But in the following round, after a left briefly dropped him again, he caught an unforgiving right that sent him horizontal for an eight count. To his credit, Parrotta, a good fighter, managed a few accurate flurries and even drew blood from Pep's muzzle in the third round. But it was not enough.

Garden matchmaker Nat Rogers, thrilled by the performance, made it clear it that it wasn't going to be the Hartford youngster's last visit to boxing's Mecca. The fight card, which drew over 15,000 fans, also saw local amateur sensation and now professional boxer Ray Robinson defeat Fritzie Zivic via a tenth-round TKO. By most counts, it was Robinson's 27th consecutive victory.[2]

A Connecticut Dream Bout

Willie Pep versus Bobby Ivy was still a dream bout to Connecticut fight fans. It was only a matter of time, or at least most thought so. Staying in Hartford, Pep grabbed three consecutive eight-round decision victories—over Abie Kaufman (1/27), Angelo Callura (2/10), and Willie Roache (2/24).[3] All took place in Foot Guard Hall. None of the three contests was challenging, which sparked the question: Were Pep's handlers being too cautious? At times it looked that way, but that wasn't the case. Behind the scenes, Lou Viscusi was artfully orchestrating every move. For example, after the Kaufman fight, Viscusi had an opportunity to ink Pep to a date against Jackie Wilson, the NBA featherweight champion, but he turned it down. The general opinion among those close to the situation was: Willie Pep was still a preliminary fighter. Systematically working his way up in competition, and rounds, was the proper path.[4] Consistent success over eight rounds was the fighter's next hurdle.

Speaking of Viscusi, he was also discreetly asking members of the media to put more emphasis on Pep's winning streak. Nothing garnered attention in big city press like consecutive victories; consequently, it could pressure a title match.

On March 9, at the 12th annual boxing show at the Connecticut School for Boys, Willie Pep served a guest referee. He joined other guest arbiters such as Billy Taylor and Stretch Noonan—the latter the tallest referee in the world at 6'11". Enjoying the task and the adulation, Pep got a taste of how difficult a role a referee had.[5]

In one of those classic Connecticut ring battles, tinged with ethnic pride, Guglielmo Papaleo, aka Willie Pep, seized an eight-round decision victory over Johnny Campagnuolo, aka Johnny Compo, the older brother of Eddie Compo (as fate had it, Pep would eventually meet Eddie as well). It took place on March 18, at the Arena in New Haven, and not surprisingly attracted over 5,000 fervent fight fans. Winning all eight rounds, the youngster's ring command, made Compo, a good fighter, look like an amateur. Pep was landing three punches to one returned. Dumbfounded by the inexorable exchanges, Compo's back was against the ropes far more times than anticipated; moreover, he couldn't believe Pep had that level of ring dominance. Compo's punches, when they landed, were hard enough to anger Pep, but not powerful enough to put him away. And, though there were no knockdowns during the contest, Compo's left eye was so badly sliced that it nearly caused a stoppage.

Bill Gore—Completing the Triumvirate

A lanky, sleepy-eyed trainer by the name of Bill Gore found his way to Hartford in March 1942. It wasn't by accident, as he was looking after a fighter named Bill Murray. A solid Ohio lightweight, Murray was making an impression by meeting and beating veterans such as Freddie Foran, as he did in Foot Guard Hall on March 10. Also working with other fighters such as former light heavy champion Melio Bettina, Gore always kept an eye open for new talent. Always. When he caught a closer glimpse of Willie Pep (he had seen him in California) in his hometown setting, it confirmed his belief in the fighter to such an extent that in a soft-pitch sales effort, he presented his corner credentials in the form of questions to Pep's handlers: Have you thought about altering the diet habits of your fighter in order to enhance his power and endurance? It wasn't about what a pugilist ate, but how and when he ate it. Having groomed Bettina, Pep's court listened intently to what Gore had to say, and they liked it. A native of Providence, Rhode Island, the phlegmatic instructor had intriguing positions about nearly every element that impacted a boxer's skills. More important, he was certain that he could craft a fighter to gain a competitive edge. Since one of Pep's finer characteristics was listening to ring scholars, he made an ideal student. Instructing the fighter once would prove enough. The triumvirate was essentially complete.[6]

New Hartford Auditorium—331 Wethersfield Avenue

Hoping to add to his victory streak (38 by most counts), Willie Pep met Toronto fighter John "Spider" Armstrong. It was the inaugural bout at the new Hartford Auditorium on April 14. The facility, with a seating capacity of 4,000, was created from the old Wethersfield Avenue car barns. Lou Viscusi and Ed Hurley, operating under V. and H. Promotions, planned on handling all the fight cards at the venue. Billed as Pep's toughest competition yet, Armstrong, who worked out of Al Weill's stable, was best known for nearly capturing a victory from Harry Jeffra. It would stay that way as Willie Pep, who scaled at 127½, knocked out Armstrong, who tipped at 126, in the fourth round. It was an impressive victory. In front of a standing room only crowd, Pep floored his adversary twice to nine counts in the opening round. However, Armstrong regained his composure and even staggered Pep in the second with a powerful left hook.[7] Scoring three impressive rights to the countenance of the Hartford feather enabled the Canadian boxer to hold on in round three, but not much longer. A flurry of combinations sent Armstrong down for a nine count in the fourth. Once Armstrong was vertical again, Pep turned out the lights with a compact right. A capacity crowd of 4,000 fight fans cheered nearly every flurry by the hometown feather. For those who couldn't make the fight, The Travelers FM radio station W53H broadcast the fight. Handling the blow-by-blow was the incomparable Bob Steele, together with Keyes Perrin. Worth noting: Pep, who was referenced as "The will o' the wisp Hartford youngster," in the *Hartford Courant,* had Bill Gore working in his corner.[8]

The following morning, Pep, still tired from the evening's events, headed over to Viscusi's office to collect his payment for services rendered. Picking up his first thousand-dollar purse ($1,032.70), the teenager was ecstatic.[9] Keeping a few bucks, Pep passed the bulk of the cash to his mother. Like many fighters, he also set aside money to purchase war bonds. After Pep's departure, Lou Viscusi and Ed Hurley continued unloading an event summary to Bill Lee, *Hartford Courant* sports editor. Viscusi confirmed three features about his fighter: popularity that appeared to be greater than Bobby Ivy; perseverance that was getting stronger with each passing bout; and potential, that everyone believed mimicked many of the former featherweight champions. Speaking of elite boxers, at a war bonds rally only a few days before the fight, Christopher "Bat" Battalino gave Willie Pep a heart-to-heart talk. Battalino reminded the youngster of the fortitude and commitment necessary to be a champion. In awe of Battalino, Pep earnestly listened to every word.

This is the front of a building that was once the Hartford Auditorium. The venue opened in 1942, at 331 Wethersfield Avenue in Hartford.

The Papaleo family made into the *Hartford Courant Magazine*, on Sunday, April 26, 1942. Bill Lee penned an inspiring article titled "Boy with a Wallop" that included a photograph of Willie Pep and kin eating Sunday dinner. The article confirmed that the 19-year-old pugilist was supporting his family due to his father's inability to work.[10]

Heading south to New Haven on May 4, Pep boxed eight rounds to a decision over Morris Curley Nichols, a Jewish scrapper from New York City; it was common for promoters to use slants to attract fight fans, be it race or religion. As every Pep bout was being proclaimed by the dailies as the toughest of his career, it was difficult for fans to get the straight dope regarding the competition. While this was a challenge, as Nichols had been training with Chalky

Wright, it lacked intensity; moreover, Nichols, who preferred in-fighting, was successfully kept at bay by Pep. Staggered in the third round and dropped briefly in the fourth, Nichols failed to execute a battle strategy, or game plan if you will.[11] Nevertheless, as matchmaker George Sheppard's first fight in the Arena, it was considered a success. Bill Gore, now officially training Pep, was matched against Nichols' trainer, who happened to be the inimitable Ray Arcel. Ironically, Gore, at this stage of his career, was being compared to Arcel.

It was back to the Auditorium in Hartford on May 12. Willie Pep, scaling at 128 or a two-pound advantage, dropped New York fighter Aaron Seltzer in the second round to a nine count, before boxing his way to an eight-round points victory. Seltzer, who had been touted as stiff competition because he

In 2011, the Hartford City Council renamed Grove Street in honor of Hall of Fame broadcaster Bob Steele. He was a former boxer and the voice of morning radio for millions of New Englanders.

held former feather champ Joey Archibald to a draw, fought cautiously after hitting the deck. And it cost him. His circumspect behavior even drew criticism from Pep, who appeared lethargic during the lackluster affair. Archibald was now being mentioned as a possible ring opponent for Pep. But first, the Hartford phenom had to get by Joey Iannotti, a tough Bronx featherweight.

On May 26, inside the Hartford Auditorium, Willie Pep controlled—he gave his adversary no time to mount an offensive—Joey Iannotti over eight rounds to add another victory to his resume. Scaling at 127 pounds, about two pounds lighter than his opponent, Pep simply unloaded the arsenal on the Bronx boxer. To the credit of Pep's iron-jawed opponent, Iannotti took it and remained vertical. Pep, who in recent fights struggled with a cut above his left eye, had the nasty wound opened again. Thankfully, it didn't impede his mission. The bout drew about 3,500 fight fans, and it was clear that Willie Pep was assisting in paying the mortgage at the new facility.

Defeating Iannotti, a talented pugilist, Pep, at least in the eyes of many, was performing at a much higher level. Talk now focused back on Joey Archibald, the former featherweight champion, who was under the care of Al Weill. Ironically, should the match be made, it would be too big for the auditorium—Pep's popularity was close to exceeding the capacity of the venue. Wisely, Viscusi, who knew Weill like a brother, had backed up the promotion by reserving Bulkeley Stadium. Details would be worked out, it was hoped, once Weill returned from New York, where his Golden Boy, Marty Servo, was battling Sugar Ray Robinson.[12]

A mere eight days into June, the transaction was complete: Willie Pep would meet Joey Archibald over ten rounds (it was initially advertised for eight) on the night of June 23 at Bulkeley Stadium, if the weather cooperated. Viscusi, as always, had a multitude of active promotions, both indoors and out. Admittedly this wasn't the Archibald of old. He hadn't won a battle since October of last year, but he was a former champion and a *name*. The Rhode Island featherweight, as many recalled, made his professional debut back in 1932 and held victories over Harry Jeffra, Leo Rodak, and Mike Belloise. A recent ankle injury had hampered him a bit, but it was healing. Speculation was that if Pep could get by Archibald, he could face a ranked fighter.

Contributing to the war effort, specifically the Victory House drive, Willie Pep conducted an exhibition on June 20. Of all places, it was held in front of the historic Old State House in downtown Hartford. Known as the venue that hosted the start of the Amistad trial back in 1839, the history behind the building was notable. To have a boxing ring set up the grounds was quit a treat for fight fans—Lord knows enough fighting had taken place inside the landmark.

While Pep was exhibiting at the State House, his opponent remained in New York, training at Stillman's gym. Archibald arrived in Hartford the day of the fight, accompanied by Al Weill, his manager and Charlie Goldman, his trainer. The fighters were ready. Over 5,500 fight fans found their way to Bulkeley Stadium to watch Willie Pep, scaling at 128½, 2½ pounds heavier than his adversary, win every round of a ten-term journey. At least that was how referee Louis "Kid" Kaplan saw it. Frustrating Pep were Archibald's swift retreats. This left the Hartford boxer little choice but to take each round one punch at a time. The highlight of the evening came in the seventh round, when a Pep left hook to the body of Archibald briefly floored the fighter. For most, Pep's victory was convincing yet uninspiring.[13]

On July 1, the team of Lou Viscusi and Ed Hurley, under the umbrella of V. and H. Promotions, made a significant change: Viscusi, who previously had a role as matchmaker and promoter, would now devote most of his time to managing Willie Pep. Hurley would handle all the firm's other responsibilities. Pep's irrefutable ring potential was what sparked the change. Devoting a full-time effort to driving Pep to the Featherweight Championship of the World had become a priority. Hurley, a legend in Connecticut fight promotion and the man who handled many of Bat Battalino's bouts, approved the changes. Engaging in a variety of promotions, from wrestling and boxing to even professional football and figure skating, the pair believed the change made sense.

Meanwhile, Willie Pep, in addition to nearly 5,000 other area youths (ages 18–20), registered for the military draft; specifically, he registered with Local Board 2B. Serial and order numbers were based on date of birth and assigned as needed.

It was announced, during the first week of July, that Willie Pep would meet

Boston boxer Abe Denner for the Featherweight Championship of New England. Scheduled to meet on July 21 at Bulkeley Stadium in Hartford, the pair planned to conduct business over 12 rounds—it would be Pep's first journey over the ten-round mark. With an awkward style, "The Boston String Bean," who held victories over Carl Guggino, Sal Bartolo, and Tony Dupre, would present a challenge.[14]

A couple of positive notes led up to Pep's next battle: He made *The Ring* magazine ratings for his 126-pound class, and it was announced that the winner of his next contest would receive a New England featherweight championship belt. That was all the incentive the Hartford youngster needed.

With Pep taking ten of 12 rounds, referee Lou Bogash held up the hand of Willie Pep. Next, State Athletic Commissioner Frank S. Coskey presented Pep with the new championship belt put up by *The Ring*. The glow on Pep's face, even with his cheeks noticeably swelled, could be seen all the way to Middletown. It was a relatively clean battle, yet Denner was warned more than once for hitting on the break. There were no knockdowns. Pep, who landed more punches, scaled at 125½, a half-pound advantage over his opponent.[15] As usual, he mixed his punches well and relied on his left hook to the body, followed with solid one-two combinations. Denner, from all accounts, failed to impress. A crowd of about 6,000 fans turned out for the entertaining Bulkeley Stadium fight card.[16]

Heading southwest about 30 miles from Hartford, Pep met the familiar face of Mexican Joey Silva on August 1 at Randolph-Clowes Stadium in Waterbury. Originally scheduled for July 31, the fight was postponed because of rain. Having taken a six-round victory over Silva last April at Foot Guard Hall, Pep hoped to be equally as successful over the eight-round jaunt. He was. The confident Hartford feather continued his unbeaten winning streak by pummeling his opposer into submission: Battered over six rounds, Silva was struggling to stand as the gong ended what would be the final round. Referee Louis "Kid" Kaplan quickly noted the surrender by Silva's corner—it was a technical knockout victory. Outweighed by nearly ten pounds, Pep, tipping at 128½, waltzed around Silva as if he was stuck in quicksand. Once again it was the Hartford fighter's left hook to the body that slowed his adversary. Driven into the ropes and even pushed through, Silva was spun by Pep much like Fred Astaire twirling Ginger Rogers. The New England feather champion was perfecting a hallmark move that was never more evident than in this battle.

Under Gore's guidance, Pep was enhancing his distinctive actions while developing an arsenal of precision punches (please see Appendix C: Skills Overview).

Viscusi, strategy in place, inked Pep to meet Pedro Hernandez, the number-two division challenger and a boxer who won over four times as many bouts as he lost. The pair would tangle for ten rounds inside Bulkeley Stadium on August 11. Since Al Weill handled Hernandez, it wasn't a hard sell to get the match. But Weill wanted a shot at Chalky Wright as much for his fighter as Viscusi did for Pep. Whereas the pair were friends, they were both clever and competitive businessmen. Hernandez planned to challenge Pep's ring prowess from a number of perspectives, if he could find a way to trap him.

Some people could catch him, like the local police. Willie Pep, who was issued a speeding ticket, faced acting Judge Max M. Savitt.[17] He had committed the violation while driving a used car that he had purchased the day before. Judge Savitt, aware of who was standing in front of him, wished the Hartford featherweight luck in his battle against Hernandez and fined him ten dollars plus costs. It appeared that Pep's speed translated beyond the ring. Regrettably, as the years passed, his foot would get heavier.

When Hernandez arrived in Hartford, Al Weill brought him over to the Charter Oak Gym for a bit of show and tell. Trainer Charlie Goldman confirmed his fighter's preparedness before sending him into the ring to spar with local welter Johnny Duke, a Pep friend and sparring partner. Weill, no stranger to every aspect of the business, was trying to use Duke to psyche out Pep or plant a level of doubt in the mind of the boxer. Ring-savvy Duke confirmed the cleverness of Hernandez but felt Pep was quicker. Not long after Weill's fighter departed, Willie Pep arrived for his sparring session with Jimmy Dolvin, Johnny Duke, Tony Falco, and Sammy Haskins. As the bulb jockeys flashed images of Pep in the ring, Bat Battalino, Louis "Kid" Kaplan, and State Commissioner Frank Coskey strolled into the gym. Both former feather champions gave Pep their blessing, while Coskey, along with Chief Inspector "Dinny" McMahon, watched and even fielded a few questions. Confirming that advance sales were strong, promoter Ed Hurley mentioned that a large contingent from New York City—not just the beat writers but also Nat Rogers, matchmaker for Madison Square Garden—also planned to be on hand.

In front of a crowd estimated at 10,000 spectators, Willie Pep scored a decisive ten-round victory over Pedro Hernandez.[18] Joining what was claimed as the largest fight crowd since the days of Bat Battalino (1927–1940), folks overflowed into the aisles and filled any area they could find for a glimpse of the action. Containment, as the local police quickly concluded, wasn't possible. Many saw it, eight rounds to one, in favor of Pep, with one even. There were no knockdowns, but both fighters slipped to the canvas after sliding on wet spots. As anticipated, Pep's speed garnered him the victory. In the fourth round, when Hernandez opted for infighting, there were a couple of moments that looked to have the Hartford boxer worried. But from the fifth onward, he had smooth sailing. This was the fight, many critics believe, that catapulted Willie Pep into a championship caliber boxer.

Of the notable beat writers covering the fight, Edward Van Every of the *New York Sun* thought Pep wasn't much of a puncher, while Lester Bromberg of the *New York World Telegram* noted the Hartford fighter's incomparable speed. Both scribes agreed on one thing: Pep was destined for the 126-pound throne.

In addition to overseeing a stable of boxers, Al Weil handled promotions at a few Connecticut venues. Two days after the fight, he signed Pep to meet veteran boxer Nat Litfin at White City Stadium in the Savin Rock-a section of West Haven. Scheduled for ten rounds, the fight took place on August 20. Litfin, who held victories over Sixto Escobar and Joey Archibald, had never been knocked out or floored. Pep, who wasn't the least bit intimidated, excited the crowd of over 4,000 fight fans by dominating the contest and capturing every round. There were no knockdowns. Scaling at 128, nearly five pounds lighter than his opponent, the Hartford pugilist meticulously picked apart the crouched and defensive-minded Litfin. The Pittsburgh fighter's ribs, a target of Pep's crushing left hooks, were cherry red by the final rounds.[19]

It was destined to be another Connecticut classic as Willie Pep was finally scheduled to meet Bobby "Poison" Ivy on September 1 at Bulkeley Stadium. Not since Louis "Kid" Kaplan met Bat Battalino back in 1930 had there been this much pent-up demand to have two area gladiators clash inside a ring. Sebastian DeMauro, aka

Bobby Ivy, began his professional career in 1938 and impressed almost immediately. Young men such as Pep admired his ring prowess. After Ivy put together a string of 14 consecutive victories, it took Sal Bartolo to end it. Defeating Bartolo in a rematch, Ivy also held victories over Eddie Letourneau, Joey Archibald, Pete DeGrasse, Harry Jeffra, and Jackie Callura. He was, in the eyes of Connecticut fight fans, the most likely Connecticut world champion since Bat Battalino. That was until Guglielmo Papaleo entered the picture. Ivy, who was formerly handled by Lou Viscusi (also by Lenny Marello and Pete Perone), was now being handled by Pete Reilly.[20] Nobody doubted, especially Reilly, that Ivy would dismember Pep.

Noting the demand, promoter Ed Hurley altered the seating arrangements to accommodate additional spectators. Hoping to make the engagement more affordable, he scaled tickets at $2, $3.50, and $5.50. His efforts paid off when over 9,000 fight fans walked through the turnstiles.

It wasn't pretty, but Willie Pep did what he had to do. Like other fighters who ended up in the ring with their mentor, he left no doubt as to who was on top of the podium. After staggering Ivy late in the ninth round, Pep delivered his rival at the halfway mark of the final round. Struggling to reach an upright position after a three-count drop, Ivy arose, hands to his side, and was out on his feet. Sensing the damage, referee Lou Bogash waved it off. And then there was an eerie silence. There was no huge ovation. Nobody shouting "I told you so!" No victory lap for Pep. The 19-year-old victor and his entourage left the ring and headed to his dressing room. Once inside, the conquering and reticent hero sat in the corner, while his battered opponent was on the opposite side of the room, tending to his wounds. Whereas Pep had yet to be beaten as a professional, he had lost as an amateur. He could empathize with Ivy and refrained from being critical of his opponent.

Pep not only defeated Ivy, he humiliated him during the first eight rounds. It wasn't exciting, nor was it close, yet everyone expected it to be. It wasn't that Ivy was that bad, it was because Pep was that good. While the Hernandez victory sold Pep to the fight critics, this battle convinced Connecticut fight fans that he had no New England peer. Nobody. The following day, offers from all around the country poured into the office of Lou Viscusi.

The March Toward
the Featherweight Championship

Originally scheduled to meet Pedro Hernandez over eight rounds in "The Garden" on September 10, Pep instead faced a substitute in Jersey boxer Frankie Franconeri. This bout was a semi-final to the Freddie Cochrane-Fritzie Zivic main event. Training at Charter Oak Gym, Pep kept loose by bouncing off the light bag and doing calisthenics. A couple of his friends dropped by to wish him well. A large contingent from Hartford was expected to make the pilgrimage to Boxing's Mecca to watch their favorite son. This was courtesy of a large ticket block that was sold over at Al's Ringside Grill on Maple Avenue. Pep was on his game, and he knew it. If there was ever a time to impress Garden management, this was it. Pep didn't disappoint. After being floored twice in the first round, Franconeri, out on his feet, had the fight waved off by referee Arthur Donovan at the 2:07 mark of the opening round.[21]

Immediately returning to Hartford after his Garden bout, Pep began preparing for a run at the title. However, doing that required successful politics on behalf of Viscusi. First, he had to get to Lulu Constantino, the number-one challenger for Wright's featherweight title. To do that, Charlie Johnston, Constantino's manager, required "a show me don't tell me" match against stablemate Vince Dell'Orto. The practice of using a "policeman," such as Dell'Orto, was common for the time and a way to protect a fighter, not to mention milking a situation for everything it was worth. Defeating Dell'Orto would get Viscusi the ear of Johnston, but there were no guarantees beyond that. A ten-round battle was set for Bulkeley Stadium on September 22.

Celebrating his reported 50th consecutive ring victory, Willie Pep, scaling at 126, dominated Vince Dell'Orto, who tipped at 129½. Taking every round on the way to a decision, the Hartford fighter enjoyed a belated 20th birthday gift. The popular feather did it in front of over 6,500 supporters. Fighting in a nonconformist crouch, Dell'Orto's unpredictability added to his defense; however, what he needed was an offense. There were no knockdowns.[22]

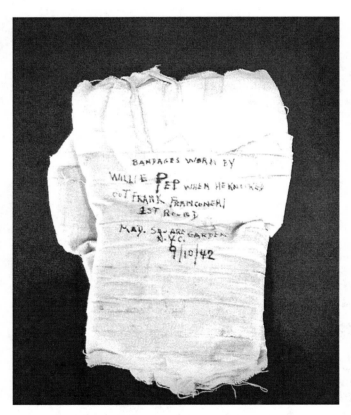

A hand wrap is a strip of cloth used by boxers to protect the hand and wrist against injuries induced by punching. Pictured is a wrap produced and worn by Willie Pep when he knocked out Frank Franconeri in the first round of their fight at Madison Square Garden (September 10, 1942).

Having recently purchased a red and yellow multiple-family house on 27–29 Standish Street, or the South Side of Hartford, Willie Pep was thrilled. While his parents weren't keen on the idea of leaving Portland Street after nine years, they needed the extra room, and they knew it. Besides, they were proud of their son, and he was their primary financial source. The wood frame house, built in 1920, occupied a lot over 6,000 square feet. It was conveniently located, less than one mile to the Hartford Auditorium. Willie always claimed his walk home was so short, he didn't even have enough time to cool down after a fight. But there was more behind the purchase of the house. Having found a love interest, Willie discreetly promised a special someone the vow of marriage should he become the featherweight champion of the world. While time would tell how the situation would play out, the purchase certainly spoke to his confidence level.

Another item flying over Pep's pursuit of a championship was New York State's rule that prohibited fighters under the age of 21 from participating in 15-round ring contests, or the distance of a championship contest. Though it wasn't a stringent rule, Lou Viscusi would still have to find a way to dance around the regulation. Also, the venue of choice for the championship bout and its promoter could create a conflict. Controlling Madison Square Garden was Mike Jacobs, a promoter who commanded loyalty and got it. Should Pep ever win in a Garden title bout, he would likely have to defend his crown in fights only promoted by Jacobs. Hey, nobody said Viscusi's job was easy.

In Holyoke on October 5, Willie Pep, scaling at 129¾, met Detroit lightweight Bobby McIntire (also spelled McIntyre), who tipped at 135¾—by contract, Pep's antagonist could not come into the ring under 135. The battle wasn't even close as Pep took all ten rounds on his way to a unanimous decision victory. At about the half-way mark, the crowd of over 2,000 fight fans began getting bored with the lackluster event. Pep stepped it up down the stretch and dropped his opponent twice—first for an eight count, then to a nine—in the ninth round. He had trouble penetrating McIntire's impressive defense for a large portion of the contest. On the undercard, Hartford youngster Julio Gallucci, aka Johnny Duke, Pep's childhood friend, won his professional debut against Red Luce.

As fate had it, Lulu Constantino lost to Chalky Wright on September 25, three days after Pep was victorious over Dell'Orto. Such was the dynamic nature of the featherweight division.[23]

World Featherweight Champion

Word came on October 7: Willie Pep would meet featherweight champion Chalky Wright, over the 15-round title route at Madison Square Garden on November 20. Did Viscusi pull the favor from his back pocket? It sure appeared that way. Oddsmakers gave Pep a 2–1 advantage. The Hartford feather, with over 50 consecutive victories, believed Wright's third defense of the crown would be his last. However, the carefree champion could care less about what any pug from Hartford thought. His compact left hooks followed by powerful right crosses had dropped many a foe, and Pep would be next. Could the Hartford fighter's "hit-and-run" strategy conquer the punching prowess of the featherweight champion? Nobody was certain.

After successfully defending his title over 15 rounds against Lulu Constantino on September 25, Wright knocked out Carlos "No No" Cuebas in the fourth round of a contest held at the Auditorium in Hartford on October 13. One of the over 2,000 in attendance was Willie Pep. Watching intently, the Hartford phenom showed no emotion. He understood that in addition to Constantino, Wright had successfully defended his crown against former champion Harry Jeffra.[24] However, Wright lost three distance battles this year, the first against Bobby Ruffin, followed by Vern Bybee and Allie Stolz. The champion was beatable.

In his final warm-up before facing Pep, Chalky Wright grabbed an eight-round

TKO victory over Henry Vasquez in New Haven on October 20. As for Pep, he took two ten-round distance victories, the first over Joey Archibald in Providence on October 16, followed by George Zengaras in Hartford on October 27. Archibald, who rode the bike the entire fight, put on a ridiculous performance. However, Zengaras, Lulu Constantino's sparring partner and stablemate, conducted a better display. At least he provided a solid defense and even reached Pep with a few precision combinations.[25]

Lending his hands to the war effort, Pep took part in a scrap metal drive on October 14. Appointed to lead one of the collection drives in Precinct 21, Pep was in charge of an area from the north side of Morgan Street to the north side of State Street (downtown Hartford). Assisting in the effort were pugilists Big Boy Carilli and Bat Battalino. It was a great example of patriotism.

Ignited by the warm-up bouts, the featherweight title hype was in full swing by mid–October. Albert Garfield "Chalky" Wright was born in 1912 but looked older. To the unknowledgeable, that cast a layer of doubt on the fighter's skills. Wright and his crafty manager didn't mind the misinterpretation one bit and used it to their advantage. Truth be told: Wright was dangerous and so good that many of the featherweights and lightweights avoided him. Possessing a knockout punch, he was labeled a "cute" fighter. Balanced, crafty, and quick, Wright could tie up a fighter in an instant. then drop him like an anvil. Before meeting Pep, he had been in a ring with Alberto "Baby" Arizmendi, Henry Armstrong, and Joey Archibald.

Tickets for the title fight, a number of blocks of which were sold in Hartford, were scaled at $2.50, $3.50, $4.00, $5.75, and $7.75. The bout had one of the best advanced sales at the Garden in years. Viscusi successfully negotiated on Pep's behalf with Jacobs and even maintained control of his fighter—something unheard of when dealing with Uncle Mike (Jacobs' moniker courtesy of Joe Louis). Pep would receive 20 percent of the net, or an estimated $10,000. As for the champion, he was guaranteed $15,000 and would grab 40 percent of the net gate if that percentage exceeded $15,000.

Training over at Charter Oak Gym, Pep had a steady stream of visitors, including his father. Sharing stories of his son's upbringing, Salvatore Papaleo enjoyed greeting members of the press as well as fight fans. Confirming Willie's desire to be a fighter, his dedication to training, and his restless, if not boundless, energy, Salvatore also mentioned that Willie's mother had never seen him box and likely would skip her son's title bout. No mother, that of a champion or not, wanted to witness their child injured or hurt. Meanwhile, Chalky Wright was holding camp at Valley Stream, Long Island. At one point, his team even offered Louis "Kid" Kaplan a few bucks to head south and share his secrets about Pep. Kaplan didn't bite.

While Hartford was familiar with Willie Pep, the city beats were not. Even Lester Bromberg and Ed Van Every, who had covered his bout against Pedro Hernandez, had already filed away their memories. Nobody was sure who the youngster was, with the exception of those conducting the performance such as Nat Rogers, the matchmaker for Madison Square Garden. Many of the beat writers turned to Rogers or reached out to Bill Lee, *Hartford Courant* sports editor, for the dope—the latter protected Pep, like a defense attorney at his client's murder trial.

Echoing across the rafters, the tenor voice of announcer Harry Balogh had all he could do merely to get the announcement out over the screams: "The decision is unanimous and the featherweight champion of the world is [pause]," and for a brief second everyone in the audience inhaled, "Willie Pep."

In front of over 19,500 fans, Willie Pep had punched his way to a 15-round unanimous decision over Chalky Wright to win the world featherweight championship. With Pep following in the footsteps of Christopher "Bat" Battalino, Hartford had another champion. It was Pep's 54th consecutive professional victory against no defeats. Wright graciously walked over to Pep's corner to shake the hands of the new champion, along with Lou Viscusi, Bill Gore, and Lenny Marello. It was a peaceful title transfer (even if Connecticut, under the National Boxing Association's jurisdiction, recognized Jackie Wilson as the feather king). Willie Pep was now the youngest featherweight champion since Terry McGovern over four decades ago. It was the largest indoor featherweight gate in history at a gross of $71,868.70.[26]

Tipping at 125½, Pep had no skating room, not against Chalky Wright, who scaled at 125¾. The champion rocked Pep in the fifth and seventh rounds, but he could not set him up for the big blow. It was Pep's fight the first four rounds, as he danced out of danger. But early in the fifth, Wright landed a left to the body and a right to the head that staggered Pep. The champion ripped into his challenger with a volley of combinations. Pep somehow found the strength to slow the effort with jabs and crosses. The sixth round was unimpressive, but Wright once again attacked in the seventh. A left hook followed by a right cross stunned Pep. It proved to be a wake-up call, as Pep began delivering his punches with greater efficiency. As his confidence grew with each passing round, Pep looked unbeatable. In the 13th round, he brought the crowd to their feet with a brilliant display—a targeted left jab followed by a tactical retreat—of pugilism. The fight was essentially his after the round, and he knew it. Pep danced for a bulk of the finally two sessions. There were no knockdowns.[27]

Later, the new champion admitted that Wright shook him a few times during the battle and said that Wright was the toughest competitor he had faced. As for the former champion, it was another day at the office; moreover, Wright appeared almost relieved to relinquish the title. While referee Art Donovan and Judges Joe Agnello and Bill Healy all voted for Pep, not everyone agreed. Journalist Dick McCann, from the *Daily News*, saw it 8–6, with one round even, in favor of Wright.

On Saturday, November 21, over 1,000 fans filled the Hartford Auditorium to welcome home the new featherweight champion. Jack Lacey, WNBC radio announcer, handled the event. Pep, dressed like a champion in a stylish double-breasted suit, even fielded a few questions. Folks needed to look no further than the fighter's swollen and discolored left cheek as proof of Wright's ability to inflict damage. Pep and trainer Bill Gore were thrilled by the hometown response. Word out of the champion's camp, was a likelihood of two or three non-title bouts before Christmas. Then Pep would be off to Florida for a well-earned vacation.

Women's Organization for War Savings was sponsoring a Women-at-Work Week, and a mere four days after his championship fight, Willie Pep was in line to purchase a $100 bond at the Italian American Home on Pearl Street, in downtown Hartford. The state of Connecticut always prided itself on being a premier supplier to the United Sates military, ever since the American Revolution. Understanding this, Willie Pep, forever patriotic, was proud to lend a hand.[28]

As every champion will tell you, regardless of the sport, once you reach the pinnacle of your profession, you will receive more invitations to sporting banquets than

It happened on November 20, 1942. Willie Pep (right) defeated Chalky Wright (left) for the NYSAC World Featherweight Championship. Pep would meet, and defeat, Chalky Wright four times during his professional career.

fan mail. While that could be a bit of an exaggeration, Pep was honored all around the area, including his birthplace of Middletown. That city hosted a banquet in Pep's honor on November 29 at the Rose Garden. Mim Daddario, Hartford Blues player and manager, acted as toastmaster. As champion, you also become a target for invitations and even violations. Upon his return to Charter Oak Gym in Hartford, Pep and a couple other pugs found their lockers cleaned out of equipment to the tune of about $400.

Knowing that Pep had six months to defend his title, the challengers began lining up. Lou Shiro, Sal Bartolo's manager, was one of the first to present his fighter's challenge, together with a check for $1,000. Most Connecticut fight fans still hoped Pep would meet Jackie Wilson, the NBA's recognized featherweight champion, to unify the division.

As the champion's final two battles of the year were being finalized, he committed to an exhibition at the Hartford Auditorium, over at 331 Wethersfield Avenue, to stay sharp. It was a favor to promoter Ed Hurley, who was conducting his usual Tuesday evening promotion at the venue, as well as to Lou Viscusi, who had a Boston fighter by the name of Freddie Cabral on the card. Unfortunately, the champion was absent without explanation. Later, it was learned that Pep had a family disagreement that provoked him to leave town.

On December 12, 1942, Willie Pep married Mary Woodcock, of Hartford, at St. Patrick's Church. The unexpected and discreet wedding was attended by Mrs. Louis Viscusi and William Gore. That, depending on how you put the pieces together, may indicate the event surprised a few people. Mrs. Papaleo, formerly of Hungerford Street and daughter of Mr. and Mrs. John Woodcock, was promised matrimony once Pep reached the pinnacle of his craft, and the champion delivered. While the romance, as romances go, was young—the pair only met a few months earlier—the two were very much in love.[29]

On December 14 at Turner's Arena in Washington, District of Columbia, Jose Aponte Torres, substituting for Lew Hanbury, who broke his right hand during a sparring session, suffered a seventh-round technical knockout against Willie Pep. The end came at the 45-second mark of the term when the Puerto Rican pugilist was out on his feet. Working behind a left jab to take command and a left hook to inflict damage, Pep, who had a cut opened under his left eye, skated past his adversary with relative ease. Torres, who hit the canvas in the sixth round, tried hard to take Pep out of his game with wild punches and round-opening assaults, but failed. Both fighters tipped at about the 130 mark.[30]

In his last battle of 1942, Willie Pep grabbed a ninth-round TKO victory over the familiar face of Joey Silva. The bout was held on December 21 at the George Washington Hotel in Jacksonville, Florida. As with many battles during the war years, a portion of the proceeds went to the community war chest. The 15-story luxury hotel, located on the corner of Adams and Julia Streets, featured a beautiful auditorium that was built the year before and was the biggest hall in town. Tipping at 128, Pep waited until the eighth round to pound Silva, who scaled at 129½, into oblivion. The cumulative damage forced Silva's handlers to inform referee Dick Gorem that their fighter could no longer continue. The swanky event promoted by Sam Butz was more of a social event—somebody pass me a shot of rye—for the estimated 1,400 well-dressed attendees than a ring battle.[31]

With a title in one hand and a bride in another, Willie Pep turned the year into the most memorable of his life. And he did it with a world at war. That was not easy when you consider that his home state was a leading supplier of America's war effort. At a time when boxing was almost the last thing anyone was thinking about, that wasn't the case in Connecticut. That was because of Willie Pep. The boxing gates attested to that fact. Pep vaulted center stage and proved there was little that the little man couldn't do. Having outgrown many of Hartford's venues, even if he still called it home, he was blazing a trail unlike few others. Streaks, especially during the 1940s, didn't solely belong to Joseph Paul DiMaggio.

1943

The Pep camp pulled into New Orleans the last week in December. They were preparing for their first battle of the year, on Monday, January 4, 1943, against the familiar but unpredictable Vince Dell'Orto. Which led some to question: why in the world was the featherweight champion risking injury against a fighter this danger-ous? Even if Viscusi believed it was an excellent tune-up for Pep's battle against Allie Stolz—a major bout scheduled for Madison Square Garden on January 15—why fight Dell'Orto in New Orleans? If it was close, the popular Dell'Orto could pull off an upset. Granted, matchmaker Lew Diamond made it clear that Pep's title was not at stake and that both fighters agreed to be over the 126-pound featherweight limit. Still, a defeat by Dell'Orto could impact Pep's confidence level.[32] Nevertheless, it was fight on.

Willie Pep eased into his battle with Vince Dell'Orto almost if he were doing a routine arsenal check. Gradually the punches got stronger as his accuracy improved. Lighter volleys were followed by power punches, and by the third round the com-binations had Dell'Orto, who always looked confused, resorting to reckless tactics. Many of the 3,000 fans in attendance appeared content to watch Pep compose his symphony, and few, if any, felt Dell'Orto had much of a chance after the third round. Picking up the ten-round decision, Pep, about four pounds lighter than his oppo-nent, headed back to the hotel to pack for his trip home. He, Mary, Viscusi, and Gore planned to catch the 1:20 afternoon train on Tuesday, arriving back in Hartford on Wednesday. But their travel plans were delayed. Receiving word from Nat Rogers that Pep's Garden battle needed to be postponed—Stolz was recovering from a ptomaine poisoning attack—the party decided to head southeast to the west coast of Florida.

Team Pep headed to Tampa on January 8, specifically to Lou Viscusi's coun-try home in Lutz, which was north of the city. After their brief vacation, the newly-weds hoped to head to New York City, where Pep would finish training for his battle with Stolz that was rescheduled for January 29. However, Viscusi wanted another warm-up battle before the Stolz fight, thus Ed Hurley arranged a fight against Bill Speary at the Auditorium on January 19. To make a long and challenging story short, everyone was back in Hartford by January 15.[33]

If it was Tuesday in Hartford, fight fans could be found at the Auditorium. The show began at 8:30 p.m., and there were four preliminary battles prior to the ten-round main event. Tickets for the champion's return to home were scaled at $1.15 for General Admission and up to $2.30 and $3.45 for Ringside Reserved. Willie Pep, scal-ing at 129, a one-pound advantage, dominated Billy Speary of Nanticoke, Pennsyl-vania over ten rounds to pick up the victory. Offering limited highlights—that is if you don't count a frustrated Pep being deducted a point for shoving his adversary—the bout was lusterless. The $3,500 gate, courtesy of a crowd of about 1,800 fans who turned out to greet the featherweight champion, wasn't bad considering it was an uncharacteristically pathetic undercard.

After the event, fans had many options for a nightcap. The old-timers headed to Kid Kaplan's Grill on the corner of Church and Trumbull (always the place to be after a battle at Foot Guard Hall because it was a short walk—a couple of blocks east on Church Street). The main dining room had high wooden booths on both sides, with small tables adorning the center aisle. Kaplan, who was often at the restaurant, loved to greet the fight fans and sign a few autographs. After battles at the Hartford Auditorium, Al's Ringside Grill, at 87 Maple Avenue, typically drew a crowd. It was a fifteen-minute walk and less than a mile from the Auditorium. If you wanted to stay in the city, Mickey's Grill at 18 Market Street was an option, or over to the Silver Tap Grille,at 571 Main Street. Of those headed across the river, some stopped at Johnny's

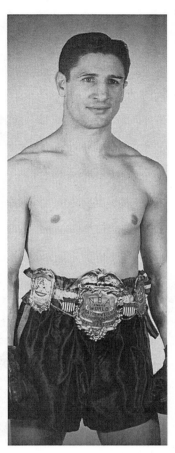

Pictured here are Allie Stolz (left), Sammy Angott (center), and Sal Bartolo. Pep defeated Stolz on January 29, 1943, lost to lightweight Angott on March 19, 1943, and defeated Bartolo on April 9, 1943.

Bar & Grill in East Hartford. The capital city was a fight town, and the time spent after the bouts was an opportunity to decompress.

On January 29, Willie Pep, tipping at 127¾, was back in Madison Square Garden to take a ten-round unanimous decision over Allie Stolz, who scaled at 133½ pounds.[34] Pep thrashed Stolz much like a Derby jockey driving a horse down the final stretch. Those at ringside saw it eight rounds to two in favor of Pep. Flooring the Jersey boy to a two-count in the second round, Pep's left hook was responsible for the bulk of the damage. Slicing the left eye of Stolz in the eighth round caused some concern in his opponent's corner. In return, Pep withstood some solid body damage in the third and fourth rounds, and he was staggered and cut in the eighth term. Over 19,000 jammed the Garden and drove the gate to nearly $66,000. Honestly, a few of the fixtures ringside, such as Benny Leonard and "Dumb Dan" Morgan, thought Pep was over his head with Stolz. They were wrong.[35]

Justified or not, the victory sparked Pep comparisons to elite fighters such as Abe Attell, Terry McGovern, Young Corbett, Tony Canzoneri, and even Henry Armstrong. These were tough shoes to fill. Whereas Pep understood the juxtapositions, he didn't like them. Willie had a bit of superstition in him, and throwing names around such as these could curse the fighter.[36] After all, Pep carried the same water bucket ("Spitzy") and bottle ("Guzz") he used in his first professional fight to every battle.

Fulfilling a favor to promoter Eddie "Old Sarge" Mack, Lou Viscusi signed the champion to a hub battle at the Mechanics Building against Davey Crawford. But that wasn't the fight everyone was talking about. A Willie Pep–Beau Jack match was on everyone's wish list, especially Nat Rogers. Yet according to Viscusi, the negotiations for such a battle weren't even close.

Davey Crawford, who had lost to his antagonist back in 1941, was proclaimed as Pep's 60th consecutive ring victim. In a one-sided affair, the champ captured every round while displaying his prizefighting expertise in front of over 3,000 fans. The February 11 event appeared more of an exhibition than a contest. Pep, who weighed 129, staggered Crawford, who scaled at 127½, but he never dropped him to the canvas.[37]

Willie Pep vs. Beau Jack

Could it be that Hartford's Golden Boy would face Augusta's premier pugilist? Or was it merely a fantasy match? It surfaced as a ten-round non-title possibility at the end of January 1943 but failed to go much further. Every promoter in the country wanted it: Merely the thought of Willie Pep, putting 60 consecutive victories on the line against a talent such as Beau Jack, with a believed record of 51–6–2, was enough to make any impresario dream of an early retirement. While logic may have concluded that it was a Garden battle, that would require NYSAC's blessing. The rub, it goes without saying, was weight. Jack would have to come into battle at 140 pounds to protect his lightweight title. However, Viscusi was not going to allow Pep to enter the ring against an opponent with a 10- or 12-pound advantage, and certainly not with the skills of Jack. Later, NYSAC Chairman John J. Phelan was emphatic that if Jack entered a contest at under 135, his title was at risk; moreover, the contest would then have to be at a 15-round title distance. At one point, a Madison Square Garden date of March 5, 1943, looked as if it might happen. But it fell through.

On February 14, Viscusi, Gore, and Pep entrained to Baltimore to do battle against Bill Speary at the Coliseum the following evening—yep, Speary once again. As a ten-round non-title fight against his familiar sparring partner, I mean opponent, Pep, who scaled at 129¾, amused a small crowd by winning every round. The Nanticoke punching bag, who tipped at 132, managed a mere two solid punches during the contest. Going horizontal for a four-count in the eighth round, Speary looked pathetic. Yet he insisted on getting back on his feet. It was a bad idea as he experienced a facial resurfacing before the final gong. Witnessing the destruction of his opponent, Pep even eased up in the final two rounds. This forced referee Ed Brockman to warn both fighters to engage. The stupefied look Pep gave Brockman could have stopped an oncoming train. Putting both fighters in a delicate position was not the way to conclude this battle. Honestly, this ten-round Pep victory didn't make a whole lot of sense.

Three days later, word came that Willie Pep would meet Sammy Angott—the talented boxer had recently vacated the lightweight title—inside Madison Square

Garden on March 19. The featherweight's title would not be at stake during the ten-round battle, and Angott agreed to weigh not more than 135 pounds.[38] While promoter Mike Jacobs and matchmaker Nat Rogers, had hoped to land Beau Jack to battle Pep, this was an attractive and economical alternative. Besides, it was a bout for the Service Boxing Equipment Fund. And, since Jack had won his NYSAC title recognition by beating Tippy Larkin after Angott's retirement, the picture had changed.[39]

A surprise dinner was held in honor of Willie Pep at Mickey's Villanova Grill on February 22. Hosted by the peerless Bob Steele, the group honored Pep with a ring. Adorned with 54 diamond chips, or one for every victory including the title, Pep proudly placed it on his finger. Other guests included: Bill Gore, Bill Lee (*Hartford Courant*), Lenny Marello, Arthur B. McGinley (*Hartford Times*), Pete Perone, and Willie's friend Jimmy "Flip" Toce. The observation of the evening was Pep's appetite, which appeared insatiable.

Like many pugilists, the champion enjoyed a good meal. His favorite was an Italian feast (preferably cooked by his mother), topped by dessert. Willie loved sweets, almost as much as he enjoyed baseball, the cinema, and games of chance—the latter a noted downfall.[40] The cinema was always a treat, and during this era Pep had his favorite actors and pictures, including George Raft in *The House Across the Bay*, Humphrey Bogart in *High Sierra*, and Edward G. Robinson in *Larceny, Inc.* The tough guy roles, even gangsters, fascinated the pugilist.

It was back to the Wethersfield Avenue confines on March 2, as Willie Pep, scaling at 129, knocked out Baltimore boxer Lou Transparenti, who tipped two pounds lighter, at the 1:20 mark of the sixth round. Even so, it didn't come easy as Pep dropped his tenacious opponent six times in the process. A left hook followed by a combination delivered the final damage. To Transparenti's credit, he nearly had Pep out in the third round when he caught him flush on the jaw with a left hook. Backing away, the champion was lucky to catch his balance and retain his composure. Understanding that Pep needed a good warm-up battle before meeting Angott, Transparenti, who held victories over Joey Archibald, Johnny Marcelline, and Lou Sallica, was a good choice. The estimated 3,000 fans enjoyed every minute of the action, which proved a good thing as the champion wouldn't box in Hartford again for over a year.

63 and Me

It was a valiant return to the ring by Sammy Angott. Having briefly retired as the undisputed lightweight champion back on November 14, 1942, he performed brilliantly by taking command early and winning four of the first five rounds. There were no knockdowns, only a few slips. Following the eighth round, which Pep won, it looked as if he might pull out the victory. But Angott would not relent and finished strong in the tenth and final round. Willie Pep, a 3–1 betting favorite who was looking to add to his incredible consecutive winning streak of 62 victories, lost the ten-round unanimous decision to Sammy Angott. The non-title fight happened on March 19, 1943, inside Madison Square Garden.

Nearly 17,000 Garden spectators contributed to a gate that reached over $70,000. Was it a surprise? That was a difficult question to answer. Granted, Angott hadn't fought since last September, but this was the same fighter who held victories over Bob

Montgomery, Lew Jenkins, and Freddie Miller—all elite boxers. While it was clear that he was fatigued in the later rounds, it wasn't enough to cost him the battle.[41] Referee Billy Cavanagh and Judge Bill Healy both had it 5–4 and one even, in favor of Angott, while Judge Joe Agnello had it 6–4 in Angott's favor. Nobody debated the decision.

Thus, the longest winning streak in professional ring history drew to a conclusion. Time for a few facts: The boxers with the fewest victories to face Pep during the streak: Joey Marcus (0), Jackie Moore (0), and James McGovern (0); The boxers with the highest number of current victories to face Pep during the streak: Chalky Wright (143), and Nat Litfin (73); The boxers with the highest number of losses to face Pep during the streak: Joey Silva (49), Davey Crawford (40), and Jimmy Gilligan (40); and, undefeated boxers Pep met during the streak: 5, Joey Marcus (debut), Jackie Moore (debut), James McGovern (debut), Augie Almeda (1–0–0), and Ruby Garcia (5–0–2). None of the fights during the streak were held outside the continental United States.

Title intact, Pep was disappointed but not distraught over his loss. Talk quickly shifted to a featherweight unification battle between Pep, the NYSAC champion, and Jackie Callura, the NBA champion—the latter having defeated Jackie Wilson. But it was merely talk. Viscusi, who wanted Willie Pep back in the ring as soon as possible, inked him for a ten-rounder against Bobby McIntire in Detroit on March 29. Meanwhile, Willie's Uncle, Sam, wanted him to take his preliminary examination for military service on March 24.[42] He did. The following day, Pep was signed to meet Sal Bartolo in the Boston Garden on April 9.

Soon to be classified as 1-A, or available for military service, Hartford's premier featherweight planned on quickly lining his pockets. Granted it was likely several weeks before Pep would report to the Army induction center, but you couldn't be certain. The responsibility of providing for his family was always in the back of his mind.

Scaling at 130, a six-pound disadvantage, Willie Pep defeated Bobby McIntire over ten rounds at Arena Gardens in Detroit. It was a unanimous decision and the beginning of another winning streak—or at least he hoped. Having trounced the fighter last year in Holyoke, the champion was understandably confident. McIntire was nearly out on his feet in the eighth round thanks to a Pep precision left to the head. There were no knockdowns. A crowd estimated at 3,500 turned out for the event. Picking up the newspaper on Tuesday morning, Pep was shocked to see that he had made it into *Ripley's "Believe It or Not."* The syndicated column recognized him as the only boxer in history to "win a world's title without having lost a fight, been held to a draw, won or lost a fight on a foul or taken part in a no-decision contest."[43]

Back to the East Coast, and in front of nearly 16,000 fight fans inside Boston Garden, Willie Pep took a ten-round split decision over Sal Bartolo. It was a non-title fight, and both fighters scaled at 128 pounds. "The Pride of East Boston," Salvatore Interbartolo was a popular and tough boxer who knew how to win. But he could be a slow starter, therefore Gore told Pep to go after him early. Targeting Bartolo's eye, Pep went right to work. Opening a cut near his antagonist's left optic began a blood flow that continued throughout the contest. Bartolo, who slipped to one knee in the first for a no-count, ignited the crowd when he managed to trap Pep against the ropes and unload an arsenal. Whereas Pep had a slight edge during the first half of the fight, Bartolo's refusal to relent didn't make it easy. Enduring more punishment than he felt was necessary, Pep, noticeably frustrated, backed off as much as he could. It was a close crusade that Pep, recovering from an infected throat, was lucky to pull off in Boston.[44]

Promising Florida promoter Bill Sallade a bout with the featherweight champion, Lou Viscusi and crew packed their bags and arrived in Tampa on April 13. While Viscusi headed out to Lutz, Willie and Mary stayed at the Hotel Thomas Jefferson in downtown Tampa. The newlyweds enjoyed the sunshine and a gorgeous view of the bay. The hotel was located near the Franklin Street Gym, where Pep was conducting his workouts. Six days later, at Municipal Auditorium, Pep grabbed a ten-round points victory over Angel Aviles, featherweight champion of Mexico. It did not come easy, however, as the wild-swinging Aviles managed to send Pep through the ropes, and to his back on the ring apron, during the final round. After a three-count, the startled champion returned to the ring. The reckless style of Aviles had the crowd of 1,500 spectators on their feet numerous times during the contest.[45] Both fighters tipped at 128 pounds.

Tampa hadn't had a visit from a world champion since 1935, when Max Baer conducted an exhibition against Tony Cancela. Ecstatic about the event, Florida fight fans enjoyed every minute of the contest. Aviles' claim to fame was recently battling Jackie Wilson, the former NBA feather champ, to a draw.[46] Since Pep was inked to battle Wilson in a 12-round non-title contest on April 27 in Pittsburgh, this bout made sense on paper even it was questioned afterwards.

The group left Tampa on April 20, bound for Pittsburgh—a journey that took 39 straight hours on the train (it was six hours late). Arriving on Thursday, April 22, Pep finished his training at the Pittsburgh Lyceum. Meanwhile, Wilson was working over at the Center Avenue Y.M.C.A. A very tired Team Pep stayed at the Pittsburgher Hotel. It was while traveling that the champion learned that he had been offered $30,000, or 50 percent of the gross gate, to defend his title outdoors, at Braves Field in Boston, on May 28. His opponent over the 15-round distance would be either Jackie Callura or Sal Bartolo.[47]

Tipping at 128, a pound heavier than his opponent, Willie Pep seized a 12-round unanimous decision over veteran Jackie Wilson at Duquesne Gardens in Pittsburgh. It happened on April 26, in front of a capacity house (7,500) of bloodthirsty spectators. As foreseen by critics, it was youth, speed, and stamina, over experience, skill, and determination. As a talented fighter who won three times as many bouts as he lost, Wilson was a crafty and evasive boxer. When Pep managed to capture his ducking, weaving, and bobbing rival, he used swift combinations to score. That said, it was only in the ninth round that he had his antagonist in trouble. Opening a cut over Wilson's left eye, Pep locked in on the gash and let loose with multiple rights. Even if it wasn't enough to drop the 33-year-old Wilson, it slowed him down.

As April closed and May began, only a few key fighters remained civilians: Beau Jack, Manuel Ortiz, and Willie Pep. But for how much longer? In the meantime, Eddie Walker, Chalky Wright's manager, was constantly in Viscusi's ear for a return bout with his fighter. It seems that Walker forgot to include a return bout clause in his initial contract. Oops! Manager Lou Viscusi received a call from NYSAC on May 7, reminding him that his fighter was running out of time to defend his title; his grace period would end on May 20. In addition to Wright, challengers included Sal Bartolo, Lulu Constantino, Pedro Hernandez, and Phil Terranova. The push was for Bartolo in Boston. Meanwhile, Willie Pep was the guest of honor in Middletown at the

Sebastian Men's Club Sports Night. There were two things, or so it seemed, that every veteran boxing champion learned to do: avoid roadwork and memorize a few one-liners for banquet speeches. Pep became an expert on the latter.

Word of Pep's title defense finally came on May 15: It would be Sal Bartolo in Boston, at Braves Field on June 8.[48] It was a sweet agreement for Pep, who was guaranteed 30 "G's." It was believed the largest sum ever promised to a featherweight champion for defense of his title. Three days later, NYSAC stated they wouldn't recognize the battle as a title defense, opting for the winner of a Chalky Wright versus Phil Terranova match to get first crack at Pep's belt. It appeared that Mike Jacobs wanted a piece of the action and planned to stage that battle on June 4. The Massachusetts Boxing Commission disagreed. Nuf Ced!

As for Willie Pep, who was enjoying some vacation time, he was fine with fighting anybody on the docket.[49] He planned on beginning training in Hartford before heading to Boston and finishing his training at Kelley and Hayes gym. While in The Hub, Pep hoped to head over to the Navy Yard to greet and salute Sergeant Barney Ross, the former lightweight and welterweight champion. The pair finally hooked up on June 1.

Since a war was taking place, the next item on the agenda for Boston boxing promoters Jack O'Brien and Eddie Mack was meeting the outdoor lighting restrictions. Thanks to special shields and bulb covers that prevented sky glow, the dimout authorities approved the lighting.

Willie Pep v. Sal Bartolo II— The First Title Defense

After the first two rounds, the title fight was all about Willie Pep, who successfully defended his NYSAC World Featherweight Championship for the first time. A crowd of about 14,000 jammed into Braves Field in Boston on June 8 to watch Hartford's golden boy, who scaled at 126, a one-pound advantage, take a 15-round unanimous decision over Sal Bartolo.

Cautious from the opening gong, Willie Pep kept his distance for the first two sessions. Then he initiated a battle plan that would defuse any hopes on the part of Sal Bartolo. Working behind a targeted left jab, Pep danced, fired, scored, then repeated. Bartolo, who looked as if he was wearing concrete shoes, was lethargic. There were no knockdowns, but the hub boxer was wrestled to the floor in the 13th term. Pep, guaranteed $30,000, was a 2–1 favorite entering the title fight, while hometown hero Bartolo, who received 12½ percent (some sources claimed 20 percent) of the net gate, grabbed a bit under $6,000. Leaving the ring with his victory scrapbook, in the form of a bruised left cheek and bloody nose, Pep headed back to his dressing room. Minutes later, a small riot ensued outside his quarters, courtesy of hundreds of inebriated servicemen and civilians. The entire event was a bit shoddy and to little surprise, the promoters incurred a loss of about $5,000.

All eyes turned to Willie Pep on June 16, as the featherweight champion passed his physical examination for military service and was sworn into the Navy. His title would be frozen for the duration. Reporting to the Navy Recruiting station in New Haven on June 23, he was assigned to a training station at Sampson, New York. In the interim, area promoters, desperate to squeeze one more fight out of Pep, were working hard to land Jackie Callura as the champion's next opponent. But it wasn't working. So a few months before his 21st birthday, Pep, like millions of others, was stepping up to defend his country.

In a spirit of uncomplaining selflessness, the featherweight champion set aside his personal goals while earning the admiration of every American. He was not alone. Serving their country: Joe Louis (Army), Billy Conn (Army), Gus Lesnevich (Coast Guard), Billy Soose (Navy), Tony Zale (Navy), Fred Apostoli (Navy), Freddie "Red" Cochrane (Navy), Marty Servo (Coast Guard), and thousands of other professional boxers.

For Apprentice Seaman William Papaleo, life in the service wasn't much different from training for a big fight. You woke up at 5:30 a.m., trained all day long, then hit your bunk by 9:30 p.m.—the notable difference being the meals. Normally, he would arise at 6:00 a.m. then head for a restaurant breakfast with Bill Gore. After breakfast, which was typically bacon and eggs, juice, toast, and coffee, he would head home to relax and read the newspaper. If there was time, he would listen to music, perhaps some Glenn Miller or Harry James, on his own private jukebox, before roadwork at 9:00 a.m. After completing a few miles, Pep hit the showers, then napped. Lunch was at 11:30, followed by personal time. By 2:30 p.m., Pep was in the gym, where he remained until 4:00 p.m. A rubdown followed, as did a shower. Dinner, which might even include a beer, varied depending upon his weight. Then bed before ten.

While Pep was drilling, Boston promoter Eddie Mack was spouting off to the local dailies that he had completed arrangements for a September fight between Pep and Henry Armstrong. Viscusi, who admitted that *he* wasn't even authorized to make such a commitment, confirmed he didn't see the sense, or is it cents, in the match. Adding to the confusion was a letter that surfaced from the Secretary of the Navy to the National Boxing Association, asking that Pep be given leave from his duties to fight Jackie Callura, NBA feather champion. What's the old line about desperation? "When you're at the end of your rope, tie a knot and hang on."[50]

Pep completed boot training on August 9 and returned to Hartford. His return address was given as that of the Woodcocks on Hungerford Street. Having to return to duty on August 12, Mary and Willie headed off to the shore for a short vacation.

Whenever Willie was back in town, he wouldn't hesitate to drop by a boxing event as he later did in West Springfield on September 27. It wasn't only the love for the sport that brought him north, but his title—he enjoyed being recognized as the featherweight champ. Naturally, his presence ringside was welcomed by the media. Asked about the rumor that he was considering new management, Pep immediately quelled any concern by confirming his loyalty to Viscusi and Gore. With the champion, or meal ticket, fulfilling his obligation, Viscusi's top horse was Johnny Cesario, a lightweight out of Cambridge, Massachusetts (later Hartford).

The war put an enormous burden on everyone in the fight game. With boxing titles frozen as numerous champions served their country, shows were conducted with whatever resources were available. Talent such as Phil Terranova, the recently crowned NBA featherweight, found its way to Hartford and into the Auditorium. But fight fans knew it wouldn't last. Many shows were substandard or pitted ancient warriors against inexperienced young talent. For example, on October 31, Johnny Bellus, a primordial New Haven pugilist, was put against the hard-hitting Ike Williams at the Hartford Auditorium—the former would prefer serving in the infantry to meeting Williams in a ring.

Seaman, Second Class William Papaleo was ordered to enroll in the Navy physical instructors' school at Bainbridge, Maryland, on November 3. As Lieutenant Forgy once quipped, "Praise the Lord and pass the ammunition!"

FOUR

The War Years,
Part 2, 1944–1945

*"The way to know about championship quality is to learn from champions,
and that I did; studying them with professional purpose during my time
in the ring and from habitual interest afterward."*—Gene Tunney

1944

The reality of war had set in, leaving many, whether soldiers or civilians, wondering if and when everything would return to normal. And, for that matter, what normal would be. For the participating professional athletes, whose careers were also impacted by the effects of time, that apprehension appeared even greater.

Life beyond the conflict continued: On Tuesday, January 18, 1944, Mary Elizabeth Papaleo, weighing six pounds and six ounces, was born to Mary and William Papaleo at St. Francis Hospital. Her father's love could be felt all the way from Bainbridge, Maryland, where Willie was hospitalized for a couple of months because of ear trouble. Banter regarding his possible medical discharge surfaced almost weekly, but nobody was certain.

Lo and behold, Hartford's favorite son was returning to civilian life after receiving a discharge from the Navy on February 15, 1944. Following 94 days in the hospital owing to ear trouble, Willie Pep was on his way home. Ironically, it came the day before his manager, Lou Viscusi, reported for his induction physical. The seasoned boxing manager was not likely to be considered for military service, but he would be on call to defend his country's freedom.

Returning home with a citation for good conduct and his discharge, Willie Pep saw his daughter for the first time on February 16. After time to reconnect with his family in Hartford, not to mention making a few ringside appearances, it was off to Tampa to soak up some Florida sunshine for a couple weeks. Pep planned to discuss his ring return at Lou Viscusi's home in Lutz (15 miles north of Tampa). Before heading south, Pep wisely visited the office of Bill Lee, *Hartford Courant* sports editor. Knowing Lee as he did, the fighter understood the columnist would gladly pen a column confirming Pep's re-entry into boxing, plus his status—this could even include a timeframe and list of possible opponents. A steadfast advocate of the fighter, Lee wasn't the least bit hesitant about providing his full support.

Speaking of news, when Willie Pep picked up the morning newspaper on March 10, he learned that Sal Bartolo had captured the National Boxing Association (NBA)

World Featherweight Title from Phil Terranova. If Pep needed any motivation to get back into shape, this was it. Beginning his morning regimen (roadwork) on March 20, he was ready to pick up where he left off. Two days later, it was announced that Pep would return to the ring on April 4, as part of an American Red Cross fight card. All expenses from the event would be underwritten to allow the organization to collect all the funds, minus government tax.

It wasn't spectacular, nevertheless it was a positive verdict. On April 4, Willie Pep, scaling at 133½, captured a challenging ten-round points victory over fledgling Leo Francis, who tipped a pound lighter. The Panamanian, who tore into his opponent as if his life depended on it, dropped the champ to a one count in the fourth round, before slicing Pep's cheek in the eighth. This left Pep thinking, where on earth was the welcome home committee? Although referee Billy Conway gave Pep nine rounds, those ringside saw the champion taking seven by a razor-thin margin. Pep was off his game, but it didn't surprise anyone.

To his disbelief, the following day he was signed to meet Manuel Ortiz, the undisputed bantamweight champion. The date for the non-title fight, which would be during the summer, was yet to be determined, while the location appeared to be Boston. Pep's handlers hoped to have him in the ring every ten days until that time. It was an aggressive undertaking, but everyone felt the formula was correct.

Inked to a ten-round non-title headliner slot against Harold "Snooks" Lacey on

April 20 at the New Haven Arena, Pep was aware that he had plenty of ring rust. Working hard at the Charter Oak Gym, he nonetheless remained confident. Lacey, a solid veteran boxer from New Haven, had posted a record of 4–5–1 during his last ten contests, with all the bouts going the distance. Never a contender, he was still a fighter you couldn't take for granted.[1] In contrast to his previous bout, Pep, tipping at 129½, seized every round to grab his 69th victory. Lacey, who scaled about two pounds lighter, was simply unable to mount an offense against Pep. That being the case, his only goal was to go the distance. Sharper than in his last outing, Pep feinted into angles, then unloaded. It was an improvement.[2]

"Pep was boxing's version of the three-card monte: Now you see him, now you don't."—Bert Randolph Sugar

If you had to pick a place to try to obtain your 70th victory in 71 bouts, Philadelphia would not be the place. Champion or not, it was always a tough boxing market for any outsider trying to grab a decision. Fortunately, Pep was tackling Jackie Leamus, a New York boxer with less than 20 battles under his belt. Viscusi, knowing how much promoter Herman Taylor desired a Pep versus Ike Williams outdoor match, pacified the producer by inking his fighter for a ten-rounder in the Arena; hence, the legendary impresario could get a good look at the featherweight champion. Taylor, who was known as "Muggsy" to his close friends, was noted for his promotion of the Jack Dempsey vs. Gene Tunney heavyweight fight at Sesquicentennial Stadium (later known as JFK Stadium). Knowing everyone in the fight game, Taylor commanded respect and got it.

Nothing sells comparable to a test drive, or was it a promotion? Weighing less than a pound over the featherweight limit of 126, Pep put on a clinic and grabbed a convincing ten-round decision over Leamus, who scaled at 131½. The only round that favored the New York fighter was the third, when a cut opened over Pep's left eye. Nearly 5,000 fight fans turned out for the event.

Speaking of impresarios: It was Jack Kearns' second show at the Coliseum, and it saw Willie Pep, tipping at 127 and outweighed by six pounds, pick up a ten-round unanimous decision over Brooklyn boxer Frankie Rubino. The battle took place on May 19, 1944, in Chicago. Working behind his left jab, Pep took control to skillfully win the battle—only the fifth round was close.[3] As a Kearns promotion, it brought out the stars. Four former champions were introduced before the battle: heavyweight Jack Johnson, bantamweight Johnny Coulon, lightweight Battling Nelson, and light heavyweight Jack Root. The price of admission meant nothing compared with being in the same venue as these elite pugilists.

If the name Jack "Doc" Kearns rang a bell, it should. Accompanied by Jack Dempsey and Tex Rickard, Kearns rode the train to immortality courtesy of the heavyweight championship of the world. Banking millions before many alive could even count that high, this trio took the fight game to a whole new level—they created, then popularized the term "million-dollar gate." If Kearns liked you, and he loved Willie Pep, you could be added to some lucrative promotions.

Buffalo was a great boxing town, as they say. On May 23, Willie Pep, tipping at 128¾, connected with a monstrous right hand that sent Joey Bagnato, who scaled at 132, to the canvas. At the 1:03 mark of the second round, it was lights out for Canadian Bagnato. The over 4,000 fans at the Memorial Auditorium were stunned by the Toronto fighter's impetuous tactics, but not by the outcome. Although the pace was brisk, it suited the champion just fine.

Returning to Hartford, Pep was scheduled to face Julie Kogon, a popular local adversary, on June 6, followed by Juan Zurita, NBA lightweight boxing champion, at Madison Square Garden on June 16. But on May 27, word came from Mexico City that Zurita had accidentally shot himself in his left hand. The wound would take at least six weeks to heal. Thus, Pep's total focus turned to Kogon, a tenacious New Haven lightweight. Greeting him at the Auditorium's first outdoor show, Willie Pep intended to make a clear statement. The ring rust from his stint in the Navy had been removed. The featherweight champion had worked that hard.

Smart, skilled, and unpredictable, Julie Kogon was an excellent counter puncher. But so was Willie Pep. This left many believing that a conflict between the two would be a cautious affair, destined to go the distance. Nevertheless, Connecticut fight fans were salivating at the mere thought. Ergo the spacious outdoor venue, adjacent to the auditorium, was fitted to accommodate a large crowd.[4]

In a "tale of the tape": Kogon had larger ankles, calves, thighs, wrists, forearms, and neck. Scaling at 130, he was two pounds heavier and was taller by an inch and a half. But Pep was quicker, smoother, and had an inch reach advantage. In his last ten bouts, Kogon posted a record of 7–1–2. Whereas he was a harder puncher than Pep, his career, unlike that of his opponent, never left the ground.

In front of the largest Hartford fight crowd in 14 years, Willie Pep dominated Julie Kogon over ten rounds and seized victory. Fighting defensively, Kogon appeared lost or perhaps intimidated. Pep took command, scored, feinted his opponent out of the neighborhood, then reset. The paid crowd of over 7,500 enthusiastic fans were as mesmerized by Pep's ring generalship as they were disenchanted by his adversary's presentation. Kogon failed to lead or mount an offensive even when he had Pep in trouble. The New Haven boxer would lose five of his next ten bouts.

By the middle of June, it was confirmed that Pep was heading back to Chicago for a battle in a ballpark. That's right, on July 7, the featherweight champion would meet Willie Joyce at Comiskey Park. It was no simple task, mind you, as Joyce had faced Henry Armstrong three times and defeated him twice; moreover, Joyce once fought Armstrong with a broken jaw and still managed to take the decision. Joyce also had a lightning-fast left jab. This would not bode well for Viscusi's fighter, or Viscusi for that matter, should they encounter a defeat. But Pep intended to take extra batting practice for this one. If he managed to pull it out, even in extra innings, he would likely earn enough money to buy his own ballpark. Was that the reason for the match, or did Viscusi sense something? It was the latter. Pep needed to step up his game to face Ortiz, and Viscusi needed to put a favor from the promoter in his back pocket. Jack Kearns had the promotion and liked the match even if Viscusi insisted that it be made for 134 pounds.[5]

Viscusi, Gore, and Pep left for Chicago on July 1. Once there, the champion and his challenger would train in the same gym. While it is hard to believe Pep had to travel such a distance to find a worthy opponent, even out of his weight class, the promotion looked promising. Kearns, always a cup of coffee from a publicity stunt, dragged his fighters over to Comiskey Park during a National Negro League double-header—yes, unfortunately some professional sports remained segregated. (Incidentally, Joyce was black, Pep was white, and Jackie Robinson was still three years from his debut with the Brooklyn Dodgers.) In front of 20,000 fans, the pair performed a battery exhibition as Pep tossed the pitches and Joyce called the signs. Two days before his fight against Joyce, the champion learned details regarding his meeting with Manuel Ortiz. That contest would be at Braves Field in Boston on July 17. The ten-round non-title bout, in another ballpark, was confirmation of the fighter's drawing power.

In his most challenging battle since he first met Sal Bartolo, Willie Pep managed to escape the confines of Comiskey Park with a ten-round, undisputed decision over Willie Joyce.

But Pep, scaling at 127¼, or six and three-quarter pounds lighter than his opponent, had to endure some damage before being awarded the verdict; specifically, his left eye was nearly closed from the third round on, and his muzzle flowed like

Niagara Falls. As usual, Pep's strength was his defense. Ducking and dodging more punches than he took, the Hartford fighter was in trouble twice. He was staggered by a right cross in the third term, and he appeared to "punch himself out" in the sixth. Surviving each instance thanks to a volley of combinations, he lived to fight another round. Notwithstanding the damage, those familiar with the featherweight champion believed it was his greatest performance to date.[6]

Pep left on a 4 p.m. train out of Chicago on July 8. Despite having little time before his bout with Ortiz, he planned to take the next three days off to spend with his family. Gore and Viscusi were worried he wasn't spending enough time at home, so they kept him in Hartford as long as they could. That delicate balance between home and career was difficult for every champion to manage. Finding enough qualified sparring partners to keep their fighter in peak condition was always the issue in Hartford.

If Pep wanted a mountain to climb, he found it with Manuel Ortiz. Shredding his opponents with deadly combinations, Ortiz hadn't lost a fight in over two and half years. Quick and deceptive, he had the power to silence an opponent. Yes, this was the same Manuel Ortiz that Pep sparred with years ago when he headed cross-country with a group of his friends. To the credit of both fighters, they would each pocket over a buck a round during this non-title dance.

Of the 9,759 fight fans in attendance at Braves Field, few found any reason to argue with the results: Willie Pep defeated Manuel Ortiz courtesy of a ten-round points verdict. According to some, Pep took seven rounds, Ortiz two, with one even. The key to Pep's success was staying out of range of his rival's heavy artillery. Believing the fight was closer than it was, Team Pep had their fighter turn on the afterburners during the final two rounds. In retrospect, it was a somewhat uninteresting battle that saw the bulk of the action taking place in the second half.[7]

Promoter George Mulligan, aka the Tex Rickard of Waterbury, booked Pep to meet Charley "Lulu" Constantino, the popular New York lightweight, outdoors at Municipal Stadium on July 28. The ten-round non-title contest promised to be the biggest Waterbury boxing event since Louis "Kid" Kaplan met Babe Herman at old Brassco Park back in 1925. If you combined the skill and popularity of both fighters, it was a formula for a winner.[8] At least it had better be, as Mulligan guaranteed the main event participants $17,500—Pep would earn $10,000, while his opponent pocketed the difference. Constantino's recent claim to fame was a five-bout winning streak, plus an impressive loss, if there was such a thing, to Beau Jack. Yet many recalled his victories over Joey Archibald, Bobby Ivy, Harry Jeffra, Nat Litfin, and Billy Speary. He could be dangerous.[9]

But word came on July 26 that the battle was postponed. It was rescheduled for August 4. Lou Viscusi, Pep's manager, contacted the State Athletic Commissioner and stated that his fighter was not prepared to engage. It appeared to be a personal problem. Viscusi, understanding that he represented a world champion, would not allow his fighter to enter the ring. Having missed recent training sessions, which was unheard of for the fighter, there was clearly concern. Thankfully, three days later, Pep was back in the gym. Later, the boxer stated that he needed personal time to sort through some issues that were bothering him.[10]

Pep was slow out of the blocks but hit his stride by the third round. Constantino, who tipped at 132½ for a four-pound advantage, had no solution as to how to

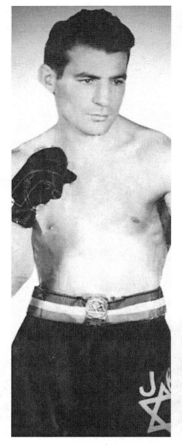  

A trio of solid opponents: (from left to right): publicity photographs of Julie Kogon, Willie Joyce, and Lulu Constantino. All three boxers lost their 10-round battles to Willie Pep via a decision.

catch his adversary. Truthfully, he looked foolish in front of over 6,600 spectators. True to form, Willie Pep captured the unanimous ten-round decision over Lulu Constantino. Referee Louis "Kid" Kaplan gave the featherweight champion every round of the colorless contest that was void of a knockdown. Witnessing Pep's 76th ring victory ringside were Bat Battalino, former featherweight champion, and Joe Shugrue, one of only a few men who ever defeated Benny Leonard. The fight was believed to be the largest-ever gate drawn by a non-title bout in the state of Connecticut; moreover, George Mulligan was the promoter behind three of the top four all-time gates.

Take a closer look at some incredible statistics: The last four opponents the champion had faced, and defeated, had a combined record of 266–52–28. Winning over five times as many bouts as they lost, these were tough opponents. Willie Joyce, for example, had only nine professional defeats, and Manuel Ortiz knocked out over 40 percent of his adversaries. For the four battles, Willie Pep drew an estimated 33,972 fans, or an average of 8,493 per contest. This happened while World War II was raging.[11] Add this: Willie Pep had made winning look effortless. It was a magnificent performance.

On August 15, NYSAC named Chalky Wright as the Number One contender for Pep's title. Hence it looked as if another battle between the talented pair was imminent. Indeed it was. Matchmaker Gus Browne wanted the rematch at Bulkeley Stadium in Hartford, but Viscusi committed to a September 8 date at Madison Square Garden. As Lou Viscusi and Eddie Walker, Wright's manager, disliked one another, Hartford appeared out of the question,[12] and it was. Walker signed with Garden promoter Mike Jacobs.

On August 17, Frank S. Coskey, state athletic commissioner, ended Connecticut's relationship with the NBA For the first time, Willie Pep was recognized as the world's featherweight titleholder in Connecticut. Coskey entered into a working agreement with the New York Boxing Commission. The actions of the NBA were absurd. They wouldn't allow Jackie Callura to meet Pep, therefore he ended up losing his title to Phil Terranova, who was stripped of his crown by Sal Bartolo. Hats off to commissioner Coskey for making the proper call.[13]

Willie Pep, partaking in his share of domestic vicissitudes, had no idea what actions were taking place regarding his next title defense. A tune-up fight against Joey Peralta, at the dog track in West Springfield on August 28, was all he was certain of. In little more than a sparring session, Pep, scaling at 128½, won every round to capture a unanimous ten-round verdict. To Peralta's praise, the seasoned boxer could in fact take a punch. The rounds were redundant but effective, as Pep slowly throttled up with left jabs, before cutting loose with vicious left hooks. However, it was the champion's accurate combinations that staggered Peralta, who scaled at 128½. With Pep bobbing, ducking, feinting, punching, slipping, and weaving, the crowd of over 4,300 enjoyed every minute of the display.

Feeling bad for Gus Browne, Viscusi agreed to have Pep meet Charles "Cabey" Lewis at the Auditorium Outdoor Arena in Hartford on September 14—this was possible because Pep's battle with Wright was moved to September 29. But Tommy Dio, the fighter's irrational manager, insisted that it be a title bout; consequently, Viscusi had the task of explaining to the nontraditional fight executive how the system works to get a crack at the championship. To make a long and silly story short, if Lewis beat Pep in this overweight contest, which was as possible as building a hotel on the sun, then Lewis would be given a title fight in Madison Square Garden. You have to hand it to Dio for sticking to his guns. After a weather postponement, the fight was rescheduled for September 19.

Celebrating his 22nd birthday, Willie Pep knocked out Charles "Cabey" Lewis in the eighth round of their scheduled ten-rounder. Lewis, who tipped at 128, managed to jolt Pep, who scaled a pound lighter, in both the first and seventh rounds. It appeared to catch everyone by surprise. Charging across the ring at the opening gong, Lewis sent a hard right to the chin of Pep that confirmed he meant business. Stunned, Pep immediately altered his distance before executing his fight plan and building a gradual lead. It worked. A precision left hook by the champion to the jaw of his adversary was responsible for the technical knockout. Referee Billy Conway, noting the defenseless fighter after two descents, had no choice but to wave it off. There were no protests from the corner of Lewis, which included eminent trainer Ray Arcel. To sum it up: The weather was miserable, which accounted for the small turnout, as was Pep, who felt a victory in a set-up bout shouldn't have been such a challenge.

Willie Pep v. Chalky Wright, II

Having witnessed Willie Pep's rain-soaked ring recital with Lewis, Mike Jacobs *formally* inked the champion to a 15-round title defense in Madison Square Garden on September 29. Chalky Wright, the premier contender, would be across the ring. Having not fought in the Garden since his loss to Angott back on March 19, 1943, Pep was excited about his return. Since that time, he had taken his skills to various cities outside of Connecticut, while adding to his impressive winning record of 78 victories in 79 fights.

Albert Garfield "Chalky" Wright was born on February 1, 1912, in Wilcox, Arizona. He was the seventh child born to James Wright and Clara Martin. Raised in Bonita, Arizona, Albert moved to Colton, California, in San Bernardino County, where he began boxing. Seeking regular employment after some frustrating years in the ring, Wright moved to Los Angeles. He became a chauffeur, bodyguard, and friend to Hollywood actress Mae West. In addition to her acting, West enjoyed boxing and encouraged her friend to return to the ring.[14]

The talented Wright was still being described in racist terms ("ancient Negro"). Truth was he was an outstanding pugilist. Wright, who had a record of 143–33–17 when he first met Pep, was now 162–35–18. He had faced only one defeat (Lulu Constantino) since he last lost to Pep. The champion always referred to him as "clever," because he was.

The pair, who held the record indoor gate for a featherweight contest, hoped to duplicate their previous performance. Jacobs, anticipating a generous contribution to his bank account, scaled tickets at $12, $10, $6, $3.50, $2.50, and $1.50 (general admission). Impressive levels, considering the times.

On September 26, the Twentieth Century Sporting Club, aka Mike Jacobs, confirmed that the Gillette Safety Razor Company would sponsor the telecasts of the next 50 fights offered by the organization, including those held at Madison Square Garden and St. Nicholas Arena. This was done primarily for the hospitalized wounded war veterans—most hospitals were equipped with television receiving sets. The Pep–Wright fight would be the first fight broadcast on a non-experimental basis.

According to Groucho Marx, "If a black cat crosses your path, it signifies that the animal is going somewhere." However, a superstitious Willie Pep begged to differ. The featherweight champion insisted that everything regarding the rematch be identical to that evening back on November 20, 1942, when he captured the title. So it was back to the 18th floor at the Hotel Lincoln, back to his tattered red robe with white lettering, and as always, his lucky water bottle and bucket in his corner. (By the way, he wore a new white robe the night he lost to Angott.)

Over 15,000 spectators produced an admirable gate for Mike Jacobs at the Garden on September 29, and they were there—at least most of them—to watch Willie Pep successfully defend his title for the second time. With both fighters scaling at 125 pounds, the champion captured the 15-round unanimous decision over Chalky Wright.[15] Pep slipped to his gloves in the seventh round, and to his knees in the eighth, but that was the closest either participant came to a knockdown. Artfully working behind the left jab, Pep scored, scooted, and scored repeatedly. The feather champ had no intention of slugging it out with his rival. For his part, Wright brought the crowd to their feet in the sixth and seventh rounds when he staggered Pep with crisp right hands matched with tenacious left hooks. Fortunately for Pep, these were the only rounds he lost. The corner trio of Gore, Viscusi, and Pete Perone (Lenny Marello was in the service) made sure of that. It was the champion's 79th victory in 80 contests and his 12th since his naval discharge.

With a puffed and discolored cheekbone, Mr. Papaleo slept in the following morning. Accompanied by his wife, he planned to spend a few days in the city, visiting the attractions and even a Broadway show. Meanwhile, Viscusi, Gore and Perone headed back to Hartford. Viscusi was reorganizing and moving. He planned on picking up more responsibilities at the Auditorium, while moving the headquarters of the Hartford Boxing Club from 1 Franklin Avenue over to 331 Wethersfield Avenue (Auditorium). A stack of offers for Pep's services also occupied his time.

In addition to spending time at home at the beginning of October, Willie Pep took part in Hartford's Columbus Day Celebration on October 12. With his first international battle less than two weeks away, Pep was gearing up for his visit to Montreal and his October 25 fight inside the Forum. There, in an overweight 10-round contest, he planned to meet Bobby Gunther. They were familiar with each other, as Gunther had sparred with Pep in Chicago for about a week prior to his battle against Willie Joyce—he was also on the undercard of the event. Montreal promoter Eddie Quinn initially liked Gunther and witnessed his rise in popularity. But three consecutive losses leading up to the fight had Quinn rethinking his choice. Later, the promoter substituted pugilist Jackie Leamus.

Pep's 80th victory, which was also his first outside the United States, was a 10-round unanimous decision over Jackie Leamus at the Forum in Montreal. Desperately trying to take the battle to close quarters, Leamus, tipping at 131½, failed. In both the fifth and the seventh rounds, he thought he had successfully trapped his opponent but was mistaken. Pep, scaling at 127¾, covered, blocked, sidestepped, and slipped like a champion.[16]

The winner of the Hartford Auditorium battle between Norman "Hi-Ho" Silver and Charles "Cabey" Lewis was promised a shot at Willie Pep. That winner was Charles "Cabey" Lewis. He would meet the champion inside the Auditorium on November 14. Truthfully, that was not the result Pep was hoping for. The fighter recalled the pain inflicted by Lewis' rib blasts back in September like it was yesterday. Nevertheless, Pep headed to the Charter Oak Gymnasium to prepare. As usual, finding qualified sparring partners was an issue. At the same time, Lewis was sparring with Lulu Constantino at Stillman's in New York.

Over 2,700 fight fans, which was below expectation, turned out to watch Willie Pep capture eight rounds on his way to a unanimous ten-round decision over Charles "Cabey" Lewis. In the fourth round, you could hear a pin drop when Pep was floored for a six count by his adversary's solid right. That, however, was the only round won by the New York fighter. Referee Louis "Kid" Kaplan scored it 8–1–1, in a fight that for the most part was uneventful. For whatever the reason, the champion did not appear at his best.

A few days later, Pep learned he had been signed to his next two fights. He would meet New York boxer Pedro Hernandez in a ten-round overweight clash at Washington on November 27, followed by Chalky Wright on December 5 at Cleveland. Pep had defeated Hernandez, a member of Al Weill's stable, back on August 11, 1942, and he had recently beaten Wright (September 29). Superfluous matches, Pep thought, but he nonetheless pushed forward.

Off they went to Washington, District of Columbia, and the Uline Arena (later renamed the Washington Coliseum), located on Third Street in the northeast portion of the city.[17] Pep and Gore arrived three hours late, so the champion lost a bit of training time. Favored at 4–1, Pep did manage to catch up with a few friends before his contest.

Tipping at 128, Willie Pep skated to a 10-round points victory over Pedro Hernandez, who scaled three and a half pounds heavier. Many saw it as Pep winning eight rounds, with two even. Poor attendance—a bit under 1,500 fight fans—hampered the excitement. There were no knockdowns, only a couple of stumbles by Hernandez. It wasn't much of an evening.[18] Pep's biggest thrill came in a pre-fight "meet and greet." The great American tap dancer Bill "Bojangles" Robinson paid him a visit. The champion, disappointed by the turnout, was glad to get back to Hartford and begin preparing for Chalky Wright.

Willie Pep v. Chalky Wright, III

Pep and trainer Bill Gore headed for Cleveland on November 30. The champion's fight with Wright on December 5 was part of a large Christmas Fund event. On the card as well: Ike Williams would meet Lulu Constantino. Much of the press was still trying to figure out why Pep was meeting Wright for a third time. The first time was a title fight, the second time was a customary return bout, by why a third? Risky, some believed, especially in Cleveland. Nevertheless, it was a for a good cause, and it was the fighter's last bout of the year.

A crowd of over 13,200 watched as Willie Pep, four and a half pounds lighter than his opponent at 128 pounds, waltz around Chalky Wright at the Arena. In the end, it was Pep by a 10-round unanimous decision. Wright managed only one solid punch, a firm right to the champion's nose in the fifth round, or the only term observers thought he won. There were no knockdowns. It was so dull that the referee warned both fighters multiple times to engage. By the way, Williams defeated Constantino in a ten-round decision. After a 17-hour train trip—in coach to add to the misery—from Cleveland, Team Pep finally arrived back in Hartford.

In a poll conducted by *Esquire* magazine, boxing writers named Willie Pep the outstanding boxer of 1944. The champion also received a medallion from the *Los Angeles Times* for being one of the leading athletes of the year.

1945

British poet Dame Edith Sitwell once quipped, "Winter is the time for comfort, for good food and warmth, for the touch of a friendly hand and for a talk beside the fire: it is the time for home." The Papaleo family agreed. Despite the occasional social commitments, such as sports banquets, Mary loved having Willie home for at least part of the holiday season. Amid the topics of discussion was moving into a newly furnished flat.

On January 6, President Franklin D. Roosevelt addressed Congress, urging the enactment of legislation making all 4Fs available in whatever capacity best suited the war effort. This meant that those either 4F or discharged from the military would now become available for service. This included professional boxers Jimmy Bivens, Ken Overlin, Willie Pep, Sugar Ray Robinson, and Bobby Ruffin. During the second week of the year, Pep was ordered by his draft board to report at 6:15 a.m. on January 16, 1945, for a pre-induction physical. Regardless of his medical discharge or possible perforated eardrum, he was reconsidered for service. On January 16, at New Haven, Willie Pep was accepted for general service in the army. Later, he received official notification from his Hartford draft board.

Willie Pep became the first notable sports personality to be inducted, then discharged from the United States military, only to be inducted once again. Regardless of his situation, or because of it, Pep took a 10-round non-title bout against Canadian lightweight Ralph Walton at the Auditorium in Hartford on January 23, 1945.[19] Aware of the ring rust collected over the holidays, he needed the work. Besides, ten percent of the receipts went to the Infantile Paralysis Fund. As a father, Pep understood the importance of the cause.[20]

Taking seven of ten rounds, Willie Pep managed an easy decision over Ralph Walton. A powerful right uppercut by his adversary, who outweighed him by 13 pounds, woke up the featherweight champion in the second round. Thereafter keeping his distance, Pep's punching efficiency increased with each passing round, though he did incur damage in the form of numerous facial cuts. The crowd of over 2,300 wasn't stirred by Pep's performance in the first five rounds, but compensation came via the action during the last half of the fight. It wasn't Pep as his finest, but he hadn't fought in over a month.

Pep's strength, he believed, originated from his straight lefts, while his control was a product of the left jab. When he failed to jab with conviction, as he did with Walton, he failed to take control of the fight and couldn't set up his other punches. It threw off his timing and distance. Needing more target practice, he was inked to a 10-rounder at the Arena in New Haven on February 5. There he would meet veteran Willie Roache, from Wilmington, Delaware, and a ranking featherweight. Having defeated Roache at Foot Guard Hall back on February 10, 1942, Pep was more concerned about finding his control than the skills of his opposition.

Willie Roache, who entered his battle with Pep with about as many wins (41), as losses, lost his 10-round bout against the champion via a decision. It wasn't even close; moreover, referee Billy Conway gave Pep all ten rounds. There was only one knockdown, but it was impressive: Near the conclusion of the opening round, Pep unloaded a vicious left hook that floored Roache to a three count. Stunned at the display of power, the New York boxer lost his rhythm and never found it. Over 5,000 spectators enjoyed the New Haven battle, and Pep's 85th victory in 86 fights. The champion, who weighed 127½, was outweighed by nearly five pounds. In one of those "say it ain't so" moments, after the battle Roache was taken into custody by military police who needed clarification of his status.

Analyzing every punch ringside was New York boxer Phil Terranova. Back on January 26, it was announced that the first championship bout of the year would be held in Madison Square Garden, and it would be a battle for the featherweight title. Willie Pep would put his belt on the line for 15 rounds against Terranova, the former NBA featherweight champion.

Willie Pep v. Phil Terranova

Phil Terranova's only excuse was that he couldn't get close enough to land a knockout punch. However, the defense fell on deaf ears. The highlight of the evening came in the tenth round as both men, sliced, bruised, and bleeding, looked vulnerable. Nevertheless, neither gladiator could deliver a death blow.

On February 19, 1945, Willie Pep successfully defended his 126-pound title by taking a 15-round unanimous decision over Phil Terranova. It was the third defense of the crown he won from Chalky Wright back on November 20, 1942, and it was an impressive one at that. Referee Art Donovan, the third man in the ring, gave Pep 10 rounds to three, with two even. Terranova's strategy was to let Pep lead; however, when he couldn't counter fast enough, he was forced to adopt an aggressive style midway through the battle. Persistent, Terranova would not capitulate. He fired endless volleys of left hooks, few of which accounted for any damage. Proof of Pep's scoring prowess came in the sixth round, when he delivered eight precision blows without a return.[21]

Attendance, at about 10,000, fell below expectations and was the smallest house the champion had ever drawn in the city.[22] At 124¼ pounds, Pep was lighter by less than a pound. Not that Lou Viscusi was worried or anything, but he did have Bobby Gleason, Terranova's manager, post a check for $10,000 as a guarantee of a return match had the Bronx fighter ended up victorious. Hey, you never know.

Shifting to the undercard: The highlight of the preliminaries was a good-looking kid from Harlem who knocked out Brooklyn boxer Joey Gatto in the opening round. His name was Joseph "Sandy" Saddler. The youngster had appeared in the Garden before, but never on a fight card with Willie Pep. That would change.

Comparing Willie Pep's skills at this juncture in his career, whether fair or not, was continued by many who covered the fight game. Names such as Abe Attell (1884–1970), George Dixon (1870–1909), Johnny Dundee (1893–1965), Johnny Kilbane (1889–1957), and Terry McGovern (1880–1918) rolled off the tongues of wordsmiths as if they had seen each in the ring. They hadn't, as a quick glance at these fighters' dates of birth and death could prove. Yet Ed Van Every, dean of New York fight writers, believed Pep was comparable to those greats, and that said a lot. Abe Attell, who needed no introduction if you follow the sweet science, believed that Pep was still improving and was destined for greatness.

On March 13, 1945, Willie Pep reported to the armed forces induction center at New Haven and headed for basic training at Fort Devens, Massachusetts. With the feather champion in the Army and Johnny Cesario, Pep's understudy, packing his bags, Lou Viscusi and Bill Gore, like many in their shoes, were left trying on various pairs. What choice did they have? Their current fistic phenom was Nick Stato, aka Nicholas Sotiropoulos, of Springfield. He broke out of Holyoke and had some noteworthy fights at the Auditorium, but he wasn't Willie Pep. It wasn't fair to compare him, which some did, to the champion.[23]

Japan accepted the terms of an unconditional surrender on August 14, 1945. The ceremonial terms of capitulation were signed aboard the U.S.S. *Missouri*. It appeared as if World War II was drawing to a conclusion, and our troops, both home and abroad, would soon be returning to civilian life.

William Patrick Papaleo was born on August 29, 1945, to Private and Mrs.

William Papaleo. He weighed in at 7½ pounds, and both he and Mrs. Papaleo were doing well. Private Willie Pep was in Bridgeport, Connecticut, on September 7, collecting his long overdue featherweight championship belt from Nat Fleischer, editor of *The Ring*—the belt was delayed because of the shortage of metals during wartime. Home on a pass from Cushing General Hospital in Framingham, Massachusetts, where he was stationed with the military police, Pep was elated by the birth of his son.

The next day, a squad of Hartford police arrested 28 men on charges of gambling and frequenting a gambling place. The incident took place on a vacant lot at the rear of 42 Charles Street. Among those arrested and booked was Willie Pep. Released under a $200 bond, Pep would have to appear in Police Headquarters on Monday, September 10. After pleading guilty, Pep

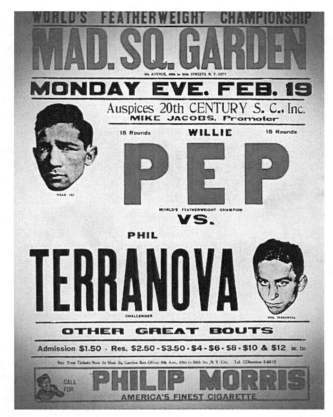

A fight poster from the World's Featherweight Championship battle, held on February 19, 1945, at Madison Square Garden. Willie Pep successfully defended his title over 15 rounds to seize the victory over Phil Terranova.

was fined $15. Appearing in his Army uniform, the elite fighter stood before Judge Cornelius J. Moylan, who reprimanded the boxer and reminded him that he was a role model.

Willie Pep became a civilian again on October 2, 1945, and immediately returned home to his family. Outside of his family members, Lou Viscusi was his first contact. Full of ginger and vinegar, Pep was ready to start training. Confident that Viscusi would work him up quickly in competition and that Gore would have him razor sharp in no time, Pep was euphoric.

The NBA's first postwar fighter ratings were released on October 16. All the champions were notified that they must defend their titles against approved contenders once they completed conditioning. Take a look at the champions, followed by the premier contenders, by division: Heavyweight—Joe Louis (champion), Billy Conn (premier contender); Light Heavyweight—Gus Lesnevich, Archie Moore; Middleweight—Tony Zale, Jake LaMotta; Welterweight—Ike Williams, Beau Jack; Featherweight—Sal Bartolo, Willie Pep; Bantamweight—Manuel Ortiz, Tony Olivera; and Flyweight—Jackie Peterson, Joe Curran. Other outstanding contenders in the

126-pound division were: Chalky Wright, Charles Chavez, Phil Terranova, Jackie Graves, Freddie Russo, Danny Webb, Chico Rosa, and Nel Tarleton. Again, these were the NBA rankings. Optimistic but cautious, Viscusi booked his fighter against Paulie Jackson over an eight-round ride.[24]

Winning every round, Willie Pep, tipping at 130, defeated Paulie Jackson, who scaled three pounds heavier, via an eight-round decision. The battle took place at the Hartford Auditorium on October 30. It was the champion's first bout in eight months, and it appeared that way with one exception: Pep sent a robust left hook to the jaw of Jackson that dropped him to a nine count in the second round. Notwithstanding his antagonist's survival, it was a classic blast and the only knockdown. Next it was off to Buffalo to meet the popular Mike Martyk, from St. Catherine's, Ontario.

On November 5, at the Memorial Auditorium in Buffalo, Willie Pep, scaling at 129½, scored a technical knockout victory over the Canadian pugilist, who tipped a pound and a half heavier. The fight, which was scheduled for ten rounds, ended at the 2:39 mark of the fifth session. Martyk, who took solid hits in the fourth round, caught a vicious left hook in the fifth that dazed him. Noting his challenger's disorientation, Pep had his opponent out on his feet in no time. Referee Eddie Seres had little choice but to call it.[25]

First Draw

Unsure of precisely how he wanted to play out the year, Viscusi inked Pep to four out-of-state battles: Eddie Giosa, in Boston on November 26; Harold Gibson, on December 5 in Lewiston, Maine; Jimmy McAllister in Baltimore on December 13; and Johnny Virgo in Buffalo on December 17 (later moved to January 15, 1946). Looking closer at the matchups: Giosa had a good record but had lost three of his last five bouts; Gibson was nothing but target practice; McAllister was a tough local fighter who could genuinely challenge Pep; and Virgo was a streaky Rochester boxer who would likely prove an easy victory. Digging even deeper: Giosa looked like easy money as promoter Sam Silverman paid $1,500 for Pep's services; Viscusi likely wanted to go ice fishing in Maine, thus Gibson; McAllister was a favor for promoter Billy Brown, and a dangerous one at that; and Viscusi liked Jack Singer of the Hudson Boxing Club, because there was no other reason to travel to Buffalo in the winter.

Inside the Mechanics Building in Boston on November 26, Willie Pep, scaling at 130 or five pounds lighter than his opposer, glided to a 10-round unanimous victory over Eddie Giosa. Under 4,000 fight fans turned out to witness the flawless performance by the champion. Giosa, who should have been paid by the punch, landed few of his own during the non-title contest—nobody could believe that this was the same tough Philly pug who held victories over Jimmy McAllister, Maxie Shapiro, and Jackie Leamus.[26]

Next on the menu: Harold "Cannonball" Gibson. The Harlem boxer, who had lost his last five fights, began boxing with good intent but turned punching bag in 1943. From that point forward, he realized he could make good money as a member of the supporting cast. To his credit, he went the distance with some good boxers, including Sandy Saddler. But Pep was an opponent beyond comparison at this point. Taking command from the start, the champion, who scaled at 128½, a half-pound advantage, systematically pounded out each round to capture the 10-round contest.

Knocking Gibson down six times, five times in the ninth round alone, Pep tried to kayo his adversary but could not do it. Still and all, a crowd of under 2,000 at the Armory enjoyed the show. This was Pep's 90th ring victory in 91 bouts.

In his final battle of the year, Pep traveled to Baltimore for a 10-round affair at the Fayette Street Garden. His opponent was Jimmy McAllister, recognized by the Maryland Commission as the Southern featherweight titleholder. The over-the-weight affair was scheduled for 10 rounds, and Pep's title was not at stake. Promoter Fred Squires assembled an engaging fight card with five good preliminaries. McAllister hailed from West Baltimore, and like Pep was on a fast track after completing a stint in the service. His last two victories, over Georgie Hansford and Vince Dell'Orto, landed him the match with Pep.

It was an anomaly, or an unexplainable deviation: Jimmy McAllister, tipping to a four-pound advantage, managed to box Willie Pep to a ten-round draw on December 13. The hometown pugilist shook Pep three times, even sending him to the floor for a count of six in the second round with a hard right to the chin. Each time Pep mounted an offensive, McAllister stood his ground. A majority saw it four rounds apiece, and two even. Both fighters, sensing the situation, tried hard for a kayo during the final two rounds. Yet it wasn't to be.

What went wrong?

Complacency. It has ruined more records and ring careers than any other feeling. Pep took his opponent lightly, and it cost him, especially early in the battle. He didn't ignite until the fifth round.

Self-control. The champion had to remember to rely on his strengths, which were his defensive skills. He didn't need to be drawn into a toe-to-toe confrontation, which occurred when he retaliated for an assault he didn't like. Knockouts were like home runs in baseball, exhilarating even if they aren't the norm. Instead of going for a home run, a barrage of left hooks to the body would have been a better call.

But there was more to the story: Unbeknownst to nearly everyone, the referee had forbidden Pep to use his trademark spin move (See Appendix C), a maneuver in which he avoided a clinch by turning his adversary around. Fairness in boxing, as every pug who has ever "laced 'em up" understood, was subject to interpretation.

A paralyzing blizzard postponed Pep's battle with Johnny Virgo. With the holidays approaching and his recent draw fresh in his mind, Pep was grateful for the break. Speaking of the gift season, *The Ring* magazine named Willie Pep "Boxer of the Year" for 1945. He was the perfect choice. Having spent stints in both the Navy and Army, Pep, unbeaten in seven non-title bouts, was the only champion to defend his title during the year.

FIVE

Postwar Pugilism,
1946–1947

"Dempsey could beat anybody he could hit. The only reason that he couldn't do anything with fellows like Tunney or Greb or myself was he couldn't hit us."—Tommy Gibbons

1946

Whether it was Viscusi's idea or that of his fighter, it was clear that the team's matchmaking criteria had changed. In 1943, Pep met one fighter with a losing record. In 1944, when he fought 16 times, he met only one fighter with a losing record. The next year, Pep again met only one fighter with a losing record. But in 1946, he would meet six opposers with losing records, with one fighter even. Was the strategy adopted to prolong the champion's title reign, or simply a way for him to spend more time with his family? Likely it was both.[1]

Talk about a series of European non-title fights for Willie Pep had Lou Viscusi intrigued. Jack Solomons, England's premier boxing promoter, wanted to host the featherweight champion in both London and Paris as early as spring; however, the details needed to be ironed out.[2] Naturally the thought of walking the streets of a postwar Europe aroused Mr. and Mrs. Papaleo, but the reality of leaving a young family behind made it difficult to comprehend. As the year began, what was certain: Willie Pep would meet Johnny Virgo at the Buffalo Auditorium on January 15. This was the postponed bout from December. The bigger questions, at least to many fight followers: Who would Pep defend his title against in 1946? And when did he intend to do it? Since Pep had beaten all the leading contenders, not to mention a few light-weight hopefuls, the list of possibilities was shrinking.

Before nearly 5,400 dedicated Buffalo fight fans, Willie Pep delivered the perfect right cross to the chin of Johnny Virgo and ended the one-sided battle at the 1:05 mark of the second round. The Rochester pug, with twice as many victories as defeats, never saw it coming. Tipping at 129¾, Pep, who was five pounds lighter than his opposer, had Virgo in trouble right from the start. While it made for a short evening, the Jack Singer promotion was still considered a success. Pep's stablemate and sparring partner, Johnny Cesario, also grabbed a victory on the fight card (over Sonny Jim Hampton). Both boxers sat together on the morning train back to Springfield. Three years younger than Pep, Cesario, undefeated at 37–0, showed considerable promise as a welterweight—boy, did he. Both were thrilled when they ran into

Jimmy Goodrich, the former lightweight champion, at the train station. Demonstrative as always, Goodrich, who owned a restaurant outside the city, asked about the Connecticut gang—folks such as Louis "Kid" Kaplan and Denny McMahon, to name a few—back in Hartford. Goodrich never fought in Connecticut—he lost to Kaplan in New York—but respected many of the individuals who were part of the local fight game. Speaking of home, Pep planned on a couple days off before heading to Ruppert's Brewery in Manhattan for the New York Boxing Writers annual dinner. Viscusi, Gore, and "Kid" Kaplan also planned to attend. Mr. Papaleo had a plaque waiting for him.

Returning to Connecticut, Pep was out at the Farmington High School Winter Carnival on January 26. Maintaining a local presence was always important to the fighter. For now, his manager was working out details for a title defense against Sal Bartolo at the Garden. When the date was finally set for March 1, everyone breathed a sigh of relief. The winner would be the *undisputed champion*—two words that every elite fighter cherished.[3]

Back to Buffalo, inside the Memorial Auditorium on February 13. Willie Pep, tipping at 128½, seven pounds lighter than his antagonist, seized a 10-round unanimous decision over Indiana pugilist Jimmy Joyce, the brother of Willie Joyce and Gene Joyce. Pep was in complete command with the exception of the eighth round, where he almost lost it. Joyce sent a pair of left hooks to Pep's midsection (some at ringside claimed they were low) that weakened the fighter. Truthfully, the champion ran on instinct until the end of the round. Thankfully, he recovered during the final two sessions. Over 6,500 spectators, many of whom had no idea of Pep's condition in the eighth round, seemed to enjoy the contest. Promoter Jack Singer had hoped Pep would meet Joey Kushner, from Syracuse, but the veteran southpaw slipped while doing roadwork and cracked a pair of ribs.

Ten days later, in another one of those "say it ain't so" moments, Sal Bartolo informed promoter Mike Jacobs that he was ill. (You can picture Jacobs on the phone, screaming at Lou Schiro, Bartolo's manager.) "Sal Bartolo Ducks New York Meeting with Champion Pep," read the headline in the *Wilmington Star*.[4] Following a physical examination that found nothing wrong with the hub fighter, the illness was confirmed as a "mental attitude." Instead of defending his title against Bartolo, Pep would engage with Jimmy McAllister in a 10-round non-title contest. Since McAllister had held the Hartford boxer to a draw last year, Jacobs considered him a respectable, but not perfect, substitution; nevertheless, disappointed ticket holders, of whom there were many, received refunds. Pep, who had trained hard for the fight, was in prime condition. Viscusi claimed that Bartolo ran out on his contract obligation, confirming who was the real featherweight champion.

On March 1, Willie Pep, tipping at 129½, shocked a Madison Square Garden crowd by knocking out Jimmy McAllister, who scaled at 128, at the 2:44 mark of the second round—sweet vindication, at least in the champion's mind. Coming out strong in the opening round, McAllister didn't look, or fight, like a substitution. Scoring immediately, he had Pep flustered to such an extent that the champion looked almost helpless. The reason behind the champion's condition: McAllister had jammed a thumb in Pep's eye that temporarily blinded the boxer. Furious but composed, Pep came out in the second round with an endless arsenal of left jabs that straightened his antagonist and transformed him into a standing target. Firing a flawless right-hand to his mark, Pep sent the Baltimore fighter back on his heels. Pep spun him around and tore into his midsection with left jabs. Noting an opening, Pep fired a lightning-fast right cross to the jaw that dropped McAllister like an anchor. The scheduled 10-round contest was over before some spectators returned from the concession stand.

Forrest City Blues

Action! Lord knows the fight game has always had its share of speculation or gambling. Its epicenter, at least for Pep's battle against McAllister, appeared to be the Forrest Hotel at 224 W. 49th Street, a bit off Broadway, in Manhattan. It was convenient, comfortable, and air-conditioned; if you were looking for decent odds, this was the place to find it. Every bookie appeared to have a connection where it mattered, in Stillman's Gym or even along Jacob's Beach (49th Street between Broadway and Eighth Avenue). Yep, they had the dope, be it good or bad, and circulated it as needed, at times even hourly. Pep, as anticipated, was favored early at 13–5. Right after lunch, word was "Pep was goin' dump the fight." Supposedly, Viscusi wanted a title fight in Hartford, and this was the only way to get it. The odds tightened quickly, all the way to even money before reversing, as thousands of dollars poured in for McAllister. The rumors spread so fast they even reached Viscusi; moreover, he was receiving phone calls from all over the country questioning the validity of the claims. Nothing irritates a fight manager more than gossip such as this. Nothing. Slowly the odds corrected, until Pep was even money a few hours before the contest. It was pure gobbledygook, but a parasite the sport couldn't shake.

Pep, awaiting news from Viscusi about his next battle, took a few days off and even tackled a few speaking engagements, such as the Windsor, Connecticut, VFW Post. Healthy and in good spirits, he soon learned he was heading to the Midwest.

Tipping about a pound

WILLIE Pep, Hartford, Conn.
Winner of

Conn. Flyweight Championship 1938
New England Featherweight Championship - 1942
World's Featherweight Championship . . . 1942
Los Angeles Times, "Fighter of Year" . . 1944
The Ring, "Fighter of the Year 1945

"Fighting Willie Pep is like trying to stamp out a grass fire."—Kid Campeche, boxer

Managed by Walter Melrose, Jackie Wilson was the light and welterweight champion of the Pacific Coast.

lighter than his opponent at 128, Willie Pep snatched a 10-round unanimous decision over Jackie Wilson at the Municipal Auditorium in Kansas City, Missouri, on March 26. Wilson, the old NBA featherweight champion (1941–1943) who began fighting back in 1929, was on the back end of a great career—he was looking for his 100th victory.[5] Pep was grateful for the opportunity to fight the talented featherweight once again—he defeated Wilson back in April 1943. Many saw it either all ten rounds for Pep or the champion taking nine rounds with one even. Regardless, it was all about the Connecticut boxer, who took command from the opening bell. There were no knockdowns, but Pep had Wilson leaning forward during the sixth frame. The non-title bout drew over 3,500 fans. Pep, Viscusi, and Gore managed an early flight out of Kansas City that arrived home on March 27. All three were looking forward to time off before preparing for their bout against Georgie Knox, at the Auditorium in Providence, on April 8.

Lending a helping hand, Pep was in the Hartford Auditorium on April 3, sparring with one of Hartford's promising talents, Dennis "Pat" Brady. The 18-year-old was receiving last-minute instructions for his battle with, of all people, Sal Bartolo on April 5. Whereas Brady was no match for Pep, he did manage to clip the champion with one of his impressive rights. Incidentally, Brady lost his battle with Bartolo via a razor-thin decision; his chief second, watching Bartolo's every move, was Bill Gore.

Inside the Rhode Island Auditorium in Providence, Willie Pep, tipping almost three pounds heavier than his opponent, captured an uninspiring third-round TKO over punching bag Georgie Knox. After spinning his adversary to the ropes, Pep used two left hooks to drop him to a nine count. Knox barely rose to his feet, wishing he was anywhere but where he was, and referee Dolly Searle called it at the 1:45 mark of the third. Knox, whose record had nearly twice as many losses as wins, performed as anticipated. The only person—among the nearly 4,800 witnesses—surprised by the conclusion was Knox.

On April 19, Willie Pep was arrested and charged with gambling and frequenting a gambling place (North Meadows).[6] It was Pep's second court appearance on gambling charges. The champion pled guilty and was fined $15 by Judge Abraham Ribicoff.[7] If you thought it was embarrassing appearing before the judge, one could only imagine the chagrin he faced when returning to his Standish Street residence.

Nearly a month after his last ring appearance, Willie Pep, scaling at 128, eight pounds lighter than his adversary, took a lackluster 10-round points victory over Philly pug Ernie Petrone. The May 6 bout at the New Haven Arena was nothing to write home about. The champion looked pitiful. Much of the battle was spent with both fighters waiting for the other to lead so they could counter—the lack of engagement appeared to have Pep off his game, as he was missing punches. Petrone, a mediocre fighter, looked even worse than Pep. The crowd, estimated at 5,000 fight fans, rode both fighters all night before ridiculing the verdict.[8]

In a tune-up bout for his upcoming clash with Sal Bartolo, Willie Pep, tipping at 128¼, captured a 10-round unanimous victory over Joey Angelo, who scaled at 133¾, at the Rhode Island Auditorium in Providence. Over 4,500 spectators turned out on May 13 to watch the champion finally perform like one against a tough young opponent. Perhaps it was exactly what Pep needed: an aggressive challenger to test his skills. Although his cut eye, acquired during the Petrone bout, kept the champion from sparring for a week, you couldn't tell by his performance. Pep appeared quicker as he ducked, side-stepped, and blocked punches to perfection.

It was off to St. Louis for a bout with Jose Aponte Torres on May 22. However, the weather failed to cooperate so the party of Pep, Viscusi, Gore, and Johnny Cesario (fighting on the undercard) missed their flight connection and ended up arriving by bus on the evening of May 21. Despite the lack of sleep, Pep entered Kiel Auditorium in front of over 3,500 spectators and put on an impressive display by taking the unanimous 10-round decision. Scaling at 129¾, nearly three pounds heavier than his challenger, Pep sliced the right eye of Torres so severely in the eighth round that the fight was nearly called—the Puerto Rican's nose was also bleeding heavily. A small crowd of over 3,500 turned out to watch what many saw as Pep's 100th fight—his record stood at 98–1–1. Team Pep left St. Louis the next morning on a flight bound for Minneapolis. They were scheduled to meet Jimmy Joyce at the Auditorium on May 27.[9] This would be Pep's final ring battle before meeting Bartolo in a title defense.

The non-title battle against Jimmy Joyce was over in eight rounds. Pep, who scaled at 127½, easily picked up the decision over his familiar opponent, who tipped at 133¾. Was Joyce selected as Pep's opponent because he was also his last opponent before the previously scheduled Bartolo title bout? Yep, somebody pass Willie a rabbit's foot. Viscusi and Gore also wanted to compare both performances. They liked what they saw. Pep, in their view, was ready.

Willie Pep v. Sal Bartolo, III

It was long overdue, and the excuses were over. Or at least everyone hoped. It was the New York and Connecticut featherweight champion versus the NBA featherweight titleholder, to determine the undisputed champion. Word was: If Willie Pep was anywhere near the same fighter he was before he entered the military, then Sal Bartolo was in for serious trouble. The pair had faced each other twice, and each time Pep was victorious. What was clear at this juncture was that Pep, like many boxers, fought to the level of competition. Facing a fighter such as Bartolo, he would lift his game to the performance level necessary to be victorious. That's what champions do, what separates them from the rest.

Pep was a 12–5 favorite entering Madison Square Garden on June 7, and with about 10,000 fight fans observing, he proved why. The bout was close until the ninth round, when Bartolo took a tremendous beating from his rival. Pep struck his antagonist so hard in the face that Bartolo, inundated with blood from what appeared to be a broken nose, thought he had fractured his jaw; moreover, the punch had that uncanny snap that resonates with those ringside. To his credit, the hub fighter, pinched, prodded, and plastered, was able to survive the 10th and 11th frames. At the 2:41 mark of the 12th term, a horizontal Bartolo was counted out. A short right uppercut to the chin, set up by a left hook, was the last thing he remembered.

Mission Accomplished! In his third meeting with Sal Bartolo, Willie Pep, who tipped at 126, about a pound heavier than his adversary, unified the title. Pep thought he had it won before the first round began as ring announcer Harry Balogh referred to him as "Featherweight champion of the world," while calling Bartolo "The Challenger." It was a good sign.

After the fight, Bartolo was rushed to St. Clare's Hospital, where X-rays confirmed he had fractured his jaw.[10] He was operated on the next day by Dr. Vincent Nardiello, who believed that Bartolo's ring career was over.

Lou Schiro, Sal Bartolo's manager, could stick the comments that he made to the press back in January in his ear. Also, Jack Healy and Dan Morgan could do the same. If Bartolo was the perfect boxer, as all three claimed, then why didn't he show it during this championship bout? What was he waiting for?

Returning to Hartford, the undisputed champion planned a few days off before heading to Buffalo for the Tommy Gomez–Phil Muscato fight on June 12. Speaking of the Queen City, Pep was scheduled to meet Harold "Cannonball" Gibson, in a non-title benefit bout, at Civic Stadium on June 26. However, that fight was rescheduled. Instead, Pep would meet Gibson on July 10 before heading off for Minneapolis to meet Jackie Graves later in the month (July 25).

On July 8, while training in Buffalo, Pep was asked to present the trophy to the winner of the Willie Pep Special at Buffalo raceway in Hamburg, New York. The featherweight champion accepted the invitation. How in the world can you decline an opportunity such as this when a race was named after you? Camilla, the horse driven by Levi Harner, was the winner. And Pep, no stranger to a track, enjoyed every minute.

Flooring his adversary four times, including twice in the seventh round, Willie Pep defeated Harold "Cannonball" Gibson via a seventh-round technical knockout. Referee Lou Scozza, one of many legendary light heavyweights hailing from Buffalo, called an end to the action at the 2:21 mark. Gibson, tipping at 127¾ or less than a pound heavier than the champion, was dropped for an eight count in the fourth round. He endured a nine count in the sixth round and another nine in the seventh, before the final knockdown. "Cannonball," who certainly dropped like one, fired little artillery during the bout and seldom hit his target.

The Acclaimed "No Punch" Round

If any boxer in history could win a round without throwing a punch, it would be Willie Pep. But did he?

Jackie Graves was a Midwest matinee idol who hailed from Austin, Minnesota, a city in the southeastern portion of the state. Known as "SPAM Town USA," it was the home to Hormel's corporate headquarters. Whether the talented southpaw fancied the canned delicacy or not was unknown, but should he defeat Willie Pep, he would have every kid in America eating the canned meat product.

Graves, who won the 1942 National Golden Gloves bantamweight championship, had lost only twice as a professional (to Bernard Docusen and Jimmy Joyce) and was certain to test Pep's skills. With power in both hands, he held victories over Harry Jeffra and Tony Olivera, and he ranked third in his weight division. Well-spoken and extraordinarily popular (especially in his hometown), he was merely 22 years of age. Nevertheless, Graves was already married and the father of three children.

Gore, Pep, and Cesario (who had a spot on the card), flew to Minneapolis on July 17 to prepare for the 10-round non-title battle in the Auditorium. To say the Minnesota fans were excited would be an understatement, as more than 500 spectators turned out to watch Pep spar a few rounds against Buffalo southpaw Walter Kolby at Nicollet Park.

On July 25, Willie Pep, who tipped at 126½, over a pound lighter than his opposer, defeated Jackie Graves via an eighth-round technical knockout. Pep gave his adversary an unmerciful beating in a one-sided affair. The end came at the 1:52 mark of the term in front of over 9,000 enthusiastic fight fans. Though the fight was scheduled for ten rounds, not a soul in the Auditorium felt deprived despite the shortened contest. Pep hit his stride in the sixth round and from that point forward dropped Graves ten times. It was a right to the jaw of the Austin Atom that did the damage. The hometown fighter tried hard to reach his feet at nine, but failed. Graves, who scored enough punches to electrify the crowd, couldn't control the speed of his opposer. After being put down for the first time, the southpaw did manage to drop Pep to his knees in the sixth round, but it was more luck than skill.[11]

Once the fight concluded, nobody thought twice about what they had witnessed. But the next morning, the newspapers were filled with contradictory accounts. This was because those writers not at the contest received accounts via phone or telegraph lines that were impacted by sunspot activity. Sunspots are areas of intense magnetic activity, often appearing on roughly an 11-year cycle, that disrupt an array of sensitive electronic systems. Thus, the accounts the writers received were difficult to decipher and led to numerous inaccurate transcriptions; for example, some had Pep being floored multiple times and nearly knocked out.[12]

Taking this a bit farther, later an article surfaced, believed to be penned by St. Paul sportswriter Don Riley, that claimed Pep won a round without throwing a punch. It was the third round of this battle with Graves. Even though few read it— and of those who did, few believed it—the story, as they say, "had legs." Like the assassination of President John F. Kennedy, the article, not to mention the fight, began to be dissected from every angle. While there was no question that Willie Pep, at this stage of his career, could have accomplished such a feat, none of the eyewitness accounts supported the claim.

In truth: Reporting on the fight the next day, the *Minneapolis Star Tribune* referred to the third round as "another furious session," while the *Minneapolis Star* noted "toe to toe slugging" and even a Pep "right to the body."[13] Both the *St. Cloud Times* and *Winona Daily News* didn't even bother acknowledging the third round. Nevertheless, the term, and thus the fight, took on mythical proportions—as George Washington had his cherry tree, Willie Pep now had his round.

Heading back to Hartford, Pep hoped to enjoy a two-week vacation before preparing for his 10-round overweight match on August 26 against Doll Rafferty. On August 16, the champion turned up at Madison Square Garden and was one of the boxing luminaries introduced before the Jersey Joe Walcott versus Tommy Gomez battle. The latter fighter was handled by the Leto boys (Joe and Jimmy) of Connecticut, plus Lou Viscusi. Gomez was a war hero and a tenacious Tampa fighter who packed a powerful punch. He compiled an impressive record and fought some good boxers, including Walcott.[14] Yet, he never fought for a title.

At the Auditorium in Milwaukee, Willie Pep, a three-pound underdog at 131 pounds, knocked out Doll Rafferty in the sixth round of a scheduled 10-round contest. Dropping Rafferty three times before he was finally counted out at the 1:10 mark, Pep conducted a proficient performance. The champion's display was in stark contrast to referee Dauber Jaeger, who illegally assisted Rafferty during a knockdown— so much for impartiality. Thrilling the crowd of about 5,000 spectators, Pep worked behind the left hand to dominate every round.[15]

Lou Viscusi booked the champion for two interesting challenges in September. The first was the undefeated Walter Kolby in Buffalo on September 4, followed by the popular New England veteran Lefty LaChance in Hartford on the 17th. Kolby, a young Buffalo southpaw with 20 fights' worth of experience, was in stark contrast to veteran LaChance, also a southpaw, who was approaching 200 ring appearances. Viscusi, if not Gore, felt the champion needed more left-handers for target practice.

Kolby, who held victories over Ruby Garcia and Willie Roache, was an ambitious youngster. He wasn't going to beat Pep—even if many locals thought he had a chance—but he could provide some interesting southpaw situations for the champion. Sure enough, Pep, who tipped at 131½, captured a TKO victory over Kolby, who scaled at 135¼. After Pep floored his adversary in the fourth round to a nine count, the inevitable ending took place at the 2:26 mark of the fifth session. A large crowd of 6,500 spectators were on hand at the Memorial Auditorium in Buffalo. In a region known for its legendary light heavyweights, it was always a treat for many to see the elite feather champion.[16]

Maurice "Lefty" LaChance was an established and prolific Maine pugilist who had grown tremendously popular in New England by virtue of some impressive victories, such as his 1943 decision over Phil Terranova. Yet he had only one victory in his last six outings. While LaChance was thrilled at the opportunity to meet his opposer, it was the champion's idea; in other words, before the curtain closed on the outdoor season at the Auditorium, Pep wanted to perform in front of his friends and family. The venue, located a mile from his house, was a short, 21-minute walk.[17]

Two days before his 24th birthday, Willie Pep, who scaled at 129, a seven-pound disadvantage, easily added another TKO victory to his resume. Dropped twice in the second round and twice in the third, LaChance made it as far as the 1:47 mark of the third round.

Viscusi wanted three or perhaps four battles for his champion before the end of the year. He was close to signing matches in Milwaukee (Charles "Cabey" Lewis), St. Louis (Phil Terranova), Los Angeles (Manuel Ortiz), and Havana (Manuel Acevedo). As is often the case with the sport, not one of these contests emerged.[18]

When It Rains, It Pours

On Monday, October 7, William Papaleo was arrested twice by the same policeman. The first charge claimed that he was driving the wrong way on a one-way street. At 9:45 p.m., the champion was taken into custody for reportedly traveling up Union Place and making a U-turn. Later in the evening, Pep was involved in an argument with Salvatore Ierna of 470 Edgewood Street in Hartford. Ierna asserted he was struck by Pep, a claim the champion denied. Ierna's wife, Mrs. Dolores Ierna, stated that her husband had torn her coat and knocked her down. Salvatore Ierna was charged with assault and battery and breach of peace, while Pep was charged with assault and battery. Both men were released on bond. Pep's charge was dismissed, and Ierna was found not guilty of the same charge. A witness before the court testified that at no time did Pep strike Ierna.[19]

But it ain't over until it's over. On Friday, October 25, William Papaleo was named defendant in a Superior Court suit charging alienation of affections and assault and battery, filed by Salvatore Ierna, who was asking $25,000 in damages. The champion was charged with alienating the affections of Ierna's wife, Mrs. Dolores Von Frenckell Ierna. Sal Ierna, according to counsel, was being sued for a divorce filed by Mrs. Ierna. Pep was charged with another count: assault and battery on Ierna, who claimed he sustained injuries.[20]

On December 13, Pep confirmed that he settled the Ierna suits with the payment of the counsel fees of the plaintiff.

As fate had it: Mrs. Dolores Ierna would become Willie Pep's second wife.

Hoping to leave, albeit temporarily, his troubles behind, Willie Pep headed off to Minneapolis. There he met veteran Paulie Jackson over ten rounds in a non-title fight, at the Auditorium on November 1. Tipping at 131 or less than a pound heavier than his opposer, Pep unloaded on Jackson. In the sixth round, he dropped his overwhelmed opposer three times, twice for the count of nine. The bell was the only thing that prevented further damage. Amazingly, Jackson was able to make the distance. Pep's decision victory was the champion's first start in ages without Bill Gore in his corner. The trainer was ill at his home in Lutz, Florida.

On November 15, promoter George Mulligan pulled a favor out of the back pocket of Lou Viscusi and inked Willie Pep to meet Tommy Beato, Central American champion, over 10 rounds at the State Armory in Waterbury. It would prove to be a far shorter evening than anticipated. With Beato dropped three times by Pep in the opening round and staggered at the close, it was only a matter of time. Pinning Beato into a neutral corner, Pep emptied an arsenal that finished with a short right hand to Beato's chin. Falling face-first, then onto his back, Beato took a full count to conclude the second round and the fight. Scaling a pound heavier at 128, Pep picked up his 107th victory in 109 bouts.[21]

Willie Pep v. Chalky Wright, IV

Willie Pep and Chalky Wright met for the fourth and final time on November 27. The event, held at the Auditorium in Milwaukee, drew 3,700 spectators to watch two of the finest featherweights ever battle it out for the last time. Pep, ever magnificent, made the 36-year-old veteran look foolish by picking him apart with the left jab before pounding him with left hooks to the body. Dropping Wright briefly in the second frame, Pep hoped to finish it, but the bell sounded. Wright was counted out a minute and five seconds into round three courtesy of combinations by Pep—a left hook did the final damage. After the bout, Wright, who formerly held the title, announced his retirement.[22]

On December 9, 1946, Willie Pep was made a defendant in a divorce action filed in Superior Court by Mary Woodcock Papaleo. Mrs. Papaleo requested custody of their two minor children, in addition to alimony. The suit would remain in court for 90 days before it could be heard. Later, it was reported that Pep and his wife reconciled on December 12.

A few days after Christmas, on December 28, Pep headed to Tampa for ten days of training. He needed the break. Having recently damaged his foot, the champion, like his team, was concerned about the injury.

In his first full year of boxing following World War II, Willie Pep fought 18 times, successfully defended his championship once, and never lost—11 victories came courtesy of knockouts, technical or otherwise. Eleven of the fighters he faced had winning records, and two of the fighters had over 100 victories. And he did so while losing the entire month of December as a result of injury.

1947

With Pep's frustrating ankle injury, the year began with necessary schedule alterations. British boxing promoter Jack Solomons postponed the champions match against veteran British fighter Nel Tarleton that was set for January 28, and his match against Cuban Miguel Acevedo—the latter, rescheduled for January 25, or possibly February 1. The changes would prove to be the least of the featherweight champion's worries.

A New Jersey Miracle

Late Sunday night, January 5, 1947, a terrible snowstorm hit the Northeast. A 250-mile radius around New York City was pounded by rain, wind, sleet, and snow that crippled any hopes of commuters reaching their destinations. Causing an abundance of cancellations, it was responsible for hundreds of traffic accidents and three plane crashes. One of the three airline disasters was a Nationwide Transport Service aircraft that crashed in a densely wooded section of Carmel, near Vineyard, New Jersey. Three were killed and 20 others, including Willie Papaleo, were injured. Taken to the Millville, New Jersey, hospital with numerous injuries, the fighter's condition was initially reported as "good."

The champion was returning from a vacation in Miami. The flight, bound for

Newark, encountered the bad weather—rain, snow, and even thunder snow—as they were approaching their final destination. Tired and bored by the relentless circling of the aircraft, Pep decided to get some sleep. Awakened by the pilot's announcement that they were landing in a wooded area, the next thing Pep recalled was the plane being torn apart as it struck the trees in its path. When he finally opened his eyes, he was face-down on the floor and unable to move. In terrible pain, he was eventually rolled over onto his back by the medical crew who reached the crash site. Placed on a stretcher and brought to the hospital, the champion recalled that a couple of those assisting him recognized who he was.

The plane, which just missed hitting a farmhouse, crashed two miles from Vineland at 8:55 p.m. Fortunately, there was no fire after the crash. The District of Columbia-3 aircraft was attempting an emergency landing at the Millville airport. Twenty passengers and three crewmen were reported aboard the aircraft. Co-pilot Percy W. Van Noy, 30, was one of the dead. Initially, the attendants at the hospital claimed that the champion's injuries—he was treated for ankle and rib injuries—were not serious. Later, it was learned that Pep suffered a broken left leg. Pep's relatives, including his father, Salvatore Papaleo, rushed to the hospital. Pep was transferred to Hartford on January 13. There he learned that he also had two chipped and split vertebrae. By the final week of January, there was informal chatter that Pep might have to relinquish his feather crown as a result of his injuries.

Pep was discharged from Hartford Hospital on January 29 and returned home. His back remained in a cast for six weeks—he also had a cast on his leg. Forget the sympathy, and there was plenty of that from all over the world, as Pep wanted no part of it. On February 7, the feather champion traveled to New York City to watch the battle between Phil Terranova and Maxie Shapiro. Arising on his crutches and in two casts at the sound of Harry Balogh's voice, he was announced as "one of the great champions."[23] Soon many would witness how great.

Pep made another public appearance at a semi-pro boxing card conducted on February 13. The Silver City Athletic Club had an impressive card at the City Hall Auditorium in Meriden, Connecticut. Promoter Val Callahan thought it would do both Willie and the kids good to interact with another. "Semi-pro" had replaced the term "amateur" a few years back when the State Athletic Commission wasn't sure what the latter term meant. Assisting Callahan was Pete Perone, no stranger to Nutmeg amateur boxing. It was a heartwarming experience for everyone involved.

For Mary, Willie on crutches was like a lion jammed into a shoe box. Those who knew Willie knew he was always restless, hated to feel confined, and cherished his freedom. He couldn't get comfortable on the crutches because he was encumbered by his casts, not to mention that the itching inside the restraints was driving him nuts. It was hard for the children to comprehend what had happened to their father. The life of a championship boxer, especially an extraordinary fighter such as Pep, was demanding. It was also challenging to those around them. Free time was always at a premium, and it often forced participants in his life to take on multiple roles. For example, Lou Viscusi would be the first to tell you that in addition to his role as a Pep's manager, he had to be the champion's assistant, confidant, doctor, father, financial planner, psychologist, and trainer, all rolled into one.

Willie Pep's journey back to the ring began, at least he believed, on March 14 when his back cast was removed. His leg casts had been removed weeks earlier. It would be a slow, painful, and arduous recovery. Conservative estimates had him three, if not four, months from a complete convalescence. Only then would he be able to contemplate what, if any, role he might play in professional boxing. While that assessment may ring true for some, they were not the featherweight champion of the world.

By the third week of April, Pep was trying hard to defy the odds. The initial training was living hell on the fighter, who had to endure shooting pain up his back and down his left leg. He walked with a limp courtesy of his lower left limb. The unsympathetic NBA was querying his ability to defend his feather crown almost weekly, but Willie refused to answer. The champion, who had lost a mere one fight and took a lone draw over 100 ring battles, had his own recovery timeline. An answer would be forthcoming if and when the titleholder had a response.

Pep's doctors believed he was making remarkable progress. A couple even went as far as to say he might be able to resume boxing in a few months; however, none wanted to go on record with their remarks. A level of doubt still existed as the month of May opened.[24]

During the second week of May, Pep began a regimen of light training. Roadwork, much of it conducted at Keney Park, was primarily walking, with hopes of gradually easing into jogging.[25] It was going to take time to get his confidence back, and though Willie knew it, he found it hard to accept. Regardless of his rehabilitation, Pep always had time for friends. On May 26, he joined numerous sports notables at the Veterans Home in Rocky Hill, Connecticut. He and Bill Gore, along with Kid Kaplan and Dennis "Dinny" McMahon, attended an annual event and had great fun. Pep wished he had a buck, if not more, for everyone who asked him about his return to the ring.

Incredible as it sounds, by June 1, Willie Pep believed he was ready to go between the ropes. Sure enough, matchmaker Gus Browne signed him to a 10-round battle against Victor Flores at the Hartford Auditorium's outdoor arena on June 17. It would be an overweight match against his opposer, who had lost his last five bouts, and both boxers were expected to tip at about 130. Despite his recent losses, Flores was far from a tomato can as he had snapped the winning streak of Dennis "Pat" Brady, one of Hartford's most promising fighters. It was a unique situation filled with uncertainty. Frankly speaking, not even Pep's handlers truly had a grasp on the fighter's skills at this point, in particular his ability to defend himself.

Capturing every round (you read it correctly), Willie Pep, scaling at 130, defeated Victor Flores, who tipped at 133, via a 10-round decision victory. Referee Kid Kaplan was astounded by Pep's performance. It wasn't even close as Pep scored two knockdowns: Flores was dropped in the fifth round to a seven-count courtesy a volley of body punches, then caught a sudden left hook to the jaw in the seventh term for a no count. Because Flores fought defensively, it was difficult to assess Pep's power, but his punch accuracy, ring speed, and command were clearly on display. More than 4,000 dedicated fight fans, including three of Pep's Hartford doctors, turned out to evaluate the champion's dexterity. To say his team of health experts were astonished by the display would be an understatement.

Next on the menu was Jean Barriere, on June 25 in North Adams, Massachusetts. However, the battle was rained out and rescheduled for July 11. On July 1, Willie Pep, tipping at 130, over four pounds lighter than his opposer, dropped Joey Fontana for the full count in the fifth round of scheduled 10-rounder. A solid left hook followed by an unerring right cross delivered the final damage. A crowd of over 2,000 turned out at Hawkins Stadium in Albany, New York, despite the rainy weather. Fontana, floored twice in the first round, was lucky to hang on as long as he did. It was the first time the New York boxer, who made his debut back in 1935, had ever been knocked out. In retrospect, putting Pep, in his condition, in the ring against a seasoned fighter such as Fontana—granted, he had only won half of his last six fights— had a few people questioning the match.[26]

Viscusi next inked Pep to a gig at Crystal Arena in Norwalk. In front of 2,000 fight fans on July 8, Pep sailed to an easy eight-round decision over punching bag Leo LeBrun of New York. The only knockdown came in the fifth session when a Pep left hook dropped his opposer for a two count. LeBrun's erratic rushes and wrestling tactics were entertaining, yet nothing more than signs of desperation from a fighter who had lost twice as many bouts as he won. Both fighters battled at 128 pounds.[27]

From Norwalk, Pep headed to North Adams in the northwestern corner of Massachusetts on July 11. Scaling at 130, two pounds lighter than his opponent, Pep knocked out Jean Barriere at Meadowbrook Stadium, in front of over 1,700 spectators. At first it looked like one of those momentum shifting battles, as Pep took the opening round, only to be battered during the second term. Regaining his composure, the champion took the third round and went on to drop his opposer three times before keeping him on the canvas. A left hook to the jaw turned Barriere's lights off at the 1:58 mark of round four. The seasoned Canadian pugilist, who was floored to a nine count in the opening round, proved to be a far better adversary than most anticipated. After the final count, Pep, exhibiting true sportsmanship, assisted in helping carry Barriere back to his corner.[28]

Matchmaker Jack "Knobby" King signed Willie Pep for a 10-rounder against Paulie Jackson on July 15. The non-title bout, held at Sargent Field in New Bedford, Massachusetts, attracted over 3,000 onlookers, many curious to evaluate Pep's ring prowess after his rehabilitation. As the champion held two victories over Jackson, not much was expected from the Reading, Pennsylvania veteran. The fact that Jackson, battered as he was, made the distance—you have permission to yawn—was the highlight of the evening. There were no knockdowns, only an occasional spark-yielding flurry. Pep looked tired and exhibited little speed or precision punching. This needed to change immediately as his next opponent was Humberto Sierra, a boxer with nearly 40 wins against six defeats. The pace of Pep's re-entry into fighting form appeared a bit aggressive—ya think? However, Pep had no intention of losing his title, regardless of the circumstance.

In July, noted trainer Manny Seamon, who fine-tuned fighters such as Joe Louis and Benny Leonard, turned up in Hartford. The reason was boxer Humberto Sierra, who was battling Willie Pep at the Auditorium Outdoor Arena on July 23. Seamon was hired by manager and promoter Tommy DeTardo to work his magic on his fighter and provide him with all the necessary tools to defeat Willie Pep. Although it was a 10-round non-title contest, the media exposure was enormous. Sierra, who held recent victories over Lulu Constantino, Jackie Callura, and Dennis Pat Brady, meant business. The situation was of great concern to Team Pep.

Stepping up his game (he had no choice), Willie Pep seized the 10-round unanimous decision over Humberto Sierra, claimant of the South American featherweight title. It was a convincing performance that left no doubt as to who was the feather-weight champion of the world. Referee Billy Taylor—like others, awestruck by the champion's dominance—had the fight Pep nine rounds, Sierra none, and one even. A blistering left hook to Sierra's chin in the third round flattened the fighter for a nine-count. It was more than the only knockdown of the fight, it was a clear signal of ring supremacy. Both fighters scaled at 129½ pounds. The overflow crowd, to say nothing of Matchmaker Gus Browne, were delighted by the showing from both pugilists.[29]

Willie Pep vs. Jock Leslie

Word came the last week of July that the champion would put his belt on the line against Jock Leslie, Flint's Blonde Bomber. It would happen at Atwood Stadium, in the Michigan's fighter's hometown, on August 22. After considerable negotiation, Viscusi ironed out a sweet contract that gave the champion a $25,000 guarantee and a percentage of the gate—the contracts awaited the approval of the Michigan Boxing Commission. Having never hosted a championship, Flint fight fans were salivating over the announcement.

A mere 229 days after Willie Pep was involved in a near-fatal plane crash, the featherweight champion was back in a boxing ring defending his title. Facing career-ending injuries, the champion refused to capitulate. Rejecting any thought of failure or giving up his dream, incomparable perseverance guaranteed his success.

Like so many, Jock Leslie cut his teeth in the Golden Gloves. At 23 years of age, with nearly 60 wins and fewer than 10 losses, he was turning heads. And turning them quickly. Leslie was considered a knockout artist, as over half his victories were courtesy of the "lights out" punch, and Hartford fight fans recalled his March 1944 kayo victory over Joseph "Sandy" Saddler at the Auditorium; moreover, in the third round of that contest, Saddler took three counts' worth of humiliation.

Honestly, the fighter who most wanted a shot at Pep was Miguel Acevedo. He was the talented boxer Pep planned to meet in Havana before his ankle injury. How-ever, Viscusi wisely wanted to sign Acevedo for an overweight match first before even considering a title shot; furthermore, he didn't feel Pep was physically ready to box the fighter. With Pep's title defense inked, Acevedo merely had to bide his time. Or so he hoped. Besides, promoter Tommy Cussans, as all Flint and likely Michigan knew, was behind Jock Leslie and excited about the match.

Pep, refreshed from a vacation, began training on August 2. Four days later, he managed enough time outside the ropes to judge the "Miss Hartford" contest held in the ballroom of the Hotel Bond. Hey, the life of a champion can be tough. On Mon-day, August 11, Team Pep headed out to Flint. The Hartford boxer, plus sparring part-ners Tony Falco and Nick Stato, planned to train for 10 days at the venue.[30] Flint welcomed the feather champion with open arms. Mayor Edward Vial even gave Pep a personal tour of his domain.

Media coverage was strong for the event, as writers from all over the country found their way to the city 66 miles northwest of Detroit; consequently, even Ed Van Every (*New York Sun*) and Nat Fleischer (*The Ring*) made the flight to Flint. Wil-lie's father, who seldom missed his son's fights, also made the trip. Atwood Stadium, opened in 1929, was built in a picturesque setting near the Flint River. Not surpris-ingly, folks enjoyed visiting the facility, and over 10,000 fight fans did just that.

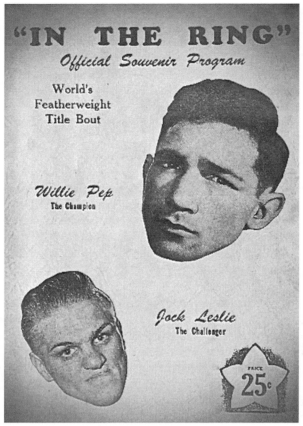

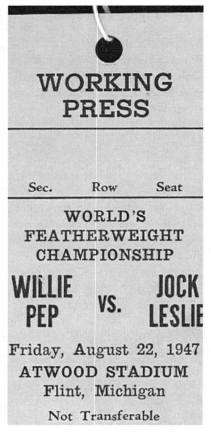

Atwood Stadium was the place to be on August 22, 1947, as World Featherweight Champion Willie Pep successfully defended his title against challenger Jock Leslie. (Souvenir Program [left], Working Pass [right]). Managed by Les Krell, Jock Leslie, who hailed from Flint, Michigan, was a knockout artist.

Scaling a pound heavier than his opponent, Willie Pep knocked out Jock Leslie in the 12th round of a championship fight slated for 15 frames. The end came at the 0:45 mark of the term when Leslie, who scaled at 125, arose from a nine count only to endure a volley of punches that concluded with a straight right to the chin. Sprawled out on the canvas, flat on his back, Leslie was motionless. The count was stopped at "4" by referee Clarence Rosen, when it was clear that it was futile.

Ahead prior to the kayo, the champion likely would have won a distance decision. However, Pep appeared exhausted by the end of the battle and did not look as sharp as anticipated. Though Leslie was persistent, he never seemed to find his rhythm. By the time he was capable of countering, Pep was gone. To his credit, the Flint resident staggered Pep in the third round and brought the crowd to their feet by unloading the chamber. But it was not enough.

After the fight, Pep wanted to get back to Hartford as soon as possible. Notwithstanding the crash that nearly ended his life, the champion believed in air travel. He had taken the train from Hartford, so the return flight was his first since the crash. Tony Falco accompanied the champion on the journey home.[31]

Basking in his newfound glory as a knockout artist, Pep was thankful to be back home in Hartford. He couldn't wait to see Mary and the kids. The champion, who loved music, took in a steak dinner and jazz show at Rocco Matarese's Circle over in Newington, Connecticut. The popular night spot was a favorite and attracted Hartford's gentry. His team, however, was watching a Garden fight that took place on August 29. Miguel Acevedo, to the astonishment of many, had his fight against Joe "Sandy" Saddler stopped because of a terrible cut over his left eye. The Cuban took a solid beating from the crafty and much-improved Saddler. The contest was an eight-round preliminary to the Ray Robinson versus Flashy Sebastian welterweight contest. With the victory, Saddler was likely to become Pep's next title defense.[32]

On September 12, boxing guru Fred J. Saddy, chairman of the NBA rating committee, ranked Willie Pep the greatest boxer of the past decade. Coming from Saddy, who once fought Jack Dempsey, it was an honor.[33]

Considered a celebrity in Hartford, Pep was news wherever he went. If he and Mary dropped by a jazz club, which they did on occasion, you would likely hear about in a newspaper column such as M. Oakley Stafford's "Informing You," which appeared in the *Hartford Courant.* Pep loved it. Being recognized, photographed, or handing out autographs was what champions did, and he savored every minute of it.

Signed to two battles in October, Pep would meet Jean Barriere—he had knocked him out in July—in Portland, Maine, inside the Exposition Building on October 21, followed by Archie Wilmer, at the Arena in Philadelphia on October 27. Both contests were non-title 10-rounders.

After dropping Barriere, who scaled at 133, for counts of nine and eight, Pep, who tipped at 129, sent his adversary horizontal with a targeted short left hook. The end came at the 2:07 mark of the opening round. It made for a quick evening.

The Philadelphia contest belonged to Herman Taylor, a promoter who every successful fight manager wanted to stay on the good side of. Tipping at 130, a pound lighter than his competition, Willie Pep took an uninspiring, yet very close, ten-round *majority* decision over Archie Wilmer.[34] The over 6,000 in attendance booed as Pep sparred and countered over nine and one-third rounds. Igniting the last two minutes of the final round kept the attention of those who hadn't walked out on the fight. Pep's performance was awful. The champion was warned twice by the referee to engage.[35]

As always, rumors regarding Pep's next title defense were as common as boats along the Connecticut River. On October 3, Humberto Sierra defeated Sandy Saddler, the number one contender, in an outstanding ring contest. The 10-round split decision that saw Saddler dropped in the opening round took place in Minneapolis. Therefore Sierra, who was outpointed by Pep back in July, catapulted into the forefront of contenders.

Early Wednesday morning, November 26, Willie Pep was arrested for speeding and reckless driving. Chased through Wethersfield at a brisk 80 miles per hour, Pep was finally caught on Wethersfield Avenue, the popular north and south thoroughfare. The fighter was fined $60 by Wethersfield Town Court on December 4. Pep, who was returning from a trip to Florida, said he lost track of how fast he was traveling.

Two bouts in December closed out the year for the World Featherweight Champion.

About 250 miles as the crow flies, Lewiston, Maine, always sounded a lot further from Hartford than it was. On December 22, Willie Pep, tipping at 128½ or three pounds lighter than his adversary, picked up an easy 10-round unanimous decision over target Alvaro Estrada. The non-title contest wasn't even close as Pep dropped Estrada six times on the road to victory. Energetic and fast afoot, Pep was a pugilistic marksman—it was a contrast from his previous ring performance 57 days earlier in Philadelphia. Before nearly 2,000 spectators at City Hall, he displayed an arsenal that included an acute left jab, spontaneous right cross, and devastating left hook.[36]

Over to Manchester, New Hampshire went Pep for his final bout of the year. Two days shy of the end of it, Willie Pep, scaling at 132, 2½ pounds lighter than his opposer, gained an eight-round technical knockout victory over Maurice "Lefty" LaChance. A small crowd of about 1,000 dedicated fight fans watched inside the Recreation Center as the featherweight master opened a cut over his antagonist's eye in the fifth term and road it to victory. Felled twice to nine counts, LaChance was little more than a holiday gift.

How do you begin to describe the incredible return of Willie Pep to the prize ring following his near-death experience? Was it a miracle? Or was it merely proof that Willie Pep was one of the greatest athletes of his time. His convalescence was extraordinary. In 164 days, or a bit under 4,000 hours, Guglielmo Papaleo went from being a crash victim lying helplessly in the New Jersey woods during the middle of winter, to defending himself in a prize ring at the Hartford Auditorium on a warm summer night. While the physical challenge alone was unfathomable, the mental competence required to succeed escaped explanation. Willie Pep pushed the bar of human physical achievement to a new level. If his illustrious career had ended in 1947, would ring historians claim he was one of the greatest gladiators ever to enter a battle? Without question. Thankfully, there was far more to the story.

Six

Ring Rivalry, 1948–1949

"I'd pay $6 to see Pep shadow box."—Mike Gibbons

1948

A year to the day since Willie Pep was involved in a life-threatening plane crash, the fighter filed a $600,000 damage suit against the airline, claiming he was "permanently and partially disabled." The petition filed in U.S. District Court in Wilmington, Delaware, was for a judgment against Nationwide Air Transport Services, Incorporated for the spinal injury he suffered during the crash. Pep claimed "negligence" on the part of the airline. Because Pep was completely disabled from January 5 until May 1947, the lawsuit filed also contended that Pep lost $500,000 in earning power. Having faced enormous medical expenses, he asked to be awarded $750 for doctor's bills. Particular to all the parties involved was a statement given to investigators by a stewardess that claimed the plane was out of gas and lost radio contact for over 20 minutes before the crash. Lou Viscusi also filed a suit against the same airlines on January 2, 1948, seeking $200,000 in damages.[1]

Speaking of Viscusi, having Pep on a weekly fight schedule since December was keeping the fighter in shape and aiding his concentration, so Viscusi hoped to maintain that pace until the champion defended his title. Certain was that Pep would meet Pedro Biesca on January 6 in Hartford, Jimmy McAllister on January 12 in St. Louis, and Joey Angelo in Boston on January 19. These three non-title bouts should prepare the champion for a February featherweight title defense—as of January, it appeared that Pep would likely face Humberto Sierra, either in Havana or Miami Beach.

Taking a solid left hook to the jaw early in round four, Willie Pep quickly found himself on the seat of his pants on the ring canvas at the Hartford Auditorium. Bemused—that smirk of knowing better painted upon his countenance—at what had occurred, the champion sat for a split second, then wisely arose to a knee while Referee Hugh Devlin conducted the count. Pep reached his feet at nine. Allowing himself time to get his bearings while Pedro Biesca punched himself out, the champion loaded the magazine, then commenced with a merciless beating of his opponent. Pep, who took by most accounts nine of ten rounds, picked up the decision. Over 2,500 fight fans enjoyed the action and cheered the champion's believed 120th ring victory in 122 fights. Pep scaled at 129½ pounds, while Biesca tipped at 134.[2]

As if you needed to be reminded: It was Jimmy McAllister who held Willie Pep to a disputed draw at Baltimore back in December 1945.[3] You didn't have to remind the champion, who redeemed himself by knocking McAllister out at Madison Square Garden in March 1946. When the pair squared off on January 12 in St. Louis, nobody was certain what might happen. Not much did. Willie Pep scored a unanimous 10-round decision in a somewhat boring overweight crusade. The highlight of the evening came in the final round when McAllister dropped to a one count after a solid left to the body, and later slipped on a misfire. Many saw it Pep seven rounds, McAllister one, and two even. The champion toyed with his opponent like a cat with a mouse, so much so that a few of the over 7,000 fans in attendance at Kiel Auditorium booed the action.

Joey Angelo, a Providence lightweight, was Pep's last bout before his scheduled featherweight title defense against a yet-to-be-determined opponent. Nearly 9,000 enthusiastic fight fans turned out on January 19 to watch the champion work his ring artistry over 10 rounds inside Boston Garden. Pep took every round on his journey to a unanimous decision. Angelo, who scaled at 135¾, seven pounds heavier than his adversary, was so confused by his opponent's proficiency that the contest was more target practice than anything else. Jabs and hooks, all from the left side, won the bout for the champion. Rarely did he opt for the heavy artillery, but when he did, the right cross was there, and damaging.[4]

An excellent wife is the crown of her husband, but nobody wears that diadem finer than the spouse of a pugilist. Nobody. They are special and always will be. Over at The Showboat of Boston, at Dock: 252 Huntington Avenue, they were lining up to watch and hear a special talent. It wasn't Peggy Lee, Dinah Shore, or even the Andrews Sisters, but Mary Papaleo. That's right, the wife of the featherweight champion of the world had talents all her own. A golden voice, not a left hook but equally as powerful, was her specialty. A large Hartford contingent was on hand not for the "Show Boat Special," which was planked porterhouse steak, but to listen and watch one of their own. As Mary delivered a stunning performance, most were still trying to figure out why some couples were blessed with so much talent. Or does talent attract talent? As the crowd filed out of the popular night club, word came that Willie had won over at the Garden. That made two victories in a single night, not a bad take for the Papaleo family.

On January 20, came word that an opponent for Pep's title defense had been approved. Lou Viscusi signed championship fight contracts with novice promoter Clarence "Kay" Kantrowitz. A seasoned Hartford movie film salesman, Kantrowitz was stepping into fight promotion. Willie Pep would defend his world featherweight crown against Humberto Sierra at Miami Beach on February 24. A guaranteed $32,500 would make its way to Pep, while Sierra would pocket 15 percent of the gate. As always there were details to iron out, but everyone felt confident about the promotion. Everyone except members of the Miami media, who believed it was a high-risk proposition.[5]

Pep, Viscusi, and Gore arrived in Tampa on February 3. Minus a few small excursions, the group stayed on the west coast of Florida and trained at the Palmetto Beach Boys' Club gym. Preparing Pep for his taller opposition were sparring partners Pat Brady, Vic Cardell, Johnny Cesario, Tony Falco (who was on the undercard), and Carey Mace. The team planned to head to Miami a short time before the fight. Expectations from all aspects of the promotion were high, especially the draw. While the promoter was aggressively—okay, unrealistically—targeting $150,000, the largest gate Pep had drawn to date was $71,000 for his Garden battle against Chalky Wright. The top of the ticket scale was $15 plus tax.[6] As for the match, they had met last summer, and Pep dominated the overweight 10-rounder. But Sierra went on to defeat Sandy Saddler, the number one contender, and everything changed. Or did it?

Regardless of the past, Sierra, a 23-year-old Cuban, was confident that he could beat Willie Pep. Having over four times as many professional wins as losses, he was a competitive adversary, and he knew it. Under the watchful eye of manager Tommy DeTardo, he completed five weeks of concentrated training and was certain it would pay dividends. With victories over Miguel Acevedo, Pat Brady, Jackie Callura, Lulu Constantino, and finally Sandy Saddler, Sierra believed he was ready to face the champion.

Employed to oversee the integrity of the championship contest was none other than Jack Dempsey, the Manassa Mauler. Promoter Kantrowitz thought it would be an appealing touch, so Dempsey drove down from Palm Beach with his manager, Max Waxman, on February 22. Dempsey, who seldom saw an appearance fee he didn't enjoy, planned on attending a dinner in honor of Babe Ruth later that evening at the Beachcomber. Joining them at "The Sportsman of the Year" dinner were Joe DiMaggio, Gar Wood, and Willie Pep.

Three days before the champion's title defense against Humberto Sierra, Mrs. Mary Woodcock Papaleo filed a new suit for divorce against her husband. A previous suit had been withdrawn after a reconciliation.

Willie Pep v. Humberto Sierra

The fight was scheduled for 15 championship rounds inside Miami's Orange Bowl, but Willie Pep, favored as much as 13–5, needed only 10 rounds to finish the job. The beginning of the end came in the ninth round when Pep, who scaled at 125½, floored Sierra, who tipped a half-pound lighter, for a five count. Once Sierra was vertical, Pep dispatched an arsenal at the Cuban that ended with two rights and an uppercut as the bell sounded. Witnessing the devastation, referee Dempsey asked the challenger if he wished to continue. Nodding in affirmation, it was on to round ten. Bounding out of his corner with both cannons hopelessly blazing, Sierra was soon out on his feet. A sweeping right hand dropped the challenger for the final time at the 0:22 mark of the term.

It was Pep's speed that overwhelmed his opponent. All Sierra's misfires made him look foolhardy. Overcast skies and intermittent rain squalls hampered the draw and the enjoyment. The canvas was soaked beneath the fighters' feet. Sierra, who slipped early in the opening round, was dropped for a two count in the second. Pep also lost his balance in the second round.

Those who had seen the champion work in the past felt he was on top of his game. Gore and Viscusi had done a magnificent job preparing their fighter. Getting Pep away from Hartford and all its distractions helped; moreover, three weeks of training in the sunshine can help anyone forget their misfortune.

Though far from a financial masterpiece—you can blame mother nature—the promotion wasn't bad. At least on the surface it appeared that way.[7] Fewer than 7,000 fight fans turned out for an event that cost the promoter over $40,000. Conducting a fight promotion below the Mason-Dixon Line was a constant reminder that though we were one country, lines of demarcation remained. Even after World War II, parts of the country still faced enormous racism. The Orange Bowl, with its "Colored Section" and its separate ticket outlets, was an irksome reminder.

After the battle, the champion was given time and space to attend to his personal issues. Naturally, everyone around the fighter offered their full support and hoped for the best for both him and Mary, along with the children.[8]

The featherweight champion surfaced at the Mills Brothers concert at the State Theater on March 5. He thought about attending the fight between Joseph "Sandy" Saddler and Bobby Timpson at the Auditorium in Hartford on March 23, but did not.

Idle since his title defense, Pep was eager to get back into the ring. He was hoping to return to fighting condition by the end of April, but he plainly couldn't do it. On May 7, he captured a 10-round unanimous decision over Leroy Willis in Detroit at Olympia Stadium—the initial date had been postponed. Testing his skills, Pep defeated his adversary while trying to work through his battle repertoire of punches and combinations. Left jabs and hooks were the mainstay of the evening as a crowd of over 6,600 spectators enjoyed the first five rounds. However, the last five rounds, which were booed for the lack of action, left a lot to be desired. There were no knockdowns. Pep scaled at 131, three and a half pounds lighter than his opposer.[9]

On a side note: The Connecticut Boxing Managers Guild gave their unanimous support to the New York Guild by agreeing to boycott the 20th Century Club, the organization that essentially controlled Madison Square Garden and St. Nicholas Arena boxing. The reason for the boycott was the fighters' right to a decent cut of television revenue. Every Connecticut boxing manager, with the exception of Lou Viscusi, belonged to the guild. As fate might have it, the President of the New York Boxing Managers' Guild was Charlie Johnston, who managed Sandy Saddler. How, or even if, the stance of either party would play into future fight negotiations remained to be seen.

Staying in the Midwest, Pep, scaling at 129, took a 10-round unanimous decision over Charley Cabey Lewis, who tipped at 130. The non-title fight on May 19 took place at the Auditorium in Milwaukee. It was the first contest to be held under a new set of state boxing guidelines. Eight-ounce gloves replaced the familiar six-ounce variety, and a boxer was required to take a count of eight during a knockdown. Pep had met Lewis twice and defeated him both times, hence the victory was no surprise.

Looking ahead, Viscusi was lining up Pep's battles over the summer months. On June 17, the champion would meet Miguel Acevedo at the Auditorium in Minneapolis in a 10-round overweight bout. The fight manager also hoped to land Pep another contest before the end of the month.

Miguel Acevedo caught the attention of Hartford fight fans when he knocked out George Dunn and disposed of Dennis "Pat" Brady back in July. Title bound until Sandy Saddler knocked him out in New York back in August 1947, the fighter was trying hard to get back in the mix. He needed an impressive victory to do so. But that victory would not be at Willie Pep's expense. The champion, tipping at 129 or two pounds lighter than his adversary, dominated the 10-round contest and was awarded a unanimous verdict. In front of 8,000 spectators, Pep rocked the Cuban in the opening round, then toyed with him the remainder of the bout. The crowd wanted to see a finishing blow, but it wasn't to be.

You should have seen the face of Luther Burgess when he found out whom he was facing instead of Jackie Graves. Staring across the ring from Burgess at Atwood Stadium on June 25 was none other than Willie Pep. The featherweight champion was there as a substitute for Graves, who suffered a hand injury. Better said, he was there as a favor to promoter Tommy Cussans. It was Cussans, you may recall, who promoted the Pep vs. Leslie battle last summer. Can you say quid pro quo? It's hard to recall anytime in boxing history when a world champion was secured as a substitute. While the situation made for a good storyline, the fight failed to impress. Burgess danced liked he was on fire, as the champion remained patient. As the rounds passed, Burgess slowed and became more confident. At the end of a boring fifth round, and noting the aplomb of his adversary, Pep dropped the 21-year-old to a no count. From this point forward, each time Burgess came out punching, there was an answer waiting for him. With multiple opportunities to deliver his opponent, Pep, a half-pound heavier, instead chose to punish him over each subsequent round. In the end, it was the champion by a 10-round unanimous decision.[10]

Returning to Hartford, Willie Pep was getting tired of his legal issues, so he reached an agreement with his wife.[11] Mrs. Mary Woodcock Papaleo was granted a divorce on July 6, 1948.

Located in the beautiful Mohawk Valley, Utica, New York,was a fight town. Their adopted son, Luigi Giuseppe d'Ambrosio, aka Lou Ambers, a former world lightweight champion, hailed from nearby Herkimer. Managed by Al Weill and trained by Charlie Goldman, Ambers, with his perpetual motion, was an inspiration to Pep and later even showed him a few ring moves. On July 7, Willie Pep, scaling at 131, three pounds heavier than his opposer, knocked out Young Junior in the first round of a non-title contest. A crowd of over 2,500 fight fans poured into Bennett's Field in Utica, prepared to watch the feather champion go ten rounds against the Springfield, Massachusetts scrapper. But before many could even find their seat and get settled in, Pep had Junior on the canvas. A left to the jaw, followed by a hard right to the same location, ended the evening at the 2:45 mark of the opening round. Pep, perturbed by Junior's aggressive approach, sparred briefly before administering the lethal blow.[12]

Back home in Hartford, Pep took back-to-back battles against Teddy "Red Top" Davis on August 3 and August 17. Both 10-round events were part of the weekly fight card at the Auditorium's outdoor arena. Davis, a transplanted California fighter who was battling regularly out of Holyoke, Massachusetts, had grown popular with fans, first by beating Timothy "Buddy" Hayes, New England featherweight champion, then Nick Stato.[13]

The fans loved having their favorite son back in town. Having not fought in the city since January 6, Willie Pep was missed by the fans. Plus he was an inspiration to the local fight scene. Action at the Auditorium began at 8:30 p.m. Matchmaker Gus Browne had an amusing card set for August 3, that began with a five-round semi-pro contest, followed by three six-round preliminaries. But the fans were on hand to see the champion. Pep came in at 128 pounds, while Davis tipped three pounds heavier. Both fighters looked prepared for battle. Referee Lou Bogash, a Connecticut boxing legend, was the third man in the ring.

Teddy Davis appeared to improve with each passing term, which concerned Pep. From the sixth round forward, the action accelerated and had the crowd mesmerized. Davis went to Pep's body early in the eighth and stayed close enough to the fighter to take the round. The match narrowed as Davis pushed Pep to the limit. Both fighters went toe-to-toe in the tenth round, giving it everything they had, much to the delight of the spectators.

When the ten rounds were completed, it was Bogash who confirmed Pep as the victor in one of the closest margins his followers could recall. It was Pep four rounds, Davis one, and five even. This contrasted with others who saw it nine rounds for Pep and one for Davis. But Bogash was in the ring, and they were not.

In the meantime, Lou Viscusi was being courted by the 20th Century Sporting Club. The group wanted to ink Pep for a battle inside Yankee Stadium against Ike Williams, lightweight title holder. But to do so would require Pep to surrender the feather crown. Viscusi, who felt insulted by the offer, politely turned it down. Eddie Compo and Paddy Demarco were two other names being tossed into the mix as possible Garden opponents for Pep.[14]

Since the challenger, Teddy "Red Top" Davis, had given the champion what many believed to be the most difficult battle he ever had in front of a hometown audience, ticket demand for the rematch was strong—over 4,200 fight fans filled the seats in Hartford. The champion, having little choice but to step up his game on August 17, did so. Lacking the intensity of the first battle, the champion wisely went out of his way to avoid the powerful body assaults of Davis. As a result, it altered the vibe of the fight. Seeing the fight slip away, Davis caught fire in the eighth round. Pep, standing firm, held his ground. Referee Billy Conway saw it nine rounds for Pep and one for Davis.

Nat Rogers, the Madison Square Garden matchmaker, attended the fight, so those who knew the fight game understood that something was up. Later it was learned that Viscusi and Rogers came to terms on a fight between Willie Pep and Paddy DeMarco. It was set for Friday night, September 10, inside the hallowed venue. It would be the first Friday night show following a series of unsuccessful Thursday evening cards. Naturally, Pep was hot and cold on the idea. It was "The Garden," but it would be his first appearance in the venue against a lightweight since his horrific loss to Sammy Angott.

Just because he could, Gus Browne, no stranger to an opportunity, was con-

A candid shot of Willie Pep next to journalist and historian Sam Cohen in 1948 (courtesy of Rick Kaletsky)

ducting a featherweight elimination tournament at the Auditorium Outdoor Arena. The goal was to find a bona fide contender for Pep's title—and naturally lift Browne's spirits and bank accounts before the holiday season.

Knowing Pep needed a tune-up fight before meeting DeMarco, Viscusi gave the nontitle assignment to Waterbury promoter and matchmaker Rocco Mara. The champion would meet Brooklyn boxer Johnny Dell over 10 rounds at Municipal Stadium in Waterbury on September 2. A club scrapper, Dell held victories over Willie Beltram, Dennis "Pat" Brady, and Chalky Wright. As anticipated, Willie Pep, who scaled at 129, was victorious over Johnny Dell, who tipped at 133. Pep closed Dell's left eye, forcing referee Billy Conway to halt the battle and award the champion an eighth-round TKO victory. Over 3,300 enthusiastic fight fans turned out to see the champion and an impressive Connecticut undercard—in addition to Pep, Tommy Bazzano, Bobby Polowitzer, and Billy Kearns were victorious.

Brooklyn had a new lightweight star, and his name was Pasquale "Paddy" Demarco. His professional career began a bit over three years earlier and had attracted attention ever since. As a top-rated fighter in the 135-pound division, he hadn't lost a ring contest since May 1946. DeMarco had won his last 21 contests. Preferring cumulative destruction over the excitement of a big blast, DeMarco was a tireless warrior. Much like Willie Pep.

Casting rules to the wind, DeMarco's charge came in the opening rounds. Pep, who was quicker, did slip a few times while avoiding DeMarco's assaults—he even ended up on the ring apron at one point. However, there were no official knockdowns. Giving Pep the benefit of the doubt, he tried to fight clean, but when DeMarco turned to butting, elbowing, and rabbit punches, it was game over—it wasn't Pep's first rodeo. Tipping at 128¼, over five pounds lighter than his opposer, Willie Pep, a 3–1 favorite, defeated Paddy DeMarco via a ten-round unanimous decision. Referee Art Donovan had it 5–3 Pep with two even, while others ringside viewed the champion's spread much greater.[15]

Lou Viscusi was doing his best to pacify an aggressive Frank "Blinky" Palermo, but it wasn't easy. As the manager of lightweight champion Ike Williams, Palermo was an irritating, yet delicate annoyance—his partner was Mafioso Frankie Carbo, a soldier in New York's Lucchese family who had been a gunman with Murder, Inc. Reminding Palermo numerous times that Pep was not willing to surrender his feather crown for a lightweight bid, Viscusi hoped to dodge what he saw as a ridiculous request for Pep's services. Besides, he had recently signed his fighter to a title defense against Sandy Saddler at Madison Square Garden on October 29. Both fighters posted a $1,000 forfeit guaranteeing their appearance and agreed to scale no more than the 126-pound limit. Trainer Bill Gore hoped to give his fighter a break, before taking two tune-up battles to bring his fighter in under the weight limit. Viscusi agreed and inked Newark tomato can Chuck Burton for an eight-round overweight bout at Jersey City on October 12, before putting Pep back into the Auditorium on October 19 against Bronx boxer Johnny LaRusso.

It was time for the champion's preparation or target practice. Willie Pep, tipping at 132 or five pounds heavier than his opposition, sailed passed punching bag Chuck Burton to capture an eight-round decision. There were no knockdowns. Estimated at 1,000 fight fans, the Jersey City Garden crowd didn't have much to cheer about because all Burton did was survive. On to Johnny LaRusso, who was no walk in

Paddy DeMarco (left), aka "The Brooklyn Billygoat," captured the Lightweight World Championship in 1954. Harold Dade (right) won the World Bantamweight championship in 1947.

Colt Park. The Bronx lightweight, who won over three times as many bouts as he lost, impressed many when he defeated contender Dennis "Pat" Brady twice. LaRusso was a clever fighter who could punch, and he provided the level of competition needed to prepare the champion for his title defense. Or so it was hoped. Prior to the contest, a rumor hit the streets: Viscusi would pull the plug on the Saddler fight if Pep failed to impress against LaRusso. Well, Pep performed marvelously in front of a crowd of about 2,000 Hartford faithful. But he did so at his own expense, as LaRusso failed to engage. It was a one-sided exhibition that did little to prepare Pep for his battle with Saddler. As a result, the pressure shifted to trainer Bill Gore to bring his fighter into the Garden at weight and primed for a title defense. It was a lot to ask.[16]

Sandy Saddler v. Willie Pep, I

Posthaste, Gore, working in the Auditorium gym with Pep, brought in Jackie Weber, the New England lightweight champion, to assist his fighter. Weber, who was on the event undercard, sparred with the feather champion, as did Billy Kearns.

Certain Pep would make weight, Gore concentrated on sharpening his fighter's skills.[17]

With his unimpeachable countenance, Sandy Saddler, who stood a *tall* five feet eight inches, didn't resemble a fighter or a vicious warrior who could use a 70-inch reach to systematically dissect an opponent like a cadaver. But the lanky fighter was precisely that. In his professional debut, the Boston-born pugilist defeated Earl Roys at the Auditorium in Hartford on March 7, 1944. If his opponent's name rings a bell, it should: Roys was the fighter Pep defeated, back in 1938, to win the Connecticut State Amateur Flyweight Championship. It was inauspicious beginning as Saddler was a substitute for a boxer named Harry Bauman. In his second professional fight, at the same location, Saddler was stopped in three rounds by Jock Leslie. Lacking the skills and polish of his opponent, Saddler needed work to become a contender. And work was precisely what brought Saddler to this point.

Charlie Johnston, Saddler's manager, understood the featherweight division. Having taken Lulu Constantino up the rank-

The incomparable Sandy Saddler, whose 103 career knockouts are more than any other featherweight champion in history, and who ranks sixth on boxing's all-time list.

ings and even to a title opportunity against Chalky Wright, he knew how to groom a fighter. He also understood Saddler and had him prepared for the task at hand. The fighter was dangerous because he could slice an opponent to ribbons with his jab before setting him up for an explosive, fight-ending blow. Like the great Jack Johnson, Saddler, merely 22 years old, could tie an opponent up in knots and, if necessary, wrestle them to the canvas. Having fought in South America and in the West Indies—the latter his father's place of birth—the youngster had picked up many tricks of the trade, and would no doubt apply them if needed. Like Pep, he disposed of sparring partners as if they were single-use tissues.

Having completed his training on October 27, Pep, accompanied by Viscusi and Gore, entrained to New York. The champion checked into the Hotel Lincoln.

Requesting and receiving his lucky suite, he was confident. In his mind, he had no reason to feel differently. But to be safe, he brought his lucky equipment—bucket, towel, water bottle, and even his red robe—with him. At the same time, his opposition was completing training over at Summit, New Jersey. Both boxers were scheduled to weigh in on Friday at 12:30 p.m. Once Pep saw he was under the limit on Friday, it was off to Gallagher's Restaurant for a steak dinner before heading back to the hotel for his nap.

Nearly six years had passed since Willie Pep won the title at "The Garden" against Chalky Wright. The gate, as you recall, set an indoor record for the featherweight championship. With the victory Pep, at the age of 20 years and two months, was the youngest champion since Terry McGovern (age 19). It was tough not to think about how much had happened since that time. From stints in the both the Army and Navy, to an airplane crash that nearly claimed his life, Pep found it hard to shake the memories.

Entering the title defense against his rival, Pep was a 3–1 favorite. As the first card arranged by Harry Markson, the new managing director of the 20th Century Sporting Club and, as fate may have it, the 11th anniversary of Mike Jacobs' first Garden battle, the date held a special meaning. Pep believed it was a good sign.

Crack! And lights out. When Willie Pep opened his eyes, he started putting the pieces of the fourth round back together. After he hit the canvas twice during the previous term, a crushing left hook found Pep's chin and sent him down again. Hurt, he reached his feet just as Ruby Goldstein counted him out—it may have been a split-second before, but it didn't matter. The coup de grâce was delivered at the 2:38 mark of round four. For the first time in 137 battles, Willie Pep, who tipped at 125, a pound heavier than Saddler, suffered a knockout defeat.

Pep's defensive skills carried him the first two rounds. But Saddler began taking him to close quarters and pounding him with left hands during the third term—his stunning left uppercut was the star of the show. A surprise left hook sent Pep down the first time, while a vicious right dropped him next. While the first knockdown looked coincidental, the second did not. The bell was his savior at the end of the third round. When Pep arrived back in his corner, Viscusi, Gore, and second Johnny Datro desperately tried to get their fighter under control. This was not the Sandy Saddler they remembered, and the situation looked grave. Across the ring, Saddler was reloading and ready for a final assault. Sensing—but not accepting—the inevitable, Pep's corner sent him out for the fourth round. The last rites came courtesy of a trio of left uppercuts, followed by a right to the skull.

A crowd of about 15,000 stunned spectators witnessed the title transfer. Those associated with Pep didn't know what to do, how to act, or what to say, because they were not familiar with defeat. Saddler had conducted a brilliant performance, and true to the behavior of a champion, he walked over to Pep's corner to shake hands. It was clear that the scrawny kid from Boston had been underestimated. Saddler attributed his victory to the study of Pep's skills during his battle against DeMarco: If an opponent reduced the efficiency of Pep's left hand—his lethal weapon—he had a chance for a victory. Using an extended right hand as his first line of defense, Saddler constantly positioned his mitt in his opponent's face. It distracted Pep and set up the Boston fighter's slicing left jab or deadly left hook.

Sitting quietly on his bench in the dressing room, head bowed, Pep mumbled every thought that entered his mind. Even though he lost to a good fighter, he felt he let everybody down. He would not raise his head or make eye contact with anyone. Short and defensive at the questions being fired at him by the media, he repeated his answers multiple times. It was as if he was trying to rationalize what had just taken place to preserve his self-image, and it was normal behavior. Convincing himself that he did everything possible to prevent the loss would allow him to put it behind him.[18]

The only thing worse than losing a title was losing a title without a return clause. Fortunately, Lou Viscusi was certain to include such a stipulation. Team Pep now had four months to regroup. Both fighters had been offered either February 11 or 12 for a return bout at Madison Square Garden.

No alibis for failure or inadequacy came out of Pep's mouth. It wasn't his style. Champions, even former ones, share a view from the top of the mountain, a view that had to be seen to be believed. Champions act like champions. Great champions come back from defeat, or as James J. Corbett always believed, live to fight another round.

Was Pep too ethical for his own good in the ring? Critics believed he was. He didn't roughhouse like Paddy DeMarco or even Sandy Saddler. It was always Pep's contention that it wouldn't get him anywhere. Losing his title altered that point of view. But could he do it? Yes. Did he want to do it? No. He wasn't merely throwing paint on a canvas to create his self-portrait, there was a genius in his brush strokes.[19] Nevertheless, there was no genius associated with losing.

Having spent the final week of November in Florida, the former champion was excited about returning home and to his training in December. Viscusi and Gore knew Pep wasn't going to sit around and feel sorry for himself. But to be certain, they had him head to Boston to assist Johnny Cesario. Gore felt a daily sparring routine with Cesario, who was training for a battle against Ralph Zanelli, would increase Pep's speed while improving his footwork.[20]

Viscusi inked Pep for a 10-round battle against Hermie Freeman, Maine State champion, at the Boston Garden on December 20. Sam Silverman, who handled the promotion up in Boston, always delivered a quality show with strong media coverage. Working out of the Auditorium gym, Pep rededicated himself to training: Four miles of morning roadwork at Keney Park, followed by sparring in the afternoon with Miguel Acevedo and Tommy Bazzano, the ideal recipe.

In a one-sided affair in front of over 8,000 fight fans, Willie Pep, scaling at 130, at least five pounds lighter than his opposer, cruised to a unanimous ten-round verdict over a seasoned Hermie Freeman.[21] Having floored his opponent in the seventh round and on a brink of a knockout in the ninth, Pep was surprised that referee Eddie Curley allowed the fight to go the distance. Despite his slow start, Pep hit his stride in the ninth round and never looked back.

It felt strange ending the year without a title, but champions never plan for defeat.

1949

Two elite fighters, middleweight Tony Zale and featherweight Willie Pep, lost their titles in 1948. As Zale had underestimated Marcel Cerdan, so too Pep with Sandy Saddler. Was it a fluke or the passing of the baton from one generation to the next? The critics believed it was the latter. But in Pep's case, there was degree of uncertainty that only a return match could confirm. As a rematch clause was contained in the initial contract, only minor details needed to be ironed out for it to become a reality; consequently, the event was confirmed for February 11 at Madison Square Garden.[22] Initial negotiations by both parties had determined the financials: Pep took 50 percent of the net receipts from the first fight, while Saddler grabbed ten percent, but a return match would see the fighters split 60 percent of the net gate.

With a tune-up battle or two in order, Pep was matched with Teddy "Red Top" Davis in St. Louis on January 17. After the fiasco with Johnny LaRusso, something Viscusi was trying hard to forget, the boxing manager's choice appeared to be the right call. Davis would challenge Pep and push the same type of buttons as Saddler; moreover, he would do so because it was in his best interest. In baseball, they have setup pitchers that typically pitch the eighth inning, with the closing pitcher handling the ninth. Davis would give his opposer a run for his money, make distance, yet not initiate any "cheap shots." In other words, if he defeated Pep, it would be a clean victory.[23] Running Pep through Davis, Gore believed, would allow him to make any needed modifications prior to sending his fighter through a lesser opponent in the Auditorium.[24] Then Pep's preparation would be complete.

On January 17, at Kiel Auditorium in St. Louis, Willie Pep took a hearty, but not challenging, 10-round unanimous decision over Teddy "Red Top" Davis. Both fighters scaled at 129 pounds. Sparring the first five rounds, Pep gradually increased his intensity. Davis, trying to take Pep out of his game plan, delivered everything from robust body assaults to round-opening charges. Whereas he failed to divert Pep from his mission, he succeeded in accomplishing his: Prepare the former featherweight champion for a challenging strike on the division crown.

Unfortunately, the process led to a slight cut near Pep's right eye that forced the cancellation of an additional tune-up bout.

Willie Pep v. Sandy Saddler, II

The mindset of a challenger has always differed from that of a champion. Holding both positions was one thing, but successfully switching between the two was another. A champion defends a title, while a challenger captures one. Comprehending the task, trainer Bill Gore had to transition his fighter. It was both a mental and physical transformation.

A champion's greatest asset is self-confidence, while his greatest downfall is complacency. Whereas a title may intimidate, it doesn't defend. Willie Pep admitted that this was a factor in losing his crown. He was smug in his position as champion, confident that what got him there was good enough to keep them there. He was wrong. Also, a champion never underestimates a challenger. Pep was guilty of this as well.

A challenger's greatest asset is desire, while his greatest downfall is failure to execute a strategic plan. Gore hoped to restore Pep's ambition, purpose, and assertiveness. To do so, he reminded Pep what it felt like to be champion. Gore created a plan to reclaim the title, then executed that strategy. If a fighter listens to his trainer, as Pep did, a strategy can be transparent to a boxer, which was why the Hartford pugilist often claimed there was no fight plan.[25] Breaking down a goal into smaller measurable steps was how Gore planned to restore Pep's self-confidence. It was a cumulative process with credit given one step at a time.

It was no secret that Sandy Saddler was going to use the same strategy he employed for the pair's initial battle. Brawling early, the Harlem boxer hoped to use his infighting to lean on Pep, while employing his short arsenal to the body. These were tactics to slow his adversary, weaken the legs, and take him out of his game. Using his hands, particularly his right, Saddler would attempt to lock Pep into a position to deliver his powerful body blows. Since Saddler couldn't outrun Pep or outbox him, roughing him at close quarters made sense. Plus, he had far more alternatives, legitimate or not, inside than out.[26] Pep understood Saddler was a turn-over southpaw. When his trademark spin failed and cost Pep a solid left hand to the head, he learned quickly just how seamless his rival could alter his stance.

It was the Garden's first fistic sellout in nearly three years. It was 15 championship rounds for the featherweight championship of the world inside the sport's premier venue. It was a Boston-born, tall, thin, unpretentious, 22-year-old champion against a virtually unbeatable former titleholder from Hartford. It was an opportunity for redemption for the former title holder, confirmation for the current. And it was fistic featherweight history at its finest.

Since they last met, the champion had fought five fights, winning four by kayo and one on points, while his challenger took two bouts, each ending in victory by decision. Media references to Pep were already being made in the past tense, while the future was reserved for Saddler. The champion, as many were certain, had yet to reach his peak, while the challenger was beyond his. It wasn't fair, but it was consistent.

All Hartford was enthralled with the battle. As the first of two sold-out trains, bound for the Garden, left the station, you could feel the excitement. Could *our* Willie do it? Everyone, even those who disliked sports, understood that the results would be front-page news in the dailies, not to mention part of Connecticut history.

Spectacular! On February 11, 1949, Willie Pep became the first undisputed featherweight champion in history to regain the title. He did it in sensational form in front of over 19,000 spectators.[27] The 15-round unanimous decision saw no knockdowns, which would have surprised anyone who caught a glimpse of either the combatants or the blood-soaked battleground at the end of the fight. For those who claimed Pep would have to deliver the fight of his career to beat Saddler, he did. Referee Eddie Joseph, no stranger to ring assignments, gave Pep ten rounds to Saddler's five, which was close to how the judges saw it. It was one of those fights you had to view ringside—owing to the frequency of clinches and infighting—to make an assessment.

Pep was the master of his own destiny until the tenth round. A right hand delivered to his chin had the boat rocking, as they say. It took all Pep had to stay afloat. It was calm water from the 11th until the 14th round. A rocking right hand to the jaw, followed by a stunning left and right, once again had Pep swaying. Almost instinctively, he avoided rough waters by bobbing, slipping, and weaving until the conclusion of the term. Saddler had little choice but to go all-out in the 15th round. Knowing this, Pep switched to the reserve tanks and danced the final three minutes. Both fighters, painted in gore, looked as if they had been through hell and back; Pep's cheeks swelled as his cuts—11 stitches' worth—bled streams over the contour of his mangled countenance, while Saddler's optic swelled to three times its normal size amidst a halo of lacerations.[28] Those making the pilgrimage from Hartford, 1,700 dedicated fight fans, already knew the result. It was that decisive a victory. Ring announcer Johnny Addie, who could not be heard over the thunderous cheering, merely confirmed the verdict.[29]

Those New York writers, many of whom wrote off Willie Pep, could now bask on a steady diet of crow; moreover, Sandy Saddler entered the record books as the feather champion with the shortest tenure since Eugene Criqui defeated Johnny Kilbane back in 1923. That's no insult to Sandy Saddler, as he clearly had a brilliant future ahead of him. Speaking of lists, Pep added to his set of accomplishments by placing the name Sandy Saddler along with the steady diet of former world's champions he had defeated.

After the fight, Charley Johnston, who piloted Saddler, criticized referee Eddie Joseph for his clear—this was stretching the definition of the word—favoritism for Pep. From Joseph shaking hands with Pep after the fight, to the gobs of Vaseline that accumulated on the Hartford boxer's neck and right arm, Joseph, at least in Johnston's mind, was not impartial. He also claimed that NYSAC Chairman Eddie Egan warned his fighter about hitting after being spun around by Pep—an action that benefited Saddler in their initial encounter—and that the action should have been questioned.[30] Johnston was doing what fight managers do, defend their fighters. Indeed, championships should always be fair and tightly regulated. If his denunciations were valid, they would be reviewed.

Johnston was also taking criticism for not protecting his fighter—his failure to have a contract for a third title bout with Pep, for insurance purposes, was an enigmatic action.

Good fortune, not to mention incomparable talent, worked in Pep's favor on this day, a salute to his unparalleled corner of Lou Viscusi, Bill Gore, and Johnny Datro. All the same, wearing a new red robe with white trim, along with a new bucket, towel, and water bottle, may have had something to do with it. Pre-fight introductions, always a reminder that history was in play, included Pat Brady, Joe Louis, and Sugar Ray Robinson.[31]

All across Connecticut, celebrations were quickly organized. Governor Chester Bowles planned to present Pep with a plaque for his feat, State Senator Rocco D. Pallotti would add an official state recognition, and a multitude of organizations would follow suit. Impressive, at least to the champion, was a state police escort from the Greenwich toll house to the limits of Hartford.[32] Awe-inspiring to his fans was Willie Pep's visit to the Newington Home for Crippled Children on February 16. For the children, some bed-ridden, it was the thrill of a lifetime to have an encounter with the champion. Willie Pep, also a proud father, appeared to those who met him a glorious figure, a hero who did what heroes were supposed to do.

Off to Miami Beach, Florida, on February 21, Pep was ready for a well-earned vacation. Word hit the news wire before the end of the month that Harry Markson, of the 20th Century Sporting Club, had rematched Pep with Saddler for June at Yankee Stadium. It caught Pep by surprise, so he planned to consult his manager about it. He would see him at an exhibition being conducted by Joe Louis in Havana, Cuba on March 5. Pep made it abundantly clear to Viscusi that he was in no rush to rematch with Saddler. Later, it was confirmed that Markson's announcement was presumptuous at best, and that other plans were in the works.

Pep was back in Hartford in time to watch Finland fighter Elis Ask, a protégé of Jack Dempsey, battle Joey Longo at the Auditorium on March 22. Having promised the legendary heavyweight champion to look the kid over, the champion complied. Let's just say: Ask, a good lightweight boxer, didn't have Pep the least bit concerned should he consider losing a few pounds.[33]

Planning to get back to his training, Pep committed to a four-round exhibition in Tampa on March 29. Realizing he had to restart the engines, exhibitions, aka easy money, were a great place to start. In his first ring appearance since he regained his feather title, Pep, who tipped at 130, boxed four rounds against local lightweight Ernest Nogues, who scaled at 139. The champion's undeniable skills were on display and thrilled the crowd. As an enormous baseball fan, the champion couldn't resist the opportunity to watch a little Spring Training action over in St. Petersburg. He even caught up with his friend Spec Shea—the Yankees pitcher hailed from Naugatuck, Connecticut.

On April 3, the Stable Room, inside the Hotel Thomas Jefferson at 307 E. Washington Street in Tampa, held a Celebrity Night in honor of Willie Pep. The gala included singing host Russ Brown, in addition to The Jesters. Everyone enjoyed it, especially the champion, who always considered the hotel his home away from home. The champion's schedule was filling up fast. Pep was booked for a six-round exhibition in New Orleans against Del Flanagan on April 25, followed by a four-round exhibition in Detroit against the aforementioned Ellis Ask on April 27—the latter was Joe Louis's first promotional venture. Since there was a testimonial dinner in honor of the champion at the Club Ferdinando in Hartford the next day, it would be a tight turnaround time for Team Pep. The champion would be presented with a new championship belt by Nat Fleischer, editor of *The Ring*, and a wealth of celebrities planned on attending.

Soaking up a bit of the lifestyle of a champion, Pep appeared in the May issue of *Sport* magazine. The cover featured Enos Slaughter of the St. Louis Cardinals. Inside, Pep was the subject of an article written by Barney Nagler. *Collier's* also had Bill Fay pen a piece about the champion, and the famed *Police Gazette* revealed the inside story, or how Pep recouped his crown, in their May issue. Even Lincoln Downs, in Lincoln, Rhode Island, got into the act by naming a feature (horse) race The Willie Pep Handicap.

Tipping at 127, Pep glided through his six-round exhibition against Del Flanagan, a promising teenager from Minneapolis who scaled at 133 pounds. Two days later, the fight promotion conducted by Joe Louis drew over 10,000 fans, much to do with the presence of the promoter, Jack Dempsey, and Willie Pep. Ellis Ask made a statement by roughing up Pep a bit, however the 12-ounce gloves worn by the fighters reduced the damage. Over 600 turned out for the banquet honoring the champion, including Bat Battalino, Johnny Dundee, Kid Kaplan, Harry Markson, Dan Morgan, and even Willie's father and brother. Many joked with Willie that the event marked the longest period time the champion had ever spent in one place.

By early May, preliminary discussions with Saddler's camp looked hopeless, owing to the overwhelming financial demands made by Johnston. The rubber match between Pep and Saddler would have to wait. Johnston, who turned down a $25,000 offer, believed his fighter would spend the summer in England and Europe. On May 10, Viscusi, seeking alternative channels, signed with Jack Dempsey as the sole promoter of Willie Pep's next title defense. If the legendary Dempsey couldn't rope in Saddler, nobody could.

Pep left Hartford on May 19 to begin an exhibition tour. Viscusi had lined up eight events, primarily in the Midwest, that would conclude in early June. However, Pep became ill (air sick) and had to quit his initial flight at a connection in Detroit. His final destination was Minneapolis. Pep later returned to Hartford. The tour, which had dates in Minneapolis, Omaha, Denver, Waterloo, Des Moines, Topeka, and Wichita, was officially canceled on May 25. The only exhibition that took place was in St. Paul, on May 25, when the champion went four rounds against Eddie Lacey. Although Viscusi claimed the Western fight tour was canceled because of potential title defenses, the champion simply was not up to it. He arrived back in Hartford on May 27.

Feeling homesick, Pep hoped to stay in New England to enjoy some of the summer. The champion joined the Cinema All-Stars in a benefit softball game for the "Jimmy Fund Drive" on June 2. The event, which saw Pep's team defeat the East Hartford Blessed Sacrament Men's Club, was held at Bulkeley Stadium in front of an estimated 500 spectators. In addition to playing, Pep contributed the necessary funds to allow the organization to reach its financial goal.

In his first Connecticut ring appearance since he regained the title, Willie Pep, scaling at 131, took a 10-round decision over Luis Ramos, who tipped at 128. The bout was held at the Arena in New Haven on June 6. Whereas it was one-sided—the champion won every round—his adversary did manage to endure considerable punishment while challenging Pep with his awkward style. Ramos set the stage when he wrestled Pep to the canvas in the opening session. In the fifth round, Ramos delivered a compressed left hook combined with a push that put Pep to his knees. The champion sprang immediately to his feet before referee John Cluney realized what happened or could begin a count. Arguably a knockdown, it was not ruled as such. The event drew an enthusiastic crowd of 3,500 fans. Rumors circulated that Pep was inked to a title bout against Eddie Compo at Waterbury on July 12. Imagine,

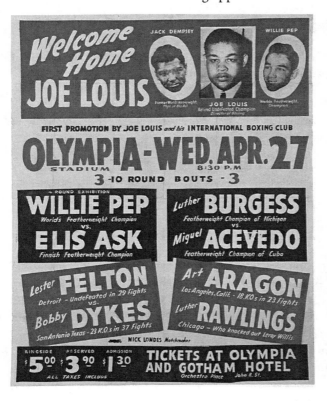

Poster for the first promotion conducted by Joe Louis and His International Boxing Club at the Olympia Stadium in Detroit on April 27, 1949. Pep is pictured in the top right corner.

as many Connecticut fight fans did, the peerless featherweight champion from Hartford in the ring against the popular New Haven scrapper Eddie Campagnuolo, aka Eddie Compo. But Viscusi, who was at the fight, claimed nothing was firm, *yet.*

Believing Pep's title defense against Eddie Compo was a "done deal" (initially scheduled for July 12), Lou Viscusi began scheduling his fighter's tune-up bouts. Bill Gore hoped for three battles to bring Pep in at 126 pounds (for his title defense), but he could probably do it with two. Brooklyn boxer Al Pennino was signed to meet Pep on June 14 at Wahconah Park in Pittsfield, Massachusetts, followed by New York lightweight Johnny LaRusso on June 20 at Century Stadium in West Springfield, Massachusetts (Viscusi believed in giving a pug a second chance). The third battle remained undetermined, but Viscusi hoped for a contest in Providence on June 27. Later, it was learned that Pep's final preparation bout would take place in Syracuse, New York.

Al Pennino had lost his last eight bouts entering his duel with Willie Pep. Chosen by Lou Viscusi because he had gone the distance with good fighters, including Sal Bartolo, and been stopped by even better fighters, such as Sandy Saddler, he was a Brooklyn scrapper who had fallen into a comfortable role as a set-up boxer since January of last year. With Pennino a low-risk, high-return pug, the fight manager liked the match.

Nothing more than a punching bag for eight rounds, the Brooklyn fighter suddenly woke up everyone in the Pittsfield ballpark by delivering a powerful right hand squarely on the chin of the champion. The ninth-round, eye-opening blast left over 2,5000 spectators in disbelief as Pep was visibly hurt. Sensing the damage, Pennino launched a reckless two-minute volley that depleted his arsenal. Dazed, Pep instinctively made it through the session with only a cut over his left eye—considering the onslaught he had endured, his survival amazed everyone. Furious entering the final round, the champion unleashed the heavy artillery, enhanced by volleys of unanswered machine gun combinations. The fact that Pennino was even standing at the final bell was a miracle. Willie Pep, tipping at 131, captured the 10-round unanimous decision over Al Pennino, who scaled a pound heavier. On went Pep to West Springfield, where matchmaker Joe DeMaria had put together an impressive evening of boxing, which included Hartford welterweight Vic Cardell on the undercard.[34]

Scaling at 129, the featherweight champion took a 10-round unanimous decision over Johnny LaRusso, who weighed 136¾. A crowd of over 3,500 spectators watched as Pep displayed some of the skills that brought him the title, but little else. LaRusso, who misfired on a majority of his punches, was never in trouble and there were no knockdowns. The city boxer landed a solid right that stunned Pep in the sixth round, but that was about the extent of the excitement. A light and intermittent rain suppressed the crowd's enthusiasm. It was the champion's 140th victory in 143 professional starts.[35]

Word came the next day that Compo had suffered a large cut over his left eye while sparring and that the title bout, scheduled for July 12, was postponed. Promoter Rocco Mara rescheduled the contest for July 28. Nevertheless, it was on to Syracuse, where Pep was scheduled to meet Freddie Russo over 10 rounds at MacArthur Stadium on June 30. When Russo pulled out of the fight, owing to lack of conditioning, he was replaced by Jean Mougin.

During World War II, Jean Mougin was a member of the French underground.

Decorated by his country for his service, he returned to the ring following the war. The previous year, he captured the French lightweight championship. But France wasn't America, and the Frenchman had lost five of his last seven battles here in the States.

Anxious about getting to Central New York, Willie Pep picked up a speeding ticket while driving his new Oldsmobile convertible coupe through Glens Falls on June 27.[36] Ironically, he wasn't driving to Syracuse. Pep was headed back to Hartford to catch a 7:00 p.m. flight to the "Salt City." Two days later, Viscusi announced that the fight was postponed on account of a back injury suffered by the champion. It was rescheduled for July 6, then rained out.

Finally, on July 12, it was fight on. Dancing 19 rounds to a lackluster unanimous decision, Willie Pep looked flawless. Scaling at 128, Pep conceded seven pounds to Mougin. Yet the power behind his punches was there as he systematically conducted his business.[37] It was Mougin's last professional fight in America.

Willie Pep v. Eddie Compo

One of 11 children in the Campagnulo family from New Haven, Eddie, like his five brothers, learned early in life the art of survival. When his older brother Johnny turned to the ring, Eddie followed. It was Johnny, as you may recall, who lost an eight-round decision to Willie Pep back in March 1942. Hanging up the gloves in 1947, Johnny was a good fighter who left behind a believed record of 51–39–17. But Eddie was one helluva boxer, who greeted Pep with nearly 60 wins and only one loss (to Tomas Beato).

At famed Madame Beys Training Camp (Ehsan's Camp) at Summit, New Jersey, Eddie Compo, under the watchful eye of his manager, Bob Mele, had worked his way into exquisite condition. The handsome and popular 21-year old wanted to be certain not to disappoint his friends or family. Was he thinking about avenging his brother's loss to Pep? Puoi scommettere la tua vita! (You bet your life!)

Defending his crown in his home state for the very first time, and against a popular Connecticut boxer, Willie Pep welcomed the challenge. The only satisfactory result was winning. Losing a battle at home, he understood, was worse than facing defeat on a national stage. Regardless of what Pep's opposer thought or where he was from, failure was not an option for the champion. Having worked himself down to fighting weight and reached the necessary mass for peak performance, the featherweight champion of the world was ready.

The only thing certain in boxing is that there was nothing certain in boxing. Willie Pep was hospitalized for a minor operation and his title defense was postponed.[38] Out of the hospital by the first week of August, Pep hoped to ease into his training and appearance schedule once his doctors approved. An announcement came the final week of August that Willie Pep would defend his title on September 20. As part of his preparation, Pep gave a four-round exhibition in Chicago on September 2.[39] The champion was ready.

It was two local beloved boxers, fighting under a championship banner, in front of their friends and family. And yes, ethnic pride was attached. Neither wanted to disappoint. If you were from Connecticut, you didn't want to pick a winner, you simply wanted to attend the fight. Over 10,000 fight fans did that as they found their way to Municipal Stadium in Waterbury. The atmosphere was electric, and the anticipation was beyond belief.

At the beginning of the seventh round, Willie Pep floored Eddie Compo with an unyielding left hook to the jaw. As it struck the face of the New Haven fighter, the impact could be heard in East Hartford. Flat on his back, Compo didn't know what hit him. Shaking his head as if to reorganize the chess pieces, he arose at the count of nine. Screams could be heard from his corner to stop the fight, and referee Billy Conway agreed. The official time of the TKO was 0:41 of round seven—it was the first time Eddie Compo had ever been knocked out. Dropped twice in the fifth term, Compo was lucky to last as long as he did as the champion battered him unmercifully. Simply punishing his adversary with combinations, Pep controlled the battle with his left jab and used his right cross to confirm his dominance. Tipping at 126, a pound and a half benefit, the champion took advantage of every ounce to deliver a spectacular performance. Handling corner duty for Pep were Bill Gore, Johnny Datro, and Jim Higgins (Lou Viscusi was working—okay, counting the money and planning his vacation—in the box office).[40]

Hans Bernstein, a prolific St. Louis promoter, spent weeks hounding Lou Viscusi to cut him a fight contract. Hoping to ink Pep for a title bout against Charley Riley, the Midwest impresario put a $30,000 offer on the table.[41] Not wanting another title defense for his fighter this year, Viscusi bartered for a non-title bout against an unidentified boxer (Harold Dade) at Kiel Auditorium in St. Louis on December 12, and pushed off the title defense until January 1950. Bernstein was elated, as it was no secret that Pep's manager was in talks with the International Boxing Club (IBC) about a title defense, or two, at Madison Square Garden.[42]

In the interim, Pep was enjoying the attention brought by the title. On October 17, he acted as a second to Bridgeport boxer Jimmy Rooney, who was battling Tito Valles at the Arena in New Haven. The latter's co-manager and chief second was Rocky Graziano, who like Pep knew a little something about the ring. Pep and Graziano would become lifelong friends, and it was through the Brooklyn-born fighter that Pep formed many other notable relationships.

Heading to Miami, Florida, to train for his upcoming battle against Harold Dade, Willie Pep also planned to soak up a little sun. Accompanying the champion was a beautiful woman by the name of Dolores Von Frenckell (the name may ring a bell as she was the former Mrs. Sal Ierna). From lounging on the beach to socializing at the Clover Club, the pair were spotted all about town.[43]

Pep arrived in St. Louis on December 11. He planned to arrive sooner, but his flight was grounded in Nashville on account of bad weather; the champion and his trainer opted for a train to the city. This happened the same time it was learned that Viscusi was negotiating with Jack Dempsey and Max Waxman for a film about Pep's life.

On December 12, the champion, tipping at 130 or about three pounds heavier than his opposer, seized a 10-round unanimous decision over Harold Dade, former bantamweight champion. Over 6,400 spectators watched as Pep rolled over Dade like a steamroller over fresh pavement. Pep could have easily knocked out Dade, but he did not, much to the chagrin of those staying awake during the uninspiring contest.[44]

Returning home, the feather champ underwent a minor eye operation to fix scar tissue at New Britain General Hospital. Viscusi must have received a discount as Pep's stablemate Johnny Cesario also had his eye operated on at the same location. All kidding aside, both fighters were doing well.

Seven

The Pinnacle, 1950–1951

"Attack is only one half of the art of boxing."—Georges Carpentier

1950

Longevity, as every boxing champion understood, was based on sound judgment. There was no room for arbitrary decisions—nonsense meant no cents in the fight game. As featherweight champion of the world, Willie Pep understood this. As a new decade began, those feathers looking up included: Miguel Acevedo (Cuba), Percy Bassett (Philadelphia), Ronnie Clayton (England), Harold Dade (Chicago), Henry Davis (Honolulu), Tirso Del Rosario (Philippine Islands), Ray Famechon (France), Glen Flanagan (St. Paul), Charley Riley (St. Louis), and the formidable Sandy Saddler (New York). It was a competitive field. Of the list, only Saddler (feather) and Dade (bantam) were former champions. Staying in the featherweight mix would be tough for all the participants, and grabbing a title shot against Pep would be even tougher.

Returning to Florida during the first week of January, Willie Pep trained at Ybor City Gym in Tampa's Latin Quarter, a region slightly northeast of downtown. Convinced that the weather contributed to his enthusiasm for training, he was in good spirits. Also, he reached his target weight quicker. Feeling great, Pep left Florida for St. Louis on January 10, 1950. Setting up shop inside the Mark Twain Hotel at 116 North Eighth Street at Pine Street, the style of the hotel reminded him of the Hotel Lincoln in New York.

Despite being champion—essentially calling the shots when it came to a title defense—Willie Pep wasn't afraid to take a contest in a challenger's hometown. That is a taboo according to boxing lore, as a champion was less likely to gain a decision in a close contest or have anything, for that matter, fall in his favor. Viscusi and Gore liked it because there were limited distractions for their fighter. Idle time never suited Pep well.[1]

The Kiel Auditorium was a prestigious-looking building located at 1401 Clark Avenue in downtown St. Louis. Optimistic about the match, promoter Hans Bernstein had the seating arranged to accommodate 10,867 fight fans. It proved a good thing as over 11,000 people showed up for the contest—more proof that good fight promoters understand their market. As this was the first time in modern boxing history that a St. Louis fighter attempted to take a world championship before local fans, nobody wanted to miss it.

Legendary sportscaster Bob Steele, of WITC in Hartford, was over the microphone ringside. For Pep, the famed broadcaster always brought a touch of home to his contests. The champion always made it point to wink at Steele as he was awaiting his ring introduction.

Willie Pep v. Charles Earl Riley

A punishing right flush on the jaw—like a baseball bat striking a ball—put Riley's lights out at the 1:05 mark of the fifth round. Flat on his back without moving, Riley was slow—still struggling five minutes later—coming back to earth.[2] The punch was delivered so fast, and at such a short range, many spectators had no idea what happened. The challenger's approach was to leap into Pep with hopes of catching the champion off-balance with a renegade left hook; Riley, with a two-inch shorter reach, had to compensate for his shortfall. The champion, having seen every approach in the book, patiently waited for his opening and then took it.

As the fight ended, many walked down to ringside, looking for information on what had taken place. Even at the hotel, hours after the contest, folks wandered up to the Pep entourage, looking for answers. To his opposer's credit: For four rounds, a somewhat cautious Riley endured numerous combinations and powerful left hooks.

A former Golden Gloves champion back in 1942, Charley Earl Riley, age 26, turned pro in 1944. Two technical knockouts over Phil Terranova thrust him into the spotlight. While he hoped to use his skills to better the champion, he failed. Riley's surname was added to Pep's list of prestigious knockout victims. The champion entered the ring a svelte 123½ pounds, two pounds lighter than his adversary.

As his second defense of the crown in four months, Pep continued to make history by defending the 126-pound honors more than any other champion. His staggering fight statistics included over 140 victories (over 40 by knockout) and consecutive winning streaks that were beyond imagination.

Leaving St. Louis, Pep headed back to Tampa. Planning to make the city his headquarters over the next three months, the champion would train at the Ybor City Gym. Quick trips to complete his fight and engagement demands appeared to work well from the location.[3] Manager Lou Viscusi was in negotiation with Boston promoter Rip Valenti for an overweight battle against, of all people, Lew Jenkins, the former lightweight champion. The pact was inked on January 24 and scheduled for February 6 at the Boston Garden. Pep's manager was also ironing out the terms and conditions for a title defense against Ray Famechon, French and European featherweight champion. If that happened, and it would, the venue of choice would be Madison Square Garden on March 17.[4]

While traveling by automobile from Hartford to Boston, Pep, accompanied by his son and Sam and Charles Greenberg, was involved in a skidding accident near Framingham, Massachusetts. The group was making the journey to start training for his fight against Roy Andrews, who substituted for Lew Jenkins, in the hub on February 6. Everyone escaped harm except Sam Greenberg, who had a slight back injury.

For 10 rounds, Willie Pep played a game of cat and mouse with Roy Andrews of Lowell, Massachusetts.[5] Flooring the youngster twice in the second round, the champion was content to coast his way to a decision victory—Andrews was saved by the bell on his second trip to the canvas.[6] The crowd of more than 7,200 spectators enjoyed the match despite its one-sidedness. Scaling at 130¼, over three pounds heavier than his adversary, Pep could have stopped his opponent at will, but opted instead for a solid workout.

After a brief stop back home in Hartford, Pep returned to Florida. Shifting his training east to Miami, the champion began preparing for a 10-round non-title fight scheduled for February 22. The contest was a favor from Viscusi to promoters Tommy DeTardo and Gus Mandell. They promised to ink a competitive adversary for Pep in preparation for his title defense against Famechon. That competitor—this may be pushing the definition of the word—turned out to be Brooklyn lightweight Jimmy Warren. Despite winning three times as many fights as he lost, the 25-year-old New Yorker wasn't expected to give Pep much of a run for his money. And he didn't; moreover, it was insulting to the promoters.

Over 3,700 fans turned out to watch the competition, but by the fourth round many were shouting their displeasure for the lack of engagement. It accomplished little in preparing Pep for Famechon. Scaling at 129¾, Pep grabbed the 10-round unanimous decision with minimal effort over Jimmy Warren, who tipped at 131¼. Many of those in attendance, to borrow a Groucho Marx line, thought their razor was dull until they saw this contest.

None too happy with the performance, the Miami boxing commission fined Pep $500 and Warren $250. As unhappy as they were, Viscusi was twice as upset. Contacting Garden matchmaker Al Weill, the embarrassed fight manager hoped to postpone Pep's battle with the Frenchman. It was both Viscusi's and Gore's opinion that Pep needed a *real* tune-up battle before facing Famechon. Weill, no stranger to the fight game, didn't buy it.

Willie Pep v. Ray Famechon

Roll the dice. That's what Viscusi did by signing Pep to a challenger he hadn't seen. Now it was a title defense his team clearly wasn't prepared for. It was the first time that the veteran manager was visibly concerned. Famechon's team had to make numerous concessions: 40 percent of the gate would go to the champion, while the challenger would receive 10. Famechon's entire purse would be held in escrow by the IBC as a guarantee that should the Frenchman win, he would give Pep a return bout within 60 days. Naturally, Viscusi addressed other items such as television revenues (each fighter to receive $1,000) and additional guarantees. When the Famechon team didn't counter the demands, it blew another hole in Viscusi's confidence. What did they know that he didn't?

Aggressive, skilled, and packing a powerful left hand, Ray Famechon, with his wide shoulders atop a muscular frame, was intimidating. The 25-year-old Frenchman won the European Featherweight Championship in 1948 and never looked back.

Pep, who began his title preparation at the end of February, decided to train out of the Hartford Auditorium gym. Bill Gore, who was traveling north from Florida, joined the fighter on March 1. The battle was scheduled for Madison Square Garden on St. Patrick's Day, March 17.

With his relentless lunging and awkward punching skills, Ray Famechon looked foolish trying to catch the champion. His heart was there even if Pep never was. There were no knockdowns, but Famechon came inches from hitting the canvas in the sixth term. Peppered by Pep jabs, the Frenchman took a solid left hook to the jaw. Yet, he somehow managed to gain his balance without falling backward. To his credit, Famechon absorbed a beating like a filthy rug hanging from a stiff clothesline. But the challenger's acclaim ends there.

To a shrill chorus of discontent, Garden announcer Johnnie Addie confirmed that the champion was still champion. Willie Pep, over 15 lackluster rounds, captured a unanimous decision over Ray Famechon. Both fighters scaled at 125 pounds. The majority of those scoring the fight gave Pep 10 rounds, Famechon three, with two even. For the over 12,000 spectators in attendance, it was a letdown, contributing to the scowl exhibited by Al Weill all evening.

Compared to his previous Garden victories, Pep looked tired and uninspired. There were no dazzling combinations ignited by the fiery heart of a champion. Instead, the Hartford Hurricane was like a tropical storm that dumped all its precipitation and gale before making landfall. It appeared that the champion was merely punching the clock.

As Pep took time off before heading back to Hartford, all the criticism of his recent performance faded quickly and was replaced by talk about a rubber match against Sandy Saddler. Having gained a six-month grace period after his defense against Famechon, the champion was in no rush to defend his title, yet alone against Saddler. Utilizing his ability to compartmentalize, Pep focused on the tasks at hand while Viscusi entertained offers. The fighter surfaced at the Broadway Arena in Brooklyn on April , to watch one of his protégés, Bobby Polowitzer of Hartford, drop a six-round decision to Phil Morizio of New York. The champion loved working with the young fighters, and they were all ears when he was around. Pep had also teamed up with Mushky Salow to handle some seasoned fighters, including Teddy "Red Top" Davis.

Idle since March 17, Pep took a 10-round non-title bout against punching bag Asuncion "Art" Llanos merely to ward off the ring rust. The fight, scheduled for May 15, took place in Hartford at the Auditorium. Scaling at 130, three pounds heavier than his opposer, Willie Pep stunned the crowd of nearly 1,500 spectators by knocking out Art Llanos at the 1:02 mark of the second round. A trio of swift punches turned the lights off: A left hook to the body, followed by a left hook to the jaw, capped off with a right cross to the chin. Dropping face-first to the canvas, Llanos, who was struggling to find his feet, was counted out by referee Hugh Devlin. It happened so quickly that many spectators missed it.[7]

Well-connected matchmaker Frank Balistrieri inked Pep to a 10-round non-title bout in Milwaukee on June 1. He was originally scheduled to oppose Sonny Boy West, but West couldn't make 133 pounds (requested by Viscusi). He was replaced with veteran Terry Young.[8] Trained by Ray Arcel and winding down a good career, Young had essentially found comfort in a setup role.

Conceding 9½ pounds to his adversary, Willie Pep, who scaled at 126, captured a 10-round unanimous decision over Terry Young. Over 6,100 Milwaukee fight fans flocked to the Arena to watch the champion work his featherweight magic. There were no knockdowns; however, there was a scare in the ninth round when a Young left, apparently south of the border, sent Pep against the ropes. The challenger besieged the champion, forcing him across the ring. With Young nearly pushing Pep through the ropes, both fighters fell in Young's corner. The wrestling display, plainly an act of frustration, prompted a warning at the end of the round.

In late May, IBC matchmaker Al Weill had progressed to an initial cut at an agreement for Willie Pep to meet Sandy Saddler at Yankee Stadium on June 14. Saddler's manager, Charley Johnston, took one look at the proposal and flatly turned it down. The rub was the percentage of the gate.[9] With the negotiations stalled, Lou Viscusi, understanding the dynamics of the fight game, was trying hard to keep the featherweight champion busy. When a bout in Cincinnati was canceled, Pep was inked for a 10-round turn against lightweight Bobby Timpson, from Youngstown, Ohio. The match was scheduled for June 26 at the Auditorium's Outdoor Arena in Hartford. Timpson, who went the distance against Sandy Saddler back in March 1948, had an initial reputation as a spoiler. However, for the last few years he had found solace as a setup fighter. Since Timpson was one of Rocky Graziano's sparring partners, maybe Pep was fulfilling a favor.

Willie Pep, tipping at 127¾, seized his believed 150th ring victory via a 10-round decision over Bobby Timpson, scaling at 134. The meaningful but not memorable victory was as dull as ditchwater. Timpson's failure to engage was as insulting to the crowd of over 1,700 as Pep's lack of ring acuity. Granted it was Pep's noted 40th Hartford victory, but it failed to impress.[10] Those sitting ringside were quick to note the familiar face of Al Weill, Madison Square Garden matchmaker. Yep, negotiations for Pep–Saddler III were getting closer. However, the only thing Weill had to say to the press was that he hoped to land something by September.

Pep was scheduled to meet southpaw Bobby Bell at Griffith Stadium in Washington, District of Columbia, on July 10, followed by Proctor Heinhold at the Catholic Youth Center in Scranton, Pennsylvania, on August 2. Or perhaps he wouldn't. On July 9 came word from the champion, via telegram to Bill Gore, that he was planning on getting married and would see him in about a week. Stunned and frantic, Viscusi and Gore tried, but failed, to locate Pep.

Wedding Bell Blues

Willie Pep, 27, married Dolores N. von Frenckll, 22, in Elkton, Maryland, on July 10, 1950. It was the second marriage for both. The simple wedding ceremony, which followed a required 48-hour waiting period after they obtained a marriage license, was conducted by the Rev. R. J. Sturgill, a Baptist minister. The marriage would last 138 days (from, Monday, July 10, until Friday, November 24, 1950, the day of the divorce filing) or, four months, 15 days including the end date.

By failing to show up for the weigh-in, Pep was indefinitely suspended by the NBA, and his bout with Bobby Bell was postponed. Once Pep was found, Viscusi and Gore went to work. The former began mending fences and apologizing for the inconvenience, while the latter prepared his fighter for his postponed, then rescheduled July 24 battle at Griffith Stadium. After another postponement, this time because of rain, the bout finally got underway on July 25. In front of over 3,300 fans, Willie Pep captured a unanimous 10-round decision over Bobby Bell. Pep took six rounds, Bell three, and one was even. Both fighters failed to lead. The bout was so drab that a Bell body assault during the seventh round became a highlight when Pep was forced to clinch. Not appearing as sharp or as fast as usual, Pep essentially sparred—as his powerful roundhouse left hook (aka "go-to punch") was blocked or missed its mark half the time, no significant damage was delivered. With Pep scaling at 130, 2½ pounds heavier than his opponent, there were glimpses of his ring majesty but not enough to satisfy anyone.

Back to the talk of the summer: Negotiations for Pep-Saddler III had stalled again as a consequence of the New York Fight Managers' boycott of the IBC. Charley Johnston, Saddler's manager, was also president of the organization. Countering the delay, Harry Markson, managing director of the IBC, was discreetly trying to reignite negotiations, and it looked promising. While Viscusi agreed to terms in the spring, Johnston never got off *his* dime, and negotiations ceased. The window of opportunity or the pinnacle of demand, as Viscusi believed, was fading. A binding contract was finally signed on July 27. In the end, Johnston took 15 percent of the gate because he felt that was a satisfactory figure for his fighter based on estimates. However, Viscusi, bargaining on behalf of the champion, waived a $100,000 guarantee in favor of 45 percent of the net receipts. IBC president Jim Norris believed the Yankee Stadium rematch could draw $300,000 gate.[11]

Willie Pep was in the Hartford Auditorium gym, preparing for what would be his last setup fight on August 2.[12] That contest would be against veteran Proctor Heinhold of Oklahoma City, at the Catholic Youth Center in Scranton, Pennsylvania. While Viscusi confirmed that the team would take an additional preparation battle if needed, Gore wasn't sure. The talented trainer did want to keep Pep out of Hartford and away from distractions.

In an impressive 10-round unanimous decision victory over Proctor Heinhold (Heinold), Willie Pep fought like a champion. Winning every round, he took command of the battle and never looked back. There were no knockdowns. The extreme heat was evident to the fighters and to the over 2,300 fight fans attending the gymnasium battle. At the end of the sixth round, referee Jack Walton went to Pep's corner to request that he "step up" his game a bit. If the champion had backed off his performance, it wasn't evident—obviously Walton had noticed something. Both fighters scaled at 131¾. On the undercard, stablemate Johnny Cesario outpointed Tommy Bazzano.

Sandy Saddler v. Willie Pep, III

Clear to every participant in the featherweight division: Willie Pep and Sandy Saddler were elite fighters capable of defeating one another on any given day. In preparation for their third battle, both gladiators trained as if their life depended on it—their careers certainly did.

Team Pep intended to eliminate every distraction. Prompted out of concern for their fighter, Viscusi and Gore moved Pep's training camp to Middletown, the city of his birth. As Pep would be living at Camp Byrne on East Road, his handlers were adamant that it was strictly private and that no visitors were welcome. Training at the Hartford Auditorium Gym, if necessary, would be limited. As for Saddler, he did preliminary work at Stillman's gym prior to heading over to Summit, New Jersey, at the camp formerly known as Madame Bey's.[13]

Tickets for the premier featherweight event at Yankee Stadium were scaled at: $20 ringside; $15, mezzanine; $10, upper and lower stand boxes; $10–$5 mezzanine stand; and $8–$5 lower stand reserved seats. Interestingly, there was no return bout clause for this fight. Both parties believed that if another fight was warranted, then

 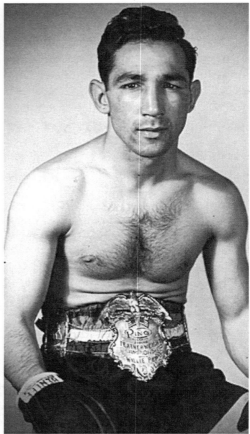

The third in a quartet of bouts between Sandy Saddler (left) and Willie Pep (right) occurred on September 8, 1950, at Yankee Stadium.

they would consider it. The demand was so strong for the event that the Greyhound Bus Line was running round-trip bus rides from Hartford to Yankee Stadium for $4.14.

Sandy Saddler had battled 10 times this year over 44 rounds and won every contest. Willie Pep fought nine times this year over 82 rounds and did not lose. This would be Pep's third title defense of the year. Of the two gladiators, Saddler had a far more difficult time making the 126-pound limit. Both fighters claimed the other fought dirty and that they would modify their behavior accordingly during the contest. The champion even went so far as to instruct his sparring partners to poke, prod, and pull him at every opportunity.

All Connecticut was behind Willie Pep. Even Governor Chester Bowles couldn't resist an opportunity to drop by Pep's training camp on August 28. While there, the Governor expressed his full confidence in the champion's ability to retain the title. He also stated that he planned on attending the Yankee Stadium event, no doubt partially thanks to four complimentary front row tickets courtesy of the champion. The next day, trying to stay in the moment, Pep held a camp birthday party for his son, who turned five years old.

Team Pep completed their Connecticut training on September 7 and immediately left for New York, where the crew checked into the Capitol Hotel. As Pep headed to his room, oddsmakers had the bout 2-to-1 in favor of Saddler.

As a reminder: Taller by 2½ inches, Sandy Saddler was four years younger and had a two-inch reach advantage. Whereas he had slightly bigger fists, he had smaller thighs. To counter, Pep would utilize his age and experience.

Suddenly, it was over. Just like that. After the seventh round, Pep slumped over on his corner stool, having suffered a dislocated left shoulder. With the fight four rounds to two and one even, the champion was ahead on the cards when Viscusi stepped in and called for a doctor to verify that his fighter could no longer continue. After a short examination by Dr. Vincent Nardiello, referee Ruby Goldstein signaled that it was indeed over. Sandy Saddler was the new champion.

The crowd of 38,781 spectators had no idea what happened. They saw the champion on his stool with the doctor massaging his left shoulder, but they couldn't put the pieces together. Saddler even dashed across the ring when the bell rang for round eight. Having taken a beating in the seventh term, Pep was unable to raise his left arm—it was not apparent during the round, but it was a serious injury. Viscusi would not let the champion continue. It was the proper call.

The new champion initially saw Pep's surrender as nothing more than an excuse. He believed that the Hartford fighter quit, because he couldn't take the beating. He was wrong. Both fighters tipped at 124¾ pounds.

In his fourth defense of his second reign as featherweight champion of the world, Willie Pep lost his prestigious title to Sandy Saddler. It happened on September 8, 1950, at Yankee Stadium. Both the attendance and the gross gate of $262,150 were featherweight bout records. The previous records (33,389 and $134,416) were set when Eugene Criqui defeated Johnny Dundee at the Polo Grounds back on July 26, 1923. Pep's cut of $92,889 was the largest purse ever earned by a fighter smaller than a lightweight. Saddler's cut was estimated at $30, 963.[14] Referee Ruby Goldstein now held the distinction of being the third man in the ring for the only two knockout defeats suffered by Willie Pep. There was no television or radio broadcast of the fight.

Saddler's best round was the third, when he dropped his rival with an accurate left hook for a nine count. He took the seventh round, but it was by a much smaller margin. Prior to the stoppage, it was only a question of Pep's ability to sustain the pace and how much longer Saddler would be able to see out of his left eye. Frustrated, Saddler wrestled with his adversary in both the sixth and seventh terms—both rounds likely contributing to Pep's shoulder injury. It wasn't pretty, but no match between these two elite warriors ever was.[15]

After the fight, you could hear a pin drop in Pep's hotel room as a small group of friends and media folks joined him. The former champion fielded questions from one corner, as his manager mumbled repetitive, yet supportive comments from another.

It was one of those fights where the record books would never do it justice, or so Willie Pep believed. They would paint a picture of a fighter who quit on his stool rather than a nearly indestructible warrior who was dominating the confrontation. The champion was on top of his game, yet few, if any fight accounts would reflect on that prowess. Nobody would believe the expert way in which he conducted business, or that he was getting stronger with each passing round. Nobody, and that bothered him.

No sooner had the fight ended, when talks of a rematch surfaced. Certainly, considering the payday, there would be a Saddler vs. Pep IV. At least Harry Markson, managing director of the International Boxing Club, believed it to be true and even stated it would happen in February. Yet much depended upon Saddler's tentative plan to wrest the lightweight championship title from Ike Williams.

A pulp fiction styled article, penned by ring wordsmith Dan Parker and illustrated by Tony Varady, appeared in the *Miami Herald* on October 15, 1950. The subject was Dolores N. von Frenkell Ierna Pep, aka Mrs. Willie Pep, who was painted as much for her pugnacity as her beauty. The fiery, yet feminine brunette, at least according to Parker, intended to become the financial planner of the family. As to the incentive behind the article, nobody was certain. But Lou Viscusi, who was mentioned six times in the piece, certainly took his fair share of punches.

Returning to Hartford, Pep, who was convalescing from his dislocated left shoulder, was also spending time with his fighters. For example, he was seen at the New Haven Arena in the corner of boxer Bobby Polowitzer.[16] Rest, together with whirlpool bath treatments at Trinity College, had healed his shoulder to the point where he hoped to resume his ring activity in December. Naturally, he would still have some pain in his left arm and shoulder, but not anything that trainer Bill Gore couldn't repair. With recent interest in the fight game sluggish, at least in Hartford, Pep was in no hurry to return to the ring. The dailies blamed everything from the fight managers and matchmakers, to the even the fighters.[17]

On November 24, 1950, Dolores N. von Frenkell Ierna Pep, aka Mrs. Willie Pep, sued for divorce on a charge of "intolerable cruelty." The former featherweight champion was ordered to appear in Superior Court in seven days. The suit came the day before the fighter planned to head to Florida. Once there, he hoped to begin easing into a training for his rematch against Sandy Saddler.[18] The action made the front page of the *Hartford Courant*, alongside world news. Pep appeared at the courthouse, per the order, but did not enter the court room. Temporary alimony of $30 per week was awarded to the fighter's bride of four months.[19] Reconciled with each other, the couple moved into an apartment in New York City on December 9.

A shining star amidst the challenging fight news was lightweight Delbert "Del" Charles Flanagan, who was handled by Lou Viscusi. Undefeated in 50 straight fights, Flanagan captured a unanimous 10-round decision over Sandy Saddler in Detroit on December 6. Needless to say, the overweight bout catapulted Flanagan up the lightweight ladder. And it put an end to the criticism Viscusi had been taking for moving Flanagan along too fast.

Speaking of Viscusi, as both he and Gore had homes in Tampa, the pair were wondering how Pep's move to New York City was going to affect their relationships. But before they could do that, they had to find a way to keep their former champion's foot off the accelerator of his automobile. The former featherweight champion, clocked at 75 miles-per-hour on the Wilbur Cross Parkway during the early hours of December 26, was arrested following a police chase. Pep's case was continued until January 18, 1951.

On December 27, Pep returned to the gymnasium for the first time since he injured his shoulder. That gym wasn't in New York City, but in Hartford at the auditorium. Pep's former cornerman, Johnny Datro, handled the workout while Viscusi was in Minneapolis steering Del Flanagan's fight against Jackie Graves, and Gore was in Florida. Viscusi, aware of Pep's legal issues, wanted Gore to evaluate Pep and requested that his fighter head to Florida as soon as possible.

1951

Not Enough Time to Heal

Everyone knew it was an aggressive schedule: Willie Pep was tentatively scheduled to fight Sandy Saddler for the featherweight championship on February 23. As he was still healing, his early January program included only drills and roadwork. It wasn't until trainer Bill Gore arrived in Hartford, during the second week of the month, that the tempo improved. Still, Pep didn't attempt boxing until January 17, late in the minds of his handlers and a major concern. Viscusi, who got his first glance of Pep in Hartford on January 21, decided to sign him to a Mile O'Dimes (March of Dimes) charity boxing event being held at the Hartford Auditorium on January 30. While he wasn't thrilled by Pep's training performance, he had Gore's word that he would have the fighter in condition for the event. On a good note, Pep's speeding arrest was dismissed by Hamden Town Court upon payment of $15. Unable to appear in front of the judge, the boxer forwarded the payment.

On January 29, the IBC announced that the Sandy Saddler vs. Willie Pep featherweight title fight, scheduled for February 23 at Madison Square Garden, had been postponed indefinitely. It was Lou Viscusi who made the decision. Phoning Garden matchmaker Al Weill, he stated that his fighter's shoulder wasn't strong enough to perform at peak performance. The news came as a complete surprise to Pep, who was preparing for his first fight since his injury. Was he disappointed? Yes, but Pep trusted his manager's judgment.

You Can't Be Serious

Tommy Baker, a mediocre featherweight from Cliffside, New Jersey, was chosen as Willie Pep's opponent for the charity event on January 30. It's fair to say: The last thing Pep's management anticipated from Baker was an injury to their fighter. An accidental headbutt by the fighter in the third round opened a deep cut on Pep's forehead. As a result, the former champion bled profusely from that point forward. Gore, trying his damnedest to control the flow, could not stop the bleeding. Sensing the damage, Pep bolted out of his corner at the start of the fourth round and unloaded the artillery. After being driven about the ring, Baker landed against the ropes and took a cold-hearted beating. Sensing the vitiation, referee Hugh Devlin stopped the bout at the 1:20 mark of the fourth.

Avoiding a possible stoppage owing to his own condition, Pep was thrilled with the cessation. However, Baker, none too happy with the result, grabbed Devlin and wrestled him to the floor. It wasn't a good idea. The crowd of over 1,900 fight fans went berserk and flowed ringside to protest the stoppage. With the fans hurling insults, not to mention anything else they could find, it was an awkward scene. Thankfully, when things finally calmed down, cooler heads prevailed. For three rounds, Pep looked strong with no outwards signs of discomfort or lost performance.

But hours after the charity contest, Gore still could not control the bleeding and became concerned. Pep was admitted to New Britain Hospital, where he underwent surgery to close his cut.[20] Twenty stitches later, and after a brief examination, Pep was released on the morning of January 31.

Needing time to recover, Pep, accompanied by his young son, headed south to Tampa. Once there, he would also conduct some light training sessions at a local gym. By the third week of February, Pep's forehead had healed, and he was ready to climb between the ropes. On February 24, Lou Viscusi, during a phone interview with the press, confirmed a few of Pep's future opportunities, which included an exhibition in Sarasota on Monday, February 26.[21]

Pep being slated to meet Marvin Ford of Charlotte, North Carolina, in a 10-round main event on the American Legion's regular weekly card didn't sound like an exhibition. Nevertheless, Pep made the short journey south to Sarasota. However, Ford couldn't make weight. So, Billy Hogan (aka Eddie Webb), who hailed from New Orleans, took the fight.[22]

As Pep toyed with his opponent during the opening round, spectators watched and waited for the inevitable. During the final seconds of the term, Pep sent a solid right to the jaw that dropped Hogan like a piano pushed off a fourth-story balcony. However, the bell sounded before referee Tony Angela could finish the count. Hogan's handlers tried frantically—and let me add inexplicably—to rejuvenate their stunned warrior before sending him out again. Can you say execution? Firing three quick shots at his mark, Pep lined up a right that struck Hogan's jaw flush and collapsed him against the ropes. Tipping at 128½ pounds, Willie Pep knocked out Billy Hogan at the 1:05 mark of the second round. The American Legion Coliseum, which held 1,500 people, was filled for the event. So was Hogan simply an exhibition victim or Pep's 154th ring victory? Most observers, including many of the Connecticut dailies, saw it as the latter, and other than Viscusi's published comments, little supports the former. It was considered an official battle.

Also, on February 26, Willie Pep filed for a divorce from his second wife on grounds of extreme cruelty. The divorce action was registered in Hillsborough Circuit Court (Florida).

Next stop, New Orleans and the Coliseum Arena, where Willie Pep, scaling at 127¼, seized a 10-round unanimous decision over Carlos Chavez, who tipped at 133. Capturing every round, Pep was pleased with his presentation and felt the shoulder held up. Viscusi, who was heading back to Hartford, agreed with his fighter's evaluation but didn't want to comment about a future title shot. Chavez, who won over three times as many battles as he lost, was clearly on the downside of a good career, having lost eight consecutive bouts. Pep, with a four-inch reach advantage, went head-hunting in the first round, then to the head and body in the second. Comfortable with his range, he began using his left hook to inflict body damage by the fourth round. When Chavez managed close quarters, Pep countered with potent, short right uppercuts. Lightning fast, the former champion was long gone before Chavez ever got set. Every time Chavez charged his target, Pep caught him with forceful lefts to the head. The entertaining bout attracted over 4,500 fight fans.

Afterwards, Pep headed back to Florida to await instructions from his team. While he hoped for a June shot against Saddler, it was a dubious circumstance. For now, Viscusi was speaking to Florida impresario Chris Dundee in Miami Beach.

Having his say over the Auditorium, located at 1700 Washington Avenue, Dundee managed to ink Pep for a 10-round battle against scrapper Pat Iacobucci on March 26—noted for his volatile behavior, the Cincinnati pugilist was the latest sensation amid Beach fight followers. Viscusi, who understood that this style of fighter was not favored by his pugilist, took the bait. Dundee, who scaled tickets at $5, $3.50, $2.50, and $1.50, was convinced the match was a hit.

In front of over 3,200 fans, Willie Pep, scaling at 127, painstakingly captured a 10-round unanimous decision over Iacobucci, who tipped a pound heavier. The free-form style of the Cincinnati scrapper overwhelmed the former featherweight champion. Viscusi should never—I'll say it for you: it was a bonehead move by somebody who knew better—have made the match and it cost him: Pep, in pain from the opening round, re-injured his left shoulder. The injury, which should have been contemplated by sense and not cents, almost cost Pep a title shot against Saddler. In the seventh round, the former champion could barely lift his arm. After he returned to Tampa, x-rays thankfully confirmed no fracture or dislocation.

Unfortunately, Pep's battles continued in Tampa as he and his wife traded verbal jabs during divorce proceedings.[23] A somewhat fatigued husband and former champion, with his arm in a sling from the injured shoulder, appeared at the proceedings. A special master would review the charges by each, then present his finding to the circuit judge, who would determine whether a divorce would be granted. The process would likely take a few weeks.[24]

While Willie Pep was healing emotionally and physically, a sorrowful Lou Viscusi began scheduling "a road" to the title—road being the perfect word as Pep was easily distracted when he was in Hartford or Tampa. Honestly, Pep wasn't thrilled by the idea, but he didn't say it in public. The former champion wanted another shot at Saddler, and the only way that made sense was working him into peak performance. That was precisely what Viscusi was trying to do. The fighter was signed to two 10-round nontitle fights in April: On the 17th, he would meet Baby Neff Ortiz in St. Louis at the Kiel Auditorium, and ten days later face Eddie Chavez in San Francisco at the Cow Palace. The latter promotion was a long way to travel, but promoter Bill Kyne offered Pep $15,000 or 30 percent of the gate for his first Bay Area appearance.

Tipping at 126½, Willie Pep scored a fifth-round TKO victory over Baby Ortiz, who scaled at 132½. The crowd of over 2,600 fight fans watched as the former champion dropped his adversary three times on the way to victory. A solid right uppercut to the jaw in the third round dropped Ortiz to all fours for an eight count, while a left to the head sent him down again in the fourth. Sending Ortiz face-first to the canvas with a right to the chin in the fifth round, Pep was surprised his opposer made it to his feet—he arose at the count of nine. The serious face lift that followed, courtesy of Pep combinations, left referee Dick Young with little choice but to wave it off.[25]

Featuring a concrete and steel roof that covered nearly six acres, the Cow Palace welcomed over 10,000 fight fans on April 27 to watch Willie Pep, who scaled at 127¾, pick up a split decision over popular hometown fighter Eddie Chavez, who tipped at 135. The latter, who held victories over Enrique Bolanos, Manuel Ortiz, Maxie Docusen, and Harold Dade, had lost only two fights in 34 ring battles. Entering the ring a 2–1 favorite, Pep maintained an early lead. While he bobbed, danced, and twisted his way to a tight decision, he was lucky. In the 10th round, Chavez, aware he was behind in points, allowed himself to be driven across the ring to lure Pep to close quarters.

Then he cut loose with a pair of solid right hands, followed by a left hook, that caught the former champion by surprise. Two left hooks followed by a right to the jaw sent a retreating Pep against the ropes. Dazed, he managed to withstand a flurry of blows before the final gong. It was, as they say, too close for comfort. Afterwards, he admitted he was reckless against the 20-year-old lightweight prospect and made far too many mistakes. Pep was not ready to face Sandy Saddler, and he knew it.[26]

By mid–May it was clear that Saddler-Pep IV, was not going to happen in June. If not June, the next month that made sense was September. These were the traditional big money months of boxing. Mutual stubbornness appeared to be stalling talks between Lou Viscusi and Charley Johnston. Frankly speaking, they needed each other if either was going to manage a big payday.

After Viscusi gave Pep time off to tend to some personal issues, it was time to get back to business in June.[27] Promoter Benny Trotta, who was handling the Coliseum in Baltimore, matched Pep with New York boxer Jesus Compos on June 4. Flashing a bit of his old form, the former champion, scaling at 131, picked up a unanimous 10-round decision over his opposer, who tipped at 127. Toying a bit—okay, at times Compos looked foolish trying catch his opponent—with his adversary, Pep worked on fine-tuning his arsenal. There were no knockdowns.

Harry Markson, managing director of the IBC, was diligently working to land Saddler-Pep IV, and while Viscusi was available, Saddler and Johnston were in South America. At first it was tentatively set for August 22 at Madison Square Garden, but it was revealed that Pep had recently undergone minor surgery (no details) and would not be able to make an August date.[28]

Finally, on August 14, it was confirmed that Sandy Saddler would meet Willie Pep for the fourth time on Wednesday, September 26 at the Polo Grounds. Saddler would take 37½ percent of the proceeds, while Pep would grab 22½ percent.[29] Both fighters desired a tune-up battle or two prior to the contest.

For his fine-tuning bout, Willie Pep met Denver boxer Corky Gonzales at the Municipal Auditorium in New Orleans on September 4. The 23-year old had faced defeat but three time in five years, and he recently upset Charley Riley. Holding victories over Eddie Bergin, Proctor Heinhold, and Harold Dade, Gonzales appeared a solid choice. The former champion planned to train in Hartford before heading to New Orleans on September 2.[30]

Coming into the fight at 129½ pounds, Willie Pep dominated his adversary, who scaled at 125½, to gain a unanimous 10-round decision. The former champion's two-handed flurries were like machine gun blasts, and by the time his opposer could react, Pep had vanished. While Gonzales forced the fighting, he did not have the speed to catch his target. Without an opportunity to inflict damage, the effort was hopeless. An invigorated Team Pep left New Orleans immediately for Hartford. Once home, they would begin three weeks of intense training for Saddler.

Sandy Saddler v. Willie Pep, IV

The line of fight fans reached around the Auditorium on Wethersfield Avenue in Hartford well before noon on Friday, September 14. Everyone was there to grab the best tickets they could afford for Saddler-Pep IV, scheduled for the Polo Grounds on September 26. Hartford Boxing Club offices opened at noon, and Eddie Sullivan, from the International Boxing Club, was there to supervise the sale of tickets scaled at $20, $12, $8, and $4.[31]

Working out of his fight camp in Middletown as well as the Auditorium gymnasium, Pep had 85 rounds of boxing under his belt by September 17—during his session on this day, he attracted over 150 fans to watch him spar with Jackie O'Brien and Ray Castello. The next day, Viscusi and Pep made the ceremonial trip to New York City to sign contracts. While there, the fight manager also intended on chatting with NYSAC chairman Eddie Eagan about who should referee the bout. None too happy with the skills of Ruby Goldstein, Viscusi insisted that the chosen arbiter enforce the command to break. His lobbying appeared successful as Ray Miller was the selection.

During the contract signing, words were exchanged by both parties. Team Pep accused their opposers of "roughhouse tactics," while Team Saddler felt their adversaries were being childish, or "crybabies." It wasn't a surprise, nor was it likely going to change anything; however, it was entertaining. Based on their previous three fights, what was certain was that both would use every trick in the book to defeat their opponent.

Anticipating his fair share of grappling against Saddler, Pep took wrestling lessons from professional wrestler "Wild Bull" Curry on September 21. Curry, a former Hartford policeman, watched films of Pep's previous encounters with Saddler, then showed Pep how to break the anticipated holds from the champion.

Since they last met, Pep, age 29, had participated in eight battles and won them all. However, he had also dislocated his left shoulder and faced a few personal problems. As for Saddler, age 25, he took 14 battles and lost two (Del Flanagan and Paddy DeMarco). Oddsmakers had Saddler a 2–1 favorite entering the battle.

Movement was the key for Pep; failure to do so would make him a target for Saddler's slicing left jab. The Hartford boxer could punch, but not with the power of his rival. He could not afford to be drawn inside, where he could be tied up or abused by the legerdemain tactics of his opponent. While Pep was certain that he could dance and dazzle the distance, he also knew he could be taken out by a single Saddler punch. Nobody on his team wanted to bring it up, yet they were all thinking the same thing: Would Pep's left shoulder hold up?

A crowd of 13,836 fight fans found their way to the Polo Grounds in New York on September 26 to watch Sandy Saddler, the featherweight champion, successfully defended his crown against Willie Pep. After the conclusion of the ninth round, Pep, whose right eye was badly sliced, stayed on his stool. He was unable to answer the bell for the tenth round. He confirmed his position with referee Ray Miller. Ringside physician, Dr. Vincent Nardiello, who did not enter the ring to examine Pep, consulted with Miller before the arbiter waved off the fight. This was the third time Saddler had won by a knockout.

Prior to the stoppage, Miller had Pep ahead in the fight 5–4 on rounds, 10–6 on points; judge Arthur Aidala had it 4–4–1 on rounds, and Pep ahead in points, 8–6; and judge Frank Forbes had Saddler ahead 5–4 on rounds and 7–5 on points. The only knockdown in the bout happened in the second round, when Saddler connected with a powerful left hook to the body that sent Pep to his knees for a count of eight.

In retrospect, it was one of the dirtiest fights in the history of boxing. Every trick in the book was used. From gouging and poking to heeling and holding, the fight got

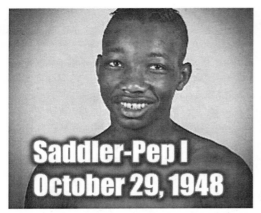
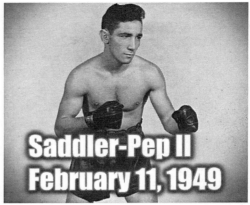
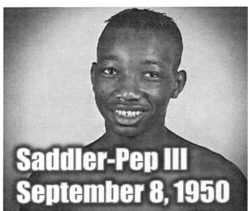
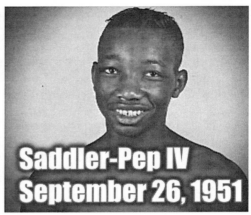

Both Sandy Saddler and Willie Pep had become household names by the time they fought their final battle at the Polo Grounds on September 26, 1951. A composite photograph shows all four battles with the victor pictured.

so bad that the referee had to warn both fighters during, and between, every round. Miller was even wrestled to the canvas in the seventh session—Pep was penalized during the term for "unnecessary roughness." Miller clearly lost control of the wrestling match, and that was precisely what it became. As a result, NYSAC revoked Pep's license and indefinitely suspended Saddler for his roughhouse tactics.[32]

The right eyelid of Willie Pep was so badly torn in the second round that the blood flow could not be contained—it blinded him in every subsequent session. During each intermission, his handlers, Johnny Datro, Bill Gore, and Jimmy Higgins, attempted to control the bleeding from the cut, only to have Saddler open it up again. Unable to see, and slowed by the champion's destructive body punches, Pep's condition waned. By the fifth round, nobody thought the fight would go the distance, and they were correct.

Sitting on the rubbing table in the dressing room that typically housed the New York Giants, Pep had his head down and was chewing on a piece of ice—it was so quite after the fight that when the sweat poured down his face and hit the floor, you could hear it. When an ice chip slipped out of the fighter's mouth and landed on the rubbing table, nobody reacted, they just watched as it melted alongside the fighter. Not a soul in the room wanted to break the silence.

WILLIE PEP

Nine Successful Featherweight Title Defenses:

* Sal Bartolo - June 8, 1943

* Chalky Wright - September 29, 1944

* Phil Terranova - February 19, 1945

* Sal Bartolo - June 7, 1946

* Jock Leslie - August 22, 1947

* Humberto Sierra - February 24, 1948

* Eddie Compo - September 20, 1949

* Charley Riley - January 16, 1950

* Ray Famechon - March 17, 1950

It is one thing to hold the featherweight title, but it is another thing to defend it. With nine successful featherweight title defenses, Willie Pep outshined many featherweight greats.

Finally, one of the reporters from the *Hartford Courant* had the guts to ask the former champion why he quit. Stunned by the question, everyone awaited Pep's response. Slowly lifting his head until his mangled right eye was clearly visible to everyone in the room, he removed the ice pack from his wet hands and mumbled, "the referee was against me."[33]

The exchange broke the silence, but not the spirit of the fighter who endeavored to answer each question. Most of the inquiries couldn't be answered, nor was it fair to continue to jab the former champion. Puffing on a fat cigar in the corner of the room was a disenchanted Lou Viscusi. He would shake his head in affirmation of his fighter's comments, but little else. Later, he would admit that Pep's decision not to continue was prudent.[34]

Many a professional boxing career would have ended at this point. Had the situation been different, from numerous perspectives, Willie Pep, with a professional record of 160–4–1, could have retired with a Hall of Fame career. But that wasn't Willie. There was still too much money on the table, and he knew he had a few good rolls left.

NYSAC License Suspension

Heading back to Hartford after six stitches to his eyelid, Pep enjoyed a few days of seclusion at his parents' house. It was time to heal. He planned to have a long talk with Lou Viscusi upon the manager's arrival back in Hartford. Needless to say, the "R" word, or retirement, appeared the next day in a local newspaper. The thought, at least in Pep's mind, wasn't an option.[35]

Concluding his suspension, Sandy Saddler resumed his boxing career. In December, he completed his trilogy against Brooklyn lightweight contender Paddy DeMarco at Madison Square Garden. It was no secret that Saddler wanted a title shot against lightweight champion Jimmy Carter, but the lanky champion had to get by DeMarco first. However, Saddler couldn't outsmart the rugged DeMarco and lost the 10-round donnybrook. A brawl it was as both fighters cast the rulebook over the ropes. Hearing the news, Pep merely shook his head while recalling how he tamed DeMarco when they met at the Garden. As a matter of course, Charley Johnston, Saddler's manager, couldn't refrain from adding his two cents in on the loss and threw out the race card. It was the first such claim heard in years in New York and unwarranted—five of the seven current champions were Black.

Pep hated being sidelined from the ring and out of the limelight. As the leading contender among featherweights, he wanted his license back. Looking at the challengers behind him—names such as Ray Famechon, Percy Bassett and Lauro Salas—he didn't feel it was time to throw in the towel. Besides, if Saddler found his way into the lightweight division, Pep was certain, none of the remaining featherweights could touch him.

EIGHT

Moving Forward, 1952–1954

"Any fool can make a rule. And any fool will mind it."—Henry David Thoreau

1952

Bothered by pressure from scar tissue around his eyes, Willie Pep underwent minor surgery in January—the procedure was successfully performed at New Britain General Hospital. Feeling much better, Pep headed to Florida in February to resume his conditioning. With trainer Bill Gore in Tampa, assisting Connecticut fighter Jackie O'Brien, the former champion couldn't wait to get back to work at Tampa City Gym.

It was hard for Pep, not to mention those around him, to get over his recent loss to Sandy Saddler. For months the comments, or criticisms, remained the same: Prompted by his opposer, Pep had little choice but to resort to dirty tactics; Pep's retaliation took him out of his comfort zone; referee Ray Miller lost control of the fight in the early rounds—a better referee could have maintained the legality and integrity of the bout; and inexperienced NYSAC Commissioner Bob Christenberry was inappropriate in his judgment and punishment of the combatants. All interesting observations and reflections, yet the result remained the same.

Knowing how badly Pep wanted to re-enter the ring, Lou Viscusi matched his fighter with Jimmy McAllister. The fight, subject to restoring Pep's license, was scheduled for Holyoke Valley Arena on March 31. However, NYSAC turned down Pep's plea for reinstatement of his boxing license. That didn't set well with the former champion, to put it mildly.[1]

It wasn't unusual for Pep to spend quiet time at Frank's Restaurant, a landmark on Asylum Street in Hartford. He would be greeted by Frank Parseliti, Sr., the owner, who would escort him to his table and personally hand him a menu. On one of the walls was a photograph of Willie Pep, age five, wearing a pair of boxing gloves. Following the Saddler fight, Parseliti asked the fighter what he was going to do next. Willie turned to Frankie and pointed at his picture. "That's all I know, Frankie," he stated, "that's all I know."[2]

A Time to Swallow Your Pride

Willie Pep, with a record of 160–4–1, met novice Santiago Gonzales, with a record of 3–0, in Tampa on April 29. Think about that for a second. From battling against an elite fighter in the Polo Grounds, in front of almost 14,000 fans, to facing a neophyte pugilist inside an Armory, in front of 4,000 spectators, the irony was difficult for the former champion to ignore.

It hurt, and it hurt bad. Yet the former champion had a job to do, and he did it. Pep took the 10-round unanimous decision with ease over his inexperienced 22-year-old opponent. Viscusi needed to establish a relationship with promoter Al Garcia, who was behind the small Fort Homer Hesterly Armory show.[3] In retrospect, it was insulting to the former champion even if he understood his manager's motivation.

Since Pep couldn't fight in Connecticut, Illinois, Massachusetts, Michigan, and New York, his options were limited. When the press used the dreaded term "comeback" to describe the bout, they were immediately corrected: Willie Pep never left.

Booking Pep for three bouts in May, Viscusi and Gore, impeded by the suspension, began bolstering the confidence of their fighter. After defeating punching bag Kenny Leach in a 10-round distance battle at Golden Park in Columbus, Georgia, on May 5, Pep, a mere five days later, knocked out Buddy Baggett in the fifth round of a bout held at Eustis Park in Aiken, South Carolina. He would next greet Claude Hammond at the Auditorium in Miami Beach on May 21.[4] Pep looked solid against Baggett when he delivered him at the 1:50 mark of the fifth round. The setup battles were serving a purpose, and Hammond was the final step before pushing Pep up a rung. Hammond, who replaced Baby Gonzalez, was a solid puncher who was working out of the Miami Beach Fifth Street gym. Outweighed by eight pounds, Pep captured a unanimous 10-round decision over Hammond, but it came at a cost. In the eighth round, he suffered a deep cut through his right eyebrow that was inflicted by a head-butt—the rupturing scar tissue shot blood in every direction. Blinded in the ninth frame, he lost the round. Yet he managed to make the distance. After the bout, Pep consulted with his Connecticut surgeon, who advised him to return home and undergo surgery. Uncomfortable and unable to get a return flight, Pep instead opted to seek medical treatment in Tampa.

Once again, Willie Pep was on the shelf. With old wounds being opened faster than they could heal, Pep was in a quandary. He had to fight to stay in the featherweight mix, yet the suspension, not to mention his healing time, presented an enormous challenge. Those around him wondered: How much longer could the former champion continue to put himself through this agonizing process?

Meantime, Sandy Saddler, whose boxing title was frozen, was in the army. He wasn't alone. The Korean Conflict was conducted from 1950–1953, between North and South Korea. United Nations troops, dominated by U.S. forces, countered the invasion of South Korea—the country had been seized by North Korean forces—by invading North Korea. The situation was complicated by China intervening on the side of the North. Thankfully, the fighting finally drew to a conclusion on July 27, 1953, when the Korean Armistice Agreement was signed.

Speaking of Saddler, Boston promoter Sam Silverman designed a series of matches to determine an interim featherweight champion. Having chatted with Lou Viscusi, the promoter learned that Willie Pep, healed from his injury, had been working out since the beginning of June. Gaining permission to utilize Pep's services— Pep's license remained revoked—in Massachusetts, Silverman booked the former champion to meet hub Irishman Tommy Collins, a former Pep sparring partner. The

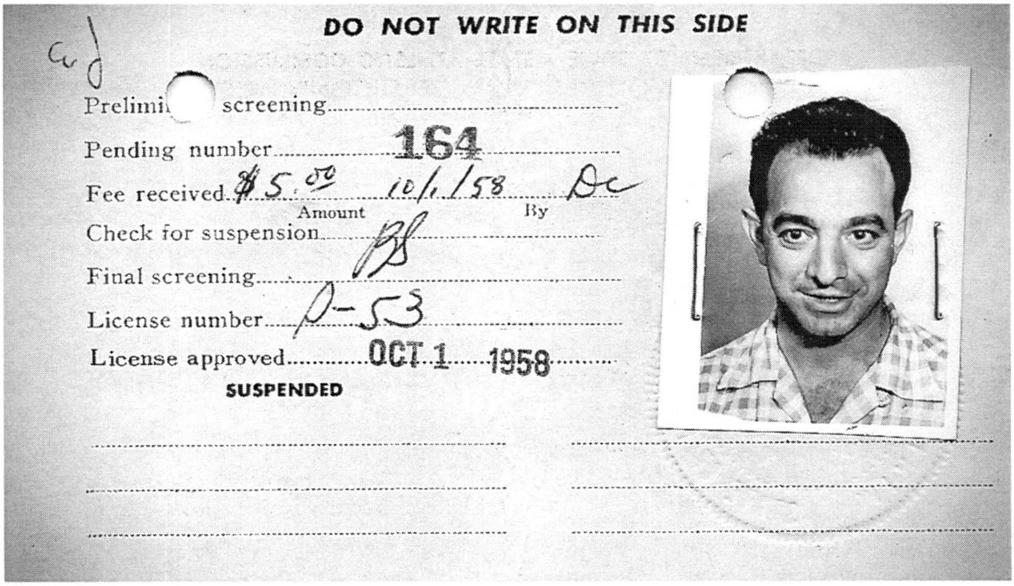

DO NOT WRITE ON THIS SIDE

Prelimi☐ screening..........................

Pending number..........**164**..............

Fee received..$5⁰⁰ 10/1/58 Dc

⎯⎯⎯⎯Amount⎯⎯⎯⎯⎯⎯⎯By⎯⎯⎯

Check for suspension.......

Final screening...............

License number......P-53

License approved............**OCT 1 1958**

SUSPENDED

Internationally known trainer Angelo Dundee, aka Angelo Mirena (pictured here in 1958), admired Willie Pep. He admitted to teaching his fighters (Ali, Basilio, Foreman, etc.) many of the defense tactics used by the featherweight legend.

move was brilliant on the part of Silverman, as Collins, a skilled and durable pugilist, was far more than a target. Scheduled for 10 rounds at Boston Garden on June 26, it would be Pep's toughest challenge since meeting Sandy Saddler.

Collins was the reigning New England featherweight champion and was extremely popular. Having won five times as many bouts as he lost, he held victories over Fabela Chavez, Jimmy McAllister, Eddie Compo, and Buddy Hayes. When a three-day heat wave forced the postponement of Pep's match with Collins, it was rescheduled for June 30. The delay gave the former champion a few more days to prepare, and word was that he needed it.

For nearly five rounds, Pep resembled his old self: mobile, quick, and confident. Firing a machine gun combination that staggered Collins at the end of the fifth term, he sent the hub fighter to the ropes. Sensing the kill, Pep charged his opposer to finish the job. It was then that Collins fired a Hail Mary left hook that found its target—it struck Pep's jaw and sent him backward to the canvas. As the crowd erupted, referee Joe Zapustas began the count that reached eight before the bell rang. Scrambling, and even falling, Pep was pulled from the canvas by his handlers, who attempted to revive him. They managed to get their dazed fighter to his feet, sweat and blood streaming from his contorted countenance. Pep, with only one eye functioning, came out for the sixth and final session.

Legs gone, the 11–5 favorite entering his battle was driven into a corner and bounced by a combination. Up at the count of eight, he was dropped again during a final assault. Viewing the lifeless form on the canvas, Zapustas didn't even bother with a count, he simply nodded to Collins and waved it off. Scaling at 127, or four pounds lighter than his opponent, Willie Pep hit the canvas for the third and final time at 55 seconds of the sixth round. It was a screaming left hook from Collins that was responsible for the damage. It was also the second loss suffered by the former champion in his last six fights.[5]

Later, Pep labeled his performance as careless: He never saw the left hook. The New England crowd of over 6,500 erupted in cheers, as they never dreamed of such an ending to the one-sided battle. Collins had beaten the odds, and a legend.

With well over 150 ring battles under his belt, Pep took time once again to heal and reflect on his incredible career. Was it over? It was hard to say, and many weren't saying. Promoter Chris Dundee was one individual who thought the former featherweight was through, but nobody was certain. During the third week of August, it was reported that Willie Pep and veteran Billy Lima, of Havana, agreed to do battle over ten rounds at Legion Field in Pensacola, Florida, on September 3. Obviously, Legion Field wasn't Boston Garden, but for a boxer with Pep's resume to battle back into the mix, it would take time and patience—the former champion was never a fan of the latter.

Scaling at 127, Willie Pep picked up a 10-round unanimous decision over Billy Lima. To the credit of the Cuban, he fought hard against Pep, and the crowd of about 2,000 fight fans appreciated the effort. There were no knockdowns but lots of solid exchanges. To provide some perspective on the event, other than the attendance figures: Of the eight fighters on the undercard, only one boxer had over ten professional fights. Despite not being an enormous financial success, the match was a solid enough performance to consider a rematch.

After the ring battle, Pep headed over 2,800 miles north to Vancouver, British Columbia. The road back to reinstatement was long, arduous, and expensive, with plenty of time for Pep to think. Later, Pep would recall how this period of his career—far from fun and exciting—gets overlooked. Was it a redundant portion of a brilliant career? Perhaps to some ring historians, but not to Pep.

On September 11, Willie Pep danced and clawed his way to a 10-round unanimous decision over Young Bobby Woods—for the record, Pep was 11 years older. Both fighters scaled at 130 pounds. In far from a clean bout, the pair grappled—Pep had Woods in a headlock during the seventh round—and roughhoused in front of over 5,000 enthusiastic fight fans. Unfortunately, the former champion had a gash ripped open over his right eye. It was a rougher scrap than Pep preferred, but nevertheless it was a victory.[6]

Back in the states—Syracuse, New York, to be exact—NYSAC Commissioner Robert Christenberry reacted to statements made by Pep to the media. The former featherweight champion believed he was treated unfairly in his fourth battle against Saddler and that his punishment didn't fit the offense. Christenberry affirmed that Pep was given the reason for the action and an open hearing. Until NYSAC received a report as to why Pep quit on his stool during the fight, he would not be welcome to do battle in New York State. The NYSAC executive claimed that fight films confirmed that it was Pep who was responsible for initiating the dirty tactics, including tripping. He said the former champion was lucky to receive his fight purse after the bout.

Ignoring—okay, refraining, at least for now, from firing back at—the comments made by Christenberry, Pep turned his attention to the Midwest. The IBC announced during the third week in September that they had signed Pep to meet Armand Savoie, Canadian lightweight champion, over 10 rounds at the Chicago Stadium on October 1. Pep was able to fight in Chicago because the Illinois State Athletic Commission reviewed his case and decided to give him a probationary license that would be subject to his performance against Savoie. It just so happened that the Canadian lightweight had defeated Sandy Saddler before the champion entered the army. Thus the timing of the nationally televised match between Pep and Savoie appeared perfect.[7]

Calm, cool, and collected, Pep conducted a symphony. His expertise kept his opponent at arm's length and off-balance. His counterpunching was magnificent. Managing to inflict some damage to Pep—a cut over his opponent's right eye in the fourth round—Savoie pounded the laceration in the fifth with hopes of a stoppage. The effort failed. By the tenth and final round, the frustration painted on Savoie's face was confirmed when he cast judgment to the wind and went for a knockout. It proved hopeless. Desperately needing an impressive victory to catapult him back into division contention, Willie Pep, five pounds lighter than his adversary at 129¼, took a unanimous 10-round decision over Armand Savoie.

While the performance was sound, the gate was not: Only 2,000 fight fans turned out. Pep netted 30 percent, or about $900, and Savoie 20 percent, or about $600. Thankfully, television rights added $2,000 to the take of each fighter. In retrospect, the victory was perfect: Pep's commanding performance—proof that the fighter's skills had not deteriorated—and national exposure brought him back into the division picture and into the hearts of fight fans. It even managed to paint a smile on the countenance of the thirty years old.

Returning to Miami Beach, Pep was scheduled for a 10-round rematch against hub fighter Billy Lima at the Jacksonville Baseball Park on October 20. It was a favor, as Miami Beach fight promoter Bill Kaye was trying to break into the Jacksonville market and needed a decent fight card. Scaling at 129, six pounds heavier than his opponent, Pep seized the 10-round unanimous decision over Lima. The former champion impressed the crowd of 3,000 dedicated fight fans—the outdoor event included rain during the final two rounds—with his commanding left jab and defensive skills.

Learning that Lou Viscusi was toying with some Midwest matches, his seasoned meal ticket reminded him that he would sooner stay south for the winter. Countering, Viscusi reminded his regionally unlicensed fighter that if he wanted to stay in the mix, he had to travel to the opportunities. They weren't coming to him. The local press was also coming down hard on Pep's handlers for matching the fighter with pugs like Lima, who was considered washed-up.[8] Later, when Viscusi explained that his fighter's match with Lima was for charity, the press backed down.

Viscusi admitted to a Florida journalist that he supported Pep quitting the ring. (This was believed the first time such an admission had appeared in print.)[9] But Pep, who loathed idle time, thought the idea was ridiculous for an athlete his age. While Viscusi and Gore were always looking for the next champion—their latest find was Cleveland Williams, a 19-year-old out of Tampa—their loyalty to Pep was unquestioned.[10]

After chatting with Miami Beach matchmaker Chris Dundee, Viscusi inked Pep to meet Manny Castro, a young Mexican fighter, on November 5 inside the Auditorium. Dundee, who liked the inexperienced Castro, was fulfilling a favor to his brother.[11] Pep planned on working out over at the famed Miami Beach Fifth Street Gym, aka the Stillman's of Florida's East Coast.

Willie Pep, tipping at 128½, took a fifth-round technical KO victory over Manny Castro, who scaled at 122½. Pulling out the stops in the fifth round, Pep unloaded the arsenal on Castro. Having dazed his opponent, Pep glanced—as if to say, is it over?—at referee Billy Regan, but the arbiter was unresponsive. So Pep repeated the action until the fight was waved off at the 0:55 mark of the term. Frankly speaking, the 18-year-old didn't belong in the ring with Pep. Angelo Dundee, the kid's trainer, thought it would be more of a fight, but that wasn't the case—nor, by the way, did Castro ever amount to much of a boxer. The Miami press, who "drank Chris Dundee's bath water," looked ridiculous with all their pre-fight hype regarding Castro. Perhaps it was necessary, as the fight attracted 2,400 spectators. After the fight, Pep was visited in his dressing room by Glen Flanagan, Rocky Graziano, and Danny Nardico. Graziano and Pep, who had become great friends, later found their way to a celebrity party at the Paddock Club.[12] The pair, dangerous as they were together, always shared a comment regarding their association: "We'll be friends until we're old and senile ... then, we'll be new friends!"[13]

St. Louis in the winter, you gotta be kidding. Pep, on the "comeback trail" according to unknowing press, headed out to the Midwest. On November 19, he would do battle against Fabela Chavez, a former sparring partner, over 10 rounds inside the Arena. Sponsored by the IBC, the fight was televised both nationally and regionally by CBS. Better stated: good money and terrific exposure.[14]

Coasting to a victory, Willie Pep deftly captured a 10-round unanimous decision over Fabela Chavez. Both fighters scaled at 129 pounds. The former champion didn't lose a single round. Controlling with the left jab, while scoring with combinations and his deadly left hook, Pep looked on top of his game. If he had lost speed, as some press claimed, none of the 2,500 fight fans in attendance noticed. Chavez, who slipped twice while attempting to catch his adversary and once as a result of doing so, looked silly. Having opened a cut near the left eye of Chavez about halfway through the battle, Pep later—in the ninth term—asked referee Ray Palmer to stop the battle because of the injury. The arbiter declined. So Pep rode the bike for the remainder of the clash. Because Pep refused to crucify Chavez, the bloodthirsty crowd booed the former champion, and the press labeled him a Florence Nightingale. A humanitarian boxer, who would have thought?

In his final battle of the year, Willie Pep, scaling at 127, three pounds heavier than his opposer, took a 10-round points victory over Jorge Sanchez, a Cuban scrapper. The fight took place at the American Legion Arena, on Clematis Street (at F.E.C. Railroad) in West Palm Beach on December 5. It set a record for a season-opening crowd by attracting 2,100 fight fans. There were no knockdowns or even near knockdowns. The lackluster battle saw Pep jab his way to victory over a defensive-minded challenger. Cheering, and occasionally jeering their friend from ringside were Rocky Graziano and jockey Con Errico.[15]

1953

In confirmation that the year 1953 would be a memorable one, Willie Pep was pleased to see his name among the contending featherweights recognized by the National Boxing Association. The others were: Ray Famechon (France), Percy Bassett (Pennsylvania), and Tommy Collins (Massachusetts). Sandy Saddler, as you didn't have to remind anyone, was on top of the mountain. In time, Pep believed, that would change.

Hoping to take a dozen or more contests during the year, the former feather-weight champion began his ring quest in of all places, Nassau, the capital and largest city of The Bahamas. Promoter Charles Major signed the former champion to meet Billy Lauderdale, from Hialeah, Florida, over 10 rounds at Nassau Stadium on January 19. It proved to be a treat for the estimated 1,600 who attended the event. Scaling at 127½, nearly ten pounds lighter than his opponent, the former champion scored a unanimous 10-round decision over his opposer. Overpowering his adversary with his ring prowess, Pep dropped Lauderdale to his knees in both the second and eighth frames. It was a comfortable start to the year, and the former champion even had a chance to meet Sir Robert Neville, Governor of the Bahamas. Pep, who returned to Miami on January 20, began training the next day at the Fifth Street Gym for his 10-round bout against Davey Mitchell. That bout was scheduled for January 27 at the Auditorium in Miami Beach.[16]

At 24 years of age, Mitchell, a lightweight from Silverton, Manitoba, had caught the eyes of many by posting a recent draw with Armand Savoie, the current Canadian lightweight champion. Training over at the Magic City Gym, Mitchell was a prolific puncher. But before he could punch any target, he had to catch it.

Tipping at 130¾, Willie Pep seized a unanimous 10-round decision over Davey Mitchell, who tipped a quarter of a pound heavier. A 3–1 favorite entering the ring, Pep rode his left jab and ducked punches to perfection. Mitchell, who was over his head, performed like it. The youngster, who was apprehensive from the start, had the crowd begging for him to engage. Nonetheless, the over 3,100 fans in attendance seemed to enjoy the event. After the fight, Pep, who remained barred in New York, made it clear that he hoped one day to settle his licensing issue; moreover, he of all people understood the value associated with his lost credentials.

Willie Pep was at Municipal Auditorium in San Antonio, Texas, on February 10. It was a long way to travel to dance 10 rounds to a decision over Jose "Pepe" Alvarez, but Viscusi had limited options, and Texas was one. Scaling at 129, Pep floored his opposer, who tipped two pounds heavier, to an eight count during the final round. It was the only knockdown of the battle. On the undercard was a West Virginia heavy-weight by the name of Tunney Hunsaker. While few would ever remember the fighter's battle on this occasion, many will recall him as the pugilist who faced a boxer making his professional debut on October 29, 1960, an Olympian named Cassius Clay, later Muhammad Ali.

In anticipation of Sandy Saddler's April discharge from the army, there were a plethora of hungry featherweights salivating for a title shot. In addition to the afore-mentioned, there were also: Teddy "Red Top" Davis, Pat Marcune, Charley Riley, Lauro Salas, and Gene Smith. Naturally whenever Pep was mentioned, he was refer-enced among the division's finest ever. His name was placed alongside Lou Ambers, Henry Armstrong, Abe Attell, Benny Bass, Bat Battalino, Tony Canzoneri, and Kid Chocolate. Which, when you think about it, was both positive and negative—good in that he didn't have to make a name for himself because he was one, and bad, in that some might not respect him as a current contender.

Florida, especially Miami Beach during this time of year, was a fun place to be. Hoping to enjoy the camaraderie, Pep asked Viscusi to try to keep him in town. As usual, a who's who in boxing enjoyed the sunshine. It wasn't unusual to find pugs like Joey Maxim and Rocky Graziano poolside enjoying the sun or an approaching

Two of Willie Pep's closest boxing friends, Rocky Graziano (left) and Jake LaMotta (right). Graziano's three-fight series with middleweight champ Tony Zale defined his career, while a six-fight series with Sugar Ray Robinson largely defined LaMotta's ring history.

mermaid. Speaking of Graziano, a recently retired boxer, he would referee Pep's next ring battle—scheduled for March 31 at the Fort Homer Hesterly Armory in Tampa, when the veteran boxer would meet novice New York pug Joey Gambino. Originally, matchmaker Al Caroly wanted to use Pep earlier in the month, but the fighter had to leave town. Fifth Street Gym was packed with pugilists from across the country, including Ralph Dupas and Willie Pastrano. Trainer Bill Gore was there working with Danny Nardico, who trained with Pep and was coming off an impressive December victory over Jake LaMotta.[17] Nardico would next meet Joey Maxim on March 4. Some called it work, but to others it was fun in the sun.

NYSAC License Suspension Lifted

On March 27, Willie Pep made a plea for reinstatement with NYSAC—the boxer appeared alone in New York, while the rest of his team remained in Miami Beach. It was the boxer's second application and came at the one-year anniversary of his first rejection—his license was revoked back on October 5, 1951. After listening to the pugilist's apology, the New York State Athletic Commission granted him a new license. After Pep served 18 months of a lifetime ban by NYSAC, the issue, not to mention embarrassment, was finally lifted from the fighter's back. Thrilled beyond belief, Pep couldn't wait to return to Florida.

Scaling at 131, two pounds heavier than his opponent, Willie Pep captured a 10-round unanimous decision over Joey Gambino.[18] The former champion had his novice New York opponent in trouble multiple times, yet neither fighter hit the canvas—Pep did slip to the floor in the second session. The crowd of over 1,200 Tampa fans were on their feet in the final round as both boxers went toe-to-toe in the most exciting term of a lackluster bout. On the undercard was undefeated heavyweight Cleveland Williams, who picked up his 30th consecutive victory. It was one of those days when both Gore and Viscusi had smiles the length of Manhattan painted on their faces.

Willie Pep loved the Miami Beach nightlife, especially if he was able to meet up with friends and see a show. A favorite stop was Mother Kelly's World-Famous Bar and Restaurant, at 1405 Dade Boulevard, where the food was great and the entertainment, both on and off the stage, was even better. Anybody who was anybody, or even thought they were, could be found there—from entertainers and politicians to questionable figures nobody dared question. Involved in plugging a comedy dance and singing team called The Goofers, the former champion allowed the group to use his name in advertisements. It was these associations that always made the former champion feel a part of the vibe.

Still in Florida, Willie Pep grabbed a 10-round unanimous decision over Montreal lightweight Noel Paquette on April 7 at the Miami Auditorium. Paquette, trained by Angelo Dundee, promoter Chris Dundee's younger brother, had little to offer his adversary. In complete command, the former champion won every round behind his left jab and deadly combinations. The mismatch, or favor if you will, attracted over 2,300 spectators.[19]

Looking ahead, Viscusi was close to firming up a Garden television date against Brooklyn's Pat Marcune on June 5. However, Pep needed a tune-up bout—his last two opponents had fewer than 20 career victories combined. Under the gun to find worthy competition, Viscusi called Texas boxing promoter Lou Gray, who offered a match against either Al Jurgens or Jackie Blair on May 13 in Dallas/Fort Worth. Later, it was learned that it would be Blair. On a positive note, because of a recent loss by Percy Bassett, the interim feather champion, Pep took over the number 1 contender position in the latest (*The Ring*) rankings.

In a nationally televised ring battle from Fort Worth, Texas, Willie Pep met southpaw Jackie Blair. The Texas lightweight king, who was once Pep's sparring partner, had over 100 professional fights' worth of experience at age 22. Winning over three times as many fights as he lost, Blair's recent victories were somewhat deceptive, as three of his last five opponents had losing records.

Pep took command early with the left jab, and it wasn't long before Blair was bleeding from the nose and cuts around his eyes. The only knockdown of the bout came in the tenth round when Blair caught Pep with a precision left to the chin and sent him down without a count. Winning only one round, on one card, Blair had plenty of heart but was not fast enough to catch the former champion. Tipping at

129¾, Willie Pep comfortably captured a 10-round unanimous decision over Jackie Blair, who scaled at 131.

Pep left for New York after the battle to prepare for his appearance at Madison Square Garden.

Triumphant Garden Return

It felt, at least to Willie Pep, that the road back to Madison Square Garden took forever. In truth, he was last inside the famed venue on March 17, 1950. That was the night he defended his featherweight title against Ray Famechon. Yet that date wasn't as fresh in his mind as the last time he fought in New York State, on September 26, 1951. Since then, 619 days had elapsed. Now 30 years old, the former champion, making another bid for the crown, greeted 24-year-old Pat Marcune, from Coney Island. Having won six straight battles this year—Pep was, after all, known for his impressive winning streaks—the seasoned warrior hoped to add Marcune's name to an uncommonly long list of victims. Depending upon how you cut the numbers, most saw Pep as having fought 183 times, losing only five, with one draw, 53 of his victories coming by way of knockout.

Not beating around the bush with the press, Pep admitted he was fighting "for the dough."[20] It was an admission that would haunt him. Unsure of when he intended to pull the plug on his ring career, he was guessing maybe another year or two. Good living, gambling, and gals, he admitted, struck hard on the balance sheet. But some decent paydays, he believed, could fix that.

To witness Pep training in Stillman's gym was like watching the Pope conduct Easter Mass. Gloves were silenced and all eyes turn toward the ring master. Dancing, bobbing, twisting, and weaving, he was majestic—it was almost as if he was floating over the ring floor, like he was painting the canvas purely with his footwork. From every corner, you could hear the whispers as trainers covered their mouths and demanded that their students watch the display. The echoes were the same: look at his feet … watch him hit and run … look at the speed … you'll never see another fighter like that, kid, never.

Pat Marcune, with over 30 victories in over 40 fights, was young, strong, reckless, and occasionally hard-headed. Hoping, no praying, that through divine intervention his ambition, together with a good right hand, could overcome Pep's experience and ability, he was mistaken.

The veteran built up an early lead and used it to coast during the middle sessions, before battering the Coney Island youngster like a flank steak. A flurry of punches had Marcune dazed before the bell ending the ninth round, and it looked like referee Pete Scalzo might stop the fight. But it wasn't to be. Drifting from his corner at the beginning of round 10, Marcune was welcomed by inexorable machine gun fire that left Scalzo no choice but to wave it off. Scaling at 127¾, Willie Pep ended the short-term dreams of Pat Marcune, who tipped at 129½, by snatching a technical knockout victory 14 seconds into the tenth round.

In the fifth round, Pep dropped Marcune to an eight count with a stinging right uppercut. It, plus an action-packed seventh term and the final two rounds represented the highlights of the evening. Entering the tenth round, ringside had it 8–1, in favor of Pep. The crowd of over 3,500 fight fans enjoyed every minute. The national exposure certainly favored the former champion. Whether fans watched on their local NBC affiliate (*Cavalcade of Sports*) or listened to ABC radio, interest was high. For posterity, Pep was favored to win the 10-rounder at 3–1. At the conclusion of the fight, NYSAC commissioner Bob Christenberry congratulated Pep for looking every bit like a featherweight champion.[21] And at that exact moment, hell froze over.

From June 6 until November 21, Willie Pep did not enter a boxing ring. His first priority was healing the cuts around his eyes—it was becoming a regimen after every battle. The damage, 15 stitches' worth, was a result of his recent encounter with Pat Marcune. After staying in New York after the fight, Pep drove back to Florida around the end of June.

By August, Willie Pep knew he should be getting back to the ring, but he lacked the desire—a peculiar and uncharacteristic attitude, not to mention excuse, for an elite fighter. In another sign that something wasn't right, his 10-round battle against Larry Mujica (a sparring partner), scheduled for August 25 at Miami Beach, was canceled because Pep was fatigued and felt he didn't have time to get back into proper condition.[22]

In September, the IBC planned to match Pep with Lulu Perez on November 13, the winner to face Sandy Saddler. However, that match faded from the radar screen when Perez delivered a poor battle against Dave Gallardo on September 4.[23] With the pieces not falling into place, Pep was ready to leave Florida.

With his new license in hand, and an impressive Madison Square Garden victory under his belt, Pep returned to New York City. It was where the action was, and besides, he had a strong friendship base there. By October, the fighter was living in midtown Manhattan. That month he made an appearance on the "All-Star Revue" television program aired by NBC. Comedian Martha Raye hosted the show, and the featherweight made a guest appearance alongside Rocky Graziano and Jake LaMotta. It was this type of New York opportunity that Pep enjoyed—he loved the exposure and delighted in the recognition—and the pay wasn't bad either (each fighter lined his pocket with $1,000). Also, with Sandy Saddler agreeing to meet Pep once he was discharged in late April, fight negotiations could be handled in person, and he obviously presumed a Pep-Saddler V bout would likely be a New York promotion.

Back in the ring on November 21, Willie Pep, scaling at 130, or eight pounds lighter than his opposer, took a 10-round unanimous decision over veteran Florida, via New Jersey, boxer Sonny Luciano, at the Armory in Charlotte, North Carolina. Luciano, at the close of a good career, failed to win a round or to aggressively engage; referee Marion Diehl had to remind him he was in a boxing match. Far from an engrossing confrontation, it served its purpose.[24]

Understanding the featherweight picture and its possibilities, Viscusi inked the former champion to three "warm weather" bouts in December; Davey Allen in West Palm Beach on December 4, Billy Lima in Houston on December 8, and Tony Longo in Miami Beach on December 15.[25]

Tipping at 129, Willie Pep took a 10-round points victory over Davey Allen, who scaled at 134. It was Allen's last professional fight. Matchmaker Al Caroly was delighted to have both Pep and Allen back at the American Legion Arena, as the opening main event of the fight season. While over 1,900 fans turned out to witness the vapid battle, not everyone stayed until the end; some even left before it was half over. Referee Billy Shell gave Pep eight of the 10 rounds. And there were no knockdowns.[26]

In Houston, it was nothing but target practice against Billy Lima, as Willie Pep, scaling at 129, captured a technical knockout over his adversary a mere 34 seconds into the second term. Pep dropped the Cuban-born fighter twice in the opening round, leaving most of the spectators in the City Auditorium on the edge of their seats—the bell saved Lima from being counted out the second time. For Lima, who worked out of Miami, this was his next-to-last professional bout. Afterwards, Pep headed back to Florida to train for his final battle of the year against Tony Longo.

On Friday, December 11, Willie Pep and Jake LaMotta turned up at the Dade County Police Benevolent Association's party being held at the Children's Home in Kendall. What better way to get into the Christmas spirit than to be around children? Pep and LaMotta, both fathers, made the perfect guest hosts.

In his final fight of the year, Willie Pep, scaling at 129, took a 10-round unanimous decision over Tony Longo, who scaled a pound heavier. The latter, an unchallenging lightweight out of Baltimore, landed only one solid punch: A right to Pep's head in the ninth round.[27] Ironically, as Longo was clearly outclassed, there were no knockdowns. Pep danced around his opposer and entertained the over 2,800 in attendance with his polished defensive skills. On the undercard of the Chris Dundee promotion was the familiar name of undefeated Connecticut boxer Larry Boardman. The lightweight, out of Marlborough, defeated his opponent via a fourth-round TKO. Overall, it wasn't a bad way to end the year.[28]

Taking 11 contests in 1953, all against fighters with winning records, the former featherweight champion performed magnificently. Three of the fighters (Blair, Luciano, and Lima) he faced had over 50 victories. With his NYSAC license suspension lifted and a triumphant return to Madison Square Garden under his belt, Pep had every reason to feel optimistic.

Lou Viscusi confirmed that Pep was offered an overweight match against ex-bantamweight champion Vic Toweel in Johannesburg, South Africa (in April 1954). But the thought of traveling by air to the African continent didn't thrill Pep, nor did he want to pursue an opportunity in a country that supported apartheid.

1954

On furlough from the United Sates Army, Sandy Saddler, hoped to be ringside at Madison Square Garden on New Year's Day. That meant traveling all the way from Germany, but he felt it was that important. He wanted to watch Lulu Perez face Dave Gallardo because it had implications on his ring career—he could face the winner following his discharge.

Lulu Perez captured a unanimous decision over Dave Gallardo, but it was a brawl. All the rules of the ring were cast aside in favor of a combination wrestling and boxing match that did nothing to elevate the sportsmanship of the fight game. Nevertheless, it was Lulu Perez who would meet Pep on February 26. The winner, according to the IBC, would then get first crack at Sandy Saddler for the featherweight title—the champion had been idle for nearly two years. However, Charley Johnston, Saddler's manager, made it abundantly clear that any covenant he *might* make would be on his terms.

Hoping to begin the year on the right foot, Willie Pep was in Jacksonville, Florida. Scaling at 128¼, he grabbed a 10-round unanimous decision over Davey Seabrook, who tipped at 131. The event took place on January 19 at the Naval Air Station. "Little David," who was born in Jacksonville, exhibited promise until 1950, when he decided it was easier to make money as set-up fighter than trying to become a contender. As anticipated, Pep ran away with the bout while picking up nearly every round on the scorecards of all three judges. As a first set-up battle for Lulu Perez, the fight might have worked, but not as a final. In retrospect, the system, aka Team Pep, failed here.[29]

In Hartford, interest in the upcoming Willie Pep versus Lulu Perez battle in Madison Square Garden was reminiscent of times past. A special section of railroad cars had even been designated for the journey. It was all folks were talking about in the city. While the fight wouldn't match the revenue figures of a Pep-Saddler fight— much to blame on television, or so many believed—it would be a respectable gate.[30]

Everybody had an opinion, and while all Connecticut residents held Pep, 31, close to their hearts, they understood that their hero had aged. When Willie Pep won his featherweight title, Lulu Perez was still in grammar school. A cocky scrapper, Perez, 20, carried his left hand so low that he appeared conceited. But attitude was one thing, and a bag of tricks another—Pep was concerned with the latter. In over 30 ring battles, Perez had lost only two; moreover, over half of his victims lost via knockout. But to knock out an opponent like Pep, well, you know the rest....

The lines were long at Union Station in Hartford. Many had their fight tickets— they were scaled at $2.40, $4, $6, and $8—but those who did not could make reservations at the Garden. The last three cars of the 4:10 train were reserved for fight fans. Anticipation was high, and the atmosphere was intoxicating. Pep's fans were everywhere. Accordion player Bill Drolet was there, warming up inside the station; he would entertain fight fans all along the southwest journey. Mayor Dominick DeLucco was also on board and though he didn't want to talk politics, folks bent his ear nearly the entire trip. Thankfully, those who didn't have their rail tickets could purchase them on the train. Had that not been the case, the wait for just train tickets could have been challenging. For those not making the odyssey, the bout was broadcast on ABC and telecast on NBC.

Say It Ain't So

The only good thing about a bad memory, as every boxer understood, was that if you carried it around long enough, everything about it would change, the only exception being it would remain a bad memory. The last thing Willie Pep needed, especially at this juncture, was a poor, if not questionable, performance. Yet it happened on February 26 at Madison Square Garden. Willie Pep, Number One ranked contender, suffered a TKO loss to Lulu Perez, the fifth-ranked 126-pounder, at the 1:53 mark of the second round. The former champion, who had tried tremendously hard to regain his footing and respect in the featherweight division, faltered. The bout, scheduled for 10 rounds, was Pep's believed 190th ring contest.

Three right hands to the chin of the former champion were responsible for three visits to the canvas. Under the New York rules, three knockdowns in a single round equated to a technical knockout. Floored on his back, Pep arose at eight. A left hook followed by a right uppercut that snapped Pep's head back was a prelude to a vicious right that dropped the Hartford boxer a second time. Waiting for referee Al Berl to reach the count of eight, a dazed Pep managed to regain his footing at nine. A shoddy retreat opened the fighter up to a left hook that sent Pep back toward the ropes, before a targeted right downed the fighter for the last time. It was over.

Taking a closer look: With a minute left in the first round, Pep noticeably slowed his footwork for no apparent reason. He also started planting his feet in front of Perez like a sitting duck. He worked behind the left jab, but when an opportunity for a solid right was there, he didn't throw it. Where was the right hand? Seconds before the end of the round, Pep was at close quarters and did not throw a punch. From the gong to the first time the former champion hit the canvas in round two, he didn't throw a right hand. Why? Was he hurt? Between the first fall and second fall, he still hadn't thrown his right. He also lowered his left, leaving himself wide-open for a right. He shook his head while sitting on the canvas—an action he had taken in other bouts—and took a nine count. Again, he refused to throw a right before the final knockdown. If he wasn't injured, the actions were difficult to understand.

Uncharacteristically, Pep was peeled like an onion from the first punch forward. As if moving in slow motion, he exhibited none of the speed, power, or ring prowess he had in nearly 200 professional battles. It was as if someone dropped kryptonite into the gloves of the Superman of all featherweights. Was it possible that in a flash, inside boxing's Mecca, after a decisive victory over his previous opponent inside the same ring, Willie Pep, who spent months fighting tooth and nail because he desperately sought the return of his New York State boxing license, was struck by Father Time? Yes. Probable? No.

Beginning with the affirmative: After the fight, Dr. Vincent Nardiello, the NYSAC physician, concluded that Pep could no longer take a punch and that he would not pass him following a physical. Dr. Ira McCown, NYSAC's medical director, and Dr. Mal Stevens, NYSAC's head of the medical advisory board, believed Pep's reflexes had deteriorated to the point that he could no longer defend himself. As a result, NYSAC suspended Willie Pep indefinitely. Both Massachusetts and the NBA sanctioning bodies agreed with the suspension. Clearly, Pep had not been satisfactorily prepared for his fight with Perez, whose skills were underrated by Pep's handlers.

As for the negative: There had been no visible signs that Pep's skills had deteriorated, to the point defined by NYSAC, in any of his previous fights. The former featherweight champion had not lost a fight since June 30, 1952. He had fought 19 times since that point and won every contest. Six of the previous opponents he defeated had more victories than Lulu Perez, though none had as few losses.

As for the unexplainable shift in odds: Perez, a 6–5 favorite on the afternoon of the fight, moved to a 3–1 favorite only an hour before the battle. Then, a half-hour before the bout began, the fight went "off the boards" (meaning no more bets were taken) as a betting proposition.[31] NYSAC Commissioner Robert K. Christenberry, who attended the bout, was asked beforehand about the significance of the odds fluctuation. Claiming it was typical, he did confirm that he had spoken to both teams; consequently, the lopsided betting phenomena had also occurred during Johnny Saxton's "no-hitter" victory over Johnny Bratton in Philadelphia on February 24 and

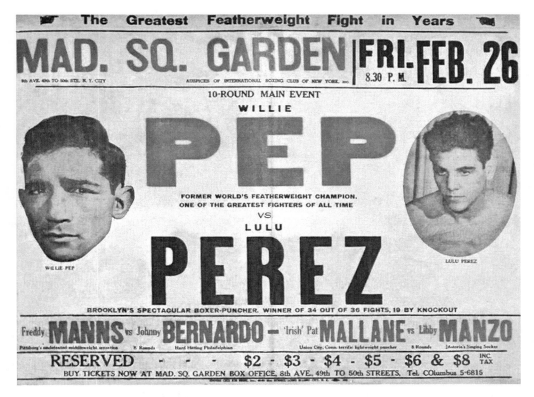

Fight poster featuring the 10-round main event at Madison Square Garden on February 26, 1954. Unfortunately, lost in the translation of this fight was that Lulu Perez had won 34 of 36 fights, 19 by knockout.

would even happen again on March 5 in New York, when Paddy DeMarco defeated favorite Jimmy Carter.[32]

After the battle, and without proof, there were rumors that Pep took a dive against Perez.[33] (Having sat down with Willie Pep and looked him in the eyes, I asked if the allegation were true: The elite fighter denied it.) Some referred to the quotes Pep made to the media before the fight as a possible motive. The former champion did state to the press that he was only boxing for the dough and that aspects of his personal life had taken a toll on his finances.[34] Which begs the question: If a fighter intended to lose a fight, would he make comments like these to the press? Not likely.

After the fight, writer Gene Ward, in his column "Inside Sports," which appeared in the *Daily News* on March 6, 1954, called the match and its conclusion "a sorry mess."[35]

The Fallout

In March, and not to anyone's surprise, Pep was dropped to the bottom of the featherweight rankings. His name became noticeably absent from the dailies. Back in Hartford during the first week of March, the former champion spent the bulk of his time with his family. Working out over at the Charter Oak Gym, he was assisting in the training of his brother Nicholas, who would turn 18 in July. Naturally, Willie couldn't resist the chance to spar with some of Pete Perone's boys. The latter's latest find was New England lightweight Graham Holmes, who sparred three rounds with Pep.

By the end of the first week in March, Viscusi was somewhat lost as to which direction he should take with Pep. It was understandable. The talented fight manager believed, as did others, that Pep's career wasn't over. But where did one go from here? Not knowing what to do next, Viscusi also started questioning his own behavior. Perhaps the timing of the battle with Perez was wrong, or maybe he should have inked Pep to another bout before Perez.[36] He was reflective, if not apologetic, in his tone. He could have given up on Willie Pep, but he did not. By the first week of April, Viscusi had a plan in place for his fighter. He would gradually increase the level of competition while evaluating his fighter's skills at the conclusion of each contest.

Even so, Willie Pep had his own calendar in mind, and he believed he was ready to fight boxer Bobby Courchesne at the Holyoke Valley Arena on April 12. Naturally, this would need NYSAC's approval, and that was subject to the results from an encephalograph, or device for recording the structure or electrical activity of the brain. However, on April 9, Willie Pep was retired by NYSAC on the advice of its medical board—the action was not binding on any other state.[37] Yet it prompted the Massachusetts Commission to withdraw their approval of Pep's match against Bobby Courchesne. Furious about the decision, Viscusi requested a copy of the medical report. Why wouldn't he be? Neither he nor Pep had any idea such a decision was impending.

In just 44 days—from Pep's battle against Perez on February 26 to the NYSAC retirement announcement that appeared in newspapers on April 10—Willie Pep went from a contender at Madison Square Garden to merely another person in a rocking chair at a retirement home. It was unconscionable treatment of an elite fighter who merited far more respect because, unlike some, he earned it.

Outside the ring, life wasn't getting any simpler for the fighter. On May 3, it was noted in the New York dailies that authorities wanted to question the fighter in regard to an incident informally labeled as the Vincent "Jim" Macri trunk murder. Macri, 48, who was a boxing fan and even fancied himself a boxer, was a former bodyguard of the notorious Albert Anastasia, of Murder Inc. fame.[38] On April 25, 1954, his body was found stuffed into the trunk of his convertible that was parked in the Bronx. Two bullet holes through the head appeared to be the cause of death. Macri's underworld connections were so complex that detectives investigating the case didn't know where to begin. Since a photograph of Macri, seated next to Willie Pep, was found in his Riverdale home, distraught detectives sought the significance, if any, between the fighter and the underworld character. The investigators—some of whom likely had their own picture taken with one or two popular fighters of the day—had already questioned dozens of individuals. They couldn't find the needle or the haystack.[39]

Back in Hartford on May 13, Pep attended the Connecticut Boxing Guild dinner in honor of Christopher "Bat" Battalino. Sitting at the dais with Battalino and Pep were three Connecticut mayors and Louis "Kid" Kaplan. Although he typically complied with these types of requests, Pep was always restless at them. Two days later, on May 15, William Papaleo, of Route 2, Box 566D, Lutz, Florida, was arrested on Center Street in Manchester, Connecticut, on a charge of speeding. His Cadillac convertible was clocked on radar at 46 miles per hour in a 30 mile an hour zone. After posting a $35 bond, Pep, who was soon leaving for Florida, gave the court permission to forfeit the bond. At the same time, Lou Viscusi was in front of the National Boxing Association in Detroit, pleading to have Pep's mandatory retirement rescinded. The matter was referred to the organization's grievance committee.

Seemingly out of nowhere, Willie Pep, tipping at 131, danced to a 10-round unanimous decision over novice Mike Tourcotte, who scaled three pounds heavier, at Hartwell Field in Mobile, Alabama.[40] For Pep, with 179 more professional bouts than his opponent, it was nothing more than a sparring session. Yet the July 24 encounter was the first headline bout in the city since prior to World War II, and Pep's first in five months. The former champion was under NYSAC's retirement ruling and the NBA's recognition of that action, but if he could find a location, as he did, and obtain the proper clearance, as he also did, then he could fight. The fight, postponed the previous day because of rain, drew a small audience.

Answering the question before you ask it: Yes, there was a strategy—or method to the madness, depending upon your perspective—being conducted by Team Pep. Knowing it would be much harder for any boxing association to maintain the position that Pep was unable to defend himself, if that fighter disproved that position through an identical circumstance, Viscusi was building his case. Each subsequent ring battle by Pep, would likely—granted the boxer could be injured in a mismatch—make it harder for both NYSAC and the NBA to hold their position.

Next, it was off to Moncton, New Brunswick, Canada, or a mere 1,638 miles as the crow flies, from Mobile, Alabama—I know what you are thinking, here we go again. It is not easy to find a territory not under supervision by both boxing boards. On August 18, inside Moncton Arena, Willie Pep, scaling at 129 or two pounds lighter than his opponent, took a 10-round unanimous decision over hometown boxer Til LeBlanc. Extraordinary speed and footwork were responsible for defeating his 24-year-old opposer.[41]

As Pep fought, Viscusi stayed in contact with NYSAC. At one point there was confusion whether Pep was retired or suspended. It was the former (for physical reasons), and the fighter could not fight in New York State until he was officially taken out of retirement. NYSAC chairman Christenberry even reminded Viscusi that this action did not prevent him from fighting in other states.

On November 1, inside the Arena at Daytona Beach, Willie Pep tipped at 128, a pound lighter than his opponent, and won a 10-round points victory over tomato can Mario "Eladio" Colon. The Puerto Rican pugilist, who lost over three times as many battles as he won, was nothing but a punching bag for the former champion.

Frustrated, bored, and with too much extra time on his hands, Willie Pep decided to take a part-time job selling used cars at Oscar & Joe, located at 166 N.W. 36th Street in Miami. No doubt being used for his celebrity status, Pep didn't seem to mind. Besides, the patina on that status had dulled a bit.

Tragedy greeted the fighter on November 3, when he learned that his cocker spaniel dog bit three-year-old Nicky DeWitt. The son of Mr. and Mrs. George DeWitt suffered a torn lip which led to the unthinkable, the child's death—doctors claimed it was a result of an anesthetic hazard. DeWitt, a nightclub comedian, was a friend and neighbor of the pugilist.

Broken up over the tragic event, Pep attempted to find solace wherever he could.

He even joined Jake LaMotta and Jerry Brandow in an act being conducted at the Black Orchid club, located at 1601 79th Street Causeway (on an island between Miami and Miami Beach). But he just couldn't get his mind off the tragic death of the neighborhood youngster.

With the holidays approaching, Pep returned to Hartford the first week of December. In addition to being with family, he would make personal appearances to fill his time and his holiday pockets. Prone to a heavy foot on the accelerator, the former champion wasn't the best at maintaining the proper speed limit while driving. On Thursday night, December 23, Pep was arrested for speeding. State Police stopped the former champion in (north) Hartford near the Wilson line. No matter where he was, he couldn't catch a break.

Ending the year on a positive note, Lou Viscusi received word from the NBA that they would grant Pep a physical examination. Should he pass, the fighter would be permitted to box in locations they governed—the fighter's examination would be conducted at Massachusetts General Hospital in Boston.

NINE

One Last Shot, 1955–1958

"A wise man will make more opportunities than he finds."—Francis Bacon

1955

W. Averill Harriman began his term as the governor of New York state on January 1, 1955. The Yale graduate, an enormous sports fan, soon named Julius Helfand as NYSAC's chairman. It was hoped that the new executive would eliminate the bad elements, in particular the criminal influences, that had crept into the sport. Also, television, which had an enormous financial impact on boxing (especially on the small venues and clubs), needed to be better managed. For example, in 1954, Dumont was televising fights on Monday night from St. Nick's Arena, ABC was also broadcasting bouts at the Eastern Parkway Arena on Monday night, Pabst Blue Ribbon was sponsoring the Wednesday evening battles on CBS, Gillette Razor Blades was behind the Friday night broadcasts by NBC, and Phillies Cigars was backing the ABC Saturday night broadcasts.[1]

In February, a month in which cupid was no stranger, Willie Pep decided to marry Miss Cynthia Regina Rhodes, of Chicago.[2] Miss Rhodes, an attractive entertainer, met the former champion while she was playing an engagement in New York. It was her first marriage and Pep's third. The civil ceremony was conducted by Joseph A. Angrisani in Hartford.[3] The maid of honor was Terrie Morin, and the best man was Rocco Presumartia. The couple planned to live at the Papaleo family home in Hartford. However, it wasn't long before both realized that life was a bit more challenging than anticipated. On April 25, Willie Pep filed for divorce in court at Tampa, Florida.[4]

The Long Road Back

Finally, on February 27, the National Boxing Association reinstated Willie Pep. Passing an exhaustive physical and mental examination in Boston, the fighter was no longer barred in the 32 states and 16 cities under the organization's umbrella. Pep, who remained retired by NYSAC, had been restricted in his fight options.[5] As Viscusi had hoped, the fighter's three victories in territories not covered by the ban did play into the decision.

It was boxing at the State Armory in Bennington, Vermont, on Friday, March 11, 1955, and the feature event was Willie Pep (billed as Former World's Champ, World

Foremost Boxer) versus Herman Gary (Myrel Olmstead, see Appendix and Chapter Notes). For $1.50, you got in the door (General Admission), and for 50 cents more you could sit ringside. The undercard featured three wrestling matches. About 500 dedicated Bennington fight fans turned out for the event, far less than anticipated. Scaling at 129, three pounds lighter than his opponent, Willie Pep took the 10-round decision. It was Bennington's first professional bout in eight years. Fighting defensively, Pep's opponent did manage a solid sixth round and even blackened Pep's eye.[6]

Wanting to get Pep a set-up bout before he headed west to face the challenging Gil Cadilli, Viscusi booked his fighter for 10 rounds at the Holyoke Arena on March 22. His opponent—and it wasn't easy to find a fighter that fit the bill—was Brooklyn boxer Charlie Titone. Pep, tipping at 130, captured a 10-round unanimous decision over Titone, who scaled at 127½. A crowd of over 1,100 fans turned out to watch the former champion display his ring magic. There were no knockdowns.[7]

After Pep's battle with Titone, both he and Bill Gore immediately returned to Hartford to take a United Airlines flight the next morning to the West Coast. Viscusi had inked his fighter to a battle at Parks Air Force Base in Dublin, California. His opponent was Gilbert Cadilli, a solid featherweight out of Los Angeles who was scouted by many, including Jack Kearns and Babe McCoy, prior to the fighter's induction into the army. Currently handled by Sid Flaherty, Bobo Olson's manager, Cadilli still appeared to have a promising future. As a recruiting event, the bout attracted an enthusiastic audience estimated at 3,000 Air Force men. When it was over, Viscusi was questioning himself as to why he agreed to the contest.

Scaling to a pound advantage at 128, Willie Pep lost an exceedingly close and disputed 10-round split decision to Gilbert Cadilli. While most of the unofficial scorecards saw it Pep, it was not to be. The former champion, having clearly outshined his opposer in the early rounds, was shocked by the verdict; moreover, most saw it 8–2 in favor of the elite boxer. In the fourth round, a robust Cadilli right opened a nasty cut over Pep's right eye, and it slowed the former champion throughout the battle—each time Gore closed the cut, it was reopened. The laceration also created the impression that the Hartford boxer was far more injured than he was.[8]

The disparity in scoring prompted a letter from State Athletic Commissioner Joe Phillips to State Attorney General Edmund Brown, asking for a ruling on whether the fight could be investigated and how to proceed. The verdict prompted immediate disputation and action from a national television audience—the switchboards filled with phone calls. Willie Pep, an elite fighter, not to mention former champion, deserved a respectable decision.

After returning to Hartford long enough to attend a few events, Pep headed to Tampa, Florida, to file his divorce suit on April 25. The couple had separated on April 11. It wasn't long before Pep learned that he had been signed for a rematch against Gil Cadilli on May 18 in Detroit. Wanting a chance to acquit himself from the loss, Pep was delighted by the news—by the way, some of the ring officials associated with that event were fired.

Scaling at 128¾ or over two pounds heavier than his adversary, Willie Pep seized a 10-round unanimous decision over Gil Cadilli. Conducting a brilliant performance that was seen on national television and by a small house of over 700 spectators, Pep easily countered Cadilli's assaults. Cadilli paid the price by losing rounds quickly and taking a beating above the shoulders—his nose began to bleed in the eighth round.

Willie Pep split a pair of back-to-back ring battles against the popular Gil Cadilli (left) in 1955. In Pep's first bout of 1958, he lost a 10-round decision to the talented Tommy Tibbs (right).

The former champion delivered solid blows, nevertheless they were not powerful enough to drop his opposer.

Outside the ring, Pep was filming *The Phil Silvers Show*, a television pilot that hoped to air in the fall on CBS. The show starred Phil Silvers as Master Sergeant Ernest G. Bilko, the officer in charge of a platoon that included Pep and fellow boxers Dan Bucceroni, Walter Cartier, and Frankie Ryff—only Cartier made the cast. While the television pilot was never shown, 143 other episodes of the show were broadcast.

When hub promoter Sam Silverman needed a substitute battle for his scheduled bout between Jimmy Carter and Walter Smith, he called Lou Viscusi. Willie Pep was quickly matched with local fighter Joey Cam at Boston Arena on June 1—the latter was once one of Pep's students. As the inaugural show for *Wednesday Night Fights* on ABC (television and radio)—the show previously aired on CBS—the exposure was good, as was the revenue: Pep would grab 25 percent of the net gate, to Cam's 20 percent, and both fighters picked up $4,000 from the television proceeds.

Opening a deep inch-and-a-half cut over Cam's left eye midway through the third round, Pep witnessed the damage and sensed what it meant: It was over.

Scheduled for ten rounds, the fight would never make it that far. Refusing to continue to inflict more harm to his opponent, Pep danced away the remainder of the round before the fight was stopped. The nearly 2,500 fans in attendance, aware of Pep's sportsmanship, applauded the veteran's actions as well as the verdict.[9]

Heading south to Miami Beach, Willie Pep, scaling at 128¼, dominated Mickey Mars, who tipped at 126, before scoring a technical knockout victory 52 seconds into the seventh session. The fight was scheduled for 10 rounds, but few of the over 2,000 fight fans at the Auditorium thought it would go the distance. The former champion bedazzled the young Ohioan before leaving him nearly collapsed in a corner. Referee Billy Regan had little choice but to stop the bout.[10]

There was never a shortage of charitable events, both in and out of the ring, for a champion such as Willie Pep. When the Bridgeport Police Department Benevolent [Society] wanted him to be part of a boxing program on July 12, the former champion complied.

Returning to Hartford, Pep trained at Sam Gulino's Main Street Gym. Traveling by car from his home in Florida, Bill Gore joined Pep the first week of July. For Pep, his morning run over in Keney Park brought back a flood of memories. Connecticut fight fans had always treated him fairly, and he appreciated it. Having won *essentially* all six of his ring battles in 1955, he was confident entering his 200th professional bout.

At Hedges Stadium (Harding Field) in Bridgeport, Willie Pep, scaling at 130½, captured a 10-round decision over Hector Rodriguez, who tipped three pounds lighter. Over 7,500 spectators turned out to watch Pep capture all 10 rounds, or at least that's how most, including referee Muravnick, saw it. Less than a handful of punches by Rodriguez managed to penetrate Pep's force field. Late in the eighth round, the former champion staggered his adversary with a left hook, but there simply wasn't enough time to finish the job. After the victory, Pep headed back to Florida.

Working out in the gym at Miami Beach the last week of August, Pep learned he was returning to Connecticut. Viscusi signed him to a flood relief bout promoted by the Connecticut Boxing Guild, on September 13 at the State Theater in Hartford. All the proceeds of the battle went to the American Red Cross. As it was all about the cause, and not about him, his opponent was of little concern. Jimmy Ithia of New York, who had fewer than 25 professional fights' worth of experience, ended up facing Pep.

Countenance shredded and bleeding from the nose and mouth, Jimmy Ithia had his evening concluded at the 1:54 mark of the sixth round. Outclassed, but certainly not out of courage, Ithia appeared grateful when Guest Referee Harry Kessler stepped forward to wave off the fight. Pep, scaling at 129¾, almost four pounds heavier than his opposer, looked fabulous in front of a small but enthusiastic crowd of over 1,200 spectators. With slight cuts over both eyes, the former champion admitted that ring rust had collected over the past two months. Truthfully, the fans didn't care, they were just happy to see him.

The former champion had two weeks to prepare for his battle against Henry Gault at the Valley Arena in Holyoke. Hailing from Spartanburg, South Carolina, William Henry "Pappy" Gault was a good boxer. The beloved pugilist won the 1948 National Golden Gloves flyweight championship before turning pro the same year. Winning over three times as many battles as he lost, Gault was on the downside of a solid career. Confident during the early rounds of his bout with Pep, Gault gradually lost his rhythm. Later, he was forced into a defensive mode while absorbing ceaseless punishment from the former champion's left jab. Scaling at 131, six pounds heavier than his adversary, Pep sailed to a 10-round unanimous decision in front of over 1,000 avid fight fans on September 27.

As the seventh-largest city in Massachusetts, Brockton was referred to as the "City of Champions," thanks primarily to Rocky Marciano.[11] Thrilled to put his skills on display at the Maple Arena in Brockton, Willie Pep, scaling at 129½, a pound heavier than his opposer, captured a 10-round unanimous decision over the familiar face of Charley Titone. The 26-year-old Brooklyn fighter, who lost to Pep in March, was dazzled once again by the bobbing, ducking, jabbing, and hooking ways of his opponent, as were the 900 fans in attendance. There were no knockdowns; however, Titone parked two shiners on Pep's optics.

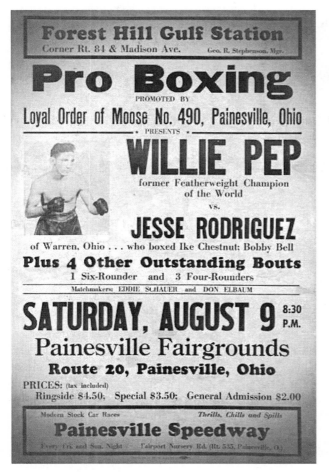

A poster from Willie Pep's bout against Jesse Rodriguez on August 9, 1958. The former champion was victorious via a 10-round decision. Matchmakers for the event were Eddie Schauer and Don Elbaum.

Criticized for greeting more stiffs than a mortician, Pep was pressing Viscusi hard for a big money fight. The manager was hoping to land a date for his fighter against Carmelo Costa, the fourth-ranked contender, but the IBC thought otherwise. So Viscusi went to New York to greet autocrat Jim Norris and flush out an opportunity. Surfacing for Pep was a possible date in Miami against Costa. The light at the end of the tunnel appeared lit, so all the former champion needed to do was to reach it.

In Tampa, Pep began training during the second week in November, for an as-yet-undetermined opponent. Following his Armory contest the final week of the month, he would head to Houston. Both of these bouts, he hoped, were nothing more than warm-ups for a potential television bout against Costa on December 28 at Miami Beach. Having made his home in Florida for most of the last decade, he hoped to make Tampa his headquarters.[12]

Back in the ring against "Pappy" Gault, this time at the Fort Homer Hesterly Armory in Tampa on November 29, Willie Pep, scaling at 127½, 3½ pounds heavier than his opposer, picked up a 10-round unanimous decision. It wasn't even close as Pep took every round. There were no knockdowns.[13] It was a redundant pairing, but Pep needed the work, and it was a benefit program.

Heading west, Willie Pep grabbed a fourth-round knockout over Leo Carter at the Auditorium in Houston. Neither of these bouts was particularly useful in preparing the former champion for a ranked fighter such as Costa, but such it was.

Wait, That Doesn't Look Like Costa

Andy Arel wasn't Carmelo Costa. The pledge Viscusi thought he had fell through—word was that promoter Chris Dundee, acting as a go-between, couldn't make it happen.[14] Resembling Billy Graham (the boxer, not the evangelist), Arel was a talented southpaw pugilist, not to mention one of Pep's former sparring partners.[15]

On December 28, inside the Auditorium in Miami Beach, Willie Pep, tipping at 128 or six pounds lighter than his opponent, took a 10round unanimous decision over Andy Arel. In front of a sold-out house (2,933 fans) and a national television audience, Pep had his way against the southpaw. Arel, who only won one round, did manage to open a cut over Pep's left eye in the ninth term, but that was the extent of the damage—later, the laceration required four stitches to close. For Pep, the year didn't end the way he expected, but he learned a long time ago not to put too much faith in the fight game.

Of 13 battles in 1955, Willie Pep officially added 12 victories and one loss to his resume. While 10 of his opponents had winning records, eight had fewer than 30 professional fights.

1956

Sandy Saddler couldn't escape the memories, and he wanted to. Not yet 30 years old, the lean and extraordinarily talented pugilist believed Willie Pep was the reason he was unpopular with fans. Yep, Pep had been badmouthing him by calling him a dirty fighter. That equated to a symphony of boos that welcomed Saddler whenever, and wherever, he entered a ring. The champion was quick to remind folks that it was Pep who was the unscrupulous pugilist, and that he only resorted to unprincipled tactics defend himself. It wasn't , but there was also not a whole lot he could do about it. Countering, Lou Viscusi found it ironic that Pep wasn't greeted in the same manner.

Granted, Sandy Saddler was on top of the mountain, with no clear contender in sight, and those looking up included: Hogan "Kid" Bassey (Nigeria), Carmelo Costa, Teddy "Red Top" Davis, Flash Elorde (Philippines), Ray Famechon (France), Fred Galiana (Spain), Shigeji Kaneko (Japan), Ciro Morasen, Willie Pep, and Lauro Salas (Mexico).

Lou Viscusi was trying hard to land two title bouts. The first was for lightweight Joe Brown, followed by Willie Pep—the former more likely than the latter. Everyone in the fight game understood that Team Pep wanted another shot at Saddler, yet it was doubtful considering the champion's views.

Training at the Tampa Boxing Club Gym, Willie Pep was preparing for his first fight of the year. His opponent was Mexican Kid Campeche, a novice pug who had defeated just one fighter with over 20 victories. Even though the bout was a bit insulting to an elite fighter such as Pep, he kept his mouth shut for a reason. Scheduled for 10 rounds at Fort Homer Hesterly Armory on March 13, the five-bout card was promoted by Lou Viscusi. Tickets were scaled at $1, $2, and $3.

Tipping at 127, a pound lighter than his opponent, Willie Pep comfortably defeated Kid Campeche via a 10-round unanimous decision. While the former champion danced and evaded his adversary, little else happened. No matter how hard the audience tried to will something significant to occur, it never did. There were no knockdowns and few solid punches. Nevertheless, the over 1,100 in attendance seemed satisfied.[16]

Distracting the former champion from the task at hand were persistent press inquiries about his questioning in the Vincent Macri affair. Pep, who had been interrogated by a Bronx investigator regarding his association, was believed a target for additional questioning. Another photograph found in Macri's home was said to be the impetus for another round of cross-examination. This photograph showed Pep, Macri, and a man identified as Johnny Roberts (alias Robilotto), who was a material witness in the murder of Willie Moretti at Cliffside, New Jersey.

There were claims that Vincent and Benedicto Macri handled big bets on certain fights, including those held in Madison Square Garden. Macri's body was found in the trunk of a convertible parked in the east Bronx on April 25, 1954, and a week after that, Benedicto disappeared. Both brothers, according to some, were witnesses before the grand jury that indicted Alfred Anastasia, an influential player with Murder Incorporated.[17] Viscusi continued to remind the hungry press that Pep, like many other boxing champions, routinely posed for thousands of photographs with fans.[18] Thousands.

On April 5, Willie Pep met with State Attorney George A. Brautigam at the courthouse in Miami. Lawyer Morton Rothenberg appeared with the former champion. At the conclusion of the 75-minute meeting, Rothenberg confirmed that Pep answered all the questions and disclosed what information he knew. This, Brautigam believed, would finally put the matter to rest.

Willie Pep headed to Beaumont, Texas, for a scheduled 10-round competition at the Sportatorium against bantamweight Buddy Baggett. It was a long way to travel to meet a boxer who hadn't won a ring contest since 1953, but if you had to end a career—which Baggett was doing his best to do—then meeting an elite fighter such as Pep was the perfect conclusion.

Scaling at 127, two pounds heavier than his opposer, Willie Pep soared to a unanimous decision over Buddy Baggett on March 27. It was Pep's second straight victory over an opponent with a losing record—as a matter of fact, three of his last four ring opponents had losing records. But before he could criticize Viscusi, he caught wind of some good news: The day after the fight, Willie Pep climbed back into *The Ring* featherweight rankings for the first time since 1954. He was now ranked tenth.

No sooner had the ink dried on the rankings when Tampa promoter Jimmy Donofrio started talking about a fifth fight between Sandy Saddler and Willie Pep. The event would be held at Al Lopez Field in Tampa on April 24. The promoter even stated that he offered $25,000 to Saddler's camp. Yet Charley Johnston, Saddler's manager, knew nothing about it—a typical response. However, he did confirm that $100,000 might be a better starting point. Regardless of what anybody thought, it certainly ignited some interest. Even if Lou Viscusi liked the idea, the timing was wrong and there were many logistical issues. The crafty fight manager realized Pep would be better off battling a ranked fighter first, then Saddler, not to mention that the Tampa television market for boxing wasn't established.[19]

On April 1, Willie Pep, always in a hurry to get somewhere, was arrested for speeding on Memorial Highway in Tampa. The 33-year-old was charged with going 50 miles an hour in a 30-miles-per-hour zone. As a result, Pep got a suspended fine of $15 on the charge in municipal court on April 3. At this time, Pep gave his address as the Bay View Hotel at 208 Jackson Street in Tampa.[20] Unfortunately, it wasn't an April Fools' Day prank.

Arriving in Hartford on April 10, Willie Pep was putting the final touches on his training over at the Main Street Gym. Working with sparring partner Aldo Menti, the former champion was looking forward to his battle against southpaw Jackie Blair. The April 17 bout would take place at the State Theatre. A mere 11 fights, as it would prove, from ending his career, Blair's skills were fading—the fighter last met Pep back on May 13, 1953. Promoted by Mushky Salow, Pep's former fight manager, the show was a (B'Nai B'Rith) benefit program.[21]

Scaling at 130, two pounds lighter than his opponent, Willie Pep captured a 10-round points victory over Jackie Blair. Promoted as the former champion's 200th professional victory, which was subject to interpretation, it drew a crowd of about 1,500 fight fans. In a one-sided fight, Pep successfully countered every offensive attack by his Texas opposer. Most saw it a clean sweep for the Hartford legend in rounds, but referee Red Moffett saw it nine rounds for Pep with one even. The former champion turned on the heat early, captured a majority of rounds, and paced himself until the finish.

Well, April 24, 1956, came and went, and the fifth meeting between Sandy Saddler and Willie Pep never happened. James O. Donofrio, 45, the man behind the Tampa offer, was denied an alcohol license (often an indicator that future licenses in all forms could be difficult to obtain) on May 29, because of a New York conviction.[22] For all intents and purposes, one of the greatest rivalries in professional sports, Saddler v. Pep, was over.[23] Yet Lou Viscusi never stopped listening to offers—it was the carrot in front of the horse, and he knew it. Boxing, like the stock market, thrived on speculation.

As for Saddler, he took seven battles in 1955, won five (Lulu Perez, Teddy Davis [Title defense], Kenny Davis, Shigeji Kaneko, and Dave Gallardo) and lost two (Joey Lopes and Flash Elorde). With over 150 professional battles behind him, Sandy Saddler fought only three battles in 1956: He defended his title against Flash Elorde, defeated George Monroe, then lost to Connecticut boxer Larry Boardman. Pep, having seen Saddler's loss to Boardman, thought the champion looked tired and was no longer strong enough to effectively use his short-armed tactics.

On May 16, boxing promoter Jimmy Parks wired a $25,000 guarantee to Sandy Saddler for a title fight, at San Antonio in July or August, against Willie Pep. Naturally, the offer was contingent on Pep being victorious over Manuel Armenteros in Park's upcoming promotion on May 22. Parks and Viscusi, were about 99 percent certain that Saddler wouldn't bite on the offer. However, Viscusi couldn't take a chance. Parks even backed his promotion with a contingent of business associations. Viscusi took the bait and inked Pep to meet Armenteros. But there was more behind it. Back in 1953, Lou Viscusi began exhibiting interest in the Texas boxing market. Hoping to establish credentials and contacts, he was signing more and more of his fighters into viable markets across the state.

Tipping at 128, three pounds heavier than his adversary, Willie Pep captured a technical knockout victory over Manuel Armenteros. The Cuban-born fighter was unable to answer the bell for the seventh round due to a bad cut inside his mouth. Slicing his adversary up like a Thanksgiving turkey, Pep begged the referee twice to stop the fight; it should have been stopped in the fifth round. Unfortunately, Pep sustained an eye injury that would sideline him for a brief period. Rather than staying in Texas and taking a fight in Corpus Christi, he returned to Florida.

It was good to be back home, even if summer, along with the hot weather, was approaching. Pep filled his time with family obligations and appearances, as his eye healed. For example, he headed over to Orlando on June 6, to make an appearance at the Turf Club at Seminole Park Raceway. The club was co-owned by Chicago Bears running back Rick Casares, who few realized was once a Golden Gloves boxing champion. Casares, who led the NFL in rushing with 235 carries for 1,126 yards in 1956, also packed a helluva punch. After an overnight stay in Orlando, Pep headed back to Tampa.

There are times in boxing when you have to shake things up a bit. You know, hurl a ridiculous challenge into the tree of opportunity to see what, if anything, falls out. Understanding this, Willie Pep sent a challenge to Larry Boardman, the lightweight sensation from Marlborough (Connecticut), who had recently beaten Sandy Saddler. (Granted it had tinges of desperation surrounding it even if it wasn't meant that way.) Without question, the popular match, if accepted, would be conducted in Connecticut. Having sparred with Boardman in Miami, Pep felt he could be competitive. Contrary to his position: Lou Viscusi purposely avoided matching Pep with lightweights (anyone recall Sammy Angott?), and Bill Gore believed Boardman was far too strong for Pep—the trainer having witnessed Boardman's defeat of Saddler. Well, the challenge picked up some press, which didn't hurt the former champion. But it died as fast as it arrived. And it was a good thing, as Larry Boardman's career was on fire and he looked unbeatable.[24]

If it was good enough strategy for Jimmy Parks to pull on Lou Viscusi, then certainly promoter Chris Dundee could do the same. It was the Miami promoter's turn to offer Sandy Saddler $25,000 to defend his title against Willie Pep, in late August. If— here comes the contingency that always accompanied the offer—Pep defeated Russell Tague at the Miami Beach Auditorium on June 19. Pep, a 3–1 favorite, wasn't worried about Tague—he had training togs in his locker older than the Iowa farm boy.

Tipping at 130½, 2½ pounds heavier than his antagonist, Willie Pep grabbed a unanimous 10-round decision over Russell Tague. Sailing through the first five rounds, Pep was enjoying the picnic until Tague found his distance and began scoring. An overhand right caught Pep's eye solidly in the sixth round and began the blood flow—later it required three stitches. After the sixth and seventh terms, some thought they might be seeing an upset. However, Pep returned to form in the eighth round and finished strong. To little surprise, Dundee's offer to Sandy Saddler was refused.[25]

Taking a few weeks to heal his exasperating eye wound, Pep headed to Lawton, Oklahoma, on July 1. He was scheduled to meet Hector "Baby Face" Bacquettes, over 10 rounds, on July 4 at Roosevelt Stadium. Anticipating a strong turnout, promoter Bob Lewis was optimistic about the match. But just in case, he obtained the services of Max Baer, the legendary heavyweight, to referee the main event.

Nobody handled a press conference like Willie Pep. Routinely asked the same questions by reporters, Pep often gave the same pitch. He reminded them that: he had over 200 victories, sought another title shot before retirement, and had those winning streaks (62 straight victories, outpointing Chalky Wright in number 54, and 72 straight victories after the loss to Sammy Angott). His next opponent was always tough, and everyone was after him "to make a name for themselves" or enhance their credibility. During this "dog and pony show," Pep found moments to kid with referee Max Baer. Playing off Baer during a press conference made the trip enjoyable for both former champions. That said—and there's always a "that said," isn't there—he was anxious to return home to Florida.

Scaling at 130, about four pounds lighter than his opposer, Willie Pep delivered a fifth-round technical knockout victory over Hector "Baby Face" Bacquettes. Outclassing his opposer, Pep put on a defensive display in front of an estimated 300 spectators.

On August 24, 1956, Joe "Old Bones" Brown, managed by Lou Viscusi, took a 15-round split decision victory over Wallace "Bud" Smith at the Municipal Auditorium in New Orleans and won the NBA and *The Ring* World Lightweight Championship. For the crafty ring manager, it was his second world champion.

Viscusi, or "Mr. Boxing" if you will, added much to the rich history of the Tampa Bay area, and he wanted to do even more. He wanted to drop more shows into the Armory, build the market base, and then attach television broadcasts. And he hoped to duplicate the effort in Texas. For the past few months, he had been working over in Houston, and it looked like the experience was paying dividends. With elite boxers under his wing, he doubled his leverage and intended to use it to his benefit.

While Pep was home healing and tending to his family affairs, Viscusi spent a considerable amount of time with Joe Brown. Obviously, he hadn't forgotten about Pep or his pursuit of another title. As a matter of fact, he presented to the National Boxing Association an idea for a featherweight tournament, which would include Pep, to be held in Houston. It was no secret that Viscusi was having trouble finding opponents for the former champion.[26]

In September, William Papaleo's divorce from Cynthia Regina Papaleo was granted in Hillsborough County.[27] Gabriel García Márquez once said, "nothing in this world was more difficult than love." It has always seemed particularly true when applied to nonpareil pugilists.

Tending to a couple of business ventures, including hosting a daily Happy Hour from 3:00 to 7:00 p.m. at Sammy Paxton's Coral Club on 412 Tampa Street, Willie Pep was enjoying his leisure time—if the former champion was getting a cut of the 55-cent cocktails, he was keeping quiet. However, Pep's inactivity on the boxing circuit sparked rumors of his retirement. There was no question that the bursitis in his arms was bugging him, as was the post-fight ritual of "lacing up his lids." But a boxer, as everyone understood, was always one good offer from reentering the ring.

In December, Pep and Al Pardo hosted guests inside the La Paix Room of the

Marseilles Hotel. Hey, if you want to meet folks, what better way? The nine-story hotel, built in 1947, was an oceanfront gem at 1741 Collins Avenue. As a major attraction in the heart of South Beach, it attracted a passionate clientele. Additionally, Pep was believed to have an interest in the Bancroft Hotel Cocktail Lounge, now called "Willie Pep's Crown Lounge," which was also along Collins Avenue. Having fun, the fighter admitted he hadn't trained since July.[28]

1957

The silence was deafening. Eleven months had passed since Sandy Saddler defended his featherweight title. Was Saddler done? His last defense was against Flash Elorde at San Francisco back on January 18, 1956, and his last ring battle was his 10-round loss to Larry Boardman in Boston on April 14. According to his management, he was recovering from injuries sustained in an automobile (taxicab) accident. Most thought otherwise; incidentally, word was that his eyesight was failing. With little choice, the NBA stripped Saddler of his feather crown on January 16 (NYSAC had yet to take action against him for his inactivity). Sandy Saddler, 30, was officially retired on January 22, 1957. Having made his pro debut back in 1944, the lanky champion had fought 162 professional bouts, winning 144, losing 16, and drawing 2. His 103 knockouts were impressive enough to put among the all-time leaders. As an elite pugilist, he had nothing left to prove.

Sensing Saddler's retirement, Willie Pep, 33, underwent a left elbow operation in Hollywood, Florida, on January 22. Cartilage and bone chips were removed during an almost two-hour operation. Admitting that he hadn't been able to extend his left arm for about two years, Pep hoped to regain his flexibility and become more competitive.

By March, rumors flew that Willie Pep would soon return to the ring. Viscusi was working on matching his fighter against Henry "Pappy" Gault at Florence, South Carolina. However, later conversations with promoter L. Glenn "Shep" Shepperd led to a pairing with Cesar Morales on April 23 at the War Memorial Auditorium in Fort Lauderdale. The show, sponsored by the Broward County Mental Health Association, also included two guest referees, Petey Sarron and Joey Maxim—the former handled Pep's bout. Tickets were scaled at $3.50 (ringside), $2.50 (reserved), and $1.25 (general admission).

Making his first appearance in ten months, the former champion conducted a clinic in front of over 1,100 spectators. Any doubts concerning the condition of his left elbow—his five-inch scar was evident to everyone ringside—were dismissed. Seeing how he utilized his complete arsenal, it was clear to everyone that Pep could deliver his opponent at will, but instead opted for a solid 10-round workout. It was the Pep of old—he twirled Morales around so fast that the fighter lost his balance and dropped to his bottom. Scaling at 130, about two pounds lighter than his opponent, Willie Pep took a 10-round unanimous decision over Cesar Morales. It was an outstanding display.

Unbeknownst to many were the conditions that surrounded the fight. Understanding that life had been a challenge for the fight promoter, Pep signed an open contract for one dollar.[29] After the fight, and in a display of empathy, the former champion put his arm around "Shep," winked, and told him to pay him when he could. There were times when Pep's heart was far bigger than the ring.

Pep was next off to Florence, South Carolina. There the Florence Boxing Club matched the former champion against tomato can Manny Castro at Memorial Stadium on May 10. The scheduled 10-round event, which was expected to draw a large audience, was a pre-race attraction for the Rebel 300-mile convertible automobile race at nearby Darlington raceway. Pep, no stranger to a heavy accelerator, was thrilled when he met and had his picture taken with Curtis Turner, Herb Thomas, Fonty Flock, and Buck Baker.

Tipping at 130, a lone pound under the weight of his antagonist, Willie Pep boxed his way to a 10-round unanimous decision over Mexican Manny Castro. Dull and uneventful, the fight took place in front of one of the smallest gates in Pep's career—about 300 fans turned out. Castro, who fought Pep back in 1952, was no match. Despite the apparent lack of interest and obvious disappointment of promoters Tommy Griffin and Jimmy Calcutt, it was a well-conducted promotion.

The most difficult part of the evening for the former champion was after the fight. There was no roar of the crowd after his victory, no folks waiting outside the dressing room for a glimpse of the elite fighter, and no autographs to sign. Reminding him of the old days, or those late evenings outside Foot Guard Hall in Hartford, it was a moment he didn't wanted to recall but couldn't avoid. While it was very difficult for Pep, he truly believed he had one more run left in him.

With his manager in Texas working with heavyweight Roy Harris, Pep anticipated a trip to "The Lonestar State." He was right. Viscusi, supporting a new boxing promotion team (Bob Capocy and Sam Ventura), inked Pep for another 10-rounder against Manny Castro. However, this time it was at the County Coliseum in El Paso. As one of Angelo Dundee's boxers, Castro, in the minds of many (but not Dundee), was vastly overrated. Arriving on July 12, Pep conducted some business with Viscusi before sparring with Jake Martinez and Pete Melendez at the El Paso Boxing Club. With both boxers tipping at 128 pounds, Pep outshined a pathetic looking Manny Castro to capture a 10-round unanimous decision. To the 1,500 spectators on hand, who booed more than they clapped, it was little more than an exhibition.

Traveling 750 miles east to Houston, Willie Pep agreed to meet Russell Tague over 10 rounds at the Sam Houston Coliseum on July 23. One of the reasons he agreed to meet his familiar opposer was that 10 percent of the gate was going to the Babe Zaharias Cancer Fund. Yet another was Tague's attitude. Believing he was an Iowa version of Johnny Kilbane, the pug uncharacteristically criticized the former champion after their June 19, 1956 battle.[30]

Piling up a large lead, Pep thought the rest of the battle would be easy. It wasn't. Tague suddenly found his distance and began to connect, so Pep was forced to keep his dancing shoes on in order to win.[31] Scaling at 131, a two-pound disadvantage, Willie Pep nabbed a unanimous decision (once again) over Russell Tague—the former champion was given all ten rounds by referee Ernie Ebb. There were no knockdowns, but Pep believed he might have injured his thumb. Cleveland Williams also picked up a knockout victory on the undercard.

Back in Tampa, Pep was looking to expand his business enterprises.[32] Having an interest in the hospitality industry, he was intrigued by the cocktail lounge environment. Frank Fungie, who used to be a fighter, owned a business called Fungie's, located at 1601 Grand Central, across the Hillsborough River from downtown Tampa. When the former champion expressed interest in the joint, Fungie sold it to him. (The Grand Opening of Willie Pep's Little Club took place on November 15 and featured a "Fabulous Parisian Review.")[33]

What Willie Pep didn't need was more drama in his life, yet it always managed to find him. Willie Pep and eight others were arrested on charges of illegal gambling in Tampa on August 10. All nine persons forfeited $15 bonds in city court. Two days later, Pep learned of the passing of Chalky Wright, 45. The former featherweight champion had accidentally drowned in his mother's home after falling in the bathtub. Like always, or so it seemed, the bad news continued. On September 4, it was learned that Willie Pep and Joe Russo, a nightclub musician, were wanted for questioning in the shooting of a woman. No formal arrest orders were made for either man. Mrs. Betty Martin, who was initially reluctant to provide information to detectives, was shot in the left leg while in her apartment—her condition was not serious.[34] She stated she was involved in the arrest of the two in a previous gambling case (see above). The police placed a hold order on the injured woman. Pep was reported to be at his home in Connecticut.[35] On September 5, Mrs. Betty Martin retracted an accusation that Pep had shot her in the left leg. Pep was immediately cleared by Tampa police, who had wanted him for questioning.

When it rains, it pours. Willie Pep was charged with reckless driving on November 21, after his car struck and injured John M. Cameron, an 83-year-old pedestrian. Cameron, who was struck by Pep's car and knocked 19 feet, was taken to Tampa Hospital with multiple injuries, and his condition was described as "serious." According to Tampa police, Pep was traveling at approximately 12 miles an hour over the 25-mile-an-hour speed limit. As bad news travels faster than good, it didn't take long for folks to hear about the incidents.

Boston promoter Sam Silverman called Lou Viscusi and told him it was time for Willie Pep to head back to the Northeast. Viscusi agreed and booked Pep for a 10-round battle against Jimmy Connors, of New Bedford, at Boston Gardens on December 17. Connors, who was undefeated, was simply destroying opponents such as Pat McCarthy, Jr., and Pappy Gault.[36] Pep, who believed that if he didn't have bad luck, he would have no luck at all (or at least in Florida), couldn't wait to head to Boston (December 12).

For four rounds, it remained a close battle.[37] Bill Gore told his fighter to step it up in the fifth frame, and that was when Pep took control with the left jab. In the eighth round, the former champion dropped Connors to a six count. It was a warning sign to the youngster, who backed off a bit. In the final frame, Pep took Connors to the ropes and unloaded a magazine before spinning him through the cords—it was ruled a knockdown. Connors was dazed, and Pep knew it, so the former champion backed off. The crowd of over 5,000 fight fans smelled a knockout, but in retrospect many were happy it didn't happen—as a matter of fact, Pep was cheered for his mercy. Tipping at 131, or four pounds heavier than his young adversary, Willie Pep took the 10-round unanimous decision over Jimmy Connors. A knockout would have been far too embarrassing for the youngster—Merry Christmas, Mr. Connors.[38]

As for a holiday wish: Willie Pep was hoping for a run of good luck.[39]

1958

There was solace in simplicity. However, exhilaration, not to mention wealth, were seldom byproducts. For some, such as Willie Pep, the euphoria was what fueled his existence, or so it seemed. The year opened with a considerable number of open issues facing the former champion both in and out of a boxing ring. Foremost was a final run at recapturing the featherweight championship.

The title belonged to Nigerian boxer Hogan "Kid" Bassey.[40] After discussing the matter with Viscusi and Gore, the decision was that the best path to the title was through New England—Pep still faced distractions, such as the Macri case, in New York. Viscusi believed promoter Sam Silverman could get Pep to Bassey. Silverman went right at the issue by offering Bassey's American agent a $35,000 guarantee or 40 percent of the gate, plus ancillary rights (television and radio, estimated at 40 percent of what could be $50,000). The prerequisite was that Pep beat Tommy Tibbs in Boston on January 14. Should Pep fail, Silverman believed his fallback position was to match Tibbs with Bassey—the key being Silverman establishing a relationship with Bassey.[41]

Scaling at 130, a pound less than his adversary, Willie Pep lost—okay, was robbed of—a close split decision to Tommy Tibbs, a ranked lightweight. It happened at the Mechanics Building in Boston. Tibbs, a 23-year-old newsboy from the hub, broke Pep's 21-bout unbeaten streak thanks to relentless pursuit and punching accuracy.[42] Unlike most of Pep's previous opposers, he was able to catch the former champion and deliver damage. Pep, who believed he won the fight, was annoyed by the constant yelling from his opposer's corner along with the referee's warning not to spin Tibbs.[43] Afterwards, Pep took home about $3,200, while Tibbs pocketed $2,000.[44] Added to the list of those who defeated Willie Pep—Sammy Angott, Gil Cadilli (disputed), Tommy Collins, Lulu Perez, and Sandy Saddler—was the name Tommy Tibbs. Now what?

A Dozen Bouts to Bassey

As Willie Pep returned to Florida, his team worked out a plan for the fighter to reach Hogan "Kid" Bassey by September—if Bassey still had the title. Taking time off, Pep was spotted at the horse track and conducting business at his Little Club on Grand Central in Tampa. Fast women and slow horses, even he admitted, were always his downfall.[45] He received word on February 12, that his mother, Mary Papaleo, 56, had suffered minor injuries when she was struck by an automobile near her home. It appeared to be a minor incident, and no arrests were made. Regardless, Pep headed back to Hartford and planned once again to work out of the city and train at the Main Street Gym.[46]

With Saddler out of the way, Pep wanted to get back between the ropes. Understanding that his ring generalship, and not his speed or punching power, could carry him to victory, he was optimistic that Viscusi, with the assistance of Jim Higgins, could put him on a path toward the title.[47] Meantime, his son William Papaleo, Jr., 13, dropped a three-rounder on Saturday, March 15. The event was part of the weekly PAL boxing matches that were being broadcast locally. To say the former champion was thrilled to see his son in the ring would be an understatement. On March 21,

Pep headed to New York City to meet with NYSAC in an attempt to regain his license. This was his second attempt. He then awaited a response.

Kicking off his pursuit of Bassey, Pep returned to the Valley Arena in Holyoke, Massachusetts, on March 31. There he took a 10-round, hard-fought, unanimous decision over Prince Johnson—both fighters scaled at 130½ pounds. One of seven opponents with a winning record that Pep would fight this year, Prince Johnson impressed the 1,200 fans on hand during the earlier rounds when he kept close quarters, but little else.

On April 8, Willie Pep, scaling at 129, a pound lighter than his opposer, scored an undemanding 10-round unanimous decision over punching bag George Stephany. The bout, held at the Bristol Arena, in Bristol, Connecticut, attracted over 750 spectators. Stephany, who lost nearly twice as many

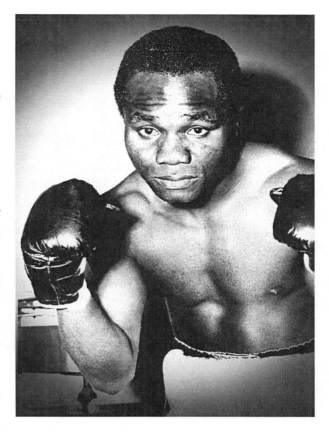

Hogan "Kid" Bassey was the first man of Nigerian descent to become a world boxing champion.

battles as he won, was helpless against the former champion. The bout, which included semi-pro contests, reminded Pep of his early days fighting under the same designation.

Six days later, this time over in Providence at the Arcadia Ballroom, Pep, still scaling at 129 or four pounds heavier than his challenger, grabbed a unanimous decision over tomato can Cleo Ortiz. Both judges and referee "Sharkey" Bouanno agreed that Pep won every round. On to Boston, where Pep would step up in challengers.

Training at Nuno Cam's Gym in Boston, Willie Pep was ready to greet undefeated Jimmy Kelly (also spelled Kelley), of Lowell, over 10 rounds at Mechanics Building in the city. Pep, favored at 10–7, was certain he could give his 19-year-old Greek opponent, with an Irish name, a ring education he would never forget. On April 29, Willie Pep accomplished the task. Scaling at 129¾, he captured a 10-round unanimous decision over Jimmy Kelley, who tipped at 132. Pep dominated every round with jabs and combinations. Kelley bled from near his left eye and nose from the second round onward. The Sam Silverman promotion attracted over 4,000 enthusiastic fight fans, many somewhat surprised at how Pep adeptly held off the charges of his young opponent.

In another paradox of pugilism: NYSAC, which four years ago retired elite boxer

Willie Pep, turned down his bid for a new license.[48] Two days later, the NBA ranked Pep number seven among division contenders. This as Boston promoter Sam Silverman was working around the clock trying to land Pep a title shot.

On May 13, Willie Pep lost one of his closest friends, Charles "Shikey" Greenberg. It tore right to the heart of the fighter. As a loyal friend, Greenberg was always there when needed, and never asked anything in return. Convinced his bad luck came in bunches, Pep tried not to think about anything except the task at hand.[49]

Back at the Mechanics Building on May 20, Pep, weighing 131 or three pounds heavier than his adversary, gained a 10-round unanimous decision victory over Bobby Singleton of Philadelphia. It wasn't even close, as Pep completely controlled the bout. Though the pace was slow during the first four rounds, the crowd of over 900 fight fans did manage to enjoy it from that point forward. Pep had his young opposer on thin ice in the final round—courtesy of two damaging left hooks—but could not put him away. There were no knockdowns, though Singleton did slip in the opening round. It was the former champion's fifth start in seven weeks, and he appeared to thrive on the pace.

A twisted leg slowed Pep down; consequently, his battle against Bobby Soares, scheduled for June 2, was moved to July 1. Later, promoter Sam Silverman inked Pep to a 10-round feature in New Bedford, Massachusetts, against Irish Pat McCoy. The June 23 contest would be held at Sargent Field. Hailing from Ireland, McCoy was a journeyman who turned punching bag a few years back—it served a purpose, as it gave him an opportunity to see the world. Scaling at 129, three pounds lighter than his opposition, Willie Pep deftly added a 10-round unanimous decision to his resume.

Heading north from Hartford, Pep traveled about 80 miles to Athol, Massachusetts, to tangle with Bobby Soares at Memorial Hall. Scaling at 127 (his lowest weight since March 1956), three pounds heavier than his opposer, Pep took a 10-round unanimous verdict.[50] Soares had only won one of his last five fights, so little was anticipated. True to form, little was delivered from the fighter. Pep took the first four rounds, took casual fire from Soares in rounds five through seven, then conducted a commanding conclusion. There were no knockdowns, however Pep did slip in the sixth frame.

As career milestones approached, Willie Pep paid more attention to the numbers. They became significant because they spoke to his career, so he didn't have to. His quoted 215 victories left him six (some believed five) victories behind Young Stribling.[51] With each passing triumph, more and more spectators realized the relevance behind what they were viewing. Promoter Sam Silverman, who deserved credit for revitalizing Pep's career, continually reminded the elite fighter of his accomplishments. Yet, Pep often felt he wasn't getting the attention he earned; moreover, at this stage of his career, the lack of television exposure was a barrier that was difficult for the former champion to overcome—he hadn't fought on TV in three years.[52]

Pep was scheduled to meet Bobby Bell in Norwood, Massachusetts, on July 14, but bad weather forced a three-day postponement. The pair last met in July 1950. Bell, a seasoned fighter from Youngstown, Ohio, had essentially welcomed the role of setup fighter three years ago. Managed by George Gainford, Sugar Ray Robinson's pilot, the wise 29 year old knew how to make an opponent work for a victory.

Tipping at 128½, Willie Pep battled Bobby Bell, who scaled at 133, over 10 rounds to take a unanimous decision. The former champion's dominant performance, against a willing opposer, captivated the over 1,400 spectators on hand.[53] There were no knockdowns. By Pep's own admission, it was his best performance in years. It soon garnered him his shot at Hogan "Kid" Bassey, granted it was a non-title affair, but it had enormous implications. It was scheduled for Boston Garden on September 20. Hallelujah.

Taking three setup bouts in August, Pep and his handlers believed should bring him into September primed for his battle against Bassey. On August 4, Pep defeated tomato can Luis Carmona, who was substituting for Cleo Ortiz, at the Northern Maine Fairgrounds in Presque Isle, Maine; five days later, Pep beat Jesse Rodriguez, at Lake County Fairgrounds in Painesville, Ohio; and on August 26, the former champion vanquished punching bag Al Duarte, substituting for Manuel Baptista, at Glovers Bowl in North Adams, Massachusetts. All three victories were a result of 10-round unanimous decisions.[54] In fact, all 11 of his battles along the journey to Bassey, that began with Prince Johnson back on March 31, concluded in successful 10-round concordant verdicts.

Hogan "Kid" Bassey

If Okon Bassey Asuquo, aka Hogan "Kid" Bassey, was as hard to beat as he was to dislike, Willie Pep had his hands full. The well-spoken, 26-year-old Nigerian, who hailed from the seaport city of Calabar, was the oldest of five children. He was a survivor in what he, along with others, viewed as a cruel world. Leaving his hometown for Lagos, the chief city of Nigeria, he met Nap Peregrino, manager of the Imperial Boxing Club. The relationship, nearly identical to that of a father and son, led to a successful amateur boxing career.

Standing five feet three inches, with a 66½-inch reach, Bassey made his professional debut in 1947. In 1952, the boxer found a new home in Liverpool, Merseyside, England. After taking the Commonwealth (British Empire) Feather Title in 1955, he set his goals even higher. On June 24, 1957, after being floored to an eight count in the second round, Kid Bassey became the new world featherweight champion by way of a 10th-round knockout of Cherif Hamia of France. However, it wasn't perfect, as he wanted to capture the title in America, in front of one, if not all three of his boxing heroes: Joe Louis, Sugar Ray Robinson, and Willie Pep.

Sensing that Pep needed to become familiar with Bassey's talents, trainer Bill Gore wisely obtained the services of Pat McCoy, of Galway, Ireland, who had over 200 rounds' worth of training sessions with Bassey. (A few days out from the fight, Bassey was a 10–7 favorite.)

The charming Nigerian promised that if Willie Pep beat him in this non-title affair, he would defend his crown against him in a fight promoted by Sam Silverman. The promoter had been a man of his word.

Floored twice by overhand rights, Willie Pep lost to Hogan Bassey via a technical knockout at 42 seconds of the ninth round. When Pep was dropped to a compulsory (eight) count in the opening seconds of the ninth round, it was a bad sign. The second blow struck Pep and sent him across the lower strand of the ropes. Dazed, with half his body outside the ring, he somehow managed to pull himself up at the count of nine (some say ten), but referee Jimmy McCarron had seen enough.

Bassey, scaling at 128¼ pounds to his adversary's 129, found his range and took control by the fifth frame. Pep, in front of an impressive crowd of over 10,400 fight fans, could not move quickly enough to avoid contact—he had a cut over his left eye and on both sides of his nose. Was this the end for Willie Pep? Willie Pep did not retire.

The poet Robert Frost once quipped, "In three words I can sum up everything I've learned about life: it goes on." Life for Willie Pep went on, and as usual his challenges came in bunches.[55]

TEN

Last Rounds, 1959–1969

"Sometimes even to live is an act of courage."—Lucius Annaeus Seneca

During an eight-hour flight from Venezuela back to the United States, Willie Pep had plenty of time to think. After losing a 10-round decision to Sonny Leon in Caracas the previous day (January 26, 1959), he decided it was over. The decision was his, and only his. It was time.

Two straight loses wouldn't impact most fighters, but Willie Pep was no ordinary fighter. Accepting the loss to Bassey was one thing, but when a fighter such as Sonny Leon can drop you three times to the canvas, well, that was food for thought. Though Pep had hoped to end his career in Hartford, it wasn't to be.

Willie Pep, the highest paid featherweight ever, could hold on to a ring victory but never a paycheck. It burned a hole in his pocket: There was always the next adrenaline rush, be it a dame, a trifecta, or a roll of the bones. Admitting that only a pittance of all his ring earnings remained, he knew it was time for a new phase of his life. That wouldn't be simple, certainly not for someone who was born to be a boxing champion.

It was a given, at least in Pep's mind, that he would stay close to the fight game. He was assisting Marty Bromberg with heavyweight Charley Marui, so training and managing were certainly options. Refereeing was also an alternative, but the former champion wasn't sure how the circumstances would play out.[1]

Along with his two children, Mary Elizabeth, 15, and William Patrick, 14, Willie Pep planned on living at the family home in Hartford. While he looked forward to it, he also knew he had to earn a living.[2]

Feeling bad about having to abandon his final fight card—he was scheduled to meet Steve Ward—on February 3 at the State Theater in Hartford, Willie Pep offered his services as a referee for one of the undercard bouts. That way those fans who purchased tickets thinking Pep, who was substituted for by Eddie Armstrong, was on the bill, could at least note his presence. Promoter Johnny Cesario, who understood the circumstances, accepted his friend's offer.[3]

A steady diet of annual events, award ceremonies, banquets, charity events, fundraisers, testimonial dinners, and tournaments would occupy the bulk of the former champion's time as he decided how to approach retirement. On April 27, he was honored by the Atlantic Athletic Club at their annual dinner. One of his first job leads was as a public relations executive for a brewery (Hampden-Harvard Brewing Company).

Remember Pep's two-car collision last November? It was learned on April 5, that

161

Pep was being sued as a result of the collision for $20,000. The suit was filed against the former boxer in New Haven Superior Court.[4]

In June, Willie Pep, comfortable in his role as a beer salesman, stated that Warner Brothers had contacted him with regard to a movie about his life, and that Sal Mineo would play the title role.[5] Pep believed that a considerable portion of the movie would be shot in Hartford, but time would tell.

Following minor surgery at the end of November, the former champion was back on his feet in a few days. His latest business venture was a nightclub, Willie Pep's Melody Lane, at 362 W. 57th Street, in Manhattan. The two occupations every boxer believed was part of their destiny were restaurant owner and entertainer. Working during the week for a firm based in Holyoke, he saved his weekends for New York City.

1960–1964

For as far back as he could remember, Willie Pep made his home in the ring. It was the epicenter of his life, an autobiography written one battle at a time. He forged his friendships from it, supported his family by it, satisfied his ego because of it. The further he was away from it, the more uncomfortable he felt. Wading into uncharted waters for the next four years wasn't always easy, pleasant, or fruitful, but it was necessary in order to find some direction in his life.

Always trying to keep one foot on the canvas, Pep would try on many hats to see if any fit. From boxing promoter and referee to entrepreneur and business executive, these four years were a preview to what lay ahead.

1960

The First Boxing Promotion

Never far from a ring, Pep began working with Kennie Lane, a lightweight out of Holyoke. Simply being around the gym was enough to get him thinking about additional opportunities. Since talent, such as Lane, had few opportunities to showcases their skills, why not create one?

On March 2, it was confirmed that the former champion was interested in promoting at the Valley Arena in Holyoke. Teaming up with matchmaker Vito Tallarita, they arranged for a seven-bout card featuring Bobby Soares, from Providence, battling Matt Mallane, from Springfield. Nine boxers on the undercard of the promotion would make their professional debut, including many Golden Glove standouts. Willie Pep even convinced Johnny Cesario to handle the ring announcing.

It looked like the team of Pep and Tallarita found a winner. Over 1,100 fight fans found their way to the Holyoke Arena for the March 14 promotion, and everyone appeared to enjoy the event. In the three-round preliminaries: Don Roy defeated

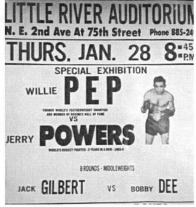

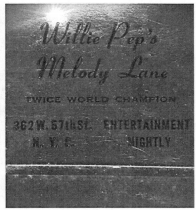

James D. Norris (left), president of the IBC from 1949 to 1958, dominated boxing in the U.S. in the 1950s. A poster (top right) from Willie Pep's comeback exhibition against Jerry Powers in Miami, Florida. A rare matchbook cover from Willie Pep's Melody Lane at 362 W. 67th Street in New York City (Library of Congress, LC-USZ62–139485 [b&w film copy neg.] Norris).

George Torres, Frank Tellafero defeated Kenny Flowers, Tony Marrero defeated Whitney Stratton, George Blake knocked out Junior Horsley, Jesus Alicia defeated Bob Campbell, and Dobie Josie knocked out Joe Taylor. In the main event: Matt Mullane scored a unanimous six-round decision over Bobby Soares. Clearly, Monday Night Boxing was a welcome, and hopefully weekly, event.[6] Unfortunately, the programs essentially came to a halt when the Arena was destroyed by fire on May 12.

When heavyweight challenger Floyd Patterson conducted his training camp at Newtown, Connecticut, in preparation for his June 20 bout against heavyweight champion Ingemar Johansson, Willie Pep couldn't resist the opportunity to visit. It happened on June 8, and it was a free publicity paradise. On hand were Joe Louis and *The Ring* magazine editor Nat Fleischer. The flash bulbs popped as all the champions mingled and posed with each other. This was a part of the fight game that Pep missed the most, the camaraderie of his fellow champions together with the recognition.

Basking in the attention, Pep's next excursion was to Boston Gardens on June 10 to watch Paul Pender win a split 15-round decision over Sugar Ray Robinson. Pep joined Jack Sharkey and Joe Louis, two former heavyweight champions during the pre-fight ceremonies. It was Willie Pep, "The Champ," enjoying the acknowledgment he so richly deserved.

The summer was filled with activity, precisely how the former boxer liked it: A quick trip down to Miami Beach to see friends, training for a possible television role, golf lessons, and as a matter of course (no pun intended), the endless speaking engagements. Pep developed a standard presentation: It began with a highlight film of Saddler–Pep IV, accompanied by a running commentary from the participant, followed by standard one-liners and a question and answer session. From Corkey's Steak House in Waterford, New York, to the Men's Club of Beth David Synagogue in Hartford, Willie Pep was a consummate entertainer.[7]

As the year drew to a close, Senate boxing investigators were tearing the lid off the fight game. James D. Norris, former president of the International Boxing Club (IBC) told a closed subcommittee session on December 9 that Frankie Carbo, who was currently serving a two-year sentence at Rikers Island, was the "expediter" and "convincer" in obtaining the services of former champions Carmen Basilio, Tony DeMarco, Jake LaMotta, and Willie Pep.[8] At this stage of the investigation, nobody was certain what to believe.

1961

Hartford winters can be cruel, making January the perfect month for the former champion to hop a plane to Florida. Since Miami Beach was where the action was, not to mention his friends, Willie Pep headed there. Staying on, or near, the beach was a must, so Pep booked a room at the Henrosa Hotel, at 1435 Collins Avenue. The Art Deco inn, built in 1935, was originally called Biarritz Hotel. Also located on Collins Avenue were The Castaways, Waikiki Resort Motel, and Tangiers Resort Motel. Just a block east, on 14th Street, was Ocean Drive, filled popular night spots.[9] After a little fun and sun, it was back home to Hartford, then on to New York City (Melody Lane, now under the watchful eye of his cousin) before the end of the month.[10]

As a popular figure at area events, Pep had perfected his oration. Most comments were variations of: Once your reflexes and legs go, a fighter's friends soon follow; he was a champ who lived like one; he was insolvent thanks to fast women, slow horses and generous judges; he had only himself to blame for his financial condition, never anyone associated with his career; Saddler, whom Pep claimed to hate (this changed over time), was a dirty fighter; it was an eye for an eye battling Saddler; and finally numbers (incredible numbers such as winning his first 62 professional fights in a row and, after a draw, winning his next 72 bouts).

Destined to be a great motion picture, *Requiem for a Heavyweight* starred Anthony Quinn, Jackie Gleason, Mickey Rooney, and Julie Harris. It was a heartfelt story of a prizefighter, Mountain Rivera, played by Anthony Quinn, who quits boxing to avoid a possible detached retina or brain damage. He confronts his alternatives and life in general. Using Rod Serling's powerful screenplay, David Susskind (producer) and Ralph Nelson (director), took their boxing motion picture into the streets of Manhattan for six weeks, beginning the second week of November. What better way to add a stroke of realism to the film than by adding popular pugilists, albeit briefly, such as: Steve Belloise, Rory Calhoun, Cassius Clay, Gus Lesnevich, Alex Miteff, Barney Ross, Abe Simon, and Willie Pep, to name a few. Most, thanks to television, were instantly recognizable during the movie's pre-credit sequence, which began with a creative shot across their blemished countenances.[11]

1962

For Willie Pep, the year 1962 was all about reentering the ring. Not as a participant—at least not yet—but as a referee. As the third person in the ring, it was as close to the action as he could get without being part of it. One

Built in 1935, Hotel Henrosa was originally called Biarritz Hotel. Willie Pep loved staying at the elegant hotel located at 1435 Collins Avenue in Miami Beach (Library of Congress, fl0160).

thing was certain: he would forever recall a few of his assignments. For example, on January 10, in the State Garden at Union City, New Jersey, he refereed a preliminary battle between Ramon Moran and Bobby Bruner. As the second bout on the undercard, everything transpired smoothly and, judging by the applause, his services were appreciated. Satisfied, Pep found an available seat to enjoy the rest of the evening. However, when it was time for the main event, a super lightweight bout between Carlos Quiles and Marcel Bizien, the atmosphere grew tense. Unhappy with the decision in favor of Quiles, a verdict based solely on referee Paul Cavalier's assessment, fight fans took issue and began throwing things before entering the ring. Attacking Cavalier, one spectator managed a solid right to the shoulder of the arbiter. Dazed, Cavalier, contrary to his surname, was concerned. Bizien was so incensed at picking up the loss that he needed to be restrained from taking apart Cavalier. Thankfully, police were able to quell the skirmish. Welcome to the Garden State, Mr. Pep, now pass me that chair.

In his first meaningful bout as a boxing referee, Willie Pep headed to Sao Paulo,

Brazil. His January 18 assignment was a bantamweight championship match between Eder Jofre, the titleholder, and unbeaten challenger John Caldwell of Great Britain. Jofre, a native of Sao Paulo, was a former Olympian (1956) and a champion in the midst of conducting an elite career—he was already considered an outstanding Latin fighter. In front of an Ibirapuera Stadium crowd estimated at 20,000, the match went smoothly for Pep, attributable to the bantam champion's vicious left hand that dropped Caldwell to a nine count in the tenth round and solidified his points victory. However, it had its moments: After a Caldwell knockdown, Pep wiped the resin off the fighter's gloves and the crowd went nuts. A common practice in America, it was considered favoritism in Brazil. And Pep did it twice.[12]

Rocky Marciano was scheduled to referee the OPBF (Oriental and Pacific Boxing Federation) lightweight title bout between Flash Elorde and Somkiat Kiatmuangyom at Rizal Memorial Sports Complex in Manilla, Philippines on March 10, but business commitments forced him to cancel the engagement. His replacement, Willie Pep, arrived in Manila on March 8 and worked until the second round, when Elorde knocked out his adversary. It was a long way to travel to count to ten.

Finger Lakes Gaming & Racetrack, a thoroughbred horse-racing track and casino located in Farmington in western New York state, opened on May 23, 1962. Located over 330 miles from Hartford, it was a beautiful drive through the heart of central New York. Willie Pep, certainly no stranger to the track, owned a filly named Gay Spangle.[13] At the track on July 14, he watched his horse beaten down the stretch, and the former champion loved the action. If he hadn't become a boxer, Pep admitted that being a jockey would have been fun.

Leaving his hometown of Hartford in late summer, Pep headed to California—his children were left in the care of his mother. Taking a job with Lino Engineering in Santa Clara on the public relations side of the business, it was a new adventure—the company manufactured firing patterns for rockets. The chips weren't falling his way in Connecticut, and the former champion felt a bit unwanted.[14]

By the end of November, still unable to find his niche, Pep moved to New Orleans, where he operated a piano lounge on busy Canal Street. His business partner was former fighter Jerome Conforto. He also hoped to continue his work as a boxing referee refereeing a bout in Harvey, Louisiana, on December 19.

1963

On January 10, Bill Gore was injured near his home in Lutz, Florida, when an automobile he was driving was struck by a freight train at a crossing off Route 41. Following the car in front of him, Gore thought he could clear the tracks. The vehicle he was driving was almost sliced in half. The talented trainer was taken to St. Joseph Hospital in Tampa for evaluation and X-rays. Thankfully, a few facial cuts and a leg injury proved the worst of the damage.

At the end of the month, Pep headed to Florida. He planned on visiting Gore before attending the Sugar Ray Robinson–Ralph Dupas fight in Miami on January 30. He would then work his way back to Louisiana.

When March 19 rolled around, the former boxing champion couldn't believe that 20 years had passed since he lost in the Garden to Sammy Angott. His streak of

62 consecutive victories was halted by the elite lightweight pugilist from Washington, Pennsylvania. While Pep appreciated being recalled in the sports anniversary columns, it always reminded him of how much he missed the ring.

Likely one of the last places Willie Pep ever thought he would turn up was Bogota, Colombia. Yet he boarded a plane on April 24, bound for the South American country. He was escorting boxer Carlos Zayas, of Holyoke, as a favor for Vito Tallarita. The manager couldn't make the trip, so he asked Pep to take his place. Zayas, a streaky bantamweight, was matched, or let's say overmatched, against undefeated Bernardo Carabello. The latter, keeping his winning streak alive, won via a fourth-round technical knockout.

Speaking of fourth, William Papaleo, who was smitten over a hat-check girl at Melody Lane, decided to marry for a fourth time. Young and strikingly beautiful, Linda Peterson was also a part-time actress. The Papaleos made their home in Hartford. The marriage lasted less than a year.[15]

Working next as a radio sales executive for a Brockton, Massachusetts company, the former featherweight champion was still struggling to find the perfect employment.

The Ring Hall of Fame

On October 15, 1963, Willie Pep became the 77th member of *The Ring* magazine Hall of Fame. One of three to enter the prestigious institution this annum, he was joined by Jem Ward, British heavyweight, and Tommy Gibbons, Minnesota, light-heavyweight. Nat Fleischer, founder and publisher of *The Ring*, formed the esteemed institution in 1954 as a way to recognize the elite of the fight game. (*The Ring* Hall of Fame inducted 155 members before it was abandoned after the 1987 inductions.)[16] Delighted at his selection, Pep was eternally grateful.

As boxing continued to sour following the ring deaths of Benny Paret (March 24, 1962) and Davey Moore (March 21, 1963), not to mention plunging gate revenues, the American Broadcasting Company (ABC) announced that it was dropping their weekly television show that aired for two decades—the chief sponsor of the show, Gillette Safety Razor Company, agreed with the decision. Regularly carried by the networks, ABC's Friday night boxing show had become a staple for fight fans and helped sustain the sport through television revenue.[17] While it was indeed a memorable year for Willie Pep, it was a tough year for boxing.

1964

In addition to planning a guest referee tour, Willie Pep made his usual number of appearances at major ring battles, beginning with the Clay-Liston bout in Convention Center at Miami Beach on February 25.

In March, the former champion was in Rhode Island as a guest referee. Feeling mouth pain, Pep returned to Hartford and was placed under observation at St. Francis Hospital ; it proved to be an infected and imbedded tooth. As he planned to head to Kingston, Jamaica in April, he wanted to be sure everything was fine.

Eddie Perkins successfully defended his junior lightweight crown against popular hometown pugilist Bunny Grant in Kingston, Jamaica on April 18. Referee Willie Pep, a mere 1,655 miles from home, maintained order in front of 25,000 highly partisan fans. It wasn't always easy, as it was difficult to hear officials ringside.

Robert Louis Stevenson once quipped, "I travel not to go anywhere, but to go. I travel for travel's sake. The great affair is to move." The quote fit Pep perfectly, as he could never sit still in the ring, at home, or even on the road. Solidifying his reputation as a ring arbiter, Pep was off to Regina, Saskatchewan, Canada on June 24. At Exhibition Stadium, Eddie Perkins, world junior welterweight champion, scored a unanimous decision over Canadian champion Les Sprague of Dartmouth, Nova Scotia, in a 10-round nontitle bout.[18]

Back in Miami Beach in December, Willie Pep was making the rounds and reestablishing contacts. By the second week of the month, the former champion was working out with light heavyweight champion Willie Pastrano at the Americana Hotel's health club. The 475-room hotel, opened on December 1, 1956, was the place to be and be seen. According to reports, Pep was going to become the acting sports director. Or perhaps there was more to the story.

It Ain't Over—The Final Ten Bouts, 1965–1966

As 1965 arrived, Willie Pep, at age 42, was in South Florida. A perpetual job-seeker, the former champion always felt like a square peg in a world filled with round holes. It wasn't easy, nor was it fun. The persistent backaches, courtesy of his 1947 plane crash, were constant reminders of days past. And the adulation was fading almost as fast as his savings.

Living in a $125-a month apartment with his wife in North Miami Beach, he wasn't destitute, but he was concerned. Yearning for the past—the Connecticut vanity license plate "WPEP," that adorned his 1964 Plymouth Fury merely one indication—he was haunted by the memories. There was only one place to turn: the ring.

What value was that feeling of once again being a contender? Once more, a force to be reckoned with? Preparing inside Miami's Fifth Street Gym, Pep felt wonderful. He wasn't kidding himself, he understood how high the mountain was. He just didn't know how far he could climb. Willie Pep was still a name—a living and breathing ring legend. Fans of all ages showed up at the gym, merely to watch him. They sought that thrill, or tingle, that goes up your spine when you realize that you are a witness to history.

On January 28, Willie Pep took a four-round exhibition against club fighter Jerry Powers—the rounds were two minutes. Promoted by Neil Composto, the display, complete with training gloves and headgear, was held at the Little River Auditorium in Miami. Perhaps it was for the dough, but perhaps, at least in Pep's mind, it was confirmation that he still had *it*—the skills of a ring craftsman.[19] As it turned out, the former champion gave a respectable display. There were shades of greatness, at least enough to satisfy onlookers—an estimated crowd of about 880 folks, well over the seating capacity, packed the hall. More important, at least to some, the pugilist was quick enough to avoid getting hurt.

Afterwards, the media was treated to "Willie-O-The-One-liners," or his usual self-deprecating humor delivered in his trademark staccato rhythm—he had been hanging around with Graziano far too long. The next evening, Pep was supposed to be the guest referee at an exhibition in Clearwater, Florida, that included Sugar Ray Robinson as part of the main event. Pep appeared, but Robinson never did.[20]

At the conclusion of the exhibition fiasco, referee Willie Pep was off to Kingston, Jamaica for a far more important event: On February 13, Bunny Grant retained his lightweight championships (British Empire and Jamaican) by seizing a challenging split-decision over fellow Jamaican Percy Hayles. In front of over 20,000 fight fans, referee Pep cast the only ballot in favor of the loser. Returning to Florida, Pep also returned to making appearances. At Island Farm Citrus Plantation, at Fort Lauderdale on February 21, he was promoting fitness as well as a healthful diet. But this type of work wasn't providing the comfortable living he had imagined.

Tossed a fight offer by Miami promoter Neil Composto, Pep bit. The former champion would meet club boxer Harold McKeever over eight rounds at the Little River Auditorium on March 12. Initially, the fighters were going to wear 14-ounce gloves, so a decision could not be made according to the Miami Commission. However, that was altered to eight-ounce gloves before the bout. Scaling at 137, two pounds heavier than his opposer, Willie Pep grabbed an eight-round unanimous decision over Harold McKeever. After the battle, Pep looked as if he had been hit by shrapnel—cuts were open over both cheeks, the left bleeding profusely, while a near-vertical gash near his right eyebrow poured blood into his eye socket.

The first four rounds went to Pep by an edge. McKeever started the blood flowing in the fifth, as Pep began retreating. A couple of solid volleys in the eighth round gave Pep the fight. There were no knockdowns. Pocketing some much-needed dough, Pep was discouraged but not enough to discontinue his comeback.[21]

Returning to Hartford, he began working out at the Golden Gloves Gym on Albany Avenue. Assisting the former champion were Johnny Datro and advisor George Sheppard. On April 26, at the Arena in Philadelphia, Willie Pep, tipping at 137½, or 2½ pounds more than his opponent, defeated Jackie Lennon via a six-round unanimous decision. Pep dominated the affair and nearly had his opponent, who was a Philly cab driver, out during the final two rounds. The battle attracted over 2,100 spectators.[22]

Fighting in Connecticut for what would prove to be the final time as a professional boxer, Willie Pep, scaling at 134 or two pounds heavier than his antagonist, took a six-round unanimous decision over Johnny Gilmore at the Crystal Arena in Norwalk. For Pep, who fought at the venue over 17 years earlier as a professional, it brought back a flood of memories. Gilmore, a former national amateur champion, was so mesmerized by the actions of the former champion that he didn't know what to do. There were no knockdowns in a fight that looked better on paper than in person. Jack Barrett was behind the promotion that attracted a small crowd.[23]

By the end of May, a bit of incertitude surrounded Pep's fight status. Though Pep was scheduled to headline a June 6 fight card up in Toronto, Canada, the Athletic Commissioner ruled that he could fight nothing more than an exhibition, owing to his age. After the judgment, George Sheppard, Pep's comeback manager, stated that his fighter was withdrawing because of illness. This led some to believe Pep was retiring, while others thought he was merely taking time off to heal a minor rib injury. Later, the former champion confirmed it was the latter.

Putting on his referee shirt, Willie Pep headed to Saint John, New Brunswick to witness heavyweight contender George Chuvalo, of Toronto, capture a first-round technical knockout over Sonny Andrews (Burns) of Boston. Pep stopped the fight at the 2:33 mark of the opening round when Andrews hit the canvas for the third time. Upon returning to Hartford, the former champion would witness the fight game also hitting the canvas for the final time.

The Connecticut General Assembly adjourned on Wednesday, June 9, 1965, after outlawing boxing.[24] In their view, boxing, having repulsed what little audience it had left with bouts such as Cassius Clay-Sonny Liston, II, had been extinct in Connecticut for several years; moreover, Willie Pep's recent Norwalk battle provided proof of the sport's inability to sustain a fan base. It was a slap in the face to the sport, fight fans, and every boxing champion, and there had been many (Tunney, Delaney, Kaplan, Rosenbloom, Battalino, and Pep), who called Connecticut home. To say that Willie Pep didn't need something such as this to happen in the middle of a potential comeback would be an understatement. The impact of the legislation was enormous. It shattered interest in Connecticut boxing and likely destroyed a half a generation's worth of future participants.[25]

Merv McKenzie, the Canadian president of the WBA, issued a press release on July 4 urging "the voluntary retirement from boxing of both Willie Pep, age 42, and Sugar Ray Robinson, age 45."[26] While the former feather champion, and everyone associated with the fighter, appreciated the concern expressed by the WBA, they disagreed. Responding on behalf of Pep, manager George Sheppard stated the business value attached to both fighters. He also affirmed Pep's ring safety and financial security (both McKenzie objections to their continued participation). Lastly, he couldn't resist reminding McKenzie that John F. Kennedy was 43 years old when he became President of the United States.

At National Stadium in Kingston, Jamaica on July 10, referee Willie Pep counted out a sitting Percy Hayles, of Jamaica, at the 2:53 mark of the third round. It was a hotly contested confrontation from the start, and over 20,000 in attendance appeared to enjoy every minute. As a result of his performance, Carlos Hernandez of Venezuela retained his world junior welterweight title.

Staying in his international mindset, pugilist Willie Pep was off to Quebec City, Quebec. Tipping at 135½, Willie Pep captured a 10-round unanimous decision over Benny "Red" Randall, who scaled at 140. The latter, who had twice as many losses as victories, hit the canvas in the opening round of a lackluster battle held on July 21 at the Old Coliseum. It would be Willie Pep's last battle for 73 days.[27]

With that chill of fall in the air, it was time to return to the ring. Tipping at 137, six pounds heavier than his familiar opposer, the former champion strolled to a six-round points victory over Johnny "Irish" Gilmore. It happened at the Arena in Philadelphia on September 28. Gilmore hadn't fought since he last faced Pep back in May, and it showed. Pep didn't perform much better. The former champion's performance was crucified by the local press. Referred to as everything from sideshow to sham, it wasn't pretty: truthfully, it was outright embarrassing. It was Pep's final bout of the year at six rounds—all his subsequent fights for the remainder of the year were scheduled for ten-rounds. The show, promoted by Jimmy Toppi, was memorable, however, as the undercard included Olympic heavyweight champion Joe Frazier, of North Philadelphia, in his third professional fight and victory.

Turn Back the Clock

It took a creative young promoter, Don Elbaum of Erie, Pennsylvania, to bring both Sugar Ray Robinson and Willie Pep back together on a fight card. The event took place at the War Memorial Arena in Johnstown, Pennsylvania. The pair weren't fighting each other, as they did back on December 2, 1938, but having their names together on the ticket brought back a flood of memories.

Willie Pep, tipping at 136 or six pounds heavier than his opponent, captured a third-round technical knockout over Willie Little. The latter was the first opponent Pep faced with a winning record since Sonny Leon back in January 1959. The end came at the 1:06 mark of the term. Dominating the contest, Pep dropped Little twice in the second round.[28] For the record: Sugar Ray Robinson defeated Peter Schmidt, Canadian welterweight champion, via a 10-round unanimous decision. It was the last time, for both fighters, that they

Don Elbaum, the talented International Boxing Hall of Fame promoter, served as matchmaker for more than 10,000 fights, including 196 over a five-year period at the Tropicana in Atlantic City.

appeared on a fight card with a fellow future member of the International Boxing Hall of Fame. Having heard the criticism that followed his performance in Philadelphia, Pep was hell-bent at rectifying the situation. The event drew only about 1,600 fans.

A mere three days later, the former champion was back in a boxing ring in Providence, Rhode Island. Scaling at 136½, Willie Pep took a third-round technical knockout over Tommy Haden, who tipped at 130¼.[29] Referee Rocky Graziano stopped the fight at the 1:33 mark of the term. Pep, who dominated the contest at the Rhode Island Auditorium, pounded and sliced Haden's bleeding left eye in the third round until Graziano had little choice but to call the fight.

Heading west to Arizona for his final two official battles of the year, Pep felt exhilarated by his recent confrontations. On October 14, at the Sportatorium in Phoenix, scaling at 138 or a pound and a half heavier than his opposer, Pep captured a fifth-round technical knockout over Sergio Musquiz. Pinning his Mexican opponent against the ropes, the veteran unleashed a volley of combinations until referee Roger Yanez waved it off. Next, it was over to Tucson, or about 106 miles as the crow flies, on October 25. At the Sports Center, Willie Pep, scaling at 132, a six-pound advantage, knocked out Ray Coleman in the fifth round. Dominating his young opposer, Pep floored Coleman in the second session before a flurry of unanswered punches finished the job a mere 30 seconds into the fifth frame. The former champion had not lost a single fight since he began his comeback. Granted, he fought only two fighters with winning records, but for any 43-year-old professional boxer, this was still impressive.

Heading back to Hartford, Pep's next battle, scheduled for November 11 at Burlington, Vermont, was postponed. Using the time wisely, Pep helped train Manny Gonzalez for his welterweight title fight against Emile Griffith at Madison Square Garden on December 10. Since he planned on attending "Sugar Ray Robinson's Farewell to Boxing," which was part of the evening's festivities, Pep killed two birds with one stone.[30]

On December 1, certain he didn't want to become the oldest professional pug, Pep once again retired. Exhibition offers poured in after the announcement. Boston promoter Sam Silverman couldn't resist the temptation of inking a Sugar Ray Robinson–Willie Pep four-round exhibition up in the hub on December 13. Over 4,000 fans turned out at the Garden to watch Pep and Sugar clown around over the distance. The main event—all clowning aside—of the evening saw Don Fullmer take a dull 12-round split decision victory over Joey Archer.

1966

One thing about a second retirement, you know what to expect. It looked as if Pep was back to the banquet circuit, at least until Connecticut boxing was once again legal. However, he still had the itch. Yep, he took a six-round preliminary bout at the Richmond Arena on March 16, 1966. Tipping at 125, one pound less than his opponent, Willie Pep lost a six-round unanimous decision to Calvin Woodland. It was an embarrassing display for a fighter of his elite stature. Was it over? Nobody was certain. Even Pep admitted that during his work life, he picked up a lot of bad habits ... like working.

Salvatore Papaleo, age 70, died on May 24, 1966. The patriarch of the family left behind his wife, Mary Marchese Papaleo; two sons, Willie Pep and Nicholas Papaleo, both of Hartford; a daughter, Mrs. Felix Nevico of Rocky Hill; and seven grandchildren. The funeral took place on May 27, with Mr. Papaleo's burial in Rose Hill Memorial Park, in Rocky Hill.

Salvatore Papaleo did his best to keep his family safe, while providing guidance, financial support (until his illness), and opportunities for his children. He was accomplished at instilling confidence in his children, while encouraging them to chase their dreams. Like any parent, there were times he was a disciplinarian. It wasn't always easy for either himself, or his oldest son.[31]

Getting over the loss of a parent is never easy. Always supportive of his family, Willie Pep filled in for his father when he could. He had always done that. Personal appearances became therapeutic for the former champion, as he fed off the adulation and enjoyed seeing old friends. Establishments such as bars, night clubs, and restaurants loved having Willie Pep, or simply "Willie," as a host or greeter because he was charming. Romano's Steak House, at 374 Asylum Street in downtown Hartford, employed Willie as host on Friday, Saturday, and Sunday. Imagine bringing a date to watch and dance to "Baby Huey and The Baby Sitters," while sitting next to the former featherweight champion of the world. This environment also gave the host the flexibility to referee an important ring battle if called upon.[32]

The former featherweight champion also had the acting bug. Willie Pep (Willie the Eye), and numerous other ring greats, including Paddy DeMarco (Dinny the Dimwit), Rocky Marciano (The Rock), Jake LaMotta (Gentleman Jim), and Petey Scalzo (Benny the Bug), appeared in a motion picture titled *Cauliflower Cupids*. The cabbage patch thugs, who play the good guys, beat up the bad guys—the moral of the story being that a boxer's talent is best left in a ring.

Inside Cobo Arena in Detroit, Michigan, on November 21, Canadian heavyweight champion George Chuvalo stopped Boston Jacobs in the third round of a scheduled 10-rounder. The third man in the ring was Willie Pep. Dropped to a mandatory nine count in the third round, Jacobs arose, only to be neutralized. Pep immediately stepped in to wave it off at the 2:33 mark.

A couple of outstanding events closed out the year for Willie Pep. On December 1, Pep and other great champions such as James J. Braddock, Rocky Graziano, Floyd Patterson, Emile Griffith, Carlos Ortiz, Sandy Saddler, and Mickey Walker appeared at Barney Ross Night at Sunnyvale Garden in New York. The benefit was for Ross, who was an outpatient at the Veterans Research Center in Chicago and was suffering from throat cancer. The program featured a two-round exhibition between Willie Pep and Sandy Saddler. The pair were a far cry from the days when they used each other as 126-pound throw rugs.

Five days later, Johnny Cesario hosted "Willie Pep Night" at Johnny's Ten Acres, his nightclub outside Meriden. The large turnout was treated to a plethora of Pep's pugilistic films, not to mention hundreds of priceless memories. Laughter was common as Cesario kidded Pep all night long about retirement with lines like, "Hey Willie, what do you call a pug who is happy on Friday Night? Retired."

On December 8, the Rockledge Country Club in West Hartford hosted a capacity crowd for a night in honor of Syd Conn, a benevolent man who raised thousands of dollars for underprivileged children. Captivating the crowd was Cassius Clay, who verbally sparred with Willie Pep over who was, in truth, the greatest of all time. Bat Battalino, Hal Goodnough, Dick McAuliffe, and Carl Yastrzemski also attended.

The last year that Willie Pep fought as a professional boxer drew to a close. His final ring performance was not glorious, nor was it memorable. Another Connecticut resident, Henry Ward Beecher, once said, "We should not judge people by their peak of excellence; but by the distance they have traveled from the point where they started." Clearly, even by 1966, you could judge Willie Pep by both.

1967

Resting comfortably at New Britain General Hospital, Willie Pep began the year with a minor nose operation on January 23. Nothing serious, just one of the annoying issues that he wanted rectified.

The Connecticut Boxing Guild named Willie Pep their "honorman" for 1967. It was the one organization that appeared to be doing what they could to keep the spirit of Connecticut boxing alive and well in the state. Under new Guild president Manny Leibert, things looked promising for the group.

The former champion was back in New York City and hitting the nightclub circuit. During the second week of February, Pep was hosting at the Chateau McLean, on McLean Avenue in Yonkers. The Westchester County city was humming with evening entertainment including Club Paddock, the Polka Dot Lounge, and the Westchester Town House. "The Champ" loved the nightlife and shared stories as fast as the staff served cocktails.

From New York, Pep headed to London as a guest of the Anglo-American Sporting Club. He had hoped to conduct an exhibition against Howard Winstone, the British and European featherweight champion, on February 27, but the British Boxing Board of Control (BBBC) nixed the idea. In their view, it would be in bad taste.

Back in Connecticut, Pep and Bat Battalino planned to appear at a public hearing on March 28 in support of a bill that would reinstate professional boxing in Connecticut. Two years had gone by, and it was time to take another look at the fight game. It was clearly an uphill battle; the torch for reconsideration was driven by stalwart supporter Manny Liebert.[33]

After his attendance at a soiree conducted by Jake LaMotta in honor of his *next* wife, Colleen Farrington, in New York City, Pep headed back to Hartford for the Connecticut Boxing Guild dinner in his honor.[34] Hundreds turned out at Valle's Steak House to celebrate the occasion with Pep, including champions Bat Battalino, Rocky Graziano, Jake LaMotta, Rocky Marciano, and Sandy Saddler. It was an incredible evening of one-liners, gags, and rare stories.

Recognition was one thing, but making the bills was another. With the hottest thing on television being shows such as *Hullabaloo, Shindig* and soon *Laugh-In*, dancing was popular. Having experienced the New York club scene, Pep put together a show that was billed as "Willie Pep and his Go-Go-Revue," and it played out in Farmington, at the Golden Horn Steak House on Route 6. Also, unable to resist being in front of the camera, Willie teamed up with sportscaster Ray Somers at station WHCT-TV, Channel 18 in Hartford. On August 14, the pair began putting together a 15-minute sports program that aired at 5:30 p.m. *Sports World*, as they called the segment, was an overview of area sports. Willie was even given his own series, appropriately called "Pep Talks," to highlight his flair for anecdotes and one-liners.[35]

Cupid struck again on November 26, as Willie Pep married delightful Geraldine M. Volpe, of White Plains, New York, at Glen Terrace in Brooklyn. The bride's father was University of Scranton basketball coach and former college All-American, Nat Volpe. A photograph of the newlyweds appeared in the *Daily News* on November 28. The marriage would last until 1982. The family lived on Middletown Avenue in Wethersfield, Connecticut.

In a unique twist, the Pep's 1967 Christmas card featured a photo of five-year-old Willie, barefoot, gloved, and posing in a pair of boxing trunks.

1968

Opening the year in New York City, Pep was scheduled for a January 10 appearance on the popular television program *To Tell the Truth*. The show used four panelists to question three contestants to determine who was telling the truth. Pep also accepted a job as host at the Cattle Baron Steakhouse in New York.

A Garden Return

Once again inside a boxing ring, Rocky Marciano had none other than Willie Pep, attired in a green sweatshirt with gray slacks, in his corner. He wanted the best second he could find for his battle against entertainer Bob "Chicken Delight" Hope, and Pep was it.

Looking across the canvas: Bob Hope had Barbara Eden, attired in a nurse's outfit, as his chief second. It was a conspicuous contrast (no offense, Willie). It was the opening of the new Madison Square Garden on February 11, 1968, and it drew a capacity crowd of about 20,000. Referee Bing Crosby did his best to keep the participants in line, however Hope was reprimanded for placing iron horseshoe inside his oversized boxing gloves. Willie had a ball, despite his skits being edited out of the television special; subsequently, Bob Hope passed along a remittance for his inconvenience in the form of a $750 watch to the former champion.[36]

Returning to New England, Pep, forever supportive of Connecticut trying to maintain a boxing presence under the law, had time to shoot up to Chicopee, Massachusetts, to watch the Bellevue Boys' Club of Hartford put on a magnificent boxing display. The youngsters performed under the watchful eye of Pep's childhood friend, Johnny Duke.[37]

Maintaining his refereeing skills, Pep handled: Marcel Bizien's points victory over Danny Andrews at the Plaza Arena in Secaucus, New Jersey, on October 14; Dick Gambino's second-round knockout of Chuck Harris at the Rhode Island Auditorium in Providence, Rhode Island, on November 20; and Gambino's first-round technical knockout of Jimmy Cherico on December 18, also in Providence. No wonder Pep always claimed he should have been paid by the mile.[38]

1969

Nobody loved being where the action was more than Willie Pep. Whether at a banquet in Elmira, New York, or a prizefight at Madison Square Garden, the former champion basked in the adoration. Can you blame him? Granted, the banquet cuisine wasn't always easy to handle, but there was nothing like that tenor voice of Johnny Addie announcing your name as it resonated through the Garden rafters. It seemed as if all of New York turned out for the fight between light heavyweight champion Bob Foster and Frankie DePaula on January 22, albeit the pre-fight introductions lasted longer than the main event. Pep was there, as were Joe Frazier, Joey Giardello, Sugar Ray Robinson, Sandy Saddler, and a variety of other sports stars. Who got the biggest ovation? "Broadway" Joe Namath, as might be expected. Hey, it was 1969.

Speaking of the Garden, 20 years had passed, or a generation in the minds of most, since Pep recaptured his featherweight crown from Sandy Saddler. It was hard to believe. From the Garden, Pep returned to earth and to Connecticut. At Willie's Steak House over on Center Street in Manchester, Willie Pep was refereeing a small boxing exhibition. Yep, the former champion was part-owner of another restaurant.

April was the month that most heard the news: Willie and Geraldine were anticipating the birth of their first child. There was still talk about a motion picture about Pep's life, but there had been talk before and nothing ever happened. Nevertheless,

Pep continued to try and work the project by contacting sponsors. He also continued to support fully all the efforts of the Connecticut Boxing Guild to legalize boxing in the state again. Redundant? At times, but Pep had to keep moving.

On May 24, Willie Pep was ringside working with Howard Cosell at the Bob Foster–Andy Kendall bout that was televised by *ABC Wide World of Sports* from West Springfield, Massachusetts. Frankly speaking, you wouldn't have known it until the third round. To little surprise, Cosell dominated the broadcast the same as Foster did the fight.

Tampa Boxing Enterprises, headed up by Lou Viscusi, had been busy promoting live sports as well as closed circuit telecasts in the "Bay Area." For example, the group handled the closed-circuit broadcast of the Joe Frazier–Jerry Quarry heavyweight championship fight on June 22. Viscusi also handled many active boxers, including welterweight Manny Gonzalez. However, it caught many by surprise to learn that Viscusi hadn't kept in contact with Willie Pep since they parted ways prior to one of the fighter's comeback efforts. That, according to both, needed to be corrected.

On June 5, Mr. and Mrs. Papaleo welcomed the birth of their daughter, Melissa Loraine, at St. Francis Hospital. She tipped at seven pounds, six ounces. The parents couldn't have been happier. The former champion shook more hands on the way out of the hospital, or so it appeared, than he ever did at the Garden.

Often Pep's refereeing assignments, both amateur and professional, were uneventful. Having worked a couple of professional bouts during the year, the new father headed off to Sydney, Australia to handle the WBC World Featherweight Championship between Johnny Famechon and Fighting Harada on July 28. The latter, having floored champion Famechon, of Australia, three times (2nd, 11th, and 14th rounds) put on an impressive display. Yet Famechon, who took considerable damage, managed to drop challenger Harada to the canvas in the fifth round. As a close fight, the decision, which was in the hands of Pep as the referee and lone judge, would not be easy. When Pep raised the hands of both fighters to signify a draw, the crowd went nuts. Amid booing from every direction inside Sydney Stadium, Pep's scorecard was amended to award the points victory to Famechon—Pep had added incorrectly (it likely saved his life). Even the partisan crowd thought Harada was the clear victor. For his own protection, Willie Pep was given a police escort as he left the stadium.[39]

On the day before his 46th birthday, August 31, 1969, Rocky Marciano died when the Cessna 172 airplane he was riding in crashed two miles short of the runway. When Willie Pep heard the news, he couldn't believe it. Heartbroken, the tears flowed. The memories of his own air crash came flooding back. But he lived, so why Rocky? Why now?

Without question, the highlight of the year was the birth of his daughter. This holiday in particular was a moment of reflection for the fighter. It was not only the end of a year, but the end of a decade. His final decade in the ring would be replaced by his first decade out of one.

ELEVEN

The Seventies, 1970–1979

"The greatest fighter I ever saw was Willie Pep. His actions in the ring were like something you would set to music. He could make moves I never saw from anyone else."—Carmen Basilio

Banquets, banquets, and more banquets. Willie Pep was Connecticut's most accommodating table guest during the 1970s. Delivering the same shtick, time after time, it was Pep's delivery that always made it entertaining. His style was a mix of Henny Youngman, Bob Hope, and Jake LaMotta, after stirring in a tinge of George Raft's suavity. "Let me tell ya how ya stay young," he'd say while altering a stolen Bob Hope line, "just hang around with older people." Before the laughter died down, he'd follow it up with "You know the best part of growing old is that it takes such a long time." He could easily transform himself into an entertainer because of who he was and what he had accomplished.

As time passes, the career of an elite athlete comes into perspective. While it was no mystery that Willie Pep was among the greats of the ring, his stature continued to grow.

1970–1975

A new decade meant new jobs, new business ventures, new promotions, and even a new book from Willie Pep. It meant more ring introductions, more community support, more articles, more radio shows, a bit more television, and more travel—Pep had more miles under his belt than Arthur Frommer. There were plenty of laughs and a few tears, but nobody was more generous with their time than Willie Pep.

The Willie Pep biopic was believed—likely stretching the definition of the word—still in the works. Teen idol Frankie Avalon had replaced Sal Mineo in the lead role. Training at the L.A. Main Street Gym, Avalon was getting in shape. The star of *Beach Blanket Bingo* was trading in the sand on the beach for the rosin on the canvas. He was even sparring with welter contender Ernie "Indian Red" Lopez.[1] As fate had it, the movie was never to be.

Always on call for an opportunity, Pep was off to Missoula, Montana, to assist light heavyweight contender Roger Rouse for his title shot against Bob Foster on April 4. Pep, who acted as the cut man in Rouse's corner, watched as his fighter was floored four times in three rounds on the way to defeat. For the record: Bob Foster was handled by Lou Viscusi, and his trainer was Bill Gore.[2]

As idle time never sat well with the former champion, Pep accepted a job offer as a state tax marshal on April 30. It appeared like a sound opportunity for Pep, who could work on his own time, and it would not interfere with his other undertakings. Of the delinquent taxes collected, Pep would pocket six percent.[3]

With his hands in everything, why not a theater show? At the end of October, Pep was appearing in "The Gordon MacRae Show" at the Colonie Coliseum Theater near Cohoes, New York. On the bill as well were MGM recording star Cathy Carlson and character actor Robert "Bogie" Sacchi.

Connecticut has always stood proud that it produced three elite featherweight boxing champions, and it began with a Russian-born fighter (1901) named Louis "Kid" Kaplan. His family, having emigrated to the United States when Louis was merely five, settled in Meriden, Connecticut. Battling out of the Lenox Athletic Club in town, Kaplan's prolific and meteoric rise found him capturing the feather crown in Madison Square Garden by January 1925. He and his manager, Dinny McMahon, also brought a degree of honesty and integrity to the sport. Kaplan, who was too ill to attend a dinner in his honor in March, died on October 26, 1970.

Never far from a ring introduction, Willie Pep was in Syracuse, New York, on December 3, 1970, to watch Canastota boxer Billy Backus ascend the welterweight throne with an impressive fourth-round technical knockout over elite boxer José Nápoles. Recognized immediately as he walked the aisles inside the War Memorial Auditorium, Pep delighted fans by signing autographs and posing for pictures.

In 1971, Willie Pep and good friend Vito Tallarita teamed up to become New England representatives of K.O. Incorporated, out of New York. They hoped to cash in on a popular technology, and the agreement allowed them to show closed circuit television boxing at select locations.

At the conclusion of his job as a state tax marshal, Pep turned briefly to teaching boxing at the Connecticut School for Boys in Meriden in June 1971. The boys' reformatory was developing a boxing program for young teens. Though Pep enjoyed the job, he resigned on August 9—the travel to and from his home wasn't cost-effective for the former champion. Trying hard to find his niche, Pep was hoping that once boxing was again legalized in Connecticut, he could find a home.

At the "Salute to Boxing" show, sponsored by the Westchester County Police, it was all about boxing nostalgia and the greatest rivalries of the ring. For one night, on September 11, 1971, at the County Center in White Plains, New York, fight fans had an opportunity to relive some classic memories. A chance to see Sandy Saddler once again dangle those endless arms of his with hopes of catching Willie Pep inside a ring. Saddler, 44, had no fear of Pep, who was only eight days shy of his 49th birthday. Why should he? Having won three of their four battles spoke volumes. The evening was for charity, and the two did their best—with 14-ounce gloves, nobody was going to get hurt—to entertain the crowd with their sparring. Besides, the past was the past, and the two *appeared* to be friends.[4]

There was nothing Willie Pep wanted to see more than boxing once again legalized in the state of Connecticut. Declared illegal in 1965, it was reinstated in 1972, but it needed regulations to be approved through the proper channels before Connecticut's first professional bout in years could take place. Willie Pep was one of many to provide advice to Barbara Dunn, the state boxing commissioner. He felt confident that 1973 would witness the return of the sweet science.

It was Rocky Graziano Night at Madison Square Garden on March 9, 1973, and the crowd was treated to the guest of honor once again entering a boxing ring against Tony Zale. Also, Willie Pep—who could stomach anything for a decent paycheck—sparred three one-minute rounds against Sandy Saddler.

In April of 1973, the former champion teamed up with author Robert Sacchi to produce *Willie Pep Remembers Friday's Heroes*. Published by F. H. incorporated, the book included a forward penned by Jimmy Breslin. Conversational in its ap-

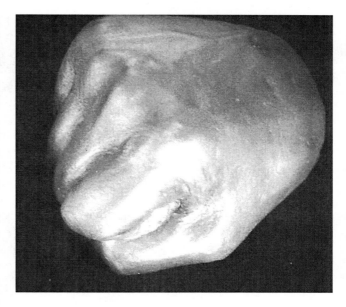

A fist casting from Willie Pep's incomparable right hand.

proach, Pep intertwined elements of his own life with ring legends: Steve Belloise, Ezzard Charles, Chuck Davey, Joey Giardello, Billy Graham, Tony Janiero, Rocky Marciano, Sandy Saddler, Chico Vejar, and Jersey Joe Walcott.

With boxing coming off the shelf, Willie Pep applied for a referee's license. His application was refused. The former champion was understandably insulted by the judgment. Connecticut's female boxing commissioner, the only woman in such a role in the United Sates, drew criticism for her decision. Later, it was learned that the denial was based on police claims that Pep had associated with underworld figures. Ironically, the decision flew in the face of other states who issued licenses to Pep as a referee, judge, and second.

The former champion next accepted a job with the Revitalization Corps. Working with area families and individuals to help turn their lives around was gratifying. Which brings up a good point: Whenever asked for assistance, regardless of the cause, Willie Pep answered. When he reapplied for a Connecticut referee's license, you would think those in charge would reconsider their initial judgment. They did not.[5]

Boxing Returns to Connecticut

Finally, professional boxing returned to Connecticut. It happened on August 7, 1973, inside of the Hartford Hilton Ballroom. A crowd estimated at 500, including Willie Pep, witnessed the first boxing show in years held in the state. Prior to watching Larry Butler take a 10-round decision over Angel Torres, the crowd gave a standing ovation to Willie Pep upon his introduction by the ring announcer. Commissioner Dunn also attended.

Denied twice for a boxing referee's license by the state Consumer Protection department, Willie Pep was offered, and accepted, a position in the organization's boxing division. He would act as an instructor, develop training programs, give clinics, and promote the fight game. Because Pep had threatened to go to court over his inability to acquire a boxing license, many believed this was a way of pacifying the former champion. Nevertheless, Pep seemed satisfied with the $8,500 annual salary. He reported to the executive director, who happened to be former Connecticut boxer Chico Vejar.[6]

A great family, good health, and a comfortable job with the state gave Willie Pep much to be grateful for and look forward to in 1974. Granted, he couldn't stay away from a charitable cause, but that was Willie; moreover, his photograph appeared routinely in the newspapers, be it at the Elks Club signing autographs or the Boys' Club inspiring youngsters.[7]

On October 3, 1974, Muhammad Ali knocked out George Foreman in the eighth round of their contest in Kinshasa, Zaire. However, Zaire was a long way to travel for a heavyweight boxing championship. Consequently, many Connecticut fight fans watched it from closed-circuit telecasts, at the 8,600-seat Civic Center in Springfield, Massachusetts, or the 3,500-seat Palace Theater in Waterbury.[8] Both locations were promoted by Willie Pep and Vito Tallarita.

Willie Pep was more popular than the Governor of Connecticut in 1975, and folks had finally stopped asking him about reentering a boxing ring, instead encouraging him to throw his hat into a political one. But the former champion always politely declined; besides, he enjoyed his public relations job.[9]

The Passing of Bill Gore

In 1974, Tony Licata was making waves in the boxing world. He was the fighter who took a 38–0–3 record into the ring against Emile Griffith and beat him. Under the guidance of Lou Viscusi and Bill Gore (along with Willie Pep), Licata looked unstoppable. He appeared destined to become Viscusi's and Gore's fourth world champion: incidentally, Pep was their first, followed by Joe Brown, world lightweight champion, and Bob Foster, world light-heavyweight titleholder. Gore, 83, became ill in June and could not be in his fighter's corner when Licata challenged Carlos Monzón for his WBA middleweight crown at Madison Square Garden. Hence Willie Pep filled in for the gifted trainer on June 30, 1975. Unfortunately, Licata, in the midst of an impressive career, lost to the elite Argentine pugilist—he ignored Pep's instructions not to trade punches with his opponent.

William H. "Bill" Gore died in Tampa, Florida, on November 13, 1975. When the tall, thin, and sleepy-eyed stranger came to Hartford over three decades earlier, his approach to training was as innovative as it was genuine. The Providence native had done his homework with regard to conditioning, nutrition, and even weight loss, and he was confident that he could build a better boxer. He was so phlegmatic in his strategy that few questioned him; moreover, when Willie Pep became a world champion, there were no doubters. Having an eye for talent, regardless of weight, Gore knew how to communicate with fighters, nurture their skills, and make them listen. Respect, he understood, was earned by working as hard as his students. Pep was one of many who confirmed that Gore always arrived early to the gym, worked shoulder to shoulder with his boxers, and left late. Articulate, soft-spoken, and well-mannered,

Gore led by example and instilled dedication. As a result, he became a father figure to many, including Melio Bettina, Joe Brown, Johnny Cesario, Bob Foster, Manuel Gonzalez, Roy Harris, Tony Licata, Willie Pep, and Cleveland Williams.

Gore was never more efficient than the 60 seconds between rounds, when he transformed himself into a master strategist and his fighter into a contender. Like an instructor in front of a graduate class on psychology, he struck a powerful nerve with his students.

Together with Lou Viscusi and Willie Pep, he was part of an unmatched boxing triumvirate—arguably, the greatest ever.[10]

1976–1979

Thanks to his prolific personal appearances, Willie Pep was still relevant. It was not a simple accomplishment considering: Over a decade, or half a generation, had passed since he was last in the ring, and it had been over a quarter-century since he was last face-to-face in a championship battle against his archenemy, Sandy Saddler.

From a Hope for Animals benefit in Poughkeepsie, on June 4, 1976, to refereeing women's boxing in Providence, Rhode Island, on August 3, 1976, it seemed that Willie Pep was always on the road.[11] He enjoyed making appearances around ring events, especially if some of his friends were involved. They were on October 16, 1976, at Rockland Community College in Suffern, as five-time world champion Emile Griffith gave an exhibition with 1976 Olympian Howard Davis. Pep attended as a guest, as did Rocky Graziano and Floyd Patterson.[12]

The year 1977 began with Pep plugging "Lisa & Co's sensational swingin' Saturday Nite Dance & Ms. Valentine Beauty Contest" at Reilly's Steakhouse, at 15 Asylum Street in downtown Hartford. The former champion acted as emcee and even employed the services of his boxing buddies (Maxie Atwater, Al Couture, and Billy Kearns). A few months later, at The Center Theatre in Waterbury, it was a show of a different sort as "Joe Frazier, and the Smoking Joe Revue" were joined on stage by Rocky Graziano, Willie Pep, and Chico Vejar. Hey, it's boxing, sorta.

Death of Bat Battalino

Undeniable, fierce, and competitive, Christopher "Bat" Battalino, who followed in the featherweight championship footsteps of Louis "Kid" Kaplan, died on July 25, 1977, at Hartford Hospital.

Guided by the wisdom of manager Hy Malley, Battalino knocked out four opponents in two nights to win the National AAU feather title in 1927. Turning pro that same year, the talented boxer had a meteoric rise to the top of his division. On September 23, 1929, Battalino captured the featherweight championship of the world by defeating André Routis over 15 rounds at Hurley Stadium in Hartford. By the time he retired in 1940, he had compiled a record of 57–26–3, with one no contest.[13] As one of three featherweight pillars in Connecticut boxing history, he attended numerous events with both Kaplan and Willie Pep.

Ringside during Muhammad Ali's 15-round victory over Ernie Shavers at Madison Square Garden on September 29, 1977, Pep clearly missed the vibe. Among those

The Battalino family plot located in Bloomfield, Connecticut (right). It includes the grave of Christopher "Bat" Battalino (left) world featherweight champion and member of the International Boxing Hall of Fame.

joining him: Milton Berle, Joe DiMaggio, Henry Kissinger, Robert Merrill, Tony Orlando, Sylvester Stallone, wrestler Antonio Inoki, and boxers Billy Conn, Floyd Patterson, and Sugar Ray Robinson. The ring introductions fulfilled a part of Pep that nothing else could and sustained, or so he believed, a national identity. Thankfully, television shows including *CBS Sportsworld* were still passing along assignments to Pep such as handling between rounds "color" at major bouts.

Be it ringside or at a high school gymnasium in Windsor Locks introducing the Park Department's new boxing program, Willie Pep, humbler than he needed to be, was always merely "Willie." However, there were instances when the former champion, who would give you the shirt off his back, felt he was being taken advantage of. Recognized by nearly every organization in Connecticut, he appreciated the trophies, but throw the dog a bone, in the form of cash, once in a while.[14]

As 1978 drew to a conclusion, Willie Pep was interviewed by actor Alexander Scourby for *Connecticut Profiles*, a program on Connecticut Public Television. Best known for his film role as the pitiless mob boss Mike Lagana in *The Big Heat* (1953), Scourby was well-known to Pep. The mutual intrigue between the pair was clearly apparent.[15]

The year 1979 marked the 30th anniversary of Saddler–Pep II, or the only battle of the four-bout rivalry won by Willie Pep. Awarded *Ring Magazine's* Fight of the Year award for 1949, it was confirmation that the talented youngster from Hartford was one of the greatest featherweight boxers ever. It also laid the foundation to which Sandy Saddler would validate the same.

Speaking of frameworks, matchmaker Vito Tallarita conducted his first of six boxing shows inside the Hartford Civic Center. Tallarita hoped

Elite pugilist Joseph "Sandy" Saddler (1926–2001), was ranked number five on *The Ring* magazine's list of "100 Greatest Punchers of All Time."

to make the four-year-old facility the cornerstone of a resurrected Hartford fight game. Tireless in his support of the sport he loved, Willie Pep was there.

When Congressman Ed Beard of Providence, Rhode Island, planned to introduce a bill to create a Federal boxing commission, he invited a few key individuals in support: John Condon (Madison Square Garden), Howard Cosell (Sportscaster), Floyd Patterson (NYSAC Commissioner), and Willie Pep (Connecticut Boxing Commission). The idea wasn't new, even if the effort was. The issue: Why should boxing be the only sport in the country under Federal control? After the laughter surrounding Pep's opening statement dissipated, on April 3, 1979, the former champion fielded questions from a Congressional subcommittee. It wasn't an outright endorsement of the bill, but quality support for its objectives.[16]

Gloves off for a full decade, Willie Pep, like other retired former champions, was making the adjustment to being out of the limelight. Whereas his name at the end of this decade was five times less likely to appear in local sports pages than during his fighting years three decades ago, his public appearances guaranteed some level of exposure.[17] Most elite fighters fade away to references only in anniversary filler pieces inside newspapers, but the strength of Pep's ring prowess made him a source of nearly constant comparison.

TWELVE

Retirement, 1980–2006

"What I wouldn't have given to be in Willie Pep's corner."—Ray Arcel

If the goal of every human is living a meaningful life, then discovering the secrets to successful aging is a subset of that objective. Many have concluded that it appears to be a custom recipe. In other words, those secrets differ from one person to the next. To enjoy life, Willie Pep, like many others, wanted to remain productive and continue doing the things he was good at.

Boxing may look easy, if you watch an elite fighter such as Willie Pep, but to most it was challenging and dangerous. On January 18, 1980, Charles Newell, 26, died at St. Francis Hospital from a brain injury. An inmate from Enfield prison, Newell was knocked out in the seventh round of a contest held at the Hartford Civic Center. The tragedy was a shock to most, including Pep, who witnessed the injury.

Not only was the sport dangerous inside the ring, it could be a challenge outside of it. On July 21, 1980, Willie Pep's attorney filed a libel suit in Hartford on his behalf. Damages were sought, to the tune of a reported $75 million, from *Inside Sports*.[1] The publication of Newsweek, Incorporated, published an article called "The Fix" on July 31, 1980. In the article, written by Paul Good, a boxer called "The Champ" threw a 1950s fight for $16,000. Pep, who was not named in the article, believed members of the boxing community discerned similarities between the main character of the article and the elite fighter. Pep contended the fight at the heart of the article was his battle against Lulu Perez at Madison Square Garden in 1954. The suit claimed Pep suffered "mortification" as a result of the article.[2] In 1984, a six-member jury took just 15 minutes to return a verdict throwing out Pep's suit after a two-week civil trial at U.S. District Court in Manhattan.[3]

Maintaining his celebrity status in Connecticut, Pep continued making appearances and even hosting events at popular area establishments, such as the Candlelight Restaurant and Lounge in Windsor. What many didn't see, or hear about, was how many times Willie Pep came to the assistance of a friend or former colleague. For example, he made the drive from Hartford to Waterbury, Connecticut, to sit in on a court hearing involving one of his former ring opponents. Very few participants in the fight game end up a champion, and for some that destiny was difficult to handle; subsequently, alcohol and drug addiction could present a problem. Understanding this, Pep, a true champion, lent a hand.[4]

Dr. Joyce Brothers, who knew more than most about the sweet science, once quipped facetiously, "My husband and I have never considered divorce ... murder sometimes, but never divorce." She agreed that boxing marriages always presented the greatest challenges. Always. Pep's marriage to Geraldine M. Volpe would draw to a conclusion during this period.

On September 19, 1982, Willie Pep celebrated his 60th birthday at a private party in Hartford. Greeting friends and family, the former champion was delighted that folks hadn't forgotten about him. One of the special birthday gifts he received was the robe he wore during his Garden battle against Chalky Wright. After four decades, it still fit.

Connecticut boxing, in a state of recovery after being outlawed for years, was showing signs of promise despite the tragic loss of Charles Newell. One of Hartford's own, Marlon Starling, a product of local development and guidance, won the NABF, WBA, WBC, and USBA welterweight championships before the end of the decade. Slowly, new managers, trainers and fighters were emerging. Like the swallows returning to San Juan Capistrano in California, it was good sign.

When asked his opinions on current aspects of the fight game, Pep never pulled any punches. He believed that championship fights should be 15 rounds, and that any *real* champion should be able to make the distance without being put at risk. He had mixed views regarding thumbless gloves; specifically, he believed the advantage went to the aggressor. A defensive boxer couldn't open his hands to block punches. Forever a conditioning advocate, the former champion believed in aggressive, but not overly aggressive management, and quality trainers.

"A mother is the truest friend we have, when trials heavy and sudden fall upon us; when adversity takes the place of prosperity; when friends desert us; when trouble thickens around us, still will she cling to us, and endeavor by her kind precepts and counsels to dissipate the clouds of darkness, and cause peace to return to our hearts." So wrote author Washington Irving. Mary Ann (Marchesi) Papaleo, widow of Salvatore Papaleo, died on December on December 12, 1983. A communicant of St. Luke's Church in Hartford, she had befriended and charmed everyone she came in contact with during her half-century in Hartford. She was survived by her two sons, William and Nicholas, and a daughter, Mrs. Frances Nevico; a brother, sister, eight grandchildren, and two great-grandchildren.[5]

Complacent in his role as an inspector for the Department of Consumer Protection's Athletic Division in 1986, Willie Pep believed he had finally found a home.[6] The job, interspersed with appearances and promotions, he felt, kept him out of trouble—one minute he was pushing Berettas at Zoppi's Police Supplies & Paraphernalia in Southington, and the next thing you know he's at an all-star softball game to benefit Camp Courant and Channel 3 Country Camp.

Cupid struck again. Willie Pep married Barbara A. Moskus on September 19, 1987. Delightful and kind-hearted, Moskus seemed the perfect fit for the former champion. Speaking of relationships, Pep, 65, and Sandy Saddler, 61, managed to have lunch together at Carmichael's Restaurant on Wethersfield Avenue in Hartford. Both were attending a gala at Valle's Steak House in Hartford. The former featherweight champions enjoyed their day, a bulk of which was spent signing autographs or commenting about the current condition of boxing.

Connecticut boxing was trying hard to plant itself firmly in the fight game in 1988, but it wasn't easy. Granted some stars had emerged from the amateur ranks, such as WBA welterweight champion Marlon Starling, but the opportunities, not to mention purses, weren't there. It was going to take time.

Willie Pep was in Deadwood, South Dakota, at the end of January 1988, attending an amateur boxing show. When questioned about the location, Pep admitted he hadn't been there before—he was not alone.[7]

Pep always enjoyed the Connecticut Boxing Guild dinners (now in their 40th year), so when he discovered another event to add to his growing list, he was delighted. The Old Time Fighters Reunion, which began in 1984, quickly became one of the former champion's favorites. Angelo Fuggetta headed up the evening, which attracted a great crowd. For example, in 1988 guests included: Max Atwater, Johnny Cesario, Al Couture, Tony DeMarco, Sal DiMartino, Johnny Duke, Rocky Graziano, Billy Kearns, Manny Leibert, Billy Lynch, Carey Mace, Sal Maltempo, Pep, and Bob Steele (emcee). Oh, what most would have given to be a fly on the wall for conversations among these ring heroes.

A resurgence of the sport was underway as evidenced in the gymnasiums across the state by the end of the decade. Granted, the national exposure generated by stars such as Roberto Duran, Marvin Hagler, Thomas Hearns, Sugar Ray Leonard, and Mike Tyson certainly didn't hurt. The Hartford Boxing Club, on Charter Oak Avenue in the capitol city, was one such example—the beat of the bag could be heard as far north as Springfield, Massachusetts.

The Death of Sugar Ray Robinson

The only other man who could be compared to Willie Pep as the best pound-for-pound fighter ever, Sugar Ray Robinson, died on April 12, 1989, in Culver City, California, at age 67. Born Walker Smith, Jr., the legendary boxer suffered from Alzheimer's disease, diabetes, and high blood pressure. In a career that spanned three decades, the boxer set the standard for greatness. And Willie Pep agreed. Naturally, the memories came flooding back. From an amateur battle in Norwich, Connecticut, to even appearing on the same fight card later in their careers, the surnames Robinson and Pep, or was it Smith and Papaleo, will forever be etched in the minds of fight fans.

On September 29, 1989, Willie Pep retired from his job as a state boxing inspector. Did this mean the elite fighter, who never sat still in a ring, might finally stand still outside of one? Not a chance. Pep was later named a partner in the boxing management company International Great Fights, Incorporated.[8] He was also sworn in on November 1, 1989, as a special deputy sheriff and assigned to Superior Court in Hartford.

The Nineties

"Now is no time to think of what you do not have. Think of what you can do with what there is."—Ernest Hemingway, *The Old Man and the Sea*

The idea of a Boxing Hall of Fame wasn't new. There had been a few, notably that established by *The Ring* magazine in 1954. However, that effort had been abandoned. Not blind to an opportunity, nor unfamiliar with the sport of boxing, the small village of Canastota, in upstate New York, launched the International Boxing Hall of Fame. As the former home of world champions Carmen Basilio and his nephew Billy Backus, the backdrop was ideal and the effort genuine. As it set off to prove its legitimacy, only time would tell if it could be sustained. The museum opened in June 1989.

In 1990, Willie Pep was one of 53 people inducted into the shrine. Among the others were Muhammad Ali, Henry Armstrong, Jack Dempsey, and Jake LaMotta, to name merely a few. On June 8, Willie Pep made the pilgrimage to Canastota, New York, 15 miles east of Syracuse. His enshrinement into the International Boxing Hall of Fame would take place on June 10. About 600 people witnessed the induction of the charter members, and while Muhammad Ali grabbed the spotlight, it was clear that Willie Pep was

Boxing Hall of Fame

Welcome to the International Boxing Hall of Fame Museum

Our mission is to honor and preserve boxing's rich heritage, chronicle the achievements of those who excelled, provide an educational experience for our many visitors, and operate our facility in a manner that enhances the image of the sport.

Inaugural Induction – June 10, 1990

This program cover is from the Inaugural Induction, June 10, 1990, at the International Boxing Hall of Fame in Canastota, New York (image courtesy of International Boxing Hall of Fame).

destined to become a fan favorite—this despite a separated shoulder that forced him to wear a sling.

More important than Willie Pep's induction was the creation of the institution. He now had an outlet, which he took advantage of, to confirm his immortality. It was a mere 230 miles (or 3 hours and 30 minutes) from his Connecticut home.

From Canastota, Pep headed to Las Vegas to attend an event in his honor, "Salute to Willie Pep," that was held at the Dunes Hotel. From there it was back to Hartford, where he and his wife took a table at a special concert given by Al Martino. The event was held at Hartford Civic Center's Assembly and Exhibition Hall on June 28, 1990. Pep and Martino had been friends for decades, and neither would miss an opportunity to spend time with the other.

The boom in sports memorabilia gave stars, including Willie Pep, who believed they were forgotten a new revenue stream and proof that they were remembered and appreciated. From trading card shows with football great Y.A. Tittle to sitting next to baseball stars such as George Kell and Monte Irvin, Pep had a blast. If this was his future, he liked it.[9]

And things got even better: The emergence of casino boxing in Connecticut began on April 23, 1992. Foxwoods High Stakes Bingo & Casino hosted its first

Outside the Boxing Hall of Fame in Canastota, Willie Pep strikes a pose for the media (image courtesy of International Boxing Hall of Fame).

boxing show that saw Tommy Morrison knock out Kimmuel Odum in the main event. Ringside celebrities included University of Connecticut basketball coach Jim Calhoun, WBA junior middleweight champion Vinny Pazienza, and Willie Pep. It didn't take a Yale economist to realize that the 2,200 fight fans at the venue were witnessing the future of the fight game.

It's a Matter of Age

It was Willie Pep's 70th birthday on September 19, 1992, and over 500 fans bought tickets to the celebration that was held at the Sheraton Ballroom. The former champion knew he was getting old because the candles cost more than the cake. Joining the boxing legend were Carmen Basilio, Tony DeMarco, and Joey Giardello. New York comedian Pat Cooper planned to keep the night rolling with laughter. As if Pep's birthday wasn't enough to celebrate, those in attendance could also commemorate the half-century mark of another event: It had been that long since Pep won the featherweight championship from Chalky Wright.[10]

As you age, change, be it the loss of a friend or family member, or even a local venue, gets harder to accept. Like an iceberg, pieces break away or slowly melt. When Pep, like many others, learned that Frank's Restaurant downtown was closing, it stung like a left jab to the shoulder. Owner Frank Parseliti, 88, was calling it a day. He opened his first restaurant at the corner of Asylum and Ann streets back in 1944. It was *the* place to see and be seen. Later, Parseliti moved the restaurant to 159 Asylum Street, then on to City Place, where it was today. Pep loved it there and knew that

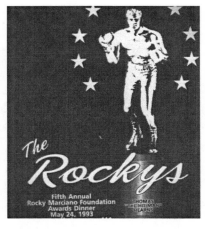

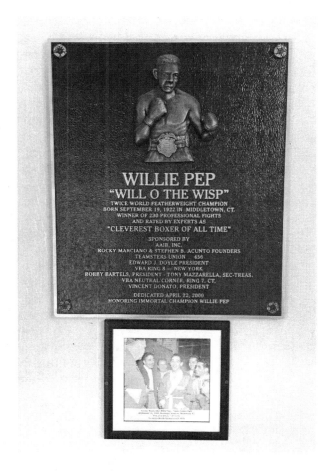

Forever attending banquets and award ceremonies, Willie Pep was often the guest of honor. A plaque (left) honoring immortal champion Willie Pep (Middletown, CT). A program (top right) from the Fifth Annual Rocky Marciano Foundation Awards Dinner (1993). A program (bottom right) from the Oldtime Fighter's Reunion sponsored by The Neutral Corner (1998).

Frankie would always "take care of him," pamper him. But as in many cities, the vibe that once existed downtown faded with the growth of suburbia.[11]

A native of Schenectady, New York, and cherished in Hartford and Tampa, Lou Viscusi had been living in Houston over the past decade. A stroke paralyzed one side of his body in 1986, and four years later another stroke left him completely disabled. Viscusi died on August 10, 1997, in Houston. Though he lacked the ability to respond, his family held the phone to his ear whenever a familiar voice, such as that of Willie Pep, called to cheer him up. Viscusi meant the world to Pep, and vice versa.

Over 200 admirers turned out to celebrate Willie Pep's 75th birthday at Marc Anthony's Café on 1000 Wethersfield Avenue in Hartford. It was also the 15th year of The Neutral Corner boxing fraternity, and the 10th wedding anniversary for Willie and his charming wife, Barbara. With Pep praised by everyone from Bob Steele to Angelo Dundee, it was a wonderful evening.[12]

Johnny Cesario and Willie Pep spent a lot of good times together. Not a surprise, considering both were guided by Lou Viscusi. Through the 1940s and into the 1950s, they traveled together and shared stories like brothers. Cesario won his first 40 professional fights, which likely would have garnered more press had Pep not won even more. Although he fought champions such as Carmen Basilio and Willie Pastrano, he never fought for a title. Cesario was always fighting along that edge between good and great. In the end it didn't matter, because outside the ring he was a champion. His altruistic acts on behalf of local charities, such as the Connecticut Children's Medical Center and Hartford's Alcohol and Drug Recovery Center, were admirable and, above all, genuine. Johnny Cesario lost his battle to cancer on October 5, 1997.

As the decade and century wound down, a five-member panel for the Associated Press named Willie Pep the fifth-best fighter of the 20th century. They also named him the top featherweight boxer of the 20th century. Sugar Ray Robinson was voted fighter of the century.[13] Not bad for a bootblack born in Middletown.[14]

An Irrevocable Condition

"Perhaps," as author James Baldwin once quipped, "home is not a place but simply an irrevocable condition." For Willie Pep, that condition could be found in two places, the Casa Loma in Hartford and Graziano's World Famous Restaurant & Inn in Canastota. Paul A. LaRosa, owner of The Casa Loma on Wethersfield Avenue, was

Inside the Boxing Hall of Fame in Canastota, Willie Pep compares his fist to other legends of the fight game (image courtesy of International Boxing Hall of Fame).

Forever linked, both Willie Pep (top) and Sandy Saddler (bottom) were frequent visitors to Canastota, New York.

not only a lifelong friend to the elite fighter, but was more like a brother. They knew what each other was thinking before either of them said it. LaRosa, the same age as Pep, was ringside when the fighter won the feather crown at the Garden in 1942, and tableside next to his friend at the turn of the century. Welcomed each time he dropped into the restaurant, Pep loved seeing his old friends and sharing in forgotten stories. And he never left without a smile on his face.

Tony Graziano, owner of Graziano's World Famous Restaurant & Inn on North Peterboro Street, filled in for LaRosa when Pep was in Canastota. They even named a room after "Will o' the Wisp" at the Inn. Like LaRosa and Pep, Graziano was a World War II veteran. Like Paul, Tony could spin a war or ring tale quicker than Pep could spin his opponents. The former featherweight champion was always welcome at "Graz's."

Not only a staple at induction weekends, Willie Pep would also visit Canastota on a whim. For him, these places were his scrapbook of memories. From dusty old black & white wire photos to torn fight posters, a remembrance was often a wall or booth away. Whether daily life was working in your favor or not, consolation was assured.

The Final Rounds

Every boxer's life ends the same way: The final bell sounds and he awaits the decision. Determining that will not only be his performance during the rounds, but his life led between them.

As the century turned, signs surfaced that Willie Pep might be facing some challenges of old age. Things such as forgetting dates, trouble driving (Pep's keys to his automobile were taken away in 2000), not wanting to do certain activities, and even conversations that were a bit hard to follow, were common with many older individuals. They could also be signs of trouble. In September 2000, Pep took a bad fall down a flight of stairs at his apartment and hurt his head. Concern for his care grew and led to the former champion being placed in the West Hill Nursing Home at Rocky Hill.

Individual sports, such as boxing, are prone to rivalries. Jack Dempsey brought Gene Tunney into the limelight, or was it the other way around? Did Zale make Graziano, or did Graziano make Zale? Like it or not, Sandy Saddler brought out the best and worst of Willie Pep, and the crafty "Will o' the Wisp" returned the favor. The final meeting between the gladiators was one of the dirtiest matches in championship boxing history, and although folks wanted to turn away from it, they could not. It was a riveting, no-holds-barred street brawl between the two greatest featherweights in boxing history. On September 18, 2001, Sandy Saddler, a former featherweight champion renowned for his four battles with Willie Pep, died at the Schervier Nursing Care Center in the Bronx. He was 75.

Doctors believed Pep exhibited early-stage dementia, a progressive condition in which the brain degenerates, causing severe memory, speech, and motor-skills loss.[15] Many of the symptoms, including memory loss and confusion, can occur in dementia diseases as well as Alzheimer's. This makes an early diagnosis difficult. If you thought a boxing match was challenging to witness, viewing a person suffering from either of these cruel diseases can be heartbreaking.

In a challenging piece of journalism, Johnny Mason of the *Hartford Courant* penned an emotional account titled, "Fight of Pep's Life, as the Former Champ's Memory Slips Away, His Loved Ones Spar Over His Care," on Sunday, February 18, 2001. It extracted every level of human sentiment and left

"If a man can bridge the gap between life and death, if he can live after he's died, then maybe he was a great man. Immortality is the only true success."—James Dean

you in a ball of tears—you cried not only for the greatest boxer who ever lived, but for his incredible friends and family. While multiple marriages can create complexities, they can also provoke love like you have never seen before. The endearment exhibited by Pep's family, many of whom were with him daily, along with his friends, was as strong and sincere as anything you could hope to witness. The courage they exemplified was as great as what Willie brought to the ring each and every battle.

Willie Pep died on November 23, 2006 (Thanksgiving Day). He was 84.[16]

Appendix A:
A Canastota Scrapbook

"There is no final bell for a fighter who makes it to Canastota, only immortality."

For fight fans, Willie Pep's many visits to Canastota, home of the International Boxing Hall of Fame, were priceless memories. For those born after his career, this was how they recalled the elite pugilist. "The Champ" loved the adulation, the charm of the little village, dining at Graziano's Casa Mia Italian Restaurant, the hospitality of the volunteers, and the friendship of Hall of Fame Director Edward "Eddie" Brophy. Pep's final attendance at the Hall of Fame Induction Weekend came in 1999.

This section includes a handful of photos taken during Pep's visits.

Left: **Theodore Roosevelt, an amateur pugilist and professional politician, once quipped, "Believe you can and you're halfway there." In the ring, Willie Pep never doubted his skills (image courtesy of International Boxing Hall of Fame).**

Left: Two elite featherweights, Alexis Argüello (left) and Willie Pep, posing for pictures at the International Boxing Hall of Fame (image courtesy of International Boxing Hall of Fame).

Below: Alexis Argüello (right) and Willie Pep became an entertaining duo during Induction weekend at the International Boxing Hall of Fame.

Alexis Argüello throws a vicious left hook from behind Willie Pep during Induction weekend at the International Boxing Hall of Fame (image courtesy of International Boxing Hall of Fame).

Willie Pep pointing out the replica poster of his fight with Phil Terranova on February 19, 1945, at Madison Square Garden (image courtesy of International Boxing Hall of Fame).

José ("Chegüi") Torres (right), an Olympic silver medalist (1956), greets Willie Pep inside a Canastota restaurant during Induction Weekend.

Always accommodating to fight fans, Willie Pep looks down to sign an autograph.

"I've got it made. I've got a wife and a TV set—and they're both working."—Willie Pep

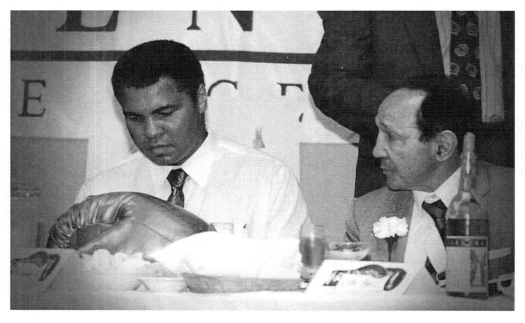

Be not afraid of greatness. Perhaps the two greatest pugilists ever: Muhammad Ali (left) and Willie Pep (image courtesy of International Boxing Hall of Fame).

Without boxing, or a canvas, life for Willie Pep, or Pablo Picasso, would likely have been far less gratifying. And not just for them.

Appendix B:
Guglielmo Papaleo—Boxing Record

Born: September 19, 1922, in Middletown, Connecticut
[There were times, such as an application for his boxing license (No. 5355) in Wisconsin, that William Papaleo stated his date of birth as September 19, 1920.]

Died: November 23, 2006

Alias: Willie Pep, "Hartford's fighting baby," Will O' The Wisp (circa 1947), The Hartford Hammer

Measurements: At age 24: Height: 5'5½" Weight: 126 lbs., Neck: 15", Reach: 68 inches, Chest Normal: 32¾ inches, Chest Expanded: 35 inches, Forearm: 10½ inches, Fist: 11 inches, Biceps: 12 inches, Thigh: 18½ inches, Wrist: 6 inches, and Ankle: 8¾ inches.

Punch Analysis: outstanding left hook, commanding left jab, solid right cross, good right uppercut and a superb use of combinations.

Boxing Inspirations: Bobby "Poison" Ivy, Lou Ambers, Tony Canzoneri, Jimmy Leto, Joe Louis, and Rocky Marciano

Fight Managers: Mushky Salow (amateur), Lenny Marello, along with Pete Perone (beginning in 1940), Lou Viscusi & Pete Reilly, Lou Viscusi & Ed Hurley, Lou Viscusi (July 1942–1959), George Sheppard/Jim Higgins (1965–1966)

Pre-fight Meal: Steak, salad, jello, hot tea with lemon.

Superstitions: Pep wrapped his own hands before a bout; always kept good-luck water bucket ("Spitzy") and bottle ("Guzz.") in his corner; like Willie Pastrano, Pep often tied his wedding ring into his shoelaces; on every fight night during his winning streaks, he wore the same suit. When a streak was broken by a loss, his friend Charley "Shikey" Greenberg, who was the same size, was given the suit.

Notes: As an amateur, Guglielmo Papaleo was identified as Willie Pep, Willie Papaleo, Willie Pepp, and even Willie Pepe. Please also note: a George Pepp (also spelled Pepe), of Meriden, fought at 130 pounds; and Willie Pipp, a lightweight from Willimantic, also fought as an amateur.

Abbreviations:

AC=Athletic Club; Aud=Auditorium; Bldg=Building; CABC=Connecticut Amateur Boxing Championship; D=Draw; DV=Date of fight varies; E=Exhibition; FGH=Foot Guard Hall; Fort H. H. Armory=Fort Homer Hesterly Armory; KO=Knockout Victory; L=Lost; Main=Main Event; MSG=Madison Square Garden; Post=Postponed;

SP=Spelling Variations; Stad=Stadium; Sub=Substitute; TBD=To Be Determined; TKO=Technical Knockout; W=Won.

All fights, minus those that appear in italics, were confirmed by at least three sources. Those fights that appear in italics have been confirmed by at least one reputable source.

Select Amateur Fights

1937

Date	Opponent	Location	Result	Comments
First amateur bout		Danbury, CT	W	

Notes: Guglielmo Papaleo was paid five dollars for the fight, two dollars of which was used to pay for his license.

1938

Date	Opponent	Location	Result	Comments
	Angelo Rodano	Norwalk, CT	L	Pep's 2nd bout
Graduates Barnard Junior High				
June 30	Henry Reese (as Willie Papaleo)	Hartford, CT	W3	Capitol Park
July 7	Dennis (Don) Lyons	Hartford, CT	D3	South Park
July 14	George "Georgie" Stone	Hartford, CT	—	Capitol Park-Post
July 16	George "Georgie" Stone	Hartford, CT	—	Young Berrio subs for Pep
July 28	George "Georgie" Stone	Hartford, CT	W3	Capitol Park
Aug 2	Young Levine (Lavigne)	Rockville, CT	W3	Sandy Beach Arena
Aug 4	Spike Murphy	Hartford, CT	TKO2	Capitol Park
Aug 11	George "Georgie" Stone	Hartford, CT	W3	Capitol Park
Aug 18	Chuck Wolack	Hartford, CT	W3	Capitol Park; DV
Aug 25	Young Levine (Lavigne)	Hartford, CT	—	Capitol Park-Scheduled
Sept 1	Henry Reese	Hartford, CT	W3	Capitol Park
Sept 5	George "Georgie" Stone	Norwich, CT	W3	Duwell AC
Sept 8	Joe Barisano	Hartford, CT	W3	Capitol Park
Sept 16	Bye (Prelim. Amateur Tour.)	Hartford, CT	—	Capitol Park
All contests above at age 15.				
Sept 22	Second Tournament Round	Hartford, CT	—	Capitol Park-Post
Sept 29	Second Tournament Round	Hartford, CT	—	Foot Guard Hall-Post
Sept 30	Zeno Hardy	New Haven, CT	W3	Arena
Oct 13	Vito Tallarita	New Haven, CT	W3	Arena; Semi-final
	Earl Roys	New Haven, CT	W3	Arena; Final CABC

Won Connecticut State Amateur Flyweight Championship

Date	Opponent	Location	Result	Comments
Oct 27	Earl Roys	New Haven, CT		North Carolina Arena
Nov 4	Buddy Lesso	New Britain, CT	TKO2	Stanley Arena
Nov 11	George "Georgie" Stone	Norwich, CT	W3	Duwell AC
Nov 17	Joel Meyers	New Haven, CT	W3	Arena; Pro/Amateur card
Dec 2	Ray Roberts (Ray Robinson)	Norwich, CT	L3	Duwell AC (42nd bout)

Notes: Pep did not go beyond high school. It wasn't unusual for Pep to use lead weights in his waistband to reach the minimum weight requirement. Angelo Rodano was a talented boxer from South Norwalk. Willie Pep claimed that the loss to Rodano was his 22nd amateur bout. There were likely four unverified victories between the Rodano loss in Norwalk and the loss Pep took to Ray Roberts on December 2, 1938. George "Georgie" Stone, of Willimantic, was the 1938 state flyweight (112 lbs.) champion; Stone's fight against Pep on July 14 was postponed by rain. Stone defeated Young Berrio, who substituted for Pep, on Saturday July 16. The fighter identified as Young Levine on August 2 was likely the same fighter identified as Young Lavigne on August 25. Pep's battle against Wolack, on August 18 garnered him a *Hartford Courant* headline. The Tallarita battle was during the semi-finals of the Connecticut State Amateur Championship; and the Ray Roberts (123 lbs.), aka Sugar Ray Robinson, fight was Pep's improbable early encounter with the elite boxer.

1939 (as Willie Pep, semi-pro)

Date	Opponent	Location	Result	Comments
Jan 20	George "Georgie" Stone	Norwich, CT	KO1	Duwell AC

For a period of time, Pep worked as a stock boy and clerk at a wallpaper company ($18 a week) to support the family.

May 4–9 Pep did NOT participate   New Haven, CT Arena
    Connecticut State Amateur Bantamweight Championship
    Featherweight (open) champion: Earl Roys
    Featherweight (novice): Nick Schaffer
    Bantamweight (open) champion: Russ Barnes
    Bantamweight (novice) Joey Wasnick

July 1	Earl Roys	Manchester, CT	L3	Red Man AC

(All contests below: Willie Pep classified as a semi-pro)

July 20	Joey Wasnick	Hartford, CT	—	Capitol Park
July 20	Billy Dayton	Hartford, CT	TKO3	Capitol Park; Sub
July 28	Roughhouse Vivienzo	Manchester, CT	KO3	Red Man AC
Aug 3	Russ Barnes	Hartford, CT	W3	Capitol Park

Claimed Connecticut State Amateur Bantamweight Championship

Aug 10	Roughhouse Vivienzo	Hartford, CT	KO3	Capitol Park
Aug 17	Joey Schultz	Hartford, CT	KO3	Capitol Park
Sept 1	Joey Clapps	West Haven, CT	W3	White City Stadium
Sept 6	Dom Centerino	West Haven, CT	—	White City Stadium
Sept 12	Dom Centerino	West Haven, CT	D3	White City Stadium
Sept 15	Joe DeJohn	New Haven, CT	W3	Arena

All contests above at age 16.

Sept 21	Dom Centerino	New Haven, CT	W3	Arena
Oct 5	Billy Marcus	New Haven, CT	W3	Arena
Oct 19	Billy Marcus	New Haven, CT	W3	Arena
Oct 26	Mickey Pronto	New Haven, CT	TKO3	Arena
Dec 1	Henry Davis	Manchester, CT	D3	Red Men AC
Dec 8	Charlie Hurst	New Britain, CT	—	Stanley Arena, Replaced
Dec 8	Earl Roys	New Britain, CT	—	Stanley Arena, Scheduled

Notes: The Connecticut classifications of amateur, semi-pro, and professional were nor clearly defined. On July 20, Billy Dayton was a substitute for New Haven boxer Joey Wasnick. Pete Perone was the matchmaker for Capitol Park. Pep claimed that his July 1 battle against Earl Roys, the state flyweight champions, should have been a draw; Pep also asserted that by defeating Russ Barnes on August 3, he had claim to his title.

1940

Date	Opponent	Location	Result	Comments
Jan 4	Buddy Donovan	New Haven, CT	W4	Arena
Jan 12	Eddie Cuneo	Norwich, CT	W3	Du-Well/Duwell AC
Mar 1	Vito Tallarita	New Britain, CT	TKO1	Stanley Arena
Mar 15	*Henry Davis*	*New Britain, CT*	*W3*	*Stanley Arena*
June 20	*Eddie Cuneo*	*New London, CT*	*W3*	*Drum Corp Center*
June 27	Kid Shumac	Rockville, CT	—	Sandy Beach Arena

Date	Opponent	Location	Result	Comments
July 3	*James McGovern*	*Hartford, CT*	*W 4*	*See Notes*
July 12	Jimmy Stenta	Rockville, CT	TKO1	Sandy Beach Arena

Notes: January 4 bout was billed as the "feature semi-pro contest" on the fight card (see *Record-Journal* [Meriden, CT]); the decision was extremely unpopular. Regarding the July 3 contest against James McGovern: This bout has been incorrectly noted by some sources, including the *Brooklyn Daily Eagle*, as Pep's first professional fight. Pep fought under the semi-pro designation, as he also did for his battle against Jimmy Stenta on July 12.

Willie Pep often claimed that he had an amateur record of 59–3–3, in 65 bouts.

(Likely it was 58–3–4, in 65 bouts. In addition to the unverified victories, there was also an unverified draw against Angelo Rodano, prior to 1940.)

Professional Record

1940

Date	Opponent	Location	Result	Comments
July 25	Joey Marcus	Hartford, CT	W4	Bulkeley Stadium
Aug 8	Joey Wasnick	Hartford, CT	KO3	Bulkeley Stadium
Aug 29	Tommy Burns	Hartford, CT	TKO1	Bulkeley Stadium
Sept 5	Joey Marcus	Waterbury, CT	W4	Randolph-Clowes Stad.

All contests above at age 17.

Date	Opponent	Location	Result	Comments
Sept 19	Jackie Moore	Hartford, CT	W6	Bulkeley Stadium
Oct 3	Billy Marcus	Waterbury, CT	—	Municipal Stadium
Oct 3	Jimmy Ritchie	Waterbury, CT	TKO3	Mun. Stad; Sub
Oct 24	Henry Davis	New Haven, CT	—	Arena
Oct 24	James McGovern	New Haven, CT	W4	Arena; Sub
Nov 22	Carlo Daponde (DePonte)	New Britain, CT	TKO6	Stanley Arena; SP
Nov 29	Frank (Al) Topazio	New Britain, CT	TKO5	Stanley Arena; SP
Dec 6	Jimmy Mutone	New Britain, CT	KO2	Stanley Arena

Notes: Pep made his pro debut at 123½ pounds. Joey Marcus was the first fighter that Pep met twice. Joey Wasnick was the first boxer Pep (124 lbs.) faced with a winning record; Joey Wasnick was Pep's first knockout victim. Tommy Burns, who was dropped three times, was Pep's first opening round victory. At 122½ pounds, Tommy Burns was the lightest fighter Pep faced; "Kid" Kaplan refereed Pep's battle against Burns. Jackie Moore was Pep's first six-round fight. Carlo Daponde (DePonte) was the first boxer to floor Pep (nine count), and, he did so in the opening round. The October 24 bout has been listed by some sources as Jimmy McAllister (*Record-Journal*, Meriden, CT). When Pep finally did meet McAllister for the first time it was in 1945—there was no reference to an October 24 battle. "Kid" Kaplan refereed November 22 bout, and the December 6 battle was scheduled for six rounds.

1941

Date	Opponent	Location	Result	Comments
Jan 13	Joe Echevarria	Holyoke, MA	W6	Valley Arena
Jan 28	Jackie Harris	New Haven, CT	—	Arena
Jan 28	Augie Almeida	New Haven, CT	TKO6	Arena; Sub
Feb 3	*Joe Echevarria*	*Holyoke, MA*	*W6*	*Arena*
Feb 10	Don Lyons	Holyoke, MA	KO2	Valley Arena
Feb 17	Ruby Garcia	Holyoke, MA	W6	Valley Arena
Mar 3	Ruby Garcia	Holyoke, MA	W6	Valley Arena (late match)
Mar 25	Marty Shapiro	Hartford, CT	W6	Foot Guard Hall
Mar 31	Joey Gatto	Holyoke, MA	KO2	Valley Arena; Feature
Apr 14	Danny Carabella	Holyoke, MA	—	Valley Arena; Feature
Apr 14	Henry Vasquez	Holyoke, MA	W6	Valley Arena; Sub

Date	Opponent	Location	Result	Comments
Apr 22	Joey Silva	Hartford, CT	W6	Foot Guard Hall
May 6	Joey Stack	Hartford, CT	—	Foot Guard Hall
May 6	Lou Puglese	Hartford, CT	KO2	Foot Guard Hall; Sub *
May 12	Johnny Cockfield	Holyoke, MA	W6	Valley Arena *
June 12	Harry Hintlian	Manchester, CT	—	Rained out; SV

nose operation

Date	Opponent	Location	Result	Comments
June 19	Harry Hintlian	Manchester, CT	W6	Red Men's Arena
June 24	Eddie DeAngelis	Hartford, CT	TKO3	Bulkeley Stadium
July 15	Jimmy Gilligan	Hartford, CT	W8	Bulkeley Stadium
Aug 1	*Harry Hintlian*	*Manchester, CT*	*W6*	*Red Men's Arena*
Aug 5	Paul Frechette	Hartford, CT	TKO3	Bulkeley Stadium
Aug 11	Eddie Flores	Thompsonville, CT	KO1	Carpet City Arena
Aug 15	Terry Amico	North Adams, MA	—	Rained Out

All contests above at age 18.

Date	Opponent	Location	Result	Comments
Sept 25	Jackie Harris	New Haven, CT	TKO1	Arena
Oct 9	Carlos Manzano	New Haven, CT	W8	Arena
Oct 21	Al Dionne	Hartford, CT	—	Foot Guard Hall
Oct 21	Connie Savoie (Savoy)	Hartford, CT	KO2	Foot Guard Hall; SV; Sub
Nov 7	Kent Martinez	Hollywood, CA	—	Legion Stadium
Nov 7	Buddy Spencer	Hollywood, CA	W4	Legion Stadium; Sub
Nov 24	Davey Crawford	Holyoke, MA	W8	Valley Arena
Dec 12	Ruby Garcia	New York, NY	W4	MSG—1st Appear

Notes: * = fought as Willie Papaleo.

The Echevarria contest was Pep's first professional ring battle outside of CT; Harris fell ill with the flu and Almeida substituted for him. The Lyons contest was on a Beau Jack fight card. Ruby Garcia, Puerto Rican lightweight prospect, was Pep's first back-to-back contest with the same opponent. Pep's clash with Joey Gatto was a six-round feature, and his first real fight coverage in an Associated Press results column; Pep appeared in a large photograph on page 51 of the April 20, 1941, *Hartford Courant.* Pep's controversial clash with Jimmy Gilligan was his first to go eight rounds. Pep's bout with Flores was an outdoor show promoted by the Holyoke Valley Arena. The bout with Harris was the first for Pep in over a month. On September 25, this fight was the first time Harris failed to go the distance. Pep's first MSG performance was a preliminary to Fritzie Zivic-Al McCoy feature. Pep's fight against Ruby Garcia on December 12 was often quoted as his 32nd professional bout. If you extract the two fights that appear in italics text, this figure would be correct.

1942

Date	Opponent	Location	Result	Comments
Jan 8	Mexican Joey Rivers	Fall River, MA	TKO4	Casino
Jan 16	Sammy Parrotta	New York, NY	W4	MSG—2nd Appearance
Jan 27	Abe Kaufman	Hartford, CT	W8	Foot Guard Hall
Feb 10	Angelo Callura	Hartford, CT	W8	Foot Guard Hall
Feb 24	Willie Roache	Hartford, CT	W8	Foot Guard Hall
Mar 18	Johnny Compo	New Haven, CT	W8	Arena
Apr 14	Spider Armstrong	Hartford, CT	KO4	Auditorium; Gore 1st.
May 4	Curley Nichols	New Haven, CT	W8	Arena
May 12	Aaron Seltzer	Hartford, CT	W8	Auditorium
May 26	Joey Iannotti	Hartford, CT	W8	Auditorium
June 20	Exhibition	Hartford, CT	—	State House
June 23	Joey Archibald	Hartford, CT	W8	Bulkeley Stadium
July 1	Lou Viscusi officially takes over as sole manager.			
July 21	Abe Denner	Hartford, CT	W12	Bulkeley Stadium

Won Featherweight Championship of New England

Date	Opponent	Location	Result	Comments
July 31	Joey Silva	Waterbury, CT	—	Postponed, rain
Aug 1	Joey Silva	Waterbury, CT	TKO7	Randolph-Clowes Stad.
Aug 11	Pedro Hernandez	Hartford, CT	W10	Bulkeley Stadium
Aug 20	Nat Litfin	West Haven, CT	W10	White City Stadium
Sept 1	Bobby Ivy	Hartford, CT	TKO10	Bulkeley Stadium
Sept 10	Pedro Hernandez	New York, NY	—	MSG; Scheduled
Sept 10	Frank Franconeri	New York, NY	TKO1	MSG–3rd Appearance

All contests above at age 19.

Date	Opponent	Location	Result	Comments
Sept 22	Vince Dell'Orto	Hartford, CT	W10	Bulkeley Stad
Oct 5	Bobby McIntire	Holyoke, MA	W10	Valley Arena
Oct 16	Joey Archibald	Providence, RI	W10	Rhode Island Auditorium
Oct 27	George Zengaras	Hartford, CT	W10	Auditorium
Nov 20	Chalky Wright, I	New York, NY	W15	MSG—4th Appearance

Won Featherweight Championship of the World

Date	Opponent	Location	Result	Comments
Dec 8	Exhibition	Hartford, CT	—	Auditorium; absent
Dec 10	TBD	Jacksonville, FL	—	G.W. Hotel; moved
Dec 14	Lew Hanbury, Jr.	Washington, DC	—	Turner's Arena
Dec 14	(Jose) Aponte Torres	Washington, DC	KO7	Turner's Arena; substitute
Dec 21	Joey Silva	Jacksonville, FL	TKO9	G. Washington Hotel Aud.

Notes: January 8 bout was Pep's first main event; he was paid $48. The January 16 battle was on the undercard of Ray Robinson v. Fritzie Zivic. The Pep v. Kaufman main event was the first fight ever broadcast over W53H FM; Bob Steele and Keyes Perrin handled the call. The battle against Spider Armstrong of Toronto was part of the boxing inaugural at the new Auditorium being conducted by Hurley-Viscusi Promotions. This was also Pep's first $1,000 purse. Pep's battle against Archibald on June 23 was over eight rounds, not ten; Pep's battle with Denner was his first bout contracted over eight rounds. Pep's bout with Silva essentially premiered his trademark spin move. Following the Hernandez bout, and his $15,500 gate on August 11, Pep was picked up in Hugh Fullerton, Jr.'s national column. The September 22 contest was often referenced as the fighter's 50th pro bout. It was reported that $20,000 worth of tickets were sold to Connecticut buyers for Wright v. Pep. Wright received 40 percent of a $71,868.70 gate (19,521 attendance). The fight, according to New York Boxing Commission, was illegal as Pep was not 21 years of age and couldn't engage in a contest greater than ten rounds. Lew Hanbury, Jr., was scheduled to meet Pep on December 14, but he fractured a knuckle on his right hand during a sparring session.

1943

Date	Opponent	Location	Result	Comments
Jan 4	Vince Dell'Orto	New Orleans, LA	W10	Municipal Auditorium
Jan 15	Allie Stolz	New York, NY	—	MSG; Postponed
Jan 19	Bill Speary	Hartford, CT	W10	Auditorium
Jan 29	Allie Stolz	New York, NY	W10	MSG–5th Appearance
Feb 11	Davey Crawford	Boston, MA	W10	Mechanics Bldg.
Feb 15	Bill Speary	Baltimore, MD	W10	Coliseum
Mar 2	Lou Transparenti	Hartford, CT	KO6	Auditorium
Mar 5	Beau Jack	New York, NY	—	MSG; Tentative
Mar 19	Sammy Angott	New York, NY	L10	MSG–6th; W steak ends
Mar 29	Bobby McIntire	Detroit, MI	W10	Arena Gardens
Apr 9	Sal Bartolo	Boston, MA	W10	Boston Garden
Apr 19	Angel Aviles	Tampa, FL	W10	Municipal Auditorium
Apr 26	Jackie Wilson	Pittsburgh, PA	W12	Duquesne Gardens
June 8	Sal Bartolo, II	Boston, MA	W15	Braves Field

Won NYSAC Featherweight Championship of the World

Was sworn into the United States Navy on Wednesday, June 16 by Lieutenant Paul W. Bridwell.

Date	Opponent	Location	Result	Comments
June 25	Chalky Wright II	New York, NY	—	MSG; Scheduled

All contests above at age 20.

Notes: The tentative date for a battle with Beau Jack was listed because it was the nearest it ever came to fruition; and Promoter Mike Jacobs was hoping Pep would defend his title on March 19 against Chalky Wright.

1944

Date	Opponent	Location	Result	Comments
Apr 4	Leo Francis	Hartford, CT	W10	Auditorium
Apr 20	Harold Lacey	New Haven, CT	W10	Arena
May 1	Jackie Leamus	Philadelphia, PA	W10	Arena
May 19	Frankie Rubino	Chicago, IL	W10	Coliseum
May 23	Joey Bagnato	Buffalo, NY	KO2	Memorial Aud.
June 6	Julie Kogon	Hartford, CT	W10	Outdoor Aud. Arena
June 16	Juan Zurita	New York, NY	—	MSG; Postponed
July 7	Willie Joyce	Chicago, IL	W10	Comiskey Park
July 17	Manuel Ortiz	Boston, MA	W10	Braves Field
July 28	Lulu Constantino	Waterbury, CT	—	Municipal St.; Postponed
Aug 4	Lulu Constantino	Waterbury, CT	W10	Municipal Stadium
Aug 17	Willie Pep officially recognized by the state of Connecticut as Featherweight Champion of the World			
Aug 28	Joey Peralta	West Springfield, MA	W10	Old Dog Track
Sept 8	Chalky Wright, II	New York, NY	—	MSG; Postponed
Sept 14	Charley Cabey Lewis	Hartford, CT	—	Outdoor Aud; Postponed
Sept 19	Charley Cabey Lewis	Hartford, CT	TKO8	Outdoor Aud. Arena
Sept 29	Chalky Wright, II	New York, NY	W15	MSG–7th Appearance

NYSAC Featherweight Championship of the World

Date	Opponent	Location	Result	Comments
Oct 25	Bobby Gunther	Montreal, Canada	—	Forum; Replaced
Oct 25	Jackie Leamus	Montreal, Canada	W10	Forum. 1st Int.
Nov 14	Charley Cabey Lewis	Hartford, CT	W10	Auditorium
Nov 27	Pedro Hernandez	Washington, DC	W10	Uline Arena
Dec 5	Chalky Wright, III	Cleveland, Ohio	W10	Arena

Notes: The September 29 bout was broadcast on television as part of the *Gillette Cavalcade of Sports*. Most of the estimated 6,000 television sets in New York City were located in bars.

1945

Date	Opponent	Location	Result	Comments
Jan 23	Ralph Walton	Hartford, CT	W10	Auditorium
Feb 5	Willie Roache	New Haven, CT	W10	Arena
Feb 19	Phil Terranova	New York, NY	W15	MSG–8th Appearance

NYSAC Featherweight Championship of the World

Date	Opponent	Location	Result	Comments
Mar 13	Inducted into U.S. Army			
Oct 30	Paulie Jackson	Hartford, CT	W8	Auditorium
Nov 5	Mike Martyk	Buffalo, NY	TKO5	Memorial Aud.
Nov 26	Eddie Giosa	Boston, MA	W10	Mechanics Bldg.
Dec 5	Harold Gibson	Lewiston, ME	W10	Armory
Dec 13	Jimmy McAllister	Baltimore, MD	D10	Baltimore Garden
Dec 17	Johnny Virgo	Buffalo, NY	—	Memorial. Aud; Postponed

1946

Date	Opponent	Location	Result	Comments
Jan 15	Johnny Virgo	Buffalo, NY	KO2	Memorial Aud.

Date	Opponent	Location	Result	Comments
Feb 13	Jimmy Joyce	Buffalo, NY	W10	Memorial Aud.
Mar 1	Sal Bartolo	New York, NY	—	MSG; Scheduled
Mar 1	Jimmy McAllister	New York, NY	KO2	MSG—9th Appearance
Mar 26	Jackie Wilson	Kansas City, MI	W10	Municipal Aud.
Apr 8	Georgie Knox	Providence, RI	TKO3	Rhode Island Auditorium
May 6	Ernie Petrone	New Haven, CT	W10	Arena
May 13	Joey Angelo	Providence, RI	W10	Rhode Island Auditorium
May 22	Jose Aponte Torres	St. Louis, MI	W10	Kiel Auditorium
May 27	Jimmy Joyce	Minneapolis, MN	W8	Auditorium
June 7	Sal Bartolo, III	New York, NY	KO12	MSG—10th Appearance

NBA Featherweight Championship of the World
NYSAC Featherweight Championship of the World

Date	Opponent	Location	Result	Comments
June 26	Harold Gibson	Buffalo, NY	—	Civic Stadium; Replaced
July 10	Harold Gibson	Buffalo, NY	TKO7	Civic Stadium
July 25	Jackie Graves	Minneapolis, MN	KO8	Aud./No punch rd.
Aug 26	Doll Rafferty	Milwaukee, WI	KO6	Auditorium
Sept 4	Walter Kolby	Buffalo, NY	KO5	Memorial Auditorium
Sept 17	Lefty LaChance	Hartford, CT	KO3	Outdoor Aud. Arena
Sept 30	Paulie Jackson	Albany, NY	—	Hawkins Stadium; Post
Nov 1	Paulie Jackson	Minneapolis, MN	W10	Auditorium
Nov 15	Tomas Beato	Waterbury, CT	KO2	State Armory
Nov 27	Chalky Wright, IV	Milwaukee, WI	KO3	Auditorium
Dec	*fractured bone between ankle and toe*			
Dec 3	Bobby McQuillan	Buffalo, NY	—	Memorial Aud; Canceled
Dec 21	Miguel Acevedo	Havana, Cuba	—	Postponed

Notes: The June 7 contest was often referenced as the fighter's 100th professional victory.

1947

Date	Opponent	Location	Result	Comments
Jan 1	Charles "Cabey" Lewis	Milwaukee, WI	—	Auditorium; Canceled
Jan 5	*injured in airplane crash*			
Jan 25	Miguel Acevedo	Havana, Cuba	—	Postponed
Jan 28	Nel Tarleton	London, UK	—	Postponed
Jan-Jun	*convalescence from airplane crash*			
June 17	Victor Flores	Hartford, CT	W10	Auditorium
June 25	Jean Barriere	North Adams, MA	—	Rained Out
July 1	Joey Fontana	Albany, NY	KO5	Hawkins Stadium
July 8	Leo LeBrun	Norwalk, CT	W8	Crystal Arena
July 11	Jean Barriere	North Adams, MA	KO4	Meadowbrook Stadium
July 15	Paulie Jackson	New Bedford, MA	W10	Sargent Field
July 23	Humberto Sierra	Hartford, CT	W10	Outdoor Aud. Arena
Aug 22	Jock Leslie	Flint, MI	KO12	Atwood Stadium

Featherweight Championship of the World

Date	Opponent	Location	Result	Comments
Oct 21	Jean Barriere	Portland, ME	KO1	Exposition Bldg.
Oct 27	Archie Wilmer	Philadelphia, PA	W10	Arena
Dec 22	Alvaro Estrada	Lewiston, ME	W10	City Hall
Dec 30	Lefty LaChance	Manchester, NH	KO8	Recreation Center

1948

Date	Opponent	Location	Result	Comments
Jan 6	Pedro Biesca (Blesca)	Hartford, CT	W10	Auditorium

Date	Opponent	Location	Result	Comments
Jan 12	Jimmy McAllister	St. Louis, MO	W10	Kiel Aud.
Jan 19	Joey Angelo	Boston, MA	W10	Boston Garden
Feb 24	Humberto Sierra	Miami, FL	TKO10	Orange Bowl

Featherweight Championship of the World

Date	Opponent	Location	Result	Comments
Apr 30	Leroy Willis	Detroit, MI	—	Olympia Stadium; Postponed
May 7	Leroy Willis	Detroit, MI	W10	Olympia Stadium
May 19	Charley Cabey Lewis	Milwaukee, WI	W10	Auditorium
June 17	Miguel Acevedo	Minneapolis, MN	W10	Auditorium
June 25	Luther Burgess	Flint, MI	W10	Atwood Stadium
July 28	Young Junior	Utica, NY	KO1	Bennett's Field
Aug 3	Teddy Davis	Hartford, CT	W10	Outdoor Aud. Arena
Aug 17	Teddy Davis	Hartford, CT	W10	Outdoor Aud. Arena
Sep 2	Johnny Dell	Waterbury, CT	TKO8	Municipal Stadium
Sep 10	Paddy DeMarco	New York, NY	W10	MSG—11th Appearance
Oct 12	Chuck Burton	Jersey City, NJ	W8	Jersey City Gardens
Oct 19	Johnny LaRusso	Hartford, CT	W10	Auditorium
Oct 29	Sandy Saddler, I	New York, NY	L KO4	MSG—12th Appearance

Featherweight Championship of the World

Date	Opponent	Location	Result	Comments
Dec 20	Hermie Freeman	Boston, MA	W10	Boston Garden

Notes: Initially, Pep's title defense against Sierra was planned for Flamingo Park, a baseball field; and on June 25, in a rare occurrence, the featherweight champion was a substitute for boxer Jackie Graves.

1949

Date	Opponent	Location	Result	Comments
Jan 17	Teddy Davis	St. Louis, MO	W10	Kiel Auditorium
Jan 25	TBD	Hartford, CT	—	Auditorium; Canceled
Feb 11	Sandy Saddler, II	New York, NY	W15	MSG—13th Appearance

Featherweight Championship of the World

Date	Opponent	Location	Result	Comments
Mar 29	Ernest Nogues	Tampa, FL	E4	Fort H.H. Armory
Apr 25	Del Flanagan	New Orleans, LA	E6	
Apr 27	Elis Ask	Detroit, MI	E4	Olympia Stadium
May 19	TBD	Minneapolis, MN	E4	Canceled—Pep ill
May 23	Harold MacDonald	Omaha, NE	E4	Canceled
May 25	Eddie Lacey	St. Paul, MN	E4	Exhibition
Jun 6	Luis Ramos	New Haven, CT	W10	Arena
Jun 14	Al Pennino	Pittsfield, MA	W10	Wahconah Park
Jun 20	Johnny LaRusso	West Springfield, MA	W10	Century Stadium
June 30	Jean Mougin	Syracuse, NY	—	MacArthur Stad; Pep ill
July 6	Jean Mougin	Syracuse, NY	—	MacArthur Stad; Rained out
July 12	Jean Mougin	Syracuse, NY	W10	MacArthur Stadium
July 12	Eddie Compo	Waterbury, CT	—	Title defense; Postponed
July 28	Eddie Compo	Waterbury, CT	—	Title defense; Postponed
July	*hospitalized*			
Sep 2	Miguel Acevedo	Chicago, IL	E4	Chicago Stadium
Sep 20	Eddie Compo	Waterbury, CT	TKO7	Municipal Stadium

Featherweight Championship of the World

Date	Opponent	Location	Result	Comments
Dec 12	Harold Dade	St. Louis, MO	W10	Kiel Stadium
Dec	*hospitalized*			

Notes: Lou Viscusi wanted an additional tune-up bout for Pep prior to meeting Sandy Saddler. So he held the Auditorium for January 25. But a slight cut over Pep's right eye forced a cancellation. Some sources claim the May 25 exhibition in St. Paul was against Mel Hammond, but Viscusi verified that it was indeed Eddie Lacey. On June 6, Dennis "Pat" Brady was originally scheduled to meet Ramos. Pep underwent a minor eye operation to fix scar tissue at New Britain General Hospital in December.

1950

Date	Opponent	Location	Result	Comments
Jan 16	Charley Earl Riley	St. Louis, MO	KO5	Kiel Auditorium

Featherweight Championship of the World

Date	Opponent	Location	Result	Comments
Feb 6	Lew Jenkins	Boston, MA	—	Boston Garden
Feb 6	Roy Andrews	Boston, MA	W10	Boston Garden; Sub
Feb 22	Jimmy Warren	Miami, FL	W10	Dinner Key Auditorium
Mar 17	Ray Famechon	New York, NY	W15	MSG—14th Appearance

Featherweight Championship of the World

Date	Opponent	Location	Result	Comments
May 15	Asuncion Llanos	Hartford, CT	KO2	Auditorium
May 22	Elis Ask	St. Louis, MO	—	Kiel Auditorium
Jun 1	Sonny Boy West	Milwaukee, WI	—	Arena; Replaced
Jun 1	Terry Young	Milwaukee, WI	W10	Arena
Jun	TBD	Cincinnati, OH	—	Canceled
Jun 26	Bobby Timpson	Hartford, CT	W10	Auditorium
Jul 10	Bobby Bell	Washington, DC	—	Griffith Stad; Postponed
Jul 24	Bobby Bell	Washington, DC	—	Griffith Stad; Postponed
Jul 25	Bobby Bell	Washington, DC	W10	Griffith Stadium
Aug 2	Proctor Heinhold	Scranton, PA	W10	Catholic Youth Ctr.
Sep 6	Sandy Saddler	Bronx, NY	—	Yankee Stadium; rescheduled
Sep 8	Sandy Saddler, III	Bronx, NY	L TKO8	Yankee Stadium

Featherweight Championship of the World

| Sep | *dislocated left shoulder* | | | |

Notes: The July 10 date was postponed because Pep failed to appear at the weighing-in owing to his second marriage; According to New York rules, Pep's title loss to Saddler was listed as an eight-round knockout.

1951

Date	Opponent	Location	Result	Comments
Jan 30	Tommy Baker	Hartford, CT	KO4	Auditorium
Jan 31	*released from hospital following minor surgery*			
Feb 16	Sandy Saddler	New York, NY	—	MSG; Rescheduled
Feb 23	Sandy Saddler	New York, NY	—	MSG; Postponed
Feb 26	Marvin Ford	Sarasota, FL	—	Ford failed weigh-in
Feb 26	Billy Hogan	Sarasota, FL	KO2	Legion Coliseum; Sub
Mar 5	Carlos Chavez	New Orleans, LA	W10	Coliseum Arena
Mar 26	Pat Iacobucci	Miami, FL	W10	Auditorium
Mar	*re-injured dislocated left shoulder*			
Apr 17	Baby Neff Ortiz	St. Louis, MO	TKO5	Kiel Auditorium
Apr 27	Eddie Chavez	San Francisco, CA	W10	Cow Palace
Jun 4	Jesus Compos	Baltimore, MD	W10	Coliseum
Jun 19	Manuel Ortiz	Los Angeles, CA	—	TBD; Canceled
Aug 22	Sandy Saddler	New York, NY	—	MSG; Rescheduled
Sep 4	Corky Gonzales	New Orleans, LA	W10	Municipal Aud.
Sep 26	Sandy Saddler, IV	New York, NY	L KO9	Polo Grounds

Featherweight Championship of the World

| Oct | *NYSAC license suspension* | | | |

Notes: On February 26, Billy Hogan, aka Eddie Webb, substituted for Marvin Ford, who could not make weight. Lou Viscusi referred to the battle as an exhibition.

1952

Date	Opponent	Location	Result	Comments
Jan	*eye surgery*			
Mar 31	Jimmy McAllister	Holyoke, MA	—	Canceled
Apr 29	Santiago Gonzalez	Tampa, FL	W10	Fort H.H. Armory
May 5	Kenny Leach	Columbus, GA	W10	Golden Park
May 10	Buddy Baggett	Aiken, SC	KO5	Eustis Park
May 12	Noel Humphries	Nashville, TN	—	Canceled
May 21	Baby Gonzalez	Miami Beach, FL	—	Replaced
May 21	Claude Hammond	Miami Beach, FL	W10	Auditorium
May 28	Luis Ramos	Macon, GA	—	Canceled
May	*eye surgery*			
Jun 26	Tommy Collins	Boston, MA	—	Postponed
Jun 30	Tommy Collins	Boston, MA	L TKO6	Boston Garden
Sep 3	Billy Lima	Pensacola, FL	W10	Legion Field
Sep 11	Bobby Woods	Vancouver, BC, Can	W10	Forum
Oct 1	Armand Savoie	Chicago, IL	W10	Chicago Stadium
Oct 20	Billy Lima	Jacksonville, FL	W10	Baseball Park
Nov 5	Manny Castro	Miami Beach, FL	TKO5	Auditorium
Nov 19	Fabela Chavez	St. Louis, MO	W10	Arena
Dec 5	Jorge Sanchez	West Palm Beach, FL	W10	Legion Arena

1953

Date	Opponent	Location	Result	Comments
Jan 19	Billy Lauderdale	Nassau, Bahamas	W10	Nassau Stadium
Jan 27	Davey Mitchell	Miami Beach, FL	W10	Auditorium
Feb 10	Jose "Pepe" Alvarez	San Antonio, TX	W10	Municipal Aud.
Mar 31	Joey Gambino	Tampa, FL	W10	Fort H.H. Armory
Apr 7	Noel Paquette	Miami Beach, FL	W10	Auditorium
Apr 27	Sal DiGuardia	Brooklyn, NY	—	Postponed
May 13	Jackie Blair	Fort Worth, TX	W10	Will Rogers Coliseum
May 25	Billy Wagner	Pittsburgh, PA	—	Postponed
Jun 5	Pat Marcune	New York, NY	TKO10	MSG–15th Appearance
Jun 6	*healing from lacerations around his eyes*			
Aug 25	Larry Mujica	Miami Beach, FL	—	Withdrew
Nov 13	Lulu Perez	New York, NY	—	MSG; Postponed
Nov 21	Sonny Luciano	Charlotte, NC	W10	Armory
Dec 4	Davey Allen	West Palm Beach, FL	W10	Legion Arena
Dec 8	Billy Lima	Houston, TX	TKO2	City Auditorium
Dec 15	Tony Longo	Miami Beach, FL	W10	Auditorium

1954

Date	Opponent	Location	Result	Comments
Jan 19	David Seabrook	Jacksonville, FL	W 10	Naval Air Station
Feb 26	Lulu Perez	New York, NY	L TKO 2	MSG–16th Appearance
Feb	*suspended indefinitely*			
Apr 9	*retired by NYSAC*			

Date	Opponent	Location	Result	Comments
Apr 12	Bobby Courchesne	Holyoke, MA	—	Arena; replaced
Jul 23	Mike Turcotte	Mobile, AL	—	Hartwell Field; Rained out
Jul 24	Mike Turcotte	Mobile, AL	W10	Hartwell Field
Aug 18	Til LeBlanc	Moncton, NB, Can	W10	Moncton Arena
Nov 1	Mario "Eladio" Colon	Daytona Beach, FL	W10	Beach Arena

Notes: For the record, boxer Charlie Titone, of Brooklyn, replaced Pep on April 12.

1955

Date	Opponent	Location	Result	Comments
Mar 11	Herman Gary (Myrel Olmstead)	Bennington, VT	W10	State Armory
Mar 22	Charley Titone	Holyoke, MA	W10	Valley Arena
Mar 30	Gil Cadilli	Parks AF Base, CA	L10	Controversial
May 18	Gil Cadilli	Detroit, MI	W10	Olympia Stadium
Jun 1	Joey Cam	Boston, MA	TKO4	Arena
Jun 14	Mickey Mars	Miami Beach, FL	TKO7	Auditorium
Jul 12	Hector Rodriguez	Bridgeport, CT	W10	Hedges Stadium
Sep 13	Jimmy Ithia	Hartford, CT	TKO6	State Theater
Sep 27	Henry "Pappy" Gault	Holyoke, MA	W10	Valley Arena
Oct 10	Charley Titone	Brockton, MA	W10	Maple Arena
Nov 3	*Myrel Olmstead*	—	—	—
Nov 29	Henry "Pappy" Gault	Tampa, FL	W10	Fort H.H. Armory
Dec 12	Leo Carter	Houston, TX	KO4	Auditorium
Dec 28	Andy Arel	Miami Beach, FL	W10	Auditorium

Notes: On March 11, some sources list Pep's opponent as Myrel Olmstead, which appears incorrect. It has also been listed as both a unanimous and split decision. Mr. Olmstead's obituary, published first on March 10, 2012, claimed he met Willie Pep on November 3, 1955. Likely, this would have taken place in Holyoke, Massachusetts. (see https://obits.masslive.com/obituaries/masslive/obituary.aspx?n=myrel-olmeda-olmstead&pid=156398744); Olmstead was on the undercard of Pep's July 12, 1955, fight against Henry Rodriguez.

1956

Date	Opponent	Location	Result	Comments
Mar 13	Kid Campeche	Tampa, FL	W 10	Fort H.H. Armory
Mar 27	Buddy Baggett	Beaumont, TX	W 10	Sportatorium
Apr 17	Jackie Blair	Hartford, CT	W 10	State Theater
Apr 24	Sandy Saddler	Tampa, FL	—	Al Lopez Field; Tentative
May 22	Manuel Armenteros	San Antonio, TX	TKO 7	Municipal Auditorium
May 22	*eye injury*			
May 28	Joe Boland	Corpus Christi, TX	—	Scheduled; Withdrew
Jun 19	Russell Tague	Miami Beach, FL	W 10	Auditorium
Jun 19	*eye injury*			
Jul 4	Hector Bacquettes	Lawton, OK	KO 4	Roosevelt Stadium
Jul 24	Lulu Perez	Miami Beach, FL	—	Auditorium; Canceled
Oct 23	Russell Tague	Miami Beach, FL	—	Auditorium;

1957

Date	Opponent	Location	Result	Comments
Jan 22	*elbow operation*	—	—	—

Date	Opponent	Location	Result	Comments
Apr 23	Cesar Morales	Fort Lauderdale, FL	W10	War Memorial Aud.
May 10	Manny Castro	Florence, SC	W10	Memorial Stadium
Jul 16	Manny Castro	El Paso, TX	W10	County Coliseum
Jul 23	Russell Tague	Houston, TX	W10	Sam Houston Coliseum
Jul 23	*fractured thumb*			
Dec 17	Jimmy Connors	Boston, MA	W10	Boston Garden

Notes: During July, there were indications that Pep may have taken one, or perhaps two, bootleg battles.

1958

Date	Opponent	Location	Result	Comments
Jan 14	Tommy Tibbs	Boston, MA	L10	Mechanics Building
Mar 31	Prince Johnson	Holyoke, MA	W10	Valley Arena
Apr 8	George Stephany	Bristol, CT	W10	Arena
Apr 14	Cleo Ortiz	Providence, RI	W10	Arcadia Ballroom
Apr 29	Jimmy Kelley (Kelly)	Boston, MA	W10	Mechanics Building
May 20	Bobby Singleton	Boston, MA	W10	Mechanics Building
May	*twisted leg*			
Jun 2	Bobby Soares	Athol, MA	—	Mem. Hall; Rescheduled
Jun 23	Pat McCoy	New Bedford, MA	W10	Sargent Field
Jul 1	Bobby Soares	Athol, MA	W10	Memorial Hall
Jul 14	Bobby Bell	Norwood, MA	—	Arena; Postponed
Jul 17	Bobby Bell	Norwood, MA	W10	Arena
Aug 4	Luis "Pancho" Carmona	Presque Isle, ME	W10	No. Maine Fairgrounds; Sub
Aug 9	Jesse Rodriguez	Painesville, OH	W10	Lake County Fairgrounds
Aug 25	Al Duarte	North Adams, MA	—	Glovers Bowl; Postponed
Aug 26	Al Duarte	North Adams, MA	W10	Glovers Bowl; Sub
Sep 20	Hogan "Kid" Bassey	Boston, MA	L TKO9	Boston Garden

Notes: Jimmy Kelley also had his surname spelled as Kelly. On August 4, Carmona substituted for Cleo Ortiz, who suffered an eye injury.

1959

Date	Opponent	Location	Result	Comments
Jan 26	Sonny Leon	Caracas, Venezuela	L10	Nuevo Circo
Jan 27	*Pep announced his (temporary) retirement from the ring*			
Feb 3	Steve Ward	Hartford, CT	—	State Theater; Canceled

Notes: Sonny Leon was the last fighter Pep faced with over 50 career victories. Eddie Armstrong was substituted for Willie Pep on February 3.

1960–1964

Inactive

1965

Date	Opponent	Location	Result	Comments
Jan 28	Jerry Powers	Miami, FL	E4	Little River Aud.
Mar 12	Hal McKeever	Miami, FL	W8	Little River Aud.
Apr 26	Jackie Lennon	Philadelphia, PA	W6	Arena

Date	Opponent	Location	Result	Comments
May 21	Johnny Gilmore	Norwalk, CT	W6	Crystal Arena
Jun 8	"Irish" Bob Shaughnessy	Toronto, Ontario, Canada	E4	Maple Leaf St.; Withdrew
Jul 21	Benny "Red" Randell	Quebec City, Quebec, Can	W10	Old Coliseum
Sep 28	Johnny Gilmore	Philadelphia, PA	W6	Arena
Oct 1	Willie Little	Johnston, PA	KO3	War Memorial Arena
Oct 4	Tommy Haden	Providence, RI	TK3	Rhode Island Auditorium
Oct 14	Sergio Musquiz	Phoenix, AZ	TK5	Sportatorium
Oct 25	Ray Coleman	Tucson, AZ	KO5	Sports Center
Nov 11	Bob LeFrevre	Burlington, VT	—	Postponed
Dec 1	Emile Griffith	New York, NY	E1	MSG
Dec 1	Manny Gonzalez	New York, NY	E1	MSG
Dec 13	Sugar Ray Robinson	Boston, MA	E4	Boston Garden

Notes: The date of Pep's fight against Benny "Red" Randall varies by source—some list it as July 26. The October 1 promotion featured both Willie Pep and Sugar Ray Robinson.

1966

Date	Opponent	Location	Result	Comments
Jan 18	TBD	Philadelphia, PA	—	Marty Servo Benefit
Mar 16	Calvin Woodland	Richmond, VA	L6	City Arena
Nov 30	Sandy Saddler	New York, NY	E2	Sunnyside Garden
	Barney Ross			Testimonial Boxing Show

Notes: Following his final battle with Sandy Saddler on September 26, 1951, here is a brief overview: In 1952, faced two fighters with losing records (out of 12), lost only to Tommy Collins. In 1953, won 11 out of 11 contests, faced not a single fighter with a losing record, defeated six consecutive boxers with over 34 victories. In 1954, faced one boxer (out of five) with a losing record, lost only one contest to Lulu Perez. In 1955, faced four boxers (out of 14) with losing records, avenged his only loss against Gil Cadilli; eight of the boxers he faced had won their previous bout. In 1956, faced three boxers (out of six) with losing records; his opponents had a combined record of 195–120–23. In 1957, faced two boxers (out of five), with losing records, battled Manny Castro in back-to-back contests, and handed Jimmy Connors his first loss. In 1958, won 11 out of 13 contests (lost to Tibbs and Bassey), faced four boxers with losing records, faced one boxer with over 60 wins (Bassey), handed boxer Jimmy Kelly his first loss, and won 11 consecutive bouts. In 1959, faced only one boxer and lost. The comeback begins: in 1965, won nine consecutive bouts and battled five consecutive opponents with losing records; and in 1966, faced only one boxer and lost.

1971

Date	Opponent	Location	Result	Comments
Sep 11	Sandy Saddler	White Plains, NY	E	County Center

1972

Date	Opponent	Location	Result	Comments
Mar 20	Sandy Saddler	Philadelphia, PA	E3	One-minute rounds

1973

Date	Opponent	Location	Result	Comments
Mar 9	Sandy Saddler	New York, NY	E3	MSG; Graziano Night

1975

Date	Opponent	Location	Result	Comments
Apr 3	Rochester Sports Star	Rochester, NY	E	War Memorial Show

1977

Date	Opponent	Location	Result	Comments
Sep 24	Sal Bartolo	Boston, MA	E3	Boston Garden

Notes: Pep gave many exhibitions, both formal and impromptu, so these are selected entries. The April 3 boxing show also featured Chico Vejar, Carmen Basilio, and Sandy Saddler.

Record as Referee—Selected Entries

1942

Date	Opponent	Location	Comments
Mar 19	Connecticut School for Boys	Hartford, CT	Guest
Oct 9	Connecticut Boy's Club	Hartford, CT	Guest

Notes: It wasn't unusual for Willie Pep to be a guest or volunteer referee at events.

1947

Date	Opponent	Location	Comments
Apr 1	Paul Frechette-Henry Polowitzer	West Yarmouth, MA	Rainbow Ballroom
Sep 12	Shamus McCray-Billy Kearns	Meriden, CT	Silver City Arena

1949

Date	Opponent	Location	Comments
Dec 28	Danny Stepanovich-Ken Fields	Coconut Grove, FL	Dinner Key Auditorium
Dec 30	Pete Noka-Henry Briere	West Palm Beach, FL	Legion Arena

1959

Date	Opponent	Location	Comments
Feb 3	Jimmy Monts-Maurice Jenkins	Hartford, CT	State Theater

1960

Date	Opponent	Location	Comments
Oct 24	Dave Wyatt-Bob Church	Baltimore, MD	Coliseum; Auto accident

1962

Date	Opponent	Location	Comments
Jan 10	Ramon Moran-Bobby Bruner	Union City, NJ	State Garden
Jan 18	Eder Jofre-Johnny Caldwell	Sao Paulo, Brazil	Ginásio Estadual do Ibirapuera

Date	Opponent	Location	Comments
Jan 31	Charlie Rogan-Al Kish	Bridgeport, CT	City Arena; Semi-pro
Feb 16	Preston Crump-Sammy Richardson	Totowa, NJ	Gladiators' Arena
Feb 28	Domingo Ortiz-Joe DiDonato	Union City, NJ	State Garden
Mar 10	Flash Elorde-Somkiat Kiatmuangyom	Manila, Philippines	Rizal Memorial Sports Complex

OPBF Lightweight Title

Date	Opponent	Location	Comments
Mar 16	Ruben Carter-Jim McMillan	Jersey City, NJ	Jersey City Armory
Dec 19	Phil David-Johnny Hand	Harvey, LA	Westside Sports Center

1963

Date	Opponent	Location	Comments
Sep 11	Johnny McKinnon–Johnny Blessas	Plainfield, NJ	Seidler Field

1964

Date	Opponent	Location	Comments
Apr 18	Eddie Perkins-Bunny Grant	Kingston, Jamaica	National Stadium
Jun 24	Eddie Perkins-Les Sprague	Saskatchewan, Canada	Exhibition Stadium

1965

Date	Opponent	Location	Comments
Jan 29	Mel Winters-Jimmy Beasley	West Palm Beach, FL	Music Carnival Theatre
Feb 12	Sugar Ray Robinson-Sonny Moore	Clearwater, FL	Exhibition; Scheduled
Feb 13	Bunny Grant-Percy Hayles	Kingston, Jamaica	National Stadium
Jun 7	George Chuvalo-Sonny Andrews	New Brunswick, Canada	
Jul 10	Carlos Hernandez-Percy Hayles	Kingston, Jamaica	National Stadium

Notes: The February 12 exhibition, scheduled to be held at the Jack Tar Harrison Hotel ballroom, never took place as Robinson was not satisfied with his payment. Pep, who did receive his $100 payment, was satisfied.

1966

Date	Opponent	Location	Comments
Nov 21	George Chuvalo-Boston Jacobs	Detroit, MI	Cobo Arena

1967

Date	Opponent	Location	Comments
May 19	Curtis Cokes-Francois Pavilla	Dallas, TX	Scheduled; Protested

W.B.C. World Welterweight Title
W.B.A. World Welterweight Title

Notes: Doug Lord, manager of Curtis Cokes, objected on grounds that Pep was announced in advance of the fight. Pep had even travelled to Dallas for the engagement.

1968

Date	Opponent	Location	Comments
May 22	Julio Cruz-Dick Gambino	Providence, RI	—
Jun 26	*Eddie Owens-Juan Botta*	*Providence, RI*	*Auditorium*
Oct 14	Marcel Bizien-Danny Andrews	Secaucus, NJ	Plaza Arena
Nov 20	Dick Gambino-Chuck Harris	Providence, RI	Rhode Island Auditorium
Dec 18	Dick Gambino-Jimmy Cherico	Providence, RI	—

Notes: Pep also took a variety of judging assignments, including the Ismael Luguna-Frankie Narvaez bout on April 29 in San Juan, Puerto Rico.

1969

Date	Opponent	Location	Comments
Jan 13	Marcel Bizien-Ralph Correa	Secaucus, NJ	Plaza Arena
Jul 16	Willie McMillian-Lee Powell	Indianapolis, Indiana	Met. Softball Stadium
Jul 28	Johnny Famechon-Fighting Harada	Sydney, NSW, Australia	Sydney Stadium

WBC World Featherweight Title

Oct 30	Irish Pat Murphy-Al Hughes	North Bergen, NJ	Embassy Hall

1970

Date	Opponent	Location	Comments
Apr 27	Ricky Raimondi-Dewey Hoderick	Providence, RI	Rhode Island Auditorium
Sep 28	Dennis McNamee-Felix Viera	Providence, RI	—
Oct 14	Dennis McNamee-Charley Hill	Providence, RI	—

1971

Date	Opponent	Location	Comments
Jan 11	Denis McNamee-Henry Jeter	Providence, RI	Rhode Island Auditorium
Feb 1	Denis McNamee-Kenny Warner	Providence, RI	Rhode Island Auditorium
May 17	Denis McNamee-Clyde Taylor	Providence, RI	Rhode Island Auditorium
Nov 17	Sammy Goss-Jo-Jo Jackson	Scranton, PA	Catholic Youth Ctr.

1975

Date	Opponent	Location	Comments
Dec 19	Billy Douglas-Dave Lee Royster	Columbus, Ohio	Lausche Bldg.

1977

Date	Opponent	Location	Comments
Oct 25	Luke Irwin-John Sullivan	West New York, NJ	Recreation Ctr.

1979

Date	Opponent	Location	Comments
Jul 2	Cat Davis-Uschi Doering	Portland, ME	Portland Exposition Building

1982

Date	Opponent	Location	Comments
Oct 26	Eddie Flanning-Jerome Brooks	N. Miami Beach, FL	Victory Park Aud.

Appendix C: Skills Overview

Trying to dissect and expound on the ring craftsmanship of Willie Pep is like describing the painting techniques of Leonardo da Vinci. Much of the art of a genius lies within. While Leonardo had his sfumato, Pep possessed the art of transition. The champion's artistry began with the seamless switching, or should we say shuffling, between orthodox and southpaw. The goal was always complete freedom of movement. Deviation from conventional patterns enabled him to confuse his opponent. Although he denied it when asked, his ring movement was as if he was reacting, or dancing, to a song that was playing in his head.

Balance

A fighter's stability allows him to mount a sound offense, while maintaining a solid defense. Finding your center of gravity (CoG), which Pep understood, allowed him to maintain his balance. It has been noted that fighters who possess a lower center of gravity have an advantage.

Understanding this, Pep used his balance to avoid his opposer's attacks. Only in certain instances, like when Pep was battling Saddler, did you see him over-extend himself to throw a punch. He did it to compensate for his height (2½") and reach (2") disadvantage.

Clinches

Elite boxers incorporate clinches into their fight strategy. Used against aggressive opponents, the clinch was a momentum killer, and Pep used it that way when he was certain he could tie up his opposer. Pep was not a fighter who enjoyed in-fighting. Yes, he had a sneaky right hand, and he used his head to rest on his opposer's shoulder, then drive him into a desired position. But both took practice. Pep wouldn't enter a clinch without an exit strategy. Perfecting methods on fighting out of a clinch, he would utilize the proper method to counter his opponent's strength. Protecting himself out of a break was essential. He always kept his opponent's lead leg between his legs and used his opponent's hips as a direction signal.

Crouching

Adopting a position where the knees were bent and the upper body was brought forward and down was called a crouch. For Willie Pep, who crouched deeply, this was a defensive tactic, often combined with another move such as a roll. He did not like it as an offensive alternative because it was restrictive and required far too much energy.

Feints

Pep kept his left foot planted and stiff on feints (deceptive blows or movements), with minimal foot motion. By mastering the head feint, he distracted his opponent, created angles, and controlled the fight psychologically. It enhanced his ring generalship and was difficult for a judge to ignore. Pep understood that the closer his line of attack was to his opponents, the more likely they would react to his feint.

Footwork

Like heavyweight Joe Louis, Willie Pep would typically step and slide his way into position. It would begin with both feet together, heel to heel, with the toes facing outward (in the shape of a "V"). As the left foot stepped forward, his right foot would elevate to the balls of his toes (Cuneiform bones). He would be certain that his left foot was firmly planted before shifting his right foot behind the left foot to support the direction of his planned assault. Satisfied with that direction, he would move forward while dragging the right foot. If he was moving away from an opponent, he would move his right foot behind the left foot and slide his left foot. This would allow Pep to maintain his closed stance. Pep also perfected lateral movement, on the balls of his feet, while in an open stance. Moving to his left, he would step with his left foot, plant it, then slide his right foot into place. If he wished to close his stance, he would swing his right foot behind the left. Plant, slide, plant, slide … he did not want to put his balance at risk. That said, few will ever forget the classic Saddler-Pep II image of the Hartford fighter thrusting his body forward, with both feet off the ground, in order to reach his rival with a left hand. Unlike some fighters, Pep could, and would, move in any direction. It became instinctive.

Head Movement

A head movement master, Willie Pep always tried to keep his head off-center. He would duck after throwing a right hand in anticipation of his opponent's left hook. While a left uppercut could have been an adversary's counter, few right-handers had a powerful enough left uppercut to do damage. Lou Ambers, who mastered the left uppercut as a right-hander, taught his to Rocky Marciano. Pep was also smart enough to anticipate a sweeping right as a natural follow to a left hook.

Left

Pep would fire his left at a low enough elevation, head down, to guarantee that his lead (or left) shoulder could protect his chin from a right hand. He would do so while keeping his left foot inside the left foot of his opponent. He would then bring his head gradually upward as he slid his left foot back. Bringing his head up to quickly would be dangerous. Being right-handed, Pep understood his opponents would be looking in that direction for his power punch. So he often feinted with the right and followed with a swift and damaging left hook to the body.

Left Jab

Pep's guidance system was the left jab. It was his rudder in rough waters. Granted it wasn't as exciting as his left hook, but it was often the precursor to destruction. He used it to direct his opponents into position, create an opening, or launch window if you will, before firing his heavier artillery. Because it was quicker, used less energy, and could be executed while moving, it was the elite fighter's prolific punch. Doubling up on the left jab, he optimized it against slower opposers.

Overhand Right

Pep's tremendous overhand right was often overlooked by his opponents. Keeping it out of his opponent's line of sight, he threw his entire body into the punch with hopes of catching his opponent off-guard. Pep knew that if he missed the punch, he was going to be off-balance, so he was cautious when pulling it out of his arsenal. It was not an easy punch to land. Obviously, it was a challenging punch to use on southpaws.

Slip

To avoid being punched, Pep mastered the slip and roll. Pep would move his head to one side of his shoulder to dodge a blow, or slip. He chose slipping over blocking because he believed it used less energy and avoided an impact. Also, recovery was better, and he could counter quicker. It was one of the four basic defensive strategies, in addition to blocking, holding, and clinching, Pep would slip inside and follow with the left jab, or slip outside and follow with the right or right uppercut. Control over his movement, from the waist below, guaranteed the efficiency of the action. For elite fighters, the slip was an instinctive move; it was rarely a counter because a good opponent's punch was often quicker than a body movement.

Spin Move

As his opponent attacked, Pep would often shift to the right and used his left hand to push behind his adversary's neck. This would typically force his opponent, who now had his back toward Pep, to turn around—it left them extraordinarily vulnerable to a solid right hand.

Another option was gliding his head to the outside of his opponent's right hip, then pressing inward and upward to the back of his opponent's left shoulder. This was done while hooking his left hand around his opponent's waist. He then had the leverage needed to spin his opponent to the left and behind him.

Pep's opponents hated the spin move because it made them look foolish and vulnerable. Not surprisingly, many of his competitors would lobby the referee with hopes of prohibiting Pep from using it.

Switching Stances

To nullify an opponent's offense, a good fighter can switch stances. The more seamlessly this can be conducted, the better at catching an opposer off guard. Pep loved switching stances—from orthodox to southpaw—and learned to do so off a bounce. Anticipating a counter, such as a left hook from a right-handed opposer, he would roll right to catch his opponent off-balance. During the move, he had the option of firing a left to the breadbasket. He would then be facing his opponent's back and could fire a left hook to the chin.

Weaving

A majority of fighters step to the same side they move their head. For example, weave right, step right, throw a right. Pep would alter his patterns. He mastered the art of weaving his head to the inside while stepping to the outside.

One of his favorite moves, while weaving to the inside, was wrapping his right or left arm around his opponent's waist, while keeping his lead foot inside his opponent's lead foot, then pushing his opponent down or tripping him to the opposite side of his wrapped hand. Once his adversary had fallen or lost his balance, Pep would step aside innocently, like a matador taunting a bull.

Wrestling

To avoid being tied up like a knot by Sandy Saddler, Pep employed a professional wrestler to assist in exit strategies from holds. For example, Saddler was notorious for using his right hand to hold the back of his opponent's head before unloading with the left. Saddler also used a single underhook. He would put his arm under Pep's arm and wrap it around his shoulder while striking with his free hand. Pep struggled when an opponent used wrestling tactics. Yet Pep was not without his own arsenal. For example, he mastered wrist control. This enabled him to use overhooks to pull his opponent's hands downward before guiding them into the ropes.

Appendix D: Official Records of Associated Members of the International Boxing Hall of Fame

Inductee	Indiana Yr.	Bouts	Won	Lost	Drew	KOs	No Decision	No Contest
Willie Pep	1990	242	230	11	1	65	—	—
Sandy Saddler	1990	162	144	16	2	103	—	—
Manuel Ortiz	1996	128	97	28	3	49	—	—
Chalky Wright	1997	220	160	43	16	81	—	1
Sammy Angott	1998	135	99	28	8	23	—	—
"Bat" Battalino	2003	87	57	26	3	23	—	1
Louis "Kid" Kaplan	2003	153	104	18	12	25	19	—

Records of Associated Featherweight Champions and Selected Fighters

Champion	Reign	Bouts	Won	Lost	Drew	KOs	No Decision	No Contest
Joey Archibald	1939	107	60	42	5	29	—	—
Petey Scalzo	1940–41	112	90	15	6	48	—	—
Richie Lemos	1941	81	55	23	3	26	—	—
Jackie Wilson	1941–43	152	100	44	7	20	—	—
Jackie Callura	1943	113	60	41	12	16	—	—
Phil Terranova	1943–44	99	67	21	11	29	—	—
Sal Bartolo	1944–46	97	73	18	6	16	—	—
Hogan Bassey	1959	82	66	13	3	24	—	—

Records of Selected Fighters

		Bouts	Won	Lost	Drew	KOs	No Decision	No Contest
Jackie Blair		133	91	33	9	44	—	—
Eddie Compo		89	75	10	4	14	—	—
Lulu Constantino		136	102	28	6	19	—	—
Ray Famechon		118	101	14	3	6	—	—
Harry Jeffra		122	94	20	7	28	—	—
Lefty LaChance		185	119	57	9	38	—	—
Jock Leslie		90	63	22	5	34	—	—

Chapter Notes

Introduction

1. Lou Viscusi would often receive half of Willie Pep's ring earnings, and he was worth every penny.

2. As my dear friend Vikki LaMotta once told me, "it is not easy being married to a boxing champion." At times, Willie Pep, like many, was not circumspect about his behavior.

3. There exists a belief that a child in these role-reversal situations may regret the loss of their childhood and innocence.

4. Viscusi, who was advancing his own skills as a fight manager, knew when he made mistakes, and it was painted on his face. Was it a smart decision to put Willie Pep up against Sammy Angott in a non-title bout?

Chapter One

1. In 1942, he scaled 147 pounds. This information, which included obvious physical characteristics, was confirmed during his World War II draft registration on February 16, 1942.

2. "Studies of American Immigration, XIII–Italian Immigration to the United States," *Los Angeles Times*, September 11, 1901, 14.

3. *Ibid.*

4. One might add disease, such as malaria, to this list as well.

5. "Studies of American Immigration, XIII–Italian Immigration to the United States," *Los Angeles Times*, September 11, 1901, 14.

6. *Ibid.*

7. *Ibid.*

8. Documentation states that: Salvatore Papaleo was born on February 25, 1896, in Rosalina Mere, Rovigo, Veneto, Italy; Mary Marchese was born on July 27, 1901, in Melilli, Siracusa, Sicilia, Italy.

9. According to Salvatore Papaleo's Petition for Naturalization, Circuit Court, Connecticut District. Vol.130–133, petition no 29592: Salvatore arrived in New York, from Naples, on April 22, 1914, aboard the S.S. *Taormina*. His wife's Petition for Citizenship states her arrival in New York on July 9, 1916, aboard the S.S. *Stampalia*.

10. Feeling unsettled in Worcester, Salvatore found solace in the heavily Sicilian city of Middletown.

11. On her petition for citizenship (#19499), Willie's mother, who was residing at 85 Mather Street in Hartford, listed the date of her marriage as May 4, 1918, in Middletown, Connecticut.

12. No better evidenced than by his handling of the 1936 flood and the 1938 hurricane.

13. It is hard to recognize Delaney without mentioning the extraordinary skills of another elite Connecticut boxer, Lou Bogash (aka Luigi Nicola Buccassi). Bogash, who grew up on the North End of Bridgeport, battled champions such as Jack Britton, Jack Delaney, and Mike O'Dowd.

14. The list continues: Saverio Giannone, aka Joe Grim (1881–1939); Peter Gulotta, aka Pete Herman (1896–1973); Isadoro Jannazzo, aka Izzy Jannazzo (1915–1995); Ignacius Guiffi, aka Harry Jeffra (1914–1988); Rocco Tozzo, aka Rocky Kansas (1893–1954); Giuseppe DiMelfi, aka Young Zulu Kid (1897–1971); Fidel LaBarba (1905–1981); Pete Latzo (1902–1968); Salvatore Mandala, aka Sammy Mandell (1904–1967); Anthony Marino, aka Tony Marino (1910–1937); Jay Nova, aka Lou Nova (1913–1991); Luigi Salica, aka Lou Salica (1912–2002); Peter Scalzo, aka Petey Scalzo (1917–1993); Mario Severino, aka Marty Servo (1919–1969); Giovanni Cervati, aka Little Jackie Sharkey (1897–1970); Phil Terranova (1919–2000); and Giovanni Panica, aka Johnny Wilson (1893–1985).

15. Later, other extremely talented pugilists emerged and added their names to the list. Those born before 1930 include: Carmine Basilio, aka Carmen Basilio (1927–2012); Giovanni "Nino" Benvenuti (1938); Eddie Campagnuolo, aka Eddie Compo (1928–1998); Rocky Castellani (1926–2008), Pasquale DeMarco, aka Paddy DeMarco (1928–1997); Calogero Fusari, aka Charlie Fusari (1924–1985); Anthony Gianiro, aka Tony Janiro (1926–1985); Roland La Starza (1927–2009); Giacobbe LaMotta, aka Jake LaMotta (1922–2017); Rocco Marchegiano, aka Rocky Marciano (1923–1969); Stefano Mauriello, aka Tami Mauriello (1923–1999); and Giuseppe Berardinelli, aka Joey Maxim (1922–2001).

16. If a town or city does not have a state attached to its name, it is located in Connecticut.

17. His breakout year came in 1940, when Ivy tackled Petey Scalzo for the NBA World Featherweight crown. In a heartbreaking loss, Ivy, who sustained a badly cut lip, saw his dreams slip away in a final round technical knockout. It happened on July 10, 1940, at Bulkeley Stadium in Hartford. Posting a record of 7–3–3 in 1941, Ivy took victories over Johnny Compo, Joey Archibald, and Harry Jeffra. Fighting twice at Madison Square Garden that year, Ivy lost to Lulu Constantino in February and Beau Jack in May.

18. His middle initial likely represented Salvatore—it could not be verified through three independent legal sources because he seldom used it.

19. If a gym owner, or even a manager or trainer, called you anything but Kid, you were considered a prospect—everybody was "Kid."

20. Perone actually had a desk drawer filled with trinkets he used as prizes for fighters.

21. Capitol Park, at Wethersfield Avenue and Eaton Street in the South End of Hartford, was an amusement park.

22. With Pep unable to make the rain date, Young Berrio substituted for him.

23. Perone's shows always garnered ink, and Pep was thrilled to read his name in the newspaper. This was a time when Bobby Ivy was clearly the "can't miss" champion of the future—at least the press thought he was.

24. "Calling 'Em Right," *Hartford Courant*, August 14, 1938, 36. Lying about your age was common with youngsters, especially when it involved picking up some pocket cash. Perone was likely not accepting any fighters under the age of 16. Papaleo's amateur career began prior to age 16.

25. Pep's weight against Roberts varied over the years. However, he often stated that he scaled at 125 pounds, while Roberts tipped at 126.

26. Some recalled the venue as a railroad car repair shop, as well as Norwich's first trade school.

27. The State Athletic Commission was supposed to approve matches and review all contracts.

28. While operating under the license issued to the Garden Athletic Club, Viscusi hoped to conduct bi-monthly shows.

29. Leto, who began his career in 1924, was fading, and Carr, a solid fighter out of Meriden, ended his career in 1939. Lou Viscusi needed some new blood and liked what he saw in the Connecticut amateur scene.

30. Pep was being classified as a semi-pro bantamweight.

31. Wasnick's fight status should have been questioned. Depending on the source, he was categorized as both a semi-pro and as a professional.

32. Pep would not meet Wasnick as an amateur. Pep would defeat Wasnick on August 4, 1940, for his second professional victory. Nobody doubted Pep's claim to the title.

33. This was promoter Dick Gray's final semi-pro card of the season.

34. Pep likely squeezed a couple of bouts in before the year was completed. He was scheduled for a December 8 bout against Earl Roys in New Britain. The bout, which likely took place, could not be verified by three independent sources.

35. "Andrews and Williams on Top Thursday," *The Journal*, January 1, 1940, 4.

Chapter Two

1. Lenny Marello, Pep's manager, also handled Bobby Ivy. He was furious over many of the commission's edicts, especially the ruling that two judges and the referee were now responsible for fight decisions.

2. Willie Pep made his professional debut at the age of 17 years, 10 months and six days excluding the end date.

3. The unforgettable events of the evening played nonstop in Pep's head and made it impossible to sleep.

4. Wasnick, who made a living in the ring during the war years, fought until 1948.

5. Burns, who had over 40 professional bouts before meeting Pep, fought until about 1940.

6. With the bout, Joey Marcus becomes the first fighter to battle Willie Pep during his professional career.

7. As a counter to the weather, Viscusi wisely backed up the venue with Foot Guard Hall.

8. McGovern was incorrectly identified as Jimmy McAllister by some sources; eyewitness accounts confirmed that it was McGovern.

9. Ivy, with nearly 50 fights' worth of experience, was coming off an impressive victory over Joey Archibald.

10. Carlo Daponde had over 40 bouts' worth of experience prior to meeting Pep.

11. Bobby Ivy, a veteran of 50 ring battles, was also on this fight card.

12. As a professional, Pep fought, and won, 10 times in 1940. Just three of the fighters he faced had winning records. While Carlo Daponde had the most experience of those he faced, he also had the most losses.

13. Attendance figures varied from source to source.

14. Pep admired the tremendous footwork and defensive skills of Ambers. The Hartford fighter, who said he didn't care much for dancing, appeared to have a rhythm to his footwork. Call it a hunch, but my guess is that Al Weill, along with Lou Ambers, gave Pep more than a few pointers about his defense.

15. Both of the scheduled six-round fights against Garcia topped the fight card. Popular fight promoter Homer C. Rainault had the second promotion and may have had the first as well. This bout, as some believe, may have been Pep's first *genuine* test as a professional.

16. Bridgeport boxer Lou Bogash, an extraordinary fighter, refereed the Pep-Puglese bout.

By the way, Rodano knocked out his opponent (Frankie Terranova), while Leto lost a decision to his antagonist (Wicky Harkins).

17. Using the time wisely, Willie Pep underwent a minor nose operation.

18. This is the article that uses the adjective: "Marty Servo Signed to Fight Bobby Britton Here July 15," *Hartford Courant,* July 6, 1941, 35. Sources claim Pep, at this point, had between 23 and 26 straight victories.

19. The feature bout on this card saw an undefeated Marty Servo victorious over Bobby Britton. Some sources list Pep fighting Harry Hintlian on August 1, 1941.

20. Some sources reported Frechette's first name as Bob.

21. It was summer, it was outdoors, and the feature saw the streaky Bobby Ivy hand Angelo Radano his second loss in 29 battles.

22. Harris, who was 10–1–3 entering his battle with Pep, showed considerable promise. Unfortunately, he would lose three of his next five battles. Other results included: Joey Peralta grabbed a points victory over Harold "Snooks" Lacey, and Aldo Spoldi grabbed a TKO victory over veteran Carl Guggino.

23. Little did Pep realize how often these cuts would reopen—they would be a near-constant aggravation for the boxer. Questions regarding Crawford's lack of performance led to a warning by the State Commissioner.

24. Regardless of the good news, the New York State Athletic Commission (NYSAC), who welcomed the Hartford fighter, made it clear that Guglielmo Papaleo could fight, but not Willie Pep. Both a world war and a word war were taking place simultaneously—a bit petty to say the least. Viscusi had his first solo managerial roadblock to overcome. In a very unscrupulous contest, Zivic and McCoy battled to a draw.

Chapter Three

1. This was not the Mexican Joe Rivers, whose competitive career began in 1908 and ended in 1924.

2. Matchmaker Rogers put together a solid fight card that also saw Maxie Shapiro take a points victory over Sal Bartolo.

3. All three of these opponents were experienced and competitive, but not contenders.

4. The Jackie Wilson catchweight fight, conducted by a Pittsburgh matchmaker, was an infantile paralysis benefit. Viscusi loved the opportunity but knew his fighter wasn't ready to face Wilson. In retrospect, it was the proper call.

5. Pep was a standout athlete who enjoyed the adoration.

6. On July 1, 1942, Lou Viscusi, who had an established role as a promoter, planned to devote a majority of his time to managing Willie Pep.

7. Spider Armstrong had over 30 victories to his credit, but he began slipping at the conclusion of his loss to Jeffra.

8. "Sellout Likely for Armstrong Bout with Pep," *Hartford Courant,* April 12, 1942, 38; Armstrong was billed as the Canadian Featherweight Champion.

9. In 2021 dollars, that amount calculates to $17,296.33 (3.63% inflation rate).

10. Although Willie was forced to grow up fast, the youngster was always there to lend a helping hand—as he saw it, it was his obligation. He showed no sign of resentment, at least not in public. Lee was perhaps Willie Pep's biggest fan. Worth repeating: He never turned his back to the champion. Never.

11. Referee Lou Bogash gave Pep six rounds while calling two even; Nichols had over three times as many victories than defeats entering his battle against Pep.

12. Servo, who lost a unanimous decision to Robinson in their first battle, lost a split decision this time out. This was his last ring battle until December 1945.

13. Joey Archibald brought a record of 60–31–5 into the fight against Pep. He would lose his next six fights and decide to retire.

14. Abe Denner was a stand-up boxer and a solid in-fighter, but he lacked a knockout punch. Denner was ranked by *The Ring* magazine as the #3 featherweight in the world in 1942 after knocking out Lefty LaChance on January 30.

15. The reported weights varied source to source.

16. Tony Falco, 19–1, defeated Lennox Dingle, and Art Tatta, 14–3–3, defeated Ralph Youvella.

17. Judge Savitt's brother was Bill Savitt, who owned Bulkeley Stadium from 1932 to 1946.

18. There were about 8,700 paid customers, which created a gate gross of over $15,000.

19. Litfin was near the end of a solid career that began back in 1929.

20. Marello, who was a second to both fighters, remained neutral during this contest.

21. Phil Terranova defeated Gus Coen Levine on the undercard. Frank Franconeri was coming off a points loss to Lulu Constantino.

22. Vince Dell'Orto had won his last three ring battles (Richie Lemos, Jackie Callura, and Guy Serean).

23. Lulu Constantino would draw Bobby Ivy in Hartford on October 20, proof that a fight manager like Lou Viscusi had to anticipate every circumstance.

24. In a career that spanned from 1933 to 1950, Harry Jeffra was a World Bantamweight and NYSAC World Featherweight boxing champion.

25. Zengaras was briefly (no count) dropped in the sixth round by a stiff left jab.

26. Purse estimates: Willie Pep—$12,500 (actual $12,226.66), Chalky Wright—$25,000; The previous high was $63,656, back on February 10, 1928, when Tony Canzoneri drew Benny Bass.

The impressive gate numbers even landed a mention in *Variety*.

27. During the pre-fight glove inspection, Gore rattled General John J. Phelan, the Commission Chairman, when he demanded to examine the gloves.

28. *The Ring* promised Pep a championship belt once the sanctions in place due to the war were lifted.

29. As fate had it, Mrs. Papaleo underwent an appendectomy three days after their wedding.

30. Torres was competitive at this point, but his career turned sour not long after this bout. He ended up losing over twice as many bouts as he won and retired after a decade-long career.

31. Viscusi knew Butz and wanted a foothold in the new facility downtown.

32. Lou Viscusi understood that the management of a champion meant an occasional quid pro quo, in this case to promoters Vic Saladino, Martin Burke, and Fred Rickerfor. Pep's manager would keep the favor in his back pocket and exercise it when necessary. Nevertheless, it was still a risky scenario for the champion.

33. Naturally, Willie and Mary would have been happy to stay, but the Auditorium needed a cash infusion and Viscusi wanted Pep's mind on Stolz in advance of the fight.

34. Pep caught Allie Stolz, who entered the fight at 49–6–2, at the right time. He was coming off a Garden loss to Beau Jack and had lost two of his last five bouts. Stolz, who was always in the lightweight mix, was a solid competitor.

35. Pep and Viscusi received a NYSAC summons because they didn't finish training in NYC, which was a violation of the ring code; Stolz held recent victories over Chalky Wright, Harold "Snooks" Lacey, and Petey Scalzo. By the way, Ike Williams was on the undercard. The bout was reported as Pep's 59th consecutive victory.

36. Many of these comparisons were prompted by an AP article quoting James Joy Johnston. As a fighter, matchmaker, manager, and promoter, Johnston was best known for guiding five men to world titles.

37. Davey Crawford brought 85 fights' worth of experience, and a losing record, into the ring to greet Pep.

38. It was initially touted as a 15-round battle. The NBA still recognized Angott as the lightweight champion. Both Angott and Charley Jones, his manager, viewed his ring departure differently: Angott claimed he had an injured right hand, but Jones disagreed. Others, especially the media, viewed it differently: See "Mob Made Angott Quit, He Wouldn't Take Dive, *Daily News*, November 20, 1942, 280. One can only imagine the negotiations around this fight, as it wreaked of political undercurrents.

39. Angott also stated he had difficulty making 135 pounds. However, once Beau Jack conquered both Allie Stolz and Tippy Larkin to gain the New York State lightweight crown, the vista surrounding the division changed.

40. There were times when he never left his house without a pair of spotted cubes in his pocket. Hey, you never know.

41. His record entering his battle with Pep was 49–6–2; Angott would only win five of his next 12 bouts. He lost to Henry Armstrong in New York, drew Beau Jack in New York, lost Juan Zurita in Los Angeles, dropped two split decisions to Ike Williams in Philadelphia, lost to Jimmy McDaniels in New York, and drew Gene Burton in Pittsburgh. Williams was managed by Frank "Blinky" Palermo for a time.

42. That evening Pep attended a wrestling match at Loew-Poli Theater on East Main Street. While he was there supporting the Red Cross Fund benefit show, he also wanted to greet Lieutenant James J. Braddock, who was a guest referee.

43. *Ripley's "Believe It or Not,"* syndicated column, March 30, 1943.

44. Concerned about their son's health, Willie's parents, along with the Lou Viscusi and his wife, drove to Boston on Sunday April 4, 1943. The fight was very close; moreover, the *Boston Globe* had it 5–4–1, advantage Pep.

45. The attendance figure for this fight varied from a believed 1,500 to as much as 5,000.

46. Wilson had lost his title to Jackie Callura. Tony Cancela refereed the Pep-Aviles bout.

47. The NBA featherweight rankings had Jackie Callura as champion and Pep a logical contender, along with outstanding boxers Sal Bartolo, Chalky Wright, Lulu Constantino and Mike Raffa.

48. What little remains of the stadium is known as Nickerson Field today and was home to the Boston University's football team until 1997.

49. On Friday, May 21, 1943, Willie Pep was in Superior Court to describe a street fight he had witnessed.

50. The Naval Secretary also confirmed that prominent individuals in sports would NOT be permitted to engage in contest away from their stations, except in certain team situations. This was the Navy's position; If you were wondering where Lenny Marello ended up, he was in the Navy as well.

Chapter Four

1. Tickets were scaled at $1, $2, and $3 inside the 6,000-seat arena; the fight drew a bit over 2,500 spectators.

2. Lacey, with a winning record and over 130 career bouts, finally retired in 1947. Two consecutive losses to Phil Terranova, during July 1944, convinced him his better days were behind him.

3. Pep scored with ten straight unanswered lefts in the sixth round; The promotion, highlighted by Pep, was weak on talent due to the war.

4. Matchmaker Gus Browne complemented the main event with an entertaining undercard.

5. On June 23, Pep was once again over at the Auditorium, not fighting but assisting in the corner of another boxer. Testing the waters, Nicky Papaleo, Willie's much younger brother was there to see what, if any, ring abilities he happened to share with the champion. Suffice it to say that was a long day for the younger Papaleo.

6. Pep was a 5 to 1 betting favorite only hours before the contest. The event drew 10,000 fight fans. It was the speed of Pep's combinations that countered the left jab of Joyce. Talented, Willie Joyce finally hung up the gloves in 1947, leaving behind a career record of 71–21–10.

7. Both Pep and Ortiz scaled at 127 pounds. Pep pocketed $10,00, while Ortiz's purse was estimated at $7,000.

8. Pep's popularity was proven, while Constantino, who owned a restaurant in New York and a lunch bar in the Brass City, had built a considerable Connecticut fan base.

9. The referee voted for Constantino, while the two judges saw it Beau Jack.

10. The life of a professional boxer was challenging, particularly if you were as talented as Pep. And, as hard a life as it was, it was often even harder on his family. The demands are intense and seemingly constant.

11. Japan's formal surrender, or V-J Day, took place on September 2, 1945.

12. Walker was a fast-talking shyster who ran out of a title match when Viscusi was handling Bobby Ivy. Later, he had the gall to state he never even knew Viscusi.

13. Connecticut had been a member of the NBA since it was founded.

14. Because Wright's father was born in Mexico, many believed that "Chalky" Wright was born there also.

15. Pep scaled at 125¼ pounds, while Wright tipped at 125½.

16. Jackie Leamus, with less than 30 career fights when he faced Pep, essentially turned punching bag for the remainder of his career.

17. It was the site of one of President Dwight D. Eisenhower's inaugural balls in 1953, and the first concert by The Beatles in the United States in 1964.

18. Hernandez, declining in skills, would win one of his next eight bouts.

19. Walton, with a believed record of 16–9–6, wasn't a threat to Pep.

20. George "Red" Doty, Bobby Polowitzer, and Johnny Cesario were some familiar Connecticut faces featured on the undercard.

21. Terranova suffered a cut nose and a mouse over his left eye, all a result of Pep's targeted left jabs and an occasional overhand right.

22. The gross gate was reported as $48,701.

23. Stato evolved into a solid boxer and held victories over Joey Wasnick, Fred and Bobby Polowitzer, Victor Flores, Roy Andrews and Humberto Sierra.

24. Paulie Jackson was a distance fighter, not to mention a good sparring session for Pep.

25. Martyk did manage to excite the large crowd, estimated at about 7,000 fans, by having Pep briefly dazed in the opening round.

26. Eddie Giosa won three times as many battles as he lost and was a good fighter. However, this was not one of his better performances.

Chapter Five

1. Viscusi even backed off Mike Jacobs who was pushing hard for an early year Pep v. Bartolo title fight in Madison Square Garden. Both understood: Regardless of circumstance, a champion can always find a challenger.

2. Israel Jacob "Jack" Solomons began promoting boxing in the 1930s. His promotions would include many historical bouts such as the bout between Randy Turpin and Sugar Ray Robinson, when the latter lost his middleweight world title in 1951.

3. Each fighter posted a $1,000 guarantee (weight and appearance).

4. "Sal Bartolo Ducks New York Meeting With Champion Pep," *Wilmington Star*, February 24, 1946, p. 10-A.

5. Some sources viewed his record at 99–31–8 entering his battle with Pep.

6. North Meadows, or the former location of the Meadows Music Theatre, is where the XFINITY Theatre is now located (61 Savitt Way, Hartford, CT). Some reports had the game at nearby Riverside Park.

7. Ribicoff represented Connecticut in the United States House of Representatives and Senate and was the 80th Governor of Connecticut and Secretary of Health, Education, and Welfare in President John F. Kennedy's cabinet.

8. Reports were mixed. Petrone's best round was the eighth when he cut Pep's left eye. Attendance figures vary as high as 6,000.

9. Johnny Cesario was on this undercard. As sparring partners, Pep and Cesario worked well together.

10. Saint Clare's Hospital, which operated from 1934 until 2007, was located in the Hell's Kitchen neighborhood (415 w. 51st Street) in Manhattan.

11. This was the second richest boxing gate on record in Minnesota. Both Tom and Mike Gibbons were among those sitting ringside.

12. Far from nonsense, we were at nearly the peak point of Solar Cycle 18 in 1947.

13. "Pep Kayoes Game Graves in Eighth," *Star Tribune*, July 26, 1946, p. 14. And "Graves Kayoed in Eighth, But Sixth Rivals Firpo-Dempsey for Thrills," *Minneapolis Star*, July 26, 1946, p. 11.

14. In just under 90 recorded battles, Gomez was believed to have lost less than ten fights.

He held victories over Teddy Yarosz, Bob Sikes, Buddy Knox, Phil Muscato, and Buddy Scott.

15. Doll Rafferty, who was a solid fighter, needed to be helped to his corner following the knockout.

16. Walter Kolby, who posted a career record of 30–5–2, ended his career in 1952.

17. Lefty LaChance, by accounts, had over 180 bouts under his belt when he met Pep.

18. Pep was scheduled to meet Paulie Jackson in Albany, New York, but mother nature forced a postponement. The pair met in Minneapolis instead.

19. See: "Willie Pep Arrested Twice During Night," *Hartford Courant*, October 8, 1946, p. 2.

20. See: "Willie Pep Being Sued for $25,000," *Record-Journal*, October 26, 1946, p. 4.

21. This was Tomas Beato's thirtieth professional bout. He did hold victories over Joey Iannotti and Eddie Compo.

22. This was a solid fight card that included victories by welterweight Charley Parham, welterweight Tony Falco, and middleweight Bob Flanagan.

23. Although Shapiro was dropped to a nine-count in the seventh round, he won the ten-round majority decision inside St. Nicolas Arena.

24. Speaking of a level of doubt, Willie Pep reported to Police that he had his car stolen on the morning of May 1, and had no idea who did it. Later, it was reported that a car bearing Pep's license plate, struck a car on Farmington Avenue in Hartford. On May 2, Raymond J. Seraphin, who was known to Pep, contacted police and claimed responsibility. Convicted of three charges, Seraphin was sentenced to five months of jail time.

25. Keney Park, the largest park within the Hartford City System, was located at 471 Tower Avenue in Hartford. The park was designed by the famous landscape architectural firm of Olmsted, Olmsted and Eliot. Many good boxers did roadwork in the park including Lou Ambers.

26. Were Viscusi and Gore pushing their fighter too fast, or was Pep simply pushing himself? It was the latter, and it was the champion's one-hundred and tenth victory in 112 fights.

27. Viscusi, who took heat from critics for putting his fighter up against Fontana, countered with LeBrun. In his defense, Pep's recovery defied the belief of health experts. It was beyond what many thought possible.

28. The canvas was damp, and Pep had trouble getting his footing. He complained to Bill Gore that the flooring needed resin.

29. This was another strong Connecticut fight card that included welterweights Vic Cardell, Carey Mace and Bobby Polowitzer.

30. Pep had a stopover in Detroit to chat with the boxing Commission and to do a couple radio shows to promote the fight. Viscusi made the trip but was suffering from a bad cold.

31. Viscusi, along with Bill Gore, headed to New York State. The fight manager wanted to visit his father who had undergone a recent operation.

32. *The Matarese Circle*, a novel by Wesleyan University alumnus Robert Ludlum was inspired by the club; Pep was a guest on Sam Cohen's popular *WMMW Sports Show* on September 12, 1947.

33. Jack Dempsey defeated Fred Saddy, a former sparring partner, via an opening round knockout on March 16, 1918. The fight, that lasted 90 seconds, took place at the Phoenix Athletic Club in Memphis, Tennessee.

34. One judge had the guts to call it even. Hey, it's Philadelphia, so what else is new?

35. Pep provided no excuses, or any concise information, regarding his performance.

36. Bear in mind: Alvaro Estrada had a losing record (10–16–0), while Archie Wilmer (26–17–1) was far more than just a target.

Chapter Six

1. On various occasions, Pep claimed he never collected a dime. See: "Make Believe A Cop Is Chasing you," *Sports Illustrated*, July 16, 1990. However, other statements he made countered this with figures such as $15,000.

2. Pedro Biesca, who lost more than half the battles he entered, was shocked when he dropped Pep.

3. Viscusi wanted to maintain a solid relationship with Benny Trotta (Magliano), McAllister's manager. The reason: Trotta, who also handled Lou Transparenti and Holly Mims, was a successful promoter in the Baltimore area.

4. Joey Angelo, aka Joseph A. D'Agastino, who was coming off decision victories over Dennis Pat Brady and Bob Montgomery, was a solid distance fighter.

5. Jimmy Burns, *Miami Herald* sports editor, was skeptical about the success of the promotion claiming that South Florida had been a graveyard for many fight promotions.

6. The tickets were scaled for a gross gate of $122,000. Prices were set at $15, $10, $5, and $3 (General Admission). The ring was not placed at the center of the field, but 32 feet in front of the south stand.

7. Behind the scenes things were far different. According to press reports, as of March 11, 1948, Team Pep was still owed $11,800 and Team Sierra was still owed over half of their guarantee. Despite all the mistakes, Viscusi was confident that he would receive his full payment. However, Pep ended up filing a damage suit against promoter Clarence Kantrowitz. On October 27, 1948, Kantrowitz went to Superior Court to file a counterclaim in answer to the suit. It stated he wasn't the promoter of the fight, only a front man for Viscusi and Pep. In addition to asking for $50,000, Kantrowitz also claimed the bout was illegal under Florida law.

8. On April 9, Pep was ordered by Superior Court to pay his wife $50 per week pending trial of the divorce action. Pep claimed that he had no real estate (Hartford & Massachusetts) or automobiles in his name. They were in the name of his mother. Viscusi was subpoenaed but failed to appear—he was in Canada. Pep gave his address as 1520 Main Street in Hartford (while he was training), along with his parents' address (when he was not training). The divorce case was set to be heard as an uncontested case, but Willie changed his mind and it was moved to the contested list. Pep's counsel decided they would file an answer to his wife's suit.

9. Leroy Willis, who fought out of Detroit, was a streaky fighter who held victories over Lou Cassiano, Harold Jones, and Lulu Costantino.

10. Luther Burgess was the first fighter handled by the legendary trainer Eddie Futch. After retiring from boxing Burgess became a world-class boxing trainer and even worked under Emanuel Steward at the famed Kronk Gym, in Detroit, Michigan.

11. By agreeing to pay his wife alimony of $12,500, if she was awarded a divorce, he hoped to set the issue aside. The divorce was not disputed. See "Willie Pep to Pay Wife $12,500 Alimony," *Bridgeport Telegram*, July 1, 1948, p. 55. Testimony given by Lou Viscusi revealed that the champion's earnings were split in half between them, with each paying their share of taxes. Viscusi paid all the fighter's expenses. Pep's father, Salvatore Papaleo, received 7½ percent from each half of the purses.

12. Fortunately for fans, Rolly Johns and Joey Kushner, both popular upstate boxers, were on the undercard.

13. Davis had a disputed decision loss to New Haven feather Eddie Compo, on December 15, 1947.

14. Lou Viscusi was working with acting promoter Sol Strauss and Garden matchmaker Nat Rogers.

15. With the exception of the ninth and tenth rounds, DeMarco looked sloppy.

16. It was reported that the former Mrs. Mary Papaleo was remarried. See M. Oakley Stafford's social column "Informing You," *Hartford Courant*, October 22, 1948, p. 28.

17. At this stage of his relationship with Pep, Gore knew precisely how to bring his fighter to the pinnacle of his game. In retrospect, Pep's battle against DeMarco likely prepared him best for what he would endure against Saddler.

18. Cognitive dissonance, a term coined by the social psychologist Leon Festinger (1957), occurs whenever a person holds two conflicting ideas, beliefs, or opinions. If Pep did everything he could do to win, then why didn't he win? Finding ways to reduce the impact of a negative factor, such as defeat, in order to put our mind at ease was a common behavior. Compartmentalizing, which many boxing champions including Pep

excelled at, was a defense mechanism. An individual suppresses their thoughts and emotions in order to deal with the present. Rather than dissect them, they set them aside.

19. Pep wasn't as familiar with Saddler as he should have been. He didn't think Saddler was a stronger fighter, nor did he believe he had greater punching power.

20. Trainer Bill Gore pulled Johnny Cesario aside and told him how to work with the former champion.

21. Freeman was a solid fighter who held victories over Spider Armstrong, Al Couture, and Lefty LaChance. He won almost three times as many fights as he lost.

22. The specific date of the rematch was said to be included in the initial contract.

23. Don't get the wrong impression: Davis was tough and wasn't going to roll over for anyone.

24. Standing 5'6", with a 68" reach, Davis was 2½ inches shorter with two inches less reach than the new featherweight champion. Gore had to bring Pep down to 126 pounds without impacting any of his skills.

25. Pep would not only know what to do, he understood why he was doing it. If he did not, he would ask Gore. Part of the reason why the fighter never claimed there was a fight plan was because he didn't want to talk about it. You don't share your game plan with the opposition unless it's a feint.

26. Saddler's devious tricks, such as putting his thumb in Pep's eye, would no doubt be utilized. Pep needed to understand how to counter beyond complaining to the referee.

27. The fight established a record gross gate ($87,563).

28. So, you are asking yourself, why didn't Gore stop the bleeding? Gore took care of the cuts above Pep's eyes, but he did not stop those below for fear they would swell his eyes closed. They did not want the fight stopped; Saddler needed seven stitches after the fight.

29. This time, Pep wasn't afraid to give Saddler a taste of his own medicine by stepping on his feet, grabbing him and even jerking him off balance.

30. Charley Johnston, who was also president of the New York Managers Guild, planned an official NYSAC protest. It came as little surprise as both organizations appeared to be always be in conflict.

31. To say nothing of the throng of political parasites ringside. All optimistic, but not guaranteed, an ovation at the conclusion of their introduction.

32. Tolls once punctuated the Connecticut Turnpike, or I-95 and 395, from Greenwich through Killingly.

33. Ask, the first Finnish boxer to hold a European championship, fought until 1957. In 1950, his loses to Teddy Davis and Jackie Graves, quickly put his talent in perspective.

34. Vic Cardell defeated Marcelo Pacheco to take his record to 33–2–4.

35. The choice of LaRusso, once again, as a set-up fighter was a surprise. The city pug was two fights away from the end of a respectable career (46–23–3).

36. Pep forfeited a $10 bail when he did not appear in court later that day. Pep confided to the author that only the incidents where he received a ticket made it into the dailies. Most of the time it was a slap on the wrist to the champion, followed by an autograph request.

37. It appeared as if he alternated the intensity of each round.

38. Willie Pep underwent an operation for hemorrhoids at St. Francis Hospital.

39. Had Pep not looked good during this charity exhibition (against a stablemate), Viscusi would have postponed his title fight against Compo.

40. Tears and blood poured from Compo's eyes, but they were no longer visible through the swelling and gore that closed both optics. As Pep delivered the fifth-round damage, he would turn to Referee Conway almost pleading with him to end the fight. On the undercard: Tommy Bazzano defeated Billy Morris, Frankie Vigeant beat Rollie Johns, Charlie DeBow defeated Russ Dungy, Nazzareno Vitale beat Andy Bishop and Sal DiMartino, in his pro debut, was victorious over Bill Treadwell.

41. In addition to handling numerous Riley promotions, Bernstein had worked with Archie Moore, Phil Terranova, Joey Maxim, Lee Savold, and Beau Jack.

42. Officials of the IBC would have taken a Pep v. Ray Famechon, or Pep v. Maxie Docusen, if it could have been arranged; however, both of these fighters were busy. On November 19, it was confirmed that Pep would meet Famechon at Madison Square Garden (likely in January); Swept under the rug was how Viscusi persuaded the NBA to recognize Eddie Compo over other worthy contenders—it wasn't easy. By defeating Compo, Pep earned a six-month grace period before he needed to defend the title again. Meanwhile, Sandy Saddler was attempting to land a lightweight title match against Ike Williams.

43. Willie's son William Patrick Papaleo, along with his friends, John Dubiel and Sam Greenberg joined the champion on his trip.

44. Dade, a superb boxer, brought a record of 35–14–4 into the battle. Defeating Manuel Ortiz on January 6, 1947, he kept the bantam crown until March 11, 1947 (Ortiz defeated him in a rematch). He had won two of his last six contests before facing Pep.

Chapter Seven

1. Making the trip worthwhile: Of the over 11,000 admissions, half of the net proceeds, after taxes, went to Pep and ten percent went to Riley.

2. Charley Riley was a sound and skilled contender. In 1954, the boxer was forced to retire because he was blind in his left eye—he claimed it had been that way for five years.

3. True to form, Pep attended a rally for the March of Dimes on January 20, 1950. He also managed to attend the Connecticut Sports Writers Alliance, in New Haven, on January 30.

4. This negotiation was complex because Viscusi, wisely mind you, not only wanted a return fight in case his fighter lost but a $20,000 bond posted should Famechon's Manager Lew Burston walk out on the commitment.

5. Roy Andrews was a competitive boxer from Lowell, Massachusetts—his brothers, Dave and Eddie also fought professionally; Promoter Valenti put together a stirring undercard that included Jackie Wilson and Bobby Polowitzer.

6. Both knockdowns were to nine-counts.

7. According to the champion, it was the first time his four-year-old son witnessed one of his fights; Johnny Cesario was one of boxers on the undercard.

8. Angelo DeSanza, aka Terry Young, was murdered in New York City, November 5, 1967. He was handled by Hall of Fame Manager Irving Cohen, who looked after Rocky Graziano and Billy Graham. Later, Jackie Levine took over the task.

9. Just a reminder that two organizations supervised boxing. The NBA oversaw 47 state commissions. Outside of it was NYSAC, the New York State Athletic Commission. Unlike many other professional sports, there was no commissioner.

10. The undercard of the battle featured Johnny Cesario, along with Danny Nardico. Few realize that Danny Nardico was awarded the Silver Star in World War II.

11. As it turned out, 38,781 spectators produced a gross gate of $262,150. Both figures featherweight records.

12. The initial date of the fight was postponed due to Pep's marriage.

13. Although Pep was training, he did have time to attend a testimonial dinner honoring Sam Cohen, *Bridgeport Herald* sports editor on August 21, 1950. Also, on August 21, former featherweight champions Bat Battalino and Louis "Kid" Kaplan turned up at the Auditorium gym to watch Pep spar with Bob Fenty and Honey Elliott. The champion worked with sparring partners Jackie Blair, George Sinclair, Fabela Chavez, Ray Castillo, George Edmonds, Bob Fenty, Abu Ali, Elmer Beltz, and Johnny Carr, to name a few.

14. These were the initial figures given to the media.

15. When the fight ended, Pep was bleeding from his nose and left cheek.

16. In an interesting twist, Pep and Mushky Salow handled boxer Teddy "Red Top" Davis. When Davis fought Denis "Pat" Brady, a Pep sparring partner and stablemate, on October 31,

1950, at the Hartford Auditorium. Let's just say, Lou Viscusi, who had an interest in Brady, wasn't thrilled with the match.

17. Even the good fights that took place at the Auditorium, fell short of expectations.

18. See "Bride of Four Months Sues Pep For Divorce," *Hartford Courant*, November 24, 1950, p. 1.

19. See "Pep To Pay Wife $30 Per Week," *Record Journal*, December 2, 1950, p. 4; Dolores, who knew Willie from their old neighborhood, also knew Pep's first wife.

20. Trainer Bill Gore believed Pep's cut was the worst he had ever in the ring. Pep scaled at 133½ pounds for the bout, while Baker tipped at 130; Pep contributed his entire purse of $845.46 to the Mile O'Dimes drive, while the Hartford Boxing Club gave ten percent of the gate or $285.82.

21. Viscusi confirmed the February 26 exhibition to the *Hartford Courant* and it appeared in print in places such as: "Pep Offered $15,000 To Meet Chavez," *Tampa Tribune*, February 25, 1951, p. 28.

22. Marvin Ford, who would appear on the undercard, did not want to face the former champion; Eddie Webb fought under the names Billy Hogan and Eddie Hogan.

23. Some of the accusations made were detailed in "Willie Pep, Wife Battle Over Divorce," *Orlando Evening Star*, March 28, 1951, p. 8.

24. A bit embarrassed by having his personal life played out in the press, yet understanding that he was a public figure, Pep hoped to use some local appearances to try to repair any damage the situation had caused. For example, he joined Ralph Mills, director of the Hillsborough County Crime Commission at a weekly meeting of the Junior Chamber of Commerce on April 5.

25. Ortiz was simply target practice. This was a solid card that also included boxers Virgil Akins, Wallace Bud Smith and Tommy Bazzano.

26. Lou Viscusi, who was unable to get a last-minute flight to the West Coast, caught the fight over the Western Union wire at the *Hartford Courant*.

27. Willie Pep had settled into an apartment back in Connecticut.

28. In New Orleans on July 24 to supervise the training of Teddy "Red Top" Davis, Willie Pep remained optimistic about his chances to meet Saddler before the end of the year.

29. This figure was in contrast to a 30–30 split which was agreed to back in February; Tickets were topped at $20; A closed television network of 20 theaters and 13 cities featured the bout.

30. Pep's sixteen-year-old brother Nick was fighting in the Thompsonville Arena at the end of August.

31. In Hartford, both the Strand and Regal Theaters carried the closed-circuit broadcast of the fight.

32. Saddler's manager Charley Johnston was hit with a $100 fine and a 30-day suspension. Pep would need more than one hearing in order to obtain a new license.

33. "Pep Promises He Can Lick Saddler If Fight Is Clean," *Hartford Courant*, September 27, 1951, p. 19.

34. Viscusi's bad health didn't allow him to work Pep's corner.

35. Willie Pep was also informed that his divorce action, which he thought was complete, was still pending. The action was made final on September 28, 1951.

Chapter Eight

1. There was a rumor that Pep would be fighting Kenny Leach in Richmond, Virginia, on April 7. However, Pep failed to make a proper application for the restoration of his license. He would later fight Leach in Columbus, Georgia.

2. When in town, all the sports stars, entertainers, and politicians dined at the Italian eatery—from Joe DiMaggio to even actor Anthony Quinn, it was always a good bet you would find them at Frank's.

3. Fort Homer Hesterly Armory was located at 522 North Howard Avenue in Tampa, Florida. The National Guard used the armory until 2005. It exists today as the Tampa Jewish Community Center & Federation.

4. Pep tipped at 130 pounds, while Leach scaled at 134. Over 2,000 fans turned out for their battle; Pep scaled at 128¾ when he met Buddy Baggart—the latter fighter tipped at 121½. At least both Baggett and Hammond had winning records.

5. Pep's exact weight was 126¾ pounds, while Collins tipped at 130½.

6. South Vancouver Elks, who sponsored the event quoted a gate of $9,394, with 3,821 paid customers; Edmonton fight promoter Jack Berry offered to match Pep against George Dunn, a familiar Hartford lightweight, but Viscusi declined.

7. Savoie (pronounced Savwah) was ranked third in the featherweight rankings. Pep displayed clever use of multiple left jabs against his Canadian opposer. Looking tired early in the final round, Pep clinched more than usual—he was saving his energy for an impressive finish that included many solid combinations.

8. See "Sport-Rays," a column by Wilbur Kinley, *Tampa Times*, October 22, 1952, p. 13.

9. "Sport-Rays," a column by Wilbur Kinley, *Tampa Times*, November 1, 1952, p. 9.

10. Willie Pep, who was living in Florida, was not as frequent a topic as he once was inside Connecticut newspapers.

11. Manny Castro had a losing record and only 14 professional bouts entering his battle against Pep.

12. The Paddock Club was located at 7th and Washington (685 Washington Ave.), Miami Beach, Florida, and also featured burlesque shows.

13. Graziano retired on September 17, 1952, after losing a ten-round decision to Chuck Davey.

14. Chavez, with three times as many victories than defeats, was handled by the talented George Parnassus. As a promoter, Parnassus worked out of his base in Los Angeles, California.

15. Con Errico was an American Thoroughbred horse racing jockey who went to prison after being convicted of race-fixing in 1980.

16. For this fight Pep used sparring partners Joey DiGuardia, welterweight and Larry Mujica, lightweight.

17. Jake LaMotta was floored for the first time in his career by Danny Nardico, who was an 11–5 underdog entering their contest.

18. Joey Gambino, with a record of 9–1–3, was the least experienced of all the opponents Pep would meet in 1953.

19. Chris Dundee pulled the favor out of Viscusi's pocket for Angelo and his fledgling Canadian prospect. Nuf Ced!

20. Pep's admission hit the press the first week of June. See "Willie Pep in Need of 'Dough,'" *San Bernardino County Sun*, June 3, 1953, p. 24. The *Associated Press* wire article also appeared as "Pep, With Admiration But No Money, To Continue 'Just for the Dough,'" *(Richmond) Times Dispatch*, June 3, 1953, p. 25.

21. One of Willie Pep's first comparisons to Sugar Ray Robinson, as the best pound for pound fighters ever was noted in Orville Revelle's "Pass In Review" column carried by the *Fort Lauderdale News*, June 17, 1953, p. 6.

22. These were uncommon actions by Willie Pep. Speculation ranged from personal issues (dames, dice & debts) to even possible stipulations surrounding his license.

23. Those handling Lulu Perez did not believe their fighter fought at the level needed to face a fighter like Willie Pep.

24. Why did this fight make sense? Pep needed to get in shape, Viscusi fulfilled a favor, and both fighters earned some pocket cash. Luciano was working out of Miami and understood his place in the fight game.

25. After a victory over Lulu Perez, Pep would be matched against Sandy Saddler. Or, so Lou Viscusi hoped.

26. Viscusi and Caroly knew each other well—the latter wanted to provide Allen with the perfect valediction.

27. Anthony J. Longo hadn't been a serious fighter since 1948. He essentially turned punching bag after a loss that year to Bobby Bell. He was taking his career one paycheck at a time.

28. Larry was trained by his father Sam Boardman, a journeyman boxer. Similar to Willie Pep, Larry worked the strong semi-pro circuit in Connecticut before turning pro. In the winter

of 1952–53, Sam Boardman moved his family to Florida—a state where Larry could box under the age of 18.

29. Fighter Teddy "Red Top" Davis wanted to match with Pep, his former handler, and it might have better prepared Pep—even if Davis wanted to defeat the former champion—for his battle against Perez. The gate for the fight was $32,808.

30. The gate for the fight was $32,808.

31. So much Perez money surfaced that gamblers no longer accepted wagers on the fighter.

32. An interesting firsthand account of the Garden atmosphere during the bout was detailed in Bob Zaiman's column "The Human Touch," that appeared in the *Hartford Courant* on March 4, 1954, p. 3. Zaiman detailed his encounter with a gambler in the lobby.

33. For a current reference see: *The Ring*, News, ringtv.com, accessed Friday June 4, 2021; In the article, "Think Boxing Is Corrupt? This Is Nothing Compared to '50s," the publication uses five descriptive words ...almost certainly took a dive..." in reference to the 1954 battle.

34. The gate totaled $32,808. It was the largest for a Garden non-title fight in almost a year. Adding in the $4,000 in television revenue, Pep pocketed $11,000 and Perez took home $9,000.

35. "Inside Sports," *Daily News*, March 6, 1954, p. 173; See Chapter Twelve. In July 1980, *Inside Sports* magazine published an article written by Paul Good. In the piece Good claimed that a boxer identified as "The Champ" threw a fight against Lulu Perez. Some believed that fighter was Willie Pep. The former featherweight champion filed a $75 million defamation suit against Newsweek, Incorporated who owned the periodical. In February 1984, following a two-week trial, the jury ruled against Pep. See "Fighting For His Name," *Hartford Courant*, November 24, 2006.

36. Viscusi spoke to Bill Lee, *Hartford Courant* sports editor. Some of the details appeared in Lee's column "With Malice Toward None," on March 8, 1954, p. 11.

37. The NYSAC medical staff, who did not examine Pep personally, supported the decision.

38. Macri, ex-convict brother of Benedict Macri (who a few days later was declared missing), left behind an address book containing dozens of individuals that authorities hoped to question. It was believed that Macris were eliminated in fear of their possible testimony against the prosecution of Albert Anastasia for income tax evasion. Albert Anastasia, 55, was shot to death on October 25, 1957, by hired killers at the Park Sheraton Hotel, Seventh Ave. and 55th Street in New York. See "Willie Pep to Face Quiz in Macri Killing, *Daily News*, May 4, 1954, p. 61.

39. In reference to Federal Bureau of Investigation, Subject: Albert Anastasia, File: 62–98011; A supplementary summary, to information provided on September12, 1955, mentions Pep on page 5. Under subtitle "Friend of Guard" it states (without a source): "Pep was a close acquaintance

of Vincent Macri, ..." and under "Checking Leads" it expresses a need for additional questioning in Florida because "we also have some confidential information." However, no source was provided for the "confidential information," nor was it confirmed that the details provided were true. Numerous pages are deleted from the file.

40. Some sources reported Tourcotte's weight at 132 pounds.

41. This was the last professional bout of Tilmon LeBlanc, who began his career in 1936. He was familiar to New England fight fans because he battled out of Holyoke and Worcester in the fall of 1949.

Chapter Nine

1. Matchmaker Teddy Brenner was handling the Eastern Parkway Arena; The IBC was handling the Pabst Blue Ribbon broadcasts; Matchmaker Billy Brown was behind the Gillette broadcasts; and Matchmaker Ray Arcel was behind the Phillies Cigar broadcasts; There were numerous concerns, from the overuse of certain boxers to the allocation of television revenue.

2. Although state and city records differ, February 16, 1955, was correct. See "Willie Pep Reveals Plans for Third Marriage Here Next Week," *Hartford Courant*, February 11, 1955, p. 23.

3. The ceremony was conducted at the home of Willie's sister, Mrs. Felix Nevico at 780 Wethersfield Avenue.

4. See " Willie Pep 'Nagged' by Third Wife, Files for Florida Divorce," *The Journal*, April 26, 1955, p. 4. For additional details see related sources such as *Willie Pep Remembers.... Friday's Heroes* (with Robert Sacchi, 1973.

5. NYSAC denied Pep's pleas to come out of retirement on February 11, 1955.

6. Identity concerns, regarding Pep's opponent on this date, have surfaced. It was reported as Herman Gary by the AP, UP, and local press coverage. Some sources claim it was Myrel Olmstead as Herman Gary. Complicating matters, others believe it could have been welterweight Herman Gary from Waterbury, Connecticut.

7. Titone, who won about twice as many battles as he lost, posed little challenge to Pep. Hartford boxers Al Maglieri and Steve Ward were on the undercard.

8. Later, Pep was taken to the hospital for stitches.

9. Cam's technical knockout loss to Pep, was the final fight of a solid professional career that included victories over Tommy Tibbs, Harry LaSane and Eddie Compo.

10. Mickey Mars won the 1950 National AAU Bantamweight champion. He took a record of 17–6 into the ring against Willie Pep.

11. The heavyweight champion of the world

was coming off his last title bout, against 38-year-old Archie Moore, on September 21, 1955. Later, it goes without saying, Marvin Hagler confirmed the moniker, as did Robbie Sims, Steve Collins and Kevin Collins, along with those around the sport such as Goody and Pasquale Petronelli.

12. During this period, Pep was spending time with his friends and family while even endorsing a few products, such as The National Sports Council's *The Manly Art Course*.

13. The evening proved tragic as welterweight fighter Ferman King, 26, who fought on the undercard, died on December 1 from injuries sustained during his fight.

14. Costa, who had never fought outside New York City, had no intention of leaving town. Having not fought since November 11, he planned to meet Baby Vasquez in March inside Madison Square Garden. Was there more to the pledge, likely, but Viscusi didn't comment. He did have some Texas matches lined up for Pep, and hoped that would lead to Costa.

15. In an interesting biographical twist: After taking a few ring battles in Philadelphia, a young Andy Arel hitched a ride to Miami Beach (via St. Petersburg), in search of Angelo Dundee. Gaunt and bespectacled, the determined fighter impressed the trainer enough to join his stable.

16. Punching bag Kid Campeche had over twice as many loses than victories.

17. The Macri brothers, according to New York police records, were former bodyguards and chauffeurs for Alfred Anastasia.

18. See "Pep to Appear at Investigation of Death of Man 18 Months Ago," *Tampa Tribune*, March 14, 1956, p. 21; Pep did say that he knew Macri "vaguely" and would cooperate fully with investigators; See also "Move To Subpoena Pep In Disappearance Denied," *Hartford Courant*, March 14, 1956, p. 23.

19. Mixed fights, even during the 1950s, were never met with open arms by the commission.

20. In Connecticut, violations such as these typically resulted only in a warning for the elite boxer or, perhaps an autograph. However in Florida, Pep had yet to gain the same level of notoriety.

21. Tickets were scaled at: $5, $3, and $2; In addition to the main event, there was an eight-round semi-final, two six rounders and a four-round opener.

22. Fingerprint records, which have to be submitted for various state licenses, indicated that Donofrio was convicted in 1931 for an attempted robbery charge. This according to J.D. Williamson, state beverage director.

23. Sandy Saddler suffered the injury on July 27, 1956, when a taxicab in which he was a passenger was hit by another car.

24. One promoter who liked the pairing was Sam Gulino, of East Hartford, who even wired both fighters $10,000 for a September bout.

25. Chris Dundee controlled his market, and

the promoters in it—there were times when Viscusi appeared like his puppet.

26. Meanwhile, Promoter Chris Dundee relentlessly pursued a rematch between Pep and Russell Tague.

27. The Circuit Court ruling was noted in the *Tampa Tribune* on September 23, 1956, p. 32.

28. Pep was also training and managing a few fighters, lightweight Eldo Mente being a good example.

29. Willie Pep never received credit for his altruism, nor ever asked for it.

30. It was a unanimous decision victory for Pep. Tague believed it was much closer.

31. A determined Russell Tague, less than a handful of professional fights from the end of his career, had no intention of surrendering to Willie Pep. By the way, Tague defeated Lulu Perez by a split-decision on August 14, 1956.

32. Pep's address at this time was 3617 South DeLeon Avenue in Tampa, Florida (near Swann Estates Section); Pep still supported his parents, who lived in the house he purchased for them in Hartford.

33. Willie Pep's Little Club, as it would first be called, stayed open while it was remodeled.

34. Mrs. Martin was described by the detectives at the scene as "very intoxicated." See "Willie Pep Sought Here in Shooting," *Tampa Tribune*, September 4, 1957, p. 1 (and continued on p. 4).

35. See "Cops Recheck Woman's Story She Was Shot by Willie Pep," *Bridgeport Post*, September 5, 1957, p. 53.

36. Connors, who had an outstanding amateur career, was "Prospect for the Month," in November 1957, according to *The Ring* magazine.

37. Both fighters even fell out of the ring in the third round.

38. The attendance figures varied depending on the source. Despite his issues outside the ring, Pep was preparing for a European tour (January 1958) that never took place.

39. Becoming the first twenty-year man in boxing since Johnny Dundee was a goal for the former champion. Having begun his professional career on July 25, 1940, he was only 937 days (from the start date to the end date, end date included) from reaching the milestone.

40. Bassey won the world crown by defeating French Algerian Cherif Hamia in Paris in 1957.

41. As Viscusi also handled Joe Brown, perhaps he would play into the picture as well; Any thought of a European Tour vanquished once Team Pep targeted the title.

42. Tommy Tibbs worked at his Dover Street newsstand as time permitted.

43. Trainer Bill Gore, not prone to publicity or prompting, believed Pep won the fight.

44. The attendance reports varied; They ranged from 4,200 to 5,400 fight fans.

45. Pep often used this phrase in interviews. For an example: "Sportin' Life," Journal, February 21, 1958, p. 4.

46. It was believed that Pep disposed of all, or part, of his business interest in Willie Pep's Little Club, which still carried his moniker; The Main Street Gym was located at 1045 Main Street in Hartford, telephone: 7-5606.

47. Jim Higgins, from Middletown, assumed a portion of Viscusi's responsibilities while Lou was over in Houston, Texas. Bill Gore was also assisting with Cleveland Williams.

48. The NYSAC snub, nixed Pep's desire to fight overseas, as the organization was also a member of the World Boxing Federation.

49. Greenberg lived at 251 Burnside Avenue in East Hartford.

50. A couple sources had Pep scaling at 128 pounds.

51. Pep officially was six victories behind Stribling. He thought he was seven victories behind Freddie Miller, when in reality he had surpassed him.

52. The IBC had their claws firmly planted in the television market with many of the ring battles taking place in New York where Pep was "retired." Truman Gibson, secretary and later IBC president, also had issues with Pep's fighting style, or so the boxer was told.

53. The attendance figures reported for the event varied dramatically. A large percentage of the crowd was also there to watch 21-year-old Tom McNeeley, former Arlington High and Michigan State athlete, win his professional boxing debut.

54. Pep tipped at 128 pounds, while Carmona scaled at 130. Pep was warned by Referee Otis LaBree to engage. A crowd estimated at 2,000 attended the August 4 event; Pep's battle against Rodriguez drew 1,500 fans. There were no knockdowns; Duarte was a seasoned lightweight who was to appear on the undercard. Pep tipped at 129½ pounds, while Duarte scaled at 137. A crowd estimated at 1,500 fans turned out for the event.

55. After the Bassey fight Pep spent weeks healing; Winston S. Churchill once said, "You will never reach your destination if you stop and throw stones at every dog that barks." Despite the distractions in his life outside the ring, Pep continued to direct his motivation toward his ring success. Casting stones wasn't an option. On November 21, Willie Pep suffered a few minor scratches when his car collided with another vehicle on Route 15 in Meriden. Pep was given a warning for failure to pass to the left.

Chapter Ten

1. Pep was also working with George Edmonds of Hartford.

2. Beginning on his 39th birthday, Pep would qualify for his $50 a month annuity checks.

3. Pep was the third man in the ring for a preliminary bout between Jimmy Monts and Maurice Jenkins.

4. See "Willie Pep Draws Driving Charge," *Orlando Sentinel*, November 23, 1957, p. 11, "Victim's Condition 'Serious'—Willie Pep Charged After Car Hits Pedestrian, 83," *Tampa Tribune*, November 22, 1957, p. 2, and "Willie Pep Charged in Auto Accident," *Hartford Courant*, November 23, 1957, p. 8; Limited details regarding the suit were provided.

5. Best known for his role as John "Plato" Crawford in the film *Rebel Without a Cause*, Salvatore Mineo, Jr. (1939–1976), was a talented actor, singer and director.

6. Pep was joined later by Frankie Martin, and the promotions moved to Wahconah Park after the Arena's final fire on May 12, 1960; Pep canceled the shows on November 11, 1960, due to financial issues.

7. On October 24, Tony Galento, Willie Pep, and three other occupants were injured in an automobile collision in Edgewood, Maryland. The group was returning to New Jersey following a Baltimore boxing engagement. Galento and Pep were treated and released at a local hospital, while the three others were admitted. The unidentified driver of the other vehicle was in critical condition.

8. The transcripts of the senate hearing (Subcommittee on Antitrust and Monopoly) are available through many sources, see "Norris' Last Stand, The horrid details of the Jim Norris-Frankie Carbo alliance that ruled boxing for a decade were verified in Washington," *Sports Illustrated*, December 16, 1960. Lou Viscusi was mentioned during the hearing.

9. The neighborhood was also home to noted mobsters, however it was not where they conducted a majority of their business. For example, Meyer Lansky (1902–1983) had his last home in South Florida. It was a condominium located at 5255 Collins Avenue. Less than seven miles away from Lansky's residence was the Miami Beach mansion of Al Capone (1899–1947), located at 93 Palm Avenue, Palm Island, Florida.

10. The former champion loved chatting with Eddie Steele, his former pianist at Willie Pep's Melody Lane.

11. Arthur Mercante, who appears out-of-focus briefly in the film, worked as the film's technical advisor.

12. In Bogota, Columbia, Willie Pep was pickpocketed twice, once at the airport and once on the way to the boxing ring from his dressing room.

13. According to Pep, his friend owed him some money and suggested a horse in payment. The fighter liked the idea, until he realized he was lucky to break even.

14. See "With Malice Toward None," *Hartford Courant*, September 1, 1962, p. 13; Sports editor Bill Lee, Pep's lifetime friend and confidant, printed a letter from the former champion. While on the West Coast, and perhaps lacking confidence in his new role, Pep casually mentioned that he was considering a few exhibitions in Japan. Nerves often contributed to the spontaneity of Willie Pep's comments.

15. New York State Marriage license number: 20107; A photograph of Mrs. Papaleo appears in the *Hartford Courant* on September 4, 1963, p. 1.

16. The institution was replaced by the International Boxing Hall of Fame in Canastota, New York.

17. The first broadcast, of the two-decade run, being Pep-Wright, at the Garden, on September 29, 1944.

18. Pep never failed to drop his good friend Bill Lee, *Hartford Courant* sports editor a postcard from wherever he was refereeing. Naturally, it always brought the former champion a blurb in the prestigious newspaper.

19. Pep received fifty percent of everything over expenses; Back home to Connecticut, Pep, still traveling, found himself in an automobile fender bender at the end of August. Seems the former champion didn't slow his vehicle quick enough to avoid hitting a car in front of him. The incident took place in the coastal town of Old Lyme, and thankfully no one was injured.

20. Known for his payment disagreements, Robinson conducted his best negotiations just prior to a performance.

21. Pep's estimated take for the fight was about $400. Pep was seconded by Pat O'Malley, and Trainer Charley Titone. Two of Pep's cuts required stitches to close; During this period, Pep was also working with fighter Mike Mamareli.

22. For his efforts Willie Pep pocketed about $600. The fight was originally scheduled for eight rounds.

23. The Central Maine Civic Center at Lewiston, Maine was the place to be on May 25, 1965, as Muhammad Ali knocked out Sonny Liston at the 2:12 mark of the first round. Few spectators, even those at ringside, saw the phantom punch including Willie Pep, who was sitting next to Rocky Marciano. The pair were as confused as everybody else when they learned the fight was over.

24. The anti-boxing bill was signed into law on July 7, 1965.

25. On June 24, 1965, Willie Pep was in New York City to celebrate the 70th birthday of William Harrison "Jack" Dempsey. The celebration, held at Dempsey's restaurant, was attended by a wealth of personalities, including boxing champions Abe Attell, Tommy Loughran, Pep, and Mickey Walker. Later in the evening, the Dempsey's entertained at a dinner party at which Gene Tunney and his wife attended. Dempsey, who wasn't shy about his frustration with the sport, also didn't dwell on the matter. The day was all about the premier cultural icon of the 1920s, who happened to be a boxer.

26. Press release, World Boxing Association, Toronto, Canada, July 4, 1965.

27. It was 73 days from the start date to the

end date, end date included. Or 2 months, 11 days including the end date.

28. Columnist Jerry Izenberg stated that Pep dropped his opponent five times during the bout. See "Jerry Izenberg, At Large," *Post-Standard*, October 5, 1965, p. 18.

29. The weights varied by source—some noted Tommy Haden at 132 pounds.

30. Bill Gore was training Manny Gonzalez.

31. Growing up fast, or being mature beyond your years, can be an enormous challenge to a child. The expectations can be unrealistic and the responsibility unfair to the subject. This is often the case in role-reversal situations, such as Willie Pep had with his father. Had Pep not been blessed with such extraordinary skills, he may have faced an intolerable position.

32. Murray Cain, aka Teddy "Red Top" Davis, died on June 4, 1966. He was forty-two years old. Beginning his career in Ohio and West Virginia, he moved to New England and became Willie Pep's premier sparring partner. A break-even fighter, he became a contender in the featherweight division by the mid 1950s, and even earned a title shot against Sandy Saddler-he lost via a unanimous decision. Later, he made a living as a set-up fighter, and a good one at that. At one point, Davis, was managed by Mushky Salow and Willie Pep.

33. Also appearing at the hearing were Maxie Atwater, Johnny Cesario, Lou Dell, and Billy Lynch; Bill SB 1035 would reinstate professional boxing and another bill, HB 5093, would allow amateur boxing.

34. Jake LaMotta was married seven times.

35. Supplementing his September income, Pep was assisting at Holmes & Burns Auto Sales, at 478 Center Street, in Manchester; The program wasn't renewed for lack of a sponsor.

36. Heading to San Juan, Puerto Rico, Willie Pep put on his judge's hat on April 29. Ismael Laguna seized a ten-round unanimous decision over Frankie Narvaez in front of more than 7,000 fight fans at Hiram Bithorn Stadium. Granted, Pep would have rather been the third man in the ring, but judging was no easy stint.

37. Forever attending banquets, Pep joined Rocky Marciano at Hamilton Standard's annual sports night, in Windsor Locks, Connecticut, on June 19, 1968.

38. American service men overseas missed their boxing heroes. In response to the demand, State Department officials, in Washington, D.C., contacted a number of boxers about a visit to Vietnam on September 10. The fighters of greatest interest to our troops: Henry Armstrong, Joe Louis, Rocky Marciano, Carlos Ortiz, Willie Pep and Jersey Joe Walcott. Thrilled that folks remembered him Pep hoped to make the trip.

39. Later, after taking enormous abuse from the press, in particular the Australian boxing writers, Pep admitted his error in judgment, aka a decision for Harada.

Chapter Eleven

1. Ernie "Indian Red" Lopez was the brother of Danny "Little Red" Lopez.

2. It was believed Sid Flaherty, who likely took Viscusi's suggestion to call on Pep, was handling Rouse at this time; Rouse was chosen to represent the United States in the middleweight division at the 1956 Olympics held in Melbourne, Australia. This was Rouse's last attempt to win the light-heavyweight title.

3. The idea sounded good initially, however Pep's empathetic heart, made the task a challenge; Pep indicated to the author he always felt bad in the roll and it wasn't him; Former world bantamweight champion Manuel Ortiz died on May 31, 1970. He was 53. Pep recalled Ortiz fondly, from sparring with him in the Main Street Gym in Los Angeles, to his July 17, 1944, victory over the two-handed boxer at Braves Field in Boston. Ortiz was inducted into the International Boxing Hall of Fame in 1996.

4. The relationship between Sandy Saddler and Willie Pep became tolerable with age. The year 1971 saw Willie Pep cheering for Joe Frazier over Muhammad Ali, and even modeling for a wig that was being offered by Master Barber Mr. Joseph Bascetta at 315 Pearl Street in Hartford.

5. For the second time in three months Pep's application for a Connecticut referee's license was denied. It happened on September 19, 1973.

6. Francis Vejar, aka Chico Vejar, was a talented welter hailing from Stamford, Connecticut. During a career that spanned eleven years (1950–1961), Vejar won over four times as many fights as he lost and appeared in more than 100 professional bouts; John J. "Jim" Higgins, the former trainer and manager of Willie Pep during his final comeback, died on December 22, 1973, in Middletown. He was no stranger to boxing as he also handled Tommy Bazzano, Tony Falco, and Jackie O'Brien, all talented fighters.

7. Supporting his fellow fighters, Willie Pep was up in Syracuse, New York, on June 6, 1974, for a fund raiser. Seems the Chairman of the Central New York Heart Fund, Carmen Basilio, thought that getting his old cronies back together might create some interest in the event. Those attending included: Billy Backus, Chuck Davey, Joey Giardello, Billy Graham, Pete Scalzo, Chico Vejar, and Ike Williams, to name a few.

8. Those in Springfield were also treated to highlights of the Ali-Frazier ring battles, while in Waterbury, it was Pep-Saddler fight films; Weeks later, Willie Pep served as a second to fighter Irish Mike Morgan for his battle against Mike Rossman at Madison Square Garden.

9. In June 1975, Pep was working with Hugh Devlin (Executive Director), Dave Musco (Chico Vejar's former assistant), Sam Cohen (Public Relations Director) and Billy Taylor (Chief of Referees). Chico Vejar resigned in May.

10. Before he was a trainer, Bill Gore owned

a doughnut shop and even befriended entrepreneur Howard Johnson of restaurant and motel fame; Some sources claim Gore was 86; His last fight appearance came on January 30, 1975, when Tony Licata defeated Marcel Clay at the Fort Homer Hesterly Armory in Tampa, Fl; He was survived by his wife Hilda ,and buried in Providence, RI.

11. Pep took a liking to boxer Cat Davis, whose fighting style reminded him of himself. Pep was even best man to her groom, Sal Algieri, at the couple's wedding. Pep even appeared on the "Soupy Sales Show" sparring with Cat Davis.

12. First reference to winning a round without punching occurred in an Associated Press(AP) article picked up by dailies such as *The Ithaca Journal*, December 2, 1976.

13. He suffered only one loss by (technical) knockout, and that was to the hard-hitting Billy Petrolle in New York on March 24, 1932.

14. Pep turned a few heads when he stated that he preferred a $1,000 appearance fee over a trophy for his attendance at the resurrection of Connecticut Boxing Hall of Fame in May 1978. During this period, Pep, who was working part-time as an inspector with the state boxing commission, decided to utilize the services of Duke Antone as a business manager.

15. During this period Pep was also appearing in his fair share of local television commercials; Ray Famechon (European Featherweight Champion) died on January 28, 1978.

16. On October 22, 1979, Willie Pep headed south to Tampa to attend the 5th Annual Florida West Coast Veteran Boxers' Association (Ring 50) banquet at Dow Sherwood's Showboat Dinner Theatre. He was there at the invitation of Floyd Golden, Ring 50 president and former fight promoter, who handled five of Pep's bouts in Tampa.

17. This conclusion was based on the analysis of selected newspapers in three states where Willie Pep either once resided or was enormously popular.

Chapter Twelve

1. The libel suit was filed in a New York federal court on March 25, 1981.

2. "Former featherweight boxing champion Willie Pep took the stand...," UPI Archives, February 21, 1984. Also see "Former featherweight boxing champion Willie Pep lost a $75...," UPI Archives February 27, 1984.

3. See "Pep; Sues Newsweek," *Record-Journal*, March 26, 1981, p. 19.; The trial opened on February 14, 1984, in New York. Pep declined to talk to reporters after the verdict. Pep needed to prove by "clear and convincing evidence" that the article was indeed false and written with malice. The jury never ruled on the malice question.

According to boxing historian Bert Randolph Sugar, "...the fight smelled funny."

4. See "Pep, Couture aid ex-foe," *Record-Journal*, October 13, 1980, p. 9. It's a wonderful piece written by Richard F. Hanley, that will touch your heart.

5. Governor William O'Neill declared September 22 as Willie Pep Day in Connecticut; Sebastian Anthony DeMauro, aka, Bobby "Poison" Ivy, died on July 25, 1984, at Hartford Hospital. The former featherweight boxer, who many believed would fill the Connecticut shoes of Bat Battalino and ascend to the division thrown, was a big influence on the career of Willie Pep. In 1940, Ivy lost a bid for the featherweight crown, at Bulkeley Stadium in Hartford, when he was stopped by champion Petey Scalzo in the fifteenth round. Later, in 1942, Pep stopped Ivy in the tenth round of a contest held at the same venue.

6. Pep still felt the state should adopt a boxing commissioner rather than continue under its current organization.

7. As a child, Willie Pep heard stories about the Black Hills of South Dakota, and how it attracted outlaws, gamblers and gunslingers. Names like Wild Bill Hickok, Calamity Jane, Potato Creek Johnny, Seth Bullock and Al Swearengen created their legends in the tiny town. It was the perfect opportunity.

8. I.G.F., Inc. was established in 1988 and handled seven fighters.

9. Like many former ring champions, Willie Pep's autograph will appreciate in value over time. Recognizing where and when he participated in certain events is helpful to the provenance of a piece of boxing memorabilia. That is part of the reason why this information is presented in this work.

10. The day before the event, Pep was over at the South Park Inn, at 75 Main Street, dedicating the Willie Pep Lounge, which was donated by the Homeward Bound Foundation, a group that welcomed Pep's participation; The face of Hartford amateur boxing, and the gymnasium owner (Charter Oak Athletic Club) who told Pep to "beat it" when the youngster dropped by seeking instruction, Dominic J. "Pete" Perone died on January 3, 1993, at Hartford Hospital. He was 90 years old. During his incredible career he was a father figure to Pep, along with: Bat Battalino, Red Doty, Bobby Ivy, and Billy Kearns. Perone was also the founder and first president of the Connecticut Boxing Guild.

11. To add insult to injury for Willie Pep, they later closed Donato's Restaurant in East Hartford, a popular meeting place for members of the Neutral Corner. Pep loved his hangouts, like Freddy's Sports Nook, over at Park and John Streets.

12. While Steele was there, Dundee's praise came via telegram. Others there included "Irish Billy" Corcoran, Earle Everett, Mark Berio, Mark

Shiffrin, Danny Wamboldt, and State Senator Biagio "Billy" Ciotto.

13. Following Robinson was Muhammad Ali, Henry Armstrong, Joe Louis and then Pep. Following Pep were Jack Dempsey, Roberto Duran, Benny Leonard, Billy Conn and Harry Greb.

14. In 1999, Pep, claimed he won 62 amateur fights; This was the first time he used a figure above 59 (victories). His most often quoted amateur record was 59–3–3.

15. See an *Associated Press* wire article, published by numerous newspapers including the *New Haven Register*, dated February 19, 2001. The article speaks to Pep's days at an Alzheimer unit of a nursing home. Some family members believed he suffered from dementia pugilistica.

16. Before his need for medical care, Willie Pep lived with his wife, Barbara, and his three stepchildren, April, LJ and Holly. His surviving family also includes two daughters Mary and Melissa, and two sons, Billy and Michael, along with their relatives. See related obituaries.

Bibliography

Books

Baker, Mark Allen. *Battling Nelson, the Durable Dane.* Jefferson, NC: McFarland, 2016.
_____. *Between the Ropes at Madison Square Garden: The History of an Iconic Boxing Ring, 1925–2007.* Jefferson, NC: McFarland, 2019.
_____. *Connecticut Boxing: The Fights, the Fighters and the Fight Game.* Charleston: History Press, 2021.
_____. *The Fighting Times of Abe Attell.* Jefferson, NC: McFarland, 2017.
_____. *Lou Ambers: A Biography of the World Lightweight Champion and Hall of Famer.* Jefferson, NC: McFarland, 2021.
_____. *Title Town USA: Boxing in Upstate New York.* Charleston: History Press, 2010.
Cavanaugh, Jack. *Tunney, Boxing's Brainiest Champ and His Upset of the Great Jack Dempsey.* New York: Ballantine, 2006.
Goldman, Herbert G., ed. *Boxing: A Worldwide Record of Bouts and Boxers.* Jefferson, NC: McFarland, 2012.
_____. *The Ring Record Book and Boxing Encyclopedia.* New York: Ring Publishing, 1985.
Pep, Willie, with Robert Sacchi. *Willie Pep Remembers.... Friday's Heroes.* New York: Friday's Heroes, 1973.
Sugar, Bert Randolph. *Boxing's Greatest Fighters.* Guilford: Lyons Press, 2006.
_____. *The Ultimate Book of Boxing Lists.* Philadelphia: Running Press, 2010.
United States Amateur Boxing. *Coaching Olympic Style Boxing* Carmel: Cooper, 1995.

Articles

Ackerman, Meyer. "Willie Pep Is Fighter of the Month." *The Ring,* February 1943.
Daniel, Daniel M. "A Busy Little Champ." *The Ring,* May 1948.
Fleischer, Nat. "Pep Wins Crown." *The Ring,* February 1943, 38–39, 44.
Kane, Martin. "Willie Ran Out of Pep." *Sports Illustrated,* September 29, 1958.
Shea, Jim. "Make Believe a Cop Is Chasing You." *Sports Illustrated,* July 17, 1990.
Smith, Gil. "The Fight That Jinxed Willie Pep." *Police Gazette,* May 1962, 19.

Steele, Bob. "Willie Pep of Hartford." *Esquire,* August 1, 1943, 70–71, 151.
Swisher, Karl. "See—They've All Forgotten Me." *The Ring,* December 1993, 41, 56–61.
Thorne, Harvey. "New Faces." *The Ring,* December 1941, 27, 43.
Uncredited. "Pep's Greatest Gamble in the Ring." *Great Moments in Sports,* November 1962, 52–58.

Brochures and Programs

"In the Ring" Official Souvenir Program, World's Featherweight Title Bout, August 22, 1947
International Boxing Hall of Fame, Inaugural Induction—June 10, 1990
The Neutral Corner Presents Oldtime Fighter's Reunion, Friday, September 11, 1998
The Rockys, Fifth Annual Rocky Marciano Foundation Awards Dinner, May 24, 1993

Internet Sites

ancestry.com
boxingtreasures.com
boxrec.com
britannica.com
chronicalingamerica.loc.gov
ctboxinghof.org
cyberboxingzone.com
espn.com
facebook.com
findagrave.com
ha.com
history.com
ibhof.com
josportsinc.com
newspapers.com
wikipedia.org
worthpoint.com
youtube.com

Legal Documents

553 F. Supp. 1000 (1983) Willie Pep, Plantiff, v. Newsweek, Inc. Defendant, No. 81 Civ. 1766

(MEL)., United States District Court, South Dakota New York, January 5, 1983.

Federal Bureau of Investigation, Subject: Albert Anastasia, File: 62–98011; Obtained through FOIA.

Magazines

Boxing Monthly
Boxing News
Boxing Scene
El Boxer
KO Magazine
Liberty
Pacific Stars and Stripes
Police Gazette
The Ring
Sporting News
Sports Illustrated
Weekly Boxing World

Newspapers

Abilene Reporter-News (Abilene, Texas)
Akron Beacon (Akron, Ohio)
Apache Sentinel (Fort Huachuca, Arizona)
Arizona Sun (Phoenix, Arizona)
Austin American (Austin, Texas)
Auttaja (Ironwood, Michigan)
Baltimore Sun (Baltimore, Maryland)
Bangor Daily News (Bangor, Maine)
Battle Creek Enquirer (Battle Creek, Michigan)
Bennington Evening Banner (Bennington, Vermont)
Berkshire Eagle (Pittsfield, Massachusetts)
Birmingham News (Birmingham, Alabama)
Boston Globe (Boston, Massachusetts)
Boston Herald (Boston, Massachusetts)
Boston Post (Boston, Massachusetts)
Brattleboro Reformer (Brattleboro, Vermont)
Bridgeport Post (Bridgeport, Connecticut)
Bridgeport Telegram (Bridgeport, Connecticut)
Bristol News Bulletin (Bristol, Tennessee)
Brooklyn Citizen (Brooklyn, New York)
Brooklyn Daily Eagle (Brooklyn, New York)
Brooklyn Times Union (Brooklyn, New York)
Burlington Daily News (Burlington, Vermont)
Carbon County News (Red Lodge, Montana)
Catholic Times (Columbus, Ohio)
Chapel Hill Weekly (Chapel Hill, North Carolina)
Charlotte News (Charlotte, North Carolina)
Charlotte Observer (Charlotte, North Carolina)
Chicago Star (Chicago, Illinois)
Chicago World (Chicago, Illinois)
Cincinnati Enquirer (Cincinnati, Ohio)
Daily Express (Dayton, Ohio)
Daily Monitor (Mount Clemens, Michigan)
Daily Oklahoman (Lawton, Oklahoma)
Daily Record (Dunn, North Carolina)
Daily Times (Salisbury, Maryland)
Dayton Daily News (Dayton, Ohio)
Dayton Herald (Dayton, Ohio)

Democrat and Chronicle (Rochester, New York)
Denton Record-Chronicle (Denton, Texas)
Detroit Evening Times (Detroit, Michigan)
Detroit Free Press (Detroit, Michigan)
Detroit Tribune (Detroit, Michigan)
Diario Las Americas (Miami, Florida)
El Sol (Phoenix, Arizona)
Evening News (Buffalo, New York)
Evening Star (Washington, District of Columbia)
Evening Sun (Baltimore, Maryland)
Evening Sun (Hanover, Pennsylvania)
Express (San Antonio, Texas)
Farmville Herald and Farmer-Leader (Farmville, Virginia)
Fitchburg Sentinel (Fitchburg, Massachusetts)
Florence Morning News (Florence, South Carolina)
Fort Lauderdale News (Fort Lauderdale, Florida)
Fort Worth Star-Telegram (Fort Worth, Texas)
Fresno Bee (Fresno, California)
Frontier (O'Neill City, Nebraska)
Hartford Chronicle (Hartford, Connecticut)
Hartford Courant (Hartford, Connecticut)
Hartford Times (Hartford, Connecticut)
Intelligencer Journal (Lancaster, Pennsylvania)
Ithaca Journal (Ithaca, New York)
Jackson Advocate (Jackson, Mississippi)
Journal (Caldwell, Ohio)
Kansas City Star (Kansas City, Missouri)
Kansas City Times (Kansas City, Missouri)
Key West Citizen (Key West, Florida)
Kingston Daily Freeman (Kingston, New York)
Laurel Outlook (Laurel, Montana)
Lincoln Times (Lincolnton, North Carolina)
Lowell Sun (Lowell, Massachusetts)
Marion Progress (Marion, North Carolina)
Meriden Daily Journal (Meriden, Connecticut)
Meriden Record (Meriden, Connecticut)
Miami Herald (Miami, Florida)
Miami News (Miami, Florida)
Miami Times (Miami, Florida)
Michigan Chronicle (Detroit, Michigan)
Middletown Times Herald (Middletown, New York)
Midland Journal (Rising Sun, Maryland)
Milwaukee Journal (Milwaukee, Wisconsin)
Mississippi Enterprise (Jackson, Mississippi)
Monroe News Star (Monroe, Louisiana)
Montana Labor News (Butte, Montana)
Nashua Telegraph (Nashua, New Hampshire)
Naugatuck Daily News (Naugatuck, Connecticut)
New England Bulletin (Hartford, Connecticut)
New Haven Register (New Haven, Connecticut)
New York Age (New York, New York)
New York Daily News (New York, New York)
New York Times (New York, New York)
Newport Daily Express (Newport, Vermont)
Newport Daily News (Newport, Rhode Island)
News and Views (Jacksonville, North Carolina)
Nome Nugget (Nome, Alaska)
North Adams Transcript (North Adams, Massachusetts)
Northwest Enterprise (Seattle, Washington)

Oakland Tribune (Oakland, California)
Observer (Utica, New York)
Ohio Daily-Express (Dayton, Ohio)
Omaha Guide (Omaha, Nebraska)
Orlando Sentinel (Orlando, Florida)
Ottawa Journal (Ottawa, Ontario, Canada)
Palm Beach Post (West Palm Beach, Florida)
Philadelphia Inquirer (Philadelphia, Pennsylvania)
Pittsburgh Courier (Pittsburgh, Pennsylvania)
Portland Press Herald (Portland, Maine)
Portsmouth Herald (Portsmouth, New Hampshire)
Post-Standard (Syracuse, New York)
Post-Star (Glens Falls, New York)
Poughkeepsie Eagle-News (Poughkeepsie, New York)
Press and Sun-Bulletin (Binghamton, New York)
Press Democrat (Santa Rosa, California)
Providence Journal (Providence, Rhode Island)
Record-Journal (Meriden, Connecticut)
Roanoke Rapids Daily Herald (Roanoke Rapids, North Carolina)
St. Louis Globe-Democrat (St. Louis, Missouri)
St. Louis Post-Dispatch (St. Louis, Missouri)
St. Paul Pioneer Press (St. Paul, Minnesota)
Shreveport Journal (Shreveport, Louisiana)
Southern News (Asheville, North Carolina)
Springfield Daily Republican (Springfield, Massachusetts)
Star-Gazette (Elmira, New York)
Tampa Bay Times (St. Petersburg, Florida)
Tampa Times (Tampa, Florida)
Tampa Tribune (Tampa, Florida)

Theocrate (Zion City, Illinois)
Times-Tribune (Scranton, Pennsylvania)
Times Union (Brooklyn, New York)
Toledo Union Journal (Toledo, Ohio)
Town Talk (Alexandria, Louisiana)
Valley Times (North Hollywood, California)
Vancouver Sun (Vancouver, British Columbia, Canada)
Voice (Lincoln, Nebraska)
Washington Post (Washington, District of Columbia)
Wilmington Morning Star (Wilmington, North Carolina)
Worcester Evening Gazette (Worcester, Massachusetts)
Wyandotte News-Herald (Wyandotte, Michigan)
Ypsilanti Daily Press (Ypsilanti, Michigan)

Organizations—Research

AAIB, Inc.
Associated Press
Bureau of Labor Statistics' Consumer Price Index (CPI)
Connecticut Boxing Hall of Fame
Connecticut Historical Society Museum and Library
International Boxing Hall of Fame
International Boxing Research Organization: IBRO
The Smithsonian Institution
United Press International
United States Census Bureau

Index

Numbers in **bold italics** indicate pages with illustrations